Wilderness and Human Communities

The Spirit of the 21st Century

Proceedings from the
7TH WORLD WILDERNESS CONGRESS

Port Elizabeth, South Africa

Edited by
Vance G. Martin and Andrew Muir

Fulcrum Publishing
Golden, Colorado

Library of Congress Cataloging-in-Publication Data

World Wilderness Congress (7th : 2001 : Port Elizabeth, South Africa)
  Wilderness and human communities : the spirit of the 21st century :
proceedings from the 7th World Wilderness Congress, Port Elizabeth, South
Africa / edited by Vance G. Martin and Andrew Muir.
    p. cm.
  Includes bibliographical references and index.
    ISBN 1-55591-866-2 (pbk. : alk. paper) 1. Wilderness areas—Africa—
Congresses. 2. Wilderness areas—Congresses. 3. Nature conservation—
Citizen participation—Congresses. I. Martin, Vance. II.
Muir, Andrew. III. Title.
  QH77.A35W67 2001
  333.78'216–dc22

                                                              2004017590

Printed in the United States of America
0 9 8 7 6 5 4 3 2 1

Fulcrum Publishing	The WILD Foundation
16100 Table Mountain Parkway, Suite 300	P. O. Box 1380
Golden, Colorado, USA 80403	Ojai, California, USA 93023
(800) 992-2908 • (303) 277-1623	(805) 640-0390 • Fax (805) 640-0230
www.fulcrum-books.com	info@wild.org • www.wild.org

Table of Contents

The Port Elizabeth Accord
of the
7th World Wilderness Congress

8 November 2001

At this time in our history, when the shadow of uncertainty pervades our thoughts and the presence of peril dictates our actions, all of our aspirations and initiatives must, by necessity, be positive, determined, visionary, and collaborative.

It is with this realization that 700 delegates from 42 nations convened in Port Elizabeth, South Africa, for the 7th World Wilderness Congress.

During the course of a week of presentations, consultations, debates and decisions by a diverse array of people, cultures, professions, and perspectives, covering both challenges and solutions, some certainties were confirmed, namely that:

- Wilderness, wildlands, and wildlife—on land, in the sea, and in the air—are a resource of fundamental, irreplaceable value and substance in all human endeavour; and
- Wild nature is essentially more than a resource, rather being *The Source* of a particular gift of strength, sanity, and inspiration in a modern and fragmented world; and further,
- Wilderness—all of its many services and values—undeniably informs and supports human communities and is an essential element of the spirit and practicality of the 21st century.

Our convention recognized the inescapable truth: where vast wilderness once surrounded and supported humankind, pervading and persisting with ease, it is now small, and dispersed islands in a sea of humanity, retreating daily while assaulted by human numbers and greed, are cloaked by an atmosphere that is not of its own making, nor life-giving.

As a result, our convention reconfirmed the basic principles of international collaboration, cross-cultural cooperation, human equity, and freedom, combined with direct personal responsibility for the present and future well-being of wilderness, wildlands, and wildlife, on land, in the sea, and in the air.

Therefore, in light of this reality and these principles, we are RESOLVED to act decisively, with intention, power, and determination, on the agreements, resolutions, and actions of this 7th World Wilderness Congress.

Vance G. Martin
WWC Executive Director

Andrew Muir
7th WWC Director

Foreword

The 7th World Wilderness Congress
Returns to Its Roots in Africa

Andrew Muir

After 25 years of convening on other continents, the World Wilderness Congress returned to its roots in South Africa in November 2001. Dr Ian Player and his Zulu friend, mentor and game scout, Magqubu Ntombela conceived the idea of creating an "indaba" when introducing people to wilderness by taking them on trails, sitting under our African stars and talking around campfires. They identified the need for a gathering of likeminded people as well as the public (i.e., business, political, scientific and cultural leaders) to join forces for wilderness to be understood and to survive globally. Thus the 1st WWC took place in Johannesburg in 1977, and subsequently convened in Australia, Great Britain, the United States, Norway and India.

Despite South Africa leading the way in Africa in terms of wilderness conservation, our diverse population as a whole has not always been included in conservation and policy issues. It became vital that a wider spectrum of our citizens develop their environmental awareness and appreciation of wilderness areas. Therefore, 2001 was the right time for the World Wilderness Congress to return to Africa to focus on, amongst other important issues, the attention needed by Southern African and African wildlands. A catalyst was also needed in South Africa, to enhance its national wilderness legislation. Strategically it was important to position this event ahead of the World Summit on Sustainable Development in Johannesburg (2002) and the World Park Conference in Durban (2003), as the 7th WWC provided a valuable public platform to demonstrate that conservation is essential both from a biological perspective and from a social and economic standpoint.

The theme of this Congress—*Wilderness and Human Communities: The Spirit of the 21st Century*—was also both important and timely. Africans, and people of other continents, need to understand the valuable services provided by wilderness, and how wild nature strengthens human culture and communities. We also also need to devise new ways in which we work together to assure the protection and sustainability of important wilderness areas, such as the Baviaanskloof, the large wild area in the Eastern Cape very near to Port Elizabeth, the venue for the 7th WWC. Finally, this theme also allowed the 7th WWC to showcase the cultural diversity of our country, and enabled the spirit of Africa people, wildlife and wildlands to come through strongly in the program. It left an indelible mark on all the delegates.

Eastern Cape, South Africa
January 2003

Introduction

Wild Nature—A Positive Force

Vance G. Martin

It is impossible to recall the 7th World Wilderness Congress without the world context in which it convened. Occurring just seven weeks after the attack of September 11, 2001, it too was a victim of terrorism—albeit of a far lesser magnitude to those directly affected by the tragic event. Final planning was completely disrupted and once the go-ahead decision was made, extensive and exhaustive restructuring was necessary.

Though over 700 delegates from some 44 nations participated, over 100 registered delegates were forced to cancel and many others who wanted to attend were unable to do so. The security—while sensitively and expertly provided by both the national and local South African governments—was extraordinarily extensive, expensive, and time-consuming. The financial losses and incremental costs were significant.

That said, most other conferences and large international gatherings were canceled. Our ultimate decision to go forward, arrived at within two weeks, was simple. The majority of delegates affirmed both their intent to attend as well as the principle at stake—the protection and sustainability of wild nature must not be held hostage to politics, whether it be of the terrorist type or the more common, everyday brand.

The impact of 9-11 was not all bad. The 7th WWC benefited by being virtually the first significant public, international gathering to be held in its immediate aftermath. The Congress delegates knew that the world now, more than ever, needed a positive vision. They suffered anthrax and bomb threats, intense airline disruption, and omnipresent security, but by their participation demonstrated a stronger-than-ever commitment to wilderness as an irreplaceable resource in a healthy and sane human society, a society that understands true wealth, not just financial wealth.

So it was in an atmosphere of hope that the 7th WWC convened. Always known for collaboration, positivity, and vision, the WWC in 2001 surpassed even its own history in this regard by looking anew toward the future. From start to finish, a courageous spirit and a contagious enthusiasm was present and palpable. As a result, many practical accomplishments were achieved, new alliances formed, old conflicts transformed, funds raised, people trained, policies clarified, and more. In a phrase, delegates and their actions confirmed a fundamental reality:

**Wilderness had never been more important than it is today.
But it is not as important today as it will be tomorrow.**

Ojai, California
January 2003

Acknowledgments

The World Wilderness Congress achieves its practical objectives through the unstinting and generous support of a wide range of funders, volunteers, and cooperating organizations. For example, many of the main presenters and program participants often pay their own delegate expenses in order to assist the main budget. The WWC is a diverse, far-reaching consortium of organizations, agencies, and individuals, and we express our sincere appreciation to all of them for their help in making the 7th WWC an enjoyable, practical, and accomplished process. In addition, there are numerous main financial sponsors whom we wish to acknowledge with gratitude, as follows:

Main Program Funders
Eastern Cape Department of Finance, Tourism, Environment and Economic Affairs—SA
Unilever—SA
Board Walk Casino and Entertainment Complex—PE
Shamwari Game Reserve
Eastern Cape Tourism Board

Function and Event Funders
Audi—SA [gala evening]
Pick 'n Pay [film festival]
Sierra Foundation/Sierra Club (USA) [wilderness management training]
Kwandwe Private Game Reserve

Sponsors

Compaq—Germany

Anglo American

Wildlands Trust

South African Airways

And a special acknowledgement to Ms. Magalen Bryant, Michael Thoresen, Robert and Charlotte Baron, Fulcrum Inc., Monomoy Fund (Ms. Dielle Fleischmann), and the Gaia Foundation—UK.

Editor's Notes

The papers contained in this book have been edited for readability and style, so that the information they contain may be more easily accessible to the general public and to conservation volunteers and professionals. For example, in most cases:

- Measurements of land area are generally in metric (hectares), where 2.54 hectares equals 1 acre;
- References and bibliography, if included in the original paper, were usually omitted;
- Text references to the particular time and place—7th World Wilderness Congress, South Africa, November 2001—were omitted;
- Footnotes, if not essential, were normally omitted.
- Vernacular language was translated where possible.

For the first time in publishing the proceedings of the WWC, we have printed the PowerPoint style of notes presentation used by a speaker (pp. 76–86, and pp. 262–277). We did this in lieu of publishing nothing at all, as we deemed the information valuable and able to be referenced if used by others.

In the appendices the reader will find as complete a list as was available of all the authors and their contact information. If you have further questions, we encourage you to communicate directly with them.

Many technical sessions and workshops also met during the 7th WWC. The most extensive was the symposium on Science and Stewardship to Protect and Sustain Wilderness Values. The papers presented, and contained in the published proceedings, cover seven topics: state-of-knowledge on protected areas in South Africa; traditional and ecological values of nature; wilderness systems and approaches to protection; protection of coastal/marine and river/lake wilderness; spiritual benefits, religious beliefs, and new stories; personal and societal values of wilderness; and the role of science, education, and collaborative planning in wilderness protection and restoration. Detailed technical papers can be obtained through the following reference:

Watson, Alan; Sproull, Janet, comps. 2003. Seventh World Wilderness Congress symposium: science and stewardship to protect and sustain wilderness values; 2001 November 1–8; Port Elizabeth, South Africa. Proc.RMRS-P-27. Ogden, UT: U.S. Department of Agriculture, Forest Service, Rocky Mountain Research Station. 237 p.

For more information on the World Wilderness Congress itself, please visit www.worldwilderness.org, or contact:

The WILD Foundation
P.O. Box 1380
Ojai, California, USA 93024
Telephone: 805-640-0390, fax 805-640-0230
info@wild.org; www.wild.org

Invocation—A Plea for Africa

Baba Credo Mutwa

When the white man came to the green shores of Africa he found this land teaming with animals. He found literally millions of buffalo, he found millions of wildebeest, and he found millions of springboks that migrated through this country's valleys like living oceans.

He came with blunderbusses, he came with his muskets, he came with his Schneider rifles and slaughtered the entire living Africa with his bullets. He did not ask himself why this country was full of animals. He saw people who wore skins, he saw people who lived in grass houses and he damned them for savages and demonized them as inferiors. It never occurred to the white man that the reason why Africa was alive with animals was because our religion demanded cooperation between human beings and animals. He never asked himself why it is that we of Africa grew the best cotton in the world and yet wore skins, he put this down to savagery, to low intelligence, and he left it there. The white man never realized that our religion taught us that cloth is a dead thing that should only be used for the burial of stillborn babies, and that human beings must, under no circumstances, separate themselves from the animal world; that man must wear the animal and thereby honor it.

Our religion did not teach us that we were masters over the animal world; far from it. We were taught that we were visitors in this land and that, like visitors, we must treat the village that is the earth with respect.

Today, when you walk into many a game park in South Africa you are told that hippos kill many black people. They never used to. When I was a child my mother and other women used to go in their skin skirts, bare-breasted, covered with red ochre. They used to go into a river which was alive with hippos and crocodiles and they used to get water from there. Why? Because they smelled naturally, they smelled of sweat, they smelled of wood smoke and they smelled of sex. Today people smell of soap, which antagonizes many a noble animal in the wild. We behave toward animals as enemies and they return our enmity.

In Africa we were taught that animals were our saviors. We were taught that each one of us should have a symbolic animal within him or her. When I married my wife, Cecilia, now departed to the Land of the Stars, I gave her a symbolic animal, the Bateleur Eagle. Whenever she and I were communicating intimately she used to imitate the eagle and I knew this is my wife.

Africa mothered the human race. If you asked me what is an African, I say to you that every one of you of every race carries within him or her, genes of the first human woman who walked erect on this continent Africa. Deny it if you dare. We all share a common humanity, we all share a similar culture. Don't tell me about European culture or Native American culture. I have been to many parts of the world and I can tell you all cultures come from the same root, which is Africa.

Today Africa is being destroyed by her own people. Foreigners manipulate Africans to market Africa. Foreigners deny us our true identity, of which they were aware when the first colonist came to Africa. Some of them knew exactly who we were, but they shut that truth away from us, and today we slaughter each other, children are given machine guns to murder their parents. They are given cast-off uniforms from dead people far away, and they are called soldiers.

My plea, my appeal is that we should be allowed to return Africa back to her shining roots. We should be allowed to bring back to our children the love and the reverence of animals that our people were taught from childhood to practice. I wish to tell you this: that Africa should be brought back to her greatness, to her true identity, if the environment is to be saved. Furthermore, the saving of the environment is to our people a matter of national emergency. At this moment, Africa is swept by AIDS, a strange disease, the roots of which are directly traceable to the flagrant destruction of the environment that we have seen in the last fifty years or so. We are paying a ghastly price for this.

It was the duty of every person in our communities in olden days to protect animals. For this reason every tribe was given a coat of arms or a totem. For example, if you belonged to the Dube tribe—Dube means zebra—you were bound to protect zebra with your life if necessary. Not only the zebra, you had also to protect all animals in the bush that always closely travel with the zebra, namely the wildebeest and the warthog.

In Africa, conservation of wild animals and conservation of trees was an important part of our now-destroyed traditional religion. How can you teach our children to respect the environment without bringing back the religion, I would like to ask you? How will you teach our children not to chop down certain trees, because our mothers used to teach us that a tree was born by a bird? One of our songs tells how the tree is given birth by the bird.

The thing you call ecology now was part and parcel of African life and religion. What the world is trying to do today with materialistic means will fail. We need to bring back to Africa what she possessed before. Did you know that in the land of the Zulus, if you killed a vulture you were executed? Did you know that even now, in the land of the Botswana people, there are trees you are not allowed to cut down even if you are short of fuel wood.

I traveled through Africa before and during the Second World War. I saw Africa as she used to be: Africa then was a paradise. In Uganda you could buy bananas, a whole basin-full, for a song. In Angola you could eat all the avocados you wanted simply for the asking. But today countries in Africa are ravaged by wars that make no sense to anybody. Wars that end only when the countries concerned have become so destroyed that not even the government of that country know the rebels they were fighting. What government can gain anything from that?

But when you look at the countries being devastated by war in Africa, they are those countries which, if left to themselves, could sustain the entire African continent in food and in oil. There is oil under Angola and for that reason that beautiful country has been reduced to hell. There are places in Mozambique where if the veldt catches fire you will see jets of fire coming from under the rocks. Uganda was a paradise. In the Sudan I ate so much rice my stomach nearly burst. Today, the Sudan is sunk in one of the most brutal wars in human history.

My question is why? Africa is being destroyed, brother and sisters, deliberately and cold-bloodedly. But who is Africa, what is this continent that everybody wants so urgently to obliterate? The answer is that Africa is the shinning buckle that joins all humankind together. I have traveled to many parts of the world and I have found African words in the language of Native Americans, I have found African practices in remote parts of this planet. Humankind originated from Africa. He took from Africa a great culture that became the root of all the other cultures.

Today Mother Africa must perish. Today the beautiful Green Goddess of my grandfather must die. Why? What have we done?

Let me finish by revealing something strange and important to you. People destroy the environment at their direst peril. In South Africa there used to be a number of birds, which have now gone into the valleys of extinction. One of these birds used to eat the seeds of a certain plant, and when it defecated the seeds they could easily sprout. This plant produced miracles in the early fight against AIDS: we have been using it in secret for three years out of fear, and only now is its great value coming out. But wait, because there is no longer a bird that eats this plant, I have to rub each little seed with a sand paper before the seeds can germinate. This plant is so important, I think, that it should be known to every member of the human race, especially those parts of the world where AIDS is rife. But we destroyed the bird that used to eat this plant, and today we are paying the ghastly price.

One last thing. My hands have held many people dying of AIDS, have bathed people that doctors have abandoned and sent home to die. Some of these people we have managed to pull out of the darkness of death, using the fruits of Africans green soil. And one of the things that works a miracle, with people who got AIDS, is the special milk from an animal called an Eland. When an Eland gives birth to a calf, there is that special milk which it produces; and then what you do is let the Eland calf suckle the mother and fill its stomach, then chase it away, tie up the animal and milk it. If you give this milk to somebody suffering from AIDS, it is something that I would leave you who looking to the truth, to find out for yourself: the result is amazing.

I say this—hand back the animals to the children of Africa! When tourists arrive in South Africa they are only told about animals from the Euro-centric view. That zebra there is called Burchell's Zebra. Who the hell was Burchell? My God! When you come to the great game reserves in the United States of America you are shown animals, first from the Euro-centric perspective: the brown bear, the coyote; and then in some places you are given a Native American guide who enriches your mind with a rich full cloth about American animals. Why is this not being done in South Africa? It would bring more tourists to the land. Don't tell visitors about Burchell's Zebra; don't tell them about Felix Leo. Tell them our stories, name the real names ... the power is there.

Do you know what Africans thought about the lion? Why do modern cultures call it the King of the Beats? Because we Africans knew that it was in charge of animals, the link that unites the carnivores to the herbivores. Do you know that Africans believed that elephants were reincarnations of gods that were murdered in heaven by other gods? During the Second World War there was an elephant called Issa in Tanganyika, and a group of African tribal people fought and died against a gang of poachers, protecting Issa from being murdered? Do you know what the name Issa means? It is the Islamic rendering of Jesus Christ. Our people there believed that this elephant was a reincarnation of Christ, so they fought and died in its defense.

What more can I tell you? I appeal to all of you to care about Africa. I appeal to all of you to weep for Africa, a continent that mothered you all, no matter who you are. Africa, our Mother.

In Honor of
Ian Player

Founder of the
World Wilderness
Congress

Umadolo—A Great Son
of South Africa

The Honorable Mangosuthu Buthelezi, MP
Minister of State for Home Affairs
INkosi of the Buthelezi Clan

I am honored to pay tribute to a great son of South Africa and a long-time friend and brother, Dr. Ian Player. I have known Dr. Player for almost half a century, during which time I have developed an unshakable respect for his character and integrity. Generations to come within our own country and abroad will appreciate Dr. Player for the giant figure that he is in the world of conservation and environmental protection. In my own mind, he remains distinguished not only for his faith commitment to preserving South Africa's greatest treasure for those who are yet to come, but also because he has proven through his work that a vision worth living for is a vision worth fighting for.

I wish to recall our personal interactions, for it is in these that our friendship has become solid. At the outset, I must mention that Dr. Player has been assisted in his achievements by a rare partnership of devotion and courage. His wife Anne, a remarkable woman in her own right, has been a constant support for her husband, without which he would perhaps not have achieved the great vision of his soul.

I met Dr. Player in 1953, shortly after I was installed as Inkosi of the Buthelezi Clan in the Mahlabathini District of what is now KwaZulu-Natal province. Together with Nick Steele, Hugh Dent and several others, he worked as a ranger in the game reserves in northern part of KwaZulu Natal. At that time there was often controversy among the amaKhosi [group of chiefs] and the

3

people in the Hlabisa District concerning the so-called "corridor". It was difficult for our people to understand why a stretch of land could be reserved for animals when they themselves so desperately needed land on which to live. As the senior conservator, Ian Player, together with the Natal Parks Board, approached me in my capacity as Undunankulu, Traditional Prime Minister of the Zulu nation, to intervene in these disputes. From this early time I saw the value of what Dr. Player was trying to achieve, not only for the few who would enjoy it at the time, but for our posterity who must inherit the treasures of South Africa.

During many meetings we attempted to resolve the dispute and I appealed to my fellow compatriots, the amaKhosi and their clansmen, to understand the importance of what we would be preserving by protecting our game and having game reserves. Recognizing the passion within Ian Player for our natural heritage, tempered by his deep respect for people, the Zulu people came to affectionately call him "Madolo," Zulu for "The Knee," in respect of the debilitating knee injury he suffered and was forced to overcome everyday of his life. From that time I interacted with Madolo continuously, at his invitation even visiting Hluhluwe Game Reserve with my family. That invitation was an object of contempt for some who held fast to the apartheid notion that game reserves were the playground of white people only. Indeed, such notion had itself compounded the difficulty of our task in persuading our people about the importance of conservation.

What Dr. Ian Player and I did at the time was indeed controversial, but truly valuable. It is amazing how often the really valuable things in life are controversial and in order to create long-term value one needs to challenge present conventional wisdom. At the time I was ridiculed for my concern for animals, plants and nature as if matters of this sort were so frivolous that they should not engage the mind and attention of a person of my rank. Environmental concerns were not regarded to be mainstream politics, not only in our country but throughout the world, and were somehow considered matters to be dealt with by political lightweights. I recognized the importance of environmental issues when it was not fashionable to do so because I recognized that, in the long-term, the survival of mankind and its prosperity depend not only on political and social conditions, but also on a balanced relationship with Mother Earth. Dr. Ian Player contributed, with others, to my reaching this deep understanding in my life.

I also had the opportunity to recognize how the understanding of environmental concerns and the care for nature conservation is part and parcel of our African culture. Also in this respect I must praise Dr. Player for teasing the environmental themes out of the thematic of our own African culture. He recognized that the African people are intrinsically bound to their environment and naturally inclined toward nature conservation. It was a matter of reconciling this natural inclination with the pressing demands for land and natural resources that afflicted us once our life and existence had been relegated to a small portion of our national land, so often of poor quality. In this way in the early 80's I began conceiving with Dr. Player a genuinely African notion of development which postulated that we do not need to achieve our industrialization and social and economic development by following the same path of many western countries which, in the process of growth, ended up destroying their environment. In this sense, environmental conservation gave impetus to a much broader vision, comprising all aspects of development and a possible path toward a genuine African Renaissance.

It is through the visionary foresight of men, such as Ian Player and Nick Steele, that our heritage has been preserved and the basis for a broader vision was founded. When we began, their work was much harsher than that of any nature conservationist in other countries of the world as at the time, their battle was engaged on many fronts. Even the Parks Board did not like what they were doing or how they went about it. By breaking apartheid's color-bar in insisting that I and my family stay at Mthwazi Lodge in Hluhluwe, they risked their jobs.

Yet, I recognized in Ian Player an unusual courage and vision. I was not overly surprised when I received news after my family's visit to Mthwazi that the blankets, linen and rooms had been fumigated upon our departure. But this shows the depth of ignorance and contempt against which we struggled.

The Parks Board and its then Chairman, Mr. Douglas Mitchell, deemed me as "too controversial a figure" for them to allow substantial association of my name with that of their conservators. In the early 70's I was invited to speak at the GameCOIN conference in San Antonio, Texas, by a mutual friend, Mr. Harry Tennison. Mr. Tennison had wanted the late Nick Steele to accompany me and introduce me at the conference, yet this was forbidden. In the end, it was Ian Player who attended the conference in Texas with my wife, Irene, Ann Player, and me, as part of the delegation of the Natal Parks Board. Thus, it was not merely the ire of the Zulu people that Dr. Player had to contend with in doing his job with such excellence, but also opposition from apartheid-minded officials. Moreover, there was the added wrath of many white people who were voters of the National Party, who opposed the existence of what they, in Afrikaans, termed "Pig Parks," referring to warthogs.

At times, Dr. Player and his colleagues also met with stiff opposition from official quarters such as magistrates in the Province. I recall in particular one magistrate who, faced with the magnitude of Dr. Player's vision, decided he had become too big for his boots, prompting the caustic remark: "Who does he think he is? Does he think he's important merely because he founded the Dusi canoe race?" (now one of the world's great canoe races). Yet for those who lack vision, men of vision appear as dreamers. What Dr. Player was working to achieve was far greater than himself, and today his work has jumped the limits of time to benefit generations not yet born. I stand in awe of his fortitude and tenacity. Deservedly, he has received honors from all over the world and has been decorated with a Distinguished Meritorious Order by the Head of State of his own country. He is indeed a giant among men.

It is a pleasure and an honor for me to praise Dr. Ian Player for the outstanding work he has accomplished in the field of nature conservation and environmental protection. I honor him as a fellow conservator, a fellow visionary for South Africa, and a close friend for whom I have the greatest respect. Madolo has left his mark on our Province and among the Zulu people, and on South Africa as a whole. His life's work speaks of the noble value to be found in living for a cause that will secure a better quality of life for those who will follow in one's shadow. He is an inspiration to me and I count it a privilege to applaud his life's achievement.

Wilderness—The Spirit of
the 21st Century

Ian Player

The 7th World Wilderness Congress has both practical and symbolic importance. The number "7" has powerful symbolic significance. The Egyptian name for the supreme being was composed of seven vowels. And in seven months a human fetus acquires a life of its own. Perhaps with the grace of the creator we will soon see the birth of new understanding in our world of the vital role of wilderness areas. Let us continue to hope, and to work for that new birth.

Many people have asked me about the logo of the World Wilderness Congress. It always contains the single *green leaf,* as do the logos of all of the organizations I have founded. Its origin comes from Grey Owl, the Englishman who became an Ojibway Indian. When he was dying he said, "You are tired of years of civilization. I come and offer you what? A single green leaf."

Forty-three years ago I asked Magqubu Ntombela for a logo for the Wilderness Leadership School. He, in his own time, brought the *Erythrina* leaf (Coral Tree) to me and said almost as a Biblical injunction, "*Tata Lokho* (take this leaf). You find it in the wilds and the settlements. It is our job to take people from the cities into the wild. The leaf has three parts," he said. "One part is to honor *Mvelangani,* God. The other the Earth, and the third Humanity." The leaf has since become the logo of all previous Congresses and allied organizations. A remarkable history has ensued.

The 1st World Wilderness Congress took place in Johannesburg in 1977. This was shortly after the Soweto riots and South Africa had become a pariah among nations. Organizing the Congress was a nightmare and my poor wife had to put up with my severe depressions. But the Congress was eventually a success. People such as Nora Kreher, Michael Sweatman and Laurens van der Post—and many others of course—played critical roles in the organization of that 1st Congress. Other Congresses followed, for instance in Australia in 1980, where again Laurens played a key role. It was in Australia I met Vance Martin, and he bore the brunt of future Congresses—Scotland in 1983, America in 1987 with John Hendee, Norway in 1993, India with Partha Sarathy in 1998, and now with Andrew Muir for the 7th. None were easy, but achievements have been many, meaningful, and practical. Too many people to mention have contributed to its success, not the least of which are the many thousands of delegates from over 75 nations who have made the accomplishments practical and effective, and put the resolutions to work on the ground. The World Wilderness Congress has now acquired a life of its own and has become the longest-running international environmental forum.

The world owes America an incalculable debt for the modern movement of national parks and wilderness areas. We in South Africa took a leaf out of their book, particularly with the 1964 Wilderness Act. The U.S. Senate proceedings prior to the Act contain every argument for and against wilderness. It proved to be an invaluable help to me in our long bureaucratic struggle for wilderness wreas in Zululand. My friend and fellow game ranger, Jim Feely, introduced me to the concept in the Mfolozi Game Reserve in 1955. We must also honor Danie Ackerman and Bill Bainbridge, who were able to initiate South Africa's wilderness under our Forestry Act, and to Bill Bainbridge again and Drummond Densham for their Wilderness Management training courses.

It is out of the crucible of the small wilderness areas in Mfolozi, Zululand, that the World Wilderness Congresses emerged along with our allied organizations, both locally and internationally, which has grown into a singular and important network. It was the beginning of a new era in conservation, particularly with introduction of "wilderness trails," trekking on foot in South Africa's wilderness areas. Few people know or remember that prior to the initiation of these walking trails, while outside of the main camping areas of the game reserves and parks, it was actually illegal for tourists to be out of their automobiles. We have come a long way.

In the Eastern Cape of South Africa, history is being rewritten at this very moment. This province has become one of the new frontiers in the conservation of wildlands in Southern Africa. In the 1800s, wild game was driven to a point of extinction. Wars raged, and the land was abused by bad farming. Those wonderful little people, the San, were massacred. But in spirit and in blood, some remain with us—and so does their art. Many of us have sat in the semi-darkness of the caves and overhangs of these early people, looking at the exquisite paintings of animals, birds, snakes and human figures all glowing numinously, and in our imagination heard their voices. The San people used to say that wherever they went the animal eye was upon them, so numerous was the game.

In the Eastern Cape we have the emerging game ranches pioneered by Adrian Gardiner's Shamwari, and Angus Sholto Douglas' Kwande, and many others. The expansion of Addo National Park, and the Baviaanskloof Mega-Wilderness Complex are redressing many wrongs. The game is returning and with it the spirit and the healing of the land. We hear the echo of Pliny the Elder who in the First Century A.D. wrote, *Ex Africa semper aliquid novi.* "Out of Africa always something new." Truly a conservation miracle is taking place here. With many new initiatives including the first private wilderness area on the continent at Shamwari, South Africa can be very proud. But we will not forget our debt to America.

Harold McMillan, a former British prime minister, said there are only two forces in the world of man. One is the great spiritual force of religion, and the other is the force of common sense. In a brilliant speech in 1994, Roger Kennedy, then Director of the National Parks in America said: "Wilderness is a religious concept." The word religion comes from the Latin: to ponder, to take account of, to observe. We must distinguish between religion and creed. As C. G. Jung says, one is generic, the other specific. Wilderness has been the birthplace of many religions, Islam and Christianity amongst them. But there is ever increasing fragmentation in the formal religions. In Christianity alone there are over 400 different sects. And on television we see tanks grinding through Bethlehem, and people dying daily. What an indictment of our dangerous species, *homo sapiens.*

But what is wilderness? I am certain that almost everyone here today would have a different definition. The word "wilderness" is an inadequate description of a soul event. It is only now beginning to recover from bad connotations because wilderness was once only considered a wasteland, a dry, dusty, uncultivated, inhospitable place. In the physical sense, we have the current World Conservation Union definition of a wilderness area—which can be within a national park or game reserve, or on its own, but strict rules define its use. The definition adopted by the IUCN was formulated after much hard work through the World Wilderness Congress and our colleagues in the Sierra Club and elsewhere:

> "Large areas of unmodified or slightly modified land and/or sea, retaining its natural character and influence, which is protected and managed so as to preserve its natural condition."

South Africa was the first country in Africa to give legal status to wilderness areas, but we now need better legislation and bigger areas proclaimed so that we can continue to be an example to the rest of the continent.

Wilderness as a philosophical concept is still an ongoing debate, and we have a long way to go. Those of us who have been into wild country know that it is numinous—a religious experience, a binding to God. We can understand why it has been the font of many religions. And like the prophet in T.E. Lawrence's *Seven Pillars of Wisdom*, those of us converted return to the cities trying to convince others of our visions of God. Generally we fail because we do not have the language to describe let alone define it. Our vocabulary is too sparse.

Wilderness remains alive because nothing can eradicate mankind's archetypal belief that the world was once a paradise and we were brothers and sisters to all other life. In this 21st century, we must have new language to convey the feelings of beauty, hope, inspiration and sacredness. We need something that will stir our psychic depths and touch the images in the soul. It has to surpass creeds and be instantly recognized by all who hear it. The language is there waiting in the collective unconsciousness for revelation.

Speaking from 50 years of personal experience I can tell you I have walked, ridden and canoed in wild places: in the Yosemite mountains with Native American rangers; wild gorges on Mindoro Island in the Philippines with Batangan and Bannunoo tribesmen; in the central Australian desert with Aborigines. Last year, in the far north of Arnhemland in Australia, we experienced the unbelievable quiet in the caves, and saw the prolific and moving art of Aborigines and where they lay the bones of their dead.

But it is in Africa, like many of you, that my soul has been most deeply touched. The Arabs said "Once you have tasted the waters of Africa you must return to have your fill thereat." As a game ranger I canoed at Ndumu on the

Pongolo River amongst the hippo and crocodile, on St. Lucia with the flamingo and the pelican, and I heard the cry of the fish eagle, and in my mind heard the words of Longfellow's poem, *The Slave's Dream*:

> Before him, like a blood red flag,
> > The bright flamingoes flew;
> From morn till night he followed their flight,
> > O'er the plains where the tamarind grew,
> Till he saw the roofs of caffre huts,
> > And the ocean rose to view.
>
> At night he heard the lion roar,
> > And the hyena scream,
> And the river horse, as he crushed the reeds
> > Beside some hidden stream;
> And it passed, like a glorious roll of drums,
> > Through the triumph of his dream.
>
> The forests, with their myriad tongues,
> > Shouted of liberty;
> And the Blast of the Desert cried aloud,
> > With a voice so wild and free,
> That he started in his sleep and smiled,
> > At their tempestuous glee.

In the valleys of Hluhluwe and Mfoloze Game Reserve I walked behind my friend Magqubu Ntombela along the rhino paths and on the flood plains and up into those ancient hills, in a landscape man has known for thousands of years. I have listened with an inner ear, to the outer sounds of the African earth: the bateleur, crested francolin, the soft song of the white-throated robin, leaves dropping from Nthombothi trees, and the sound of the wind in the reeds and the long themeda grasslands. As a young game ranger I sat at night at the fire on anti-poaching patrols with Magqubu Ntombela, waiting expectantly for the great eagle owl to call; the leopard with its long, sawing cough; the hyena; and then, at dawn, the roar of the lion. I have listened to inner voices telling me of my past, and had dreams that came to me while lying on the hard ground of wild Africa, and been touched and energized by the images that seemed to come up from the ancient earth.

Somewhere among all this is a symphony of the African earth waiting to emerge. A new song that will express a flowering and our exultation of this continent of the birth of humankind—the landscape of the human soul. But oh how easily are we devastated and depressed, no matter what country we live in, when we see wild land being ripped open, seared with the bricks and mortar of high rise buildings, and roads that cut into the heart of the land as we hear the phrase: "You can't stop progress."

All those of us who are involved in the conservation and wilderness movement know how difficult it is not to be disillusioned. There is a constant inner struggle to stop oneself being overwhelmed. We know that there is not a wild area on this planet that is not under threat, and we humans are the perpetrators. There is so little left. As Jung said, "We have lost a world that once pulsed with our blood and breathed with our breath. Did the wind used to cry, and the hills shout forth praise."

How often have we called out on sleepless nights, "This is too much, I can't go on." Yet such is the power of our belief in the cause that we continue to a point of exhaustion. As Robert Johnston so eloquently put it: "There are times when we feel too wounded to live but unable to die." We have to keep going and not turn off our feelings and become insensitive. David Livingstone, our poet, once said to a group of young aspiring poets, "Make your skin—your carapace against the world and its slings and arrows—as thin as possible without bleeding to death through it." How pertinent this is to us, because we could so easily emotionally bleed to death.

But let us for the moment look at and celebrate our recent great South African successes. Many of us were deeply involved in the most critical struggle to save Lake St. Lucia. The agony of those four long years was only relieved by the wonderful international wilderness camaraderie and the unshakeable commitment to that most righteous cause. There is also the miracle in Africa of the Trans Frontier Peace Parks, which have hugely advanced the green frontier.

All of us know the western world is in an inner state of crisis. The recent attack on America has shaken the very foundations of our modern material civilization. A cry has welled out of the depths of the unconscious. Humanity has said: "The world will never be the same again." Recently someone wrote and said that because of September 11th, wilderness was now irrelevant. The fact that the 7th World Wilderness Congress convened just seven weeks following the attack, despite enormous difficulties encountered by Vance and Andrew and their staff, is in part a validation of the importance of wilderness. Is wilderness relevant? Of course it is, but we need the personal commitment and personal will to assure that it remains so.

There is a desperate need to return to the source of religious inspiration. We need wilderness as a sacred place to commune with the great spirit and our enlightened selves. Wilderness, in whatever way we describe it, has become the chance for human beings to redeem their humanity. It is the place where we go to contemplate our origins, examine our past, and plan our future. It is manna for the soul and hope for all life. … Yes—the wilderness is relevant, and we have just begun to explore the great mystery of it.

Perspectives and Reports from Around the World

The Global Environment Facility's Commitment to Wilderness Areas

Mohamed T. El-Ashry

This is the second meeting of the World Wilderness Congress on the continent of Africa, and it takes place at the beginning of a new century and a new millennium. This Congress, which represents the global wilderness movement, has grown in strength, meeting over the last twenty-five years in six countries on six continents. Its achievements are clearly manifested in the international recognition of wilderness as a distinct category in the United Nations list of protected areas maintained by IUCN, and in the current growth in legally designated wilderness and wildland areas to cover approximately 5% of the earth's surface.

I must pay tribute to the government and people of the Republic of South Africa. As they prepare to host the World Summit on Sustainable Development in September of 2002, South Africa does not shy away from hosting events such as this Congress. It is a clear reflection of their commitment to preserving and protecting nature's bounty and their stewardship in a manner that both meets the needs of present and of future generations. We welcome South Africa's commitment to these global environmental issues and are prepared to work hard with South Africans to bring their laudable efforts to fruition.

Please allow me also to recognize Dr. Ian Player and the late Mr. Magqubu Ntombela who hosted the first congress here in South Africa and the tireless unyielding efforts of Vance Martin who has ensured that the Congress remains a vibrant global event. In Vance's words, "each World Wilderness Congress serves as a benchmark against which we can measure our collective progress—or lack thereof—towards an important goal—defining a human civilization that understands natural proportion, lives sustainably, and respects life."

You may not know that the GEF owes its origins in part to the World Wilderness Congress. It grew out of the wisdom and concern of a few visionary and selfless individuals—notably environmental thinkers, businessmen and economists—at the 4th Wilderness Congress in Colorado in 1987. A working session hosted by The WILD Foundation Chairman, Michael Sweatman, conceptualized a study later done by the World Resources Institute, financed by the McArthur Foundation and others, on "Financing Nature Conservation." This study led to some of the key principles behind the Global Environment Facility. I am very proud of those beginnings.

Over the last ten years, the GEF has grown to be the principal partner of countries in taking real action to achieve sustainable development, mainly by aligning its portfolio with national biodiversity programs and country priorities. GEF was established to forge international cooperation and finance actions related to biological diversity, climate change, international waters, and the ozone layer. It also works to stem the pervasive problem of land degradation, and was recently, at a meeting here in South Africa, designated the financial mechanism for the new convention on Persistent Organic Pollutants (POPs). Since its establishment in 1991, the GEF has allocated more than US $1.3 billion to 446 biodiversity conservation and sustainable use projects in 123 developing countries—the single

largest funding worldwide. These projects have leveraged an additional $1.5 billion in government counterpart commitments and another $1.1 billion in co-financing from bilateral and multilateral agencies and the private sector.

GEF's impact on conservation of wilderness is even more evident in its support for protected areas. Some 671 protected areas in 106 countries, covering over 889 million hectares, over one-half of identified globally significant biodiversity sites, receive GEF support. 70% are forests and 29% are priority wetlands and coastal areas. More than one half of priority biodiversity sites in the *Global 200 List of the Earth's Distinctive Eco-regions* classification by WWF are supported by GEF through 86 projects. Through its support to the *Critical Ecosystems Partnerships Fund*, the GEF is helping to conserve 60% of the earth's land based life in 1.4% of the world's land area which includes globally significant eco-regions and the Meso-American Biological Corridor. GEF projects cover 80% of the home range of the top ten most threatened and endangered plant and animal species according to the IUCN Red Book.

Like the World Wilderness Congress, GEF shares your concern that matters of spirit and culture are equally important to matters of science, politics, economics and education in natural resource issues. In this respect, more than $81.2 million in grants has been allocated to projects which conserve outstanding sites linked to the cultural patrimony of mountain indigenous communities. Over 60% of the total number of *World Natural and Cultural Heritage Sites* are now conserved through GEF funding of more than $270 million to 40 projects.

This meeting of the 7th World Wilderness Congress in Africa should also be seen in terms of Africa's contribution to the global conservation movement. The African continent, although currently confronted by various socio-economic challenges, has the potential to contribute considerably to the global conservation movement through its people and through the broad range of rich cultural and natural landscapes. Africa is currently a recipient of $350 million in GEF grants in support of conservation. In this respect, the region is second only to Latin America.

The 7th World Wilderness Congress is held in the Eastern Cape, the home of Nelson Mandela, one of the greatest leaders of our time and in history. Mr. Mandela taught the world the meaning of perseverance, persistence and tolerance. Here in South Africa can be found the Baviaanskloof Mountains, an area on the verge of being declared the largest wilderness area in South Africa. This area is one of notable biological diversity and historical importance. It has over thousands of years sheltered the San people, and today provides ecological services to major industrial areas of the Eastern Cape. Moreover, it is the site of wilderness experience programs operated by the Wilderness Foundation and the Wilderness Leadership School, both for poor urban youth, as well as for members of the Environmental Portfolio Committee of the South African Parliament. Already, the GEF has committed $15.93 million in grants to support nine projects in South Africa including conservation of the Drakensberg Mountains, the Cape Floral Kingdom, Addo Elephant reserve and the Agulhas Conservation area. When regional projects of which South Africa is a participant are added, the GEF portfolio grows to $72.5 million. As part of our continued collaboration, I am pleased to announce that, at the request of the Government of South Africa, the GEF will be making a contribution of US$1 million towards the conservation of the Baviaanskloof area. South African authorities will work with the GEF's implementing agencies in the preparation and implementation of this project.

South Africa has been contributing to the establishment of transboundary conservation areas and assisting to bring peace in an area which has had more than its share of hostilities. The establishment of transboundary peace parks is a major step in bringing about conservation benefits and also in the socio-economic development of the region. I am pleased also to announce that, at the request of the Government of Angola, the GEF is moving to assist current conservation efforts to rehabilitate the Angolan parks through sharing of animal populations in the two countries. The GEF will support a $1 million effort being undertaken jointly by the Government of Angola, UNDP and the Kissama Foundation.

No amount of financial resources alone will conserve our wilderness areas and natural resources heritage. It will require the continued commitment of persons like yourselves working individually and collectively to realize the goals which we mutually share. I would like to assure you that the GEF stands ready to continue working with you towards achieving those objectives.

Toward a New Vision
for Africa's Protected Areas

Mohamed I. Bakarr[1], Humphrey Kisioh,[2] and Walter Lusigi[3]

Introduction

The African continent is endowed with a great wealth of biological diversity—from a variety of ecosystems and habitats to a cornucopia of unique species found nowhere else on earth. For hundreds of years, the world has marveled at this remarkable natural heritage, which has also served as backdrop for the myriad of cultures that have evolved since the first of our predecessors walked on this continent. Today, this natural wealth is facing an ever-increasing threat associated with factors ranging from anthropogenic to biophysical. And at the same time, efforts to safeguard biodiversity continues to face overwhelming challenges all across the continent.

During the last century, all African countries demonstrated increasing commitment to conservation by setting aside large portions of their territories as protected areas, and through ratification of international conventions and treaties related to conservation. Establishment of protected areas has been the principal means for conserving biodiversity in Africa, and their potential for contributing to sustainable development has been widely recognized. However, this commitment to conservation by African nations is not matched by capacity and resources needed to safeguard biodiversity and manage the protected areas more effectively. As a consequence, the protected areas and ecosystems within

[1]Center for Applied Biodiversity Science at Conservation International
[2]IUCN East Africa Regional Office
[3]Global Environmental Facility

which they occur, face unprecedented pressures from growing populations, the uneven and often over-exploitation and consumption of natural resources, and unsustainable patterns of development. These are leading, not only to depletion of resources, but also to degradation and destruction of natural habitats. Even more challenging is the increasing impact of biophysical factors, such as climate change, which are already exacerbating the problems created by habitat loss and degradation. This situation makes the need for enhanced management of protected areas in Africa urgent.

In this paper, we outline some of the successes and problems associated with protected areas in sub-Saharan Africa, and present a new African-led initiative that is being developed under the auspices of the IUCN's World Commission on Protected Areas (WCPA). We discuss the initiative in a wider context of global scale changes facing protected areas and their management, and WCPA's effort to address them through a learning network. We emphasize the importance of placing protected areas on a high level agenda at the regional and continental scale in Africa, and the need for a new financing mechanism to include a Trust Fund that will strengthen and reinforce management efforts of government agencies.

Africa's Protected Areas—
A Mixed History of Success and Problems

Although the concept of "protected areas" connotes parks and reserves in the sense defined by The World Conservation Union (IUCN), the act of protecting habitats and species is an integral part of most African cultures. It is only in the last few decades that the value of such traditional protection efforts, such as *Sacred Groves*, has gained some recognition in the conservation literature. Nevertheless, the overall area allocated to protection of biodiversity on the African continent since the early 1900s has been phenomenal. For example, in sub-Saharan Africa alone, the area of terrestrial habitats in protected areas (IUCN management categories I–IV only) amounts to just over two million square kilometers (near 8.5% of the total land area), almost twice the size of South Africa. [IUCN Management Categories: 1—Strict Nature Reserves/ Wilderness Areas; II—National Parks; III—Natural Monuments; IV— Habitat/Species Management Areas; Based on data from IUCN/WCPA (1999)] The benefits of setting aside such areas is almost always well justified, and indeed protected areas have influenced cultures and livelihoods throughout the continent, and played a crucial role in many national economies through direct (e.g., income from tourism) and indirect (e.g., providing jobs) opportunities. Whether their existence is solely on paper or fully supported by relevant infrastructure and institutional development, research is now showing that the mere existence of protected areas do, to a varying extent, succeed at safeguarding biodiversity that would otherwise be permanently altered by other national priority needs. [Bruner et al. 2001, *Science* Vol. 291] In Africa, these areas for the most part today represent the only remaining natural habitats in many countries, and perhaps our only hope of passing on the continent's biological treasures for generations to come. The existence of these areas is not without problems, however, and throughout the continent, protected areas are, indeed, facing increasing threat.

Among major threats widely documented are the illegal exploitation of wildlife species, degradation of habitats from human encroachment, and in many cases by invasion of alien species. In the forest region of West and Central Africa, illegal exploitation of wildlife has been so severe that most protected areas today face what has become known as the empty forests syndrome. Large mammals, such as primates, antelopes, and the elephant, have suffered the greatest impacts of such uncontrolled exploitation. And unlike the vast savannah woodlands of Eastern and Southern Africa where relatively few species occur in enormous numbers and their incredible seasonal migrations remain an ecological marvel, African forest mammal species are among the most diverse in the world, but occur in naturally low densities and often with very restricted ranges.

The only large mammal extinction to be recorded on the African continent in the last century may have occurred in West Africa's forest region, with the apparent disappearance of a sub-species of primate, Miss Waldron's Red Colobus (*Procolobus badius waldroni*), from all previously recorded localities in Ghana and Côte d'Ivoire. [Oates et al. 2000, *Conservation Biology* (14) 5: 1526–1532]. Many other species of primates, such as the western chimpanzee (*Pan troglodytes verus*), white-naped mangabey (*Cercocebus atys lunulatus*), the Roloway monkey (*Cercopithecus diana diana*), and the Drill (*Mandrillus leucophaeus*), are among some of the world's most endangered species, with remaining populations already on the brink. Today, the fate of protected forests without significant populations of these critically important species remains in doubt, since hundreds of rain forest tree species depend on animals for their regenerative and reproductive cycles.

The threats to protected areas are often associated with a diverse range of factors, including poor relations between the protected area managers and adjacent communities, insufficient trained staff, lack of funding for capital development and operations, and civil unrest. With populations increasing and settlements expanding, human communities are moving ever closer to protected areas, creating conflict situations and management challenges in areas where such close juxtapositions were once rare. Furthermore, the increasing demand for resources that have dwindled or entirely disappeared elsewhere has put pressure on protected areas where such resources are now limited. While many African countries have the basic staff for protected areas in place and well trained through many years of effort, government and public support for these protected areas has been steadily declining in recent times. More importantly, it is becoming apparent that the role of protected area managers warrants a new dimension in order to address these emergent challenges.

Global Scale Challenges and the Need for Innovation in Establishment and Management of Protected Areas

The problems outlined in the previous paragraphs underscore the need for innovation in protected management across Africa. This need extends, however, beyond Africa to include all of the world's protected areas. Throughout the world, the capacity to adequately manage and safeguard these critical areas is increasingly challenged by the suite of environmental, social, economic, and institutional changes that are taking place at accelerating rates around the world. These issues include climate change, sea level rise, fragmentation of landscapes, invasive species, population growth, rising demands for food and fiber, and the impact of biotechnology upon hinterlands. In addition, such institutional changes as decentralization of authority and responsibility for resource management, democratization, access to information, and the rise of the private sector are particularly pertinent in developing countries. Consequently, countries that have already taken major steps to protect some of the world's most valuable biotic assets are faced with a complex circumstance that is often beyond the immediate grasp of protected area managers.

Failing to respond to these rapidly evolving issues can lead to reduced quantity and quality of ecosystem services and goods at local and national scales. At the global scale, this failure risks a loss of globally important biodiversity and biological resources.

In response to these challenges, the IUCN's World Commission on Protected Areas (WCPA) is implementing a global partnership initiative entitled Ecosystems, Protected Areas, and People (EPP), to improve and strengthen the role of protected areas for conserving global biodiversity. [The EPP partnership initiative is led by WCPA and the World Resources Institute (WRI), and will be implemented over a four-year period (2001–2004). The initiative has to-date secured involvement of several major organizations and institutions including, Conservation International/Center for Applied Biodiversity Science (CI-CABS), The Nature Conservancy (TNC), UNESCO Man and Biosphere (MAB), UNESCO World Heritage Center (WHC), UNEP World Conservation Monitoring Center (UNEP-WCMC), UNEP-Global Environmental Facility (GEF), the United Nations Foundation (UNF), World Wildlife Fund (WWF), and other IUCN Programs and Commissions.] A major aim of this project is to help protected area managers, directors, and policy makers in developing countries protect their *in situ* biodiversity in the rapidly changing context of coming decades. Specifically, the WCPA and partner institutions will establish an on-going international program that will make available the lessons learned from field activities around the world that demonstrate how particular policies, strategies, and field practices can meet the challenges of accelerating change. The project seeks to develop a Protected Areas Learning Network (PALNet) that will systematically gather lessons being learned from field projects seeking to address one or several change issues around the world.

PALNet will focus on giving policy makers, directors and managers of protected areas access to clear and useful information that will help them understand the relevance of these changes and potential opportunities for their areas, and practical and credible examples of what can be done to adapt their policies, strategies and management practices. Examples include projects that are targeting landscape approaches to provide connectivity among protected areas and enable native biota to adapt to the influences of fragmentation and isolation of wild land sites, and projects that are developing the capacity of local communities to manage protected areas critical to their livelihoods in response to new government decentralization policies. The program will develop a service to gather and analyze such cases, store the information, and make it accessible on WEB-based services, and in hard copy for wide distribution in various languages. This will become a long-term on-going service that will continuously revise and renew the case materials in an effort to enable managers to upgrade their knowledge and management capacity.

The EPP initiative will encompass five major themes to serve as framework for compiling and analyzing "lessons learned" on policies, strategies and best practice from field cases.

Theme 1: Understand and Prepare for Global Change—

This theme involves the compilation of information and knowledge from analytical and field research on key factors of change that will challenge the survival and value of protected areas, and provide options for responding to these challenges. The factors are categorized as:

- Biophysical—climate change, sea-level rise, fragmentation, invasive species, fire;
- Socio-economic—growing demand for food and fiber, impact of biotechnology-generated crops, extractive industries;
- Institutional—decentralization of authority and responsibility to other levels of government, NGOs, and communities; democratization; access and use of information; etc.

Theme 2: Building the Global System—

This theme will focus on establishing criteria and procedures to identify and select the most important sites for the *in situ* conservation of biodiversity (at the species, genetic varieties, habitats and landscape levels). It will also establish procedures and criteria to link these core areas with adequate "connectivity," such as by landscape "corridors," where needed for adaptation to global change, dispersal and migration purposes; and propose methods for establishing "bioregional" programs in surrounding landscapes to develop and promote adequate social and economic equity and stewardship for each region. Lessons will include how to promote a mosaic of land uses in surrounding regions that feature biodiversity-friendly agriculture, forestry, fishing and other practices.

Theme 3: Ensuring Management Effectiveness—
This theme will examine and test methods for evaluating the effectiveness of managing protected areas in terms of their objectives, with special reference to biodiversity conservation. It will develop norms, standards, and indicators to help directors, managers, and community leaders track their performance and make appropriate improvements in their strategies, policies and practices (planning, budgeting, protection, restoration, reintroduction, fire control, etc.), and consider methods leading up to a process of "certification" of protection at the national and international levels.

Theme 4: Establishing Equity with People—
Based upon a global analysis of past and current strategies, policies, and practices, this theme will seek to propose and test new approaches for ensuring equitable arrangements with communities living in and around protected areas. It will promote new financial options, economic tools, and policies that lead to more equitable distribution of costs and benefits from ecosystem goods and services; analyze experience from co-management, approaches for management by indigenous peoples, decentralization, participatory planning, and other innovative approaches to foster social equity and stewardship.

Theme 5: Developing the Capacity to Manage—
This theme will propose criteria for the types of policies, capabilities, knowledge, and skills that directors and managers will need in coming decades to address a rapidly changing reality and context for conservation. Based upon an analysis of ongoing educational and training opportunities, and the views of current leaders, the theme will also propose options for preparing managers for the 21st century, with special emphasis on communications skills, working with scientists, information technology, monitoring, and community relations.

To ensure that lessons from the EPP initiative are fully integrated into key global endeavors, project activities and outputs will target major delivery mechanisms such as the Convention on Biological Diversity and its Subsidiary Body for Scientific, Technical, and Technological Advice (CBD/SBSTTA), the World Heritage Convention, and the IUCN's World Parks Congress to be held in Durban, South Africa, in 2003.

The African Protected Areas Initiative

The global scale effort being mounted by the WCPA to address protected area management needs around the world, and the World Parks Congress coming to Durban, offers a unique opportunities to leverage much needed benefits to Africa's protected area systems. In particular, the development of EPP offers a crucial link to the new vision for Africa's protected areas. The new vision, which is being developed in anticipation of the 2003 World Parks Congress, will be addressed through the Africa Protected Areas Initiative (APAI) [APAI is an initiative of the IUCN/WCPA and will be implemented through the IUCN East Africa Regional Office, in partnership with other IUCN Programs and Regional Offices, and several organizations including UNEP-GEF, UNEP-WCMC, Peace Parks Foundation, Conservation International, and WWF International.] APAI is an Africa-wide and African-led process aimed at addressing fundamental protected area related issues in Africa, including their very future. The program and activities of APAI are aimed at enhancing the conservation of biodiversity and management of protected areas systems. It will achieve this by catalyzing and facilitating international, regional, national and local action, promoting adaptive management approaches and technologies that reduce pressure on ecosystems, protected areas and resources.

APAI is both a timely and strategic opportunity to mobilize resources and expertise across the continent, and to consolidate international support toward the new vision for Africa's protected areas. The new vision is one that seeks to strengthen protected areas at all scales (from local to national, to regional) across the continent, and instill a sense of pride among all Africans for the special significance these areas hold in safeguarding our natural treasures. It seeks to place protected areas on the continent's highest level political agenda to ensure a deep commitment from continental bodies such as the Africa Union (AU), and emerging initiatives such as the New Partnership for African Development (NEPAD), as well as regional bodies such as the Economic Committee for West African States (ECOWAS) and the Southern African Development Community (SADC). The vision also seeks to establish a balance between the drive to enhance benefits from protected areas to people and the need to manage them effectively for biodiversity.

In an effort to improve the effectiveness of management in Africa, a myriad of strategies and action plans for protected areas, species or groups of species have been prepared. However, there has not been any continent-wide mechanism for coordinating all these initiative and synthesizing and disseminating the experience and lessons learned. This is the void that the APAI is expected to fill. Many of the pieces are in place for a consolidated and greatly enhanced set of activities to address the multiple challenges facing protected areas in Africa. So, there is not only a strong case for increased donor support, but also for a fundamental shift in its focus, towards developing competent local institutions and expertise, through supporting local initiatives, using available African technical capacity, supporting regional training institutions, improving information flow, and helping improve the working conditions of protected area staff.

The initiative is also aimed at supporting those processes and activities that enhance the sustainable management of natural resources and increase the benefits available to people. Special attention will be given to building strategic partnerships between diverse stakeholders and programs. It will seek to strengthen policy dialogue within a broad range of public and private stakeholders in all aspects of protected area management. At the international level, APAI will assist countries to meet their obligations under the international conventions, and improve management of designated sites. The governments will be assisted to draw on the continued international interest for conservation, access resources available under the conventions, and develop alternative and innovative funding mechanism for conservation. In this way, the program will help to link national activities and processes with the global conservation efforts.

The importance of trans-boundary protected areas is becoming increasingly recognized in the conservation of shared resources and migratory species. APAI will assist governments with such shared resources to develop mechanisms for collaboration in their sustainable management, and where possible or appropriate, establish cross-border protected areas.

Developing a Strategy for Integrated Protected Area Systems in Africa

The long-term goal of APAI is to develop for all sub-Saharan African countries a well-designed and well-managed system of protected areas that will meet the environmental and social needs of each country. This goal will depend on establishing innovative strategies for Africa's protected area systems based on sound science, as well as social, cultural, political and economic realities. Amongst the issues that need to be addressed include:

1. the need for a continent-wide protected area database, maintained within Africa to support the activities that are identified as of highest priority by the African countries (building on existing databases, such as WCMC);
2. an institutional framework to enhance partnership and collaboration among the many organizations interested in African protected areas.
3. greatly increased international support for protected areas in Africa, including new and innovative sustainable funding mechanisms;
4. enhanced protected area management throughout Africa through improved training, institutional development policy development, systems planning, wildlife management, cost recovery, community relations, public outreach, etc.
5. preparation in African countries of national protected area systems plans that rationalize the existing protected area networks.
6. the need to improve and strengthen political buy-in for protected area systems through relevant regional bodies, the Africa Convention and the Convention on Biological Diversity Conference of Parties.

Although the main thrust of this effort is on protected areas for conserving biodiversity, it is recognized that these areas alone are no longer adequate for effective conservation. In fact, the majority of Africa's flora and fauna species, including many that are endangered, occur outside protected areas. Furthermore, expansion of protected areas is limited by many factors, not the least of which are under-valuation of natural resources and ecosystem services. The challenge therefore is not only to ensure that existing protected areas are effectively managed, but also to establish a strategy that aims at conserving species and habitats across entire landscapes by incorporating biodiversity concerns into development and land-use planning. Where practical, protected area networks should be expanded, and factors that limit the effectiveness of their management such as lack of capacity and diminishing resources addressed.

Building and Promoting New Partnerships

Like every where else in the world, biodiversity and protected areas in Africa occur in various forms and on diverse spatial scales and contexts—on public, communal, corporate and private lands. Thus, there is need for broadening the scope for biodiversity conservation to accommodate this range of opportunities. This calls for the development of multiple approaches to management of natural resources. This, in turn, requires coordination among stakeholders with significant interests in biodiversity in order to reconcile complex web of interests from a wide range of actors.

An important element of APAI is building partnerships, and more intensive process of interaction between stakeholders, where key actors collaborate and learn from each other. This should result in evolution of more positive relationships between stakeholders, and the discarding of rigid models in favor of more proactive approaches that help build greater understanding and cooperation. Subsequently, diversified management strategies based upon complementary approaches should be built through participatory processes.

The initiative will foster a strategy to shift some government level responsibilities for protected areas to reliable groups and organizations, so that they can focus more on policy, oversight and capacity building. Through this shift, some of the costs of biodiversity conservation can be shared with a wider range of partners and investors, thereby reducing pressure on already over-stretched budgets.

Successful conservation will depend on active partnership among stakeholders, to serve as the basis upon which to build dynamic and effective management systems. The next challenge is to build an alliance between central governments, all the public, community, and private organizations that contribute to overall biodiversity conservation. All partners, whether government, NGO or community, will need to build the kind of capacity necessary to fulfill their roles and functions:

- choose institutions that can best contribute to protected area management;
- build systems that will be needed to ensure accountability between government, and civil institutions;
- administer natural resources in ways that equitably distribute the burdens of conservation and benefits of healthy ecosystems, as well as the goods and services provided.

The APAI will play an important role in meeting these challenges by promoting mechanisms for building in-country and regional capacity, and mobilizing support for the inclusion of biodiversity conservation and protected area systems in the countries' sustainable development plans. It will also provide opportunities for protected area managers to address management challenges through south-south exchanges where managers can draw from each other's strength in finding innovative approaches, field-testing of new techniques and in providing a unique forum to facilitate dialogue across multiple sectors. In this way, they will be better able to achieve the management objectives of their protected areas.

Developing and Promoting New Mechanisms for Financing Africa's Protected Areas

In Africa, protected areas are traditionally funded through government budgets. However, funding has been falling steadily since the economic down turn set in the 1990s. Donor funding to protected areas has to some extent bridged the gap between what is required and what was actually available; in 1996 alone, donors provided an estimated total $160 million to sixteen countries across the continent. But without strong institutions and homegrown management processes and systems, the expected impact has not been achieved. In many cases, this support is poorly coordinated and is not always directed to the most strategically important priorities, including biodiversity conservation and supporting national development.

Many international organizations, supported by a wide range of donors, are providing support to protected areas in Africa. But this support is poorly coordinated and is not always directed to the most strategically important priorities, including biodiversity conservation and supporting national development. There is not only a strong case for continued and increased donor support, but also for a fundamental shift in its focus, towards developing competent local institutions and expertise, through supporting local initiatives, using available African technical capacity, supporting regional training institutions, improving information flow, and helping improve the working conditions of protected area staff.

Under the CBD, nations have made a commitment not only to conserve their own biodiversity, but also to help and co-operate with each other. The international community has called for "the current trends in loss of environmental resources to be effectively reversed at both global and national levels by 2015." Greater efforts in managing biodiversity through protected areas, is required if this target is to be met.

The threats to African protected areas arise both within countries and at the international level. While countries clearly need to define their own needs, and often are doing so through the preparation of their national biodiversity strategies and action plans, protected areas are also threatened by structural problems that can only be addressed at the international level, helping to address the problems of economic pressures on African governments. Addressing problems of structural adjustment, very high debt burdens, unfavorable terms of trade, and the impact of agricultural subsidies in the north, all require a policy response at the international level. Thus the proposed initiative will have both national and international elements requiring different approaches and different kinds of expertise.

A major target for APAI is a Trust Fund for Africa's Protected Areas, which is intended to serve as major endowment that will ensure a permanent and sustainable source of co-financing for the management of protected areas on the African continent. The Trust fund will be a programmatic fund, providing multiple grants to co-finance proposals aimed at, but not limited to:

- Deepening the political commitment of African countries to implement sound environmental management practices to strengthen the role of protected areas at the local, national and regional levels across the continent.
- Strengthening the capacity of African organizations to demonstrate and promote replication of best practices, including a focus on enhancing the institutional capacity of key centers of excellence working on environmental and biodiversity issues across the continent.
- Improving networking among African institutions and relevant south-south exchanges to enhance effective sharing of tools and strategies for improved management of protected areas.

APAI will ensure that the mechanisms for establishing the fund, including the legal and institutional framework is thoroughly researched over the next two years. It is anticipated that the Fund itself will be formally launched at the World Parks Congress in Durban in 2003.

Complementary Processes to APAI

The development of APAI is the culmination of numerous consultations and efforts, over the last decade or so, aimed at seeking solutions to the problems and pressures facing protected areas in Africa. Two of the most significant processes include the European Union's Africa-Caribbean-Pacific initiative and the Skukuza strategy.

The European Union Initiative for Protected Areas and Biodiversity Conservation in African-Caribbean-Pacific (ACP) Countries

The European Union has, since 1977, been supporting the signatories to the Lome IV Convention in their efforts to protect and enhance their environment, including halting the destruction of their land and forests, restoring ecological balances, and preserving natural resources. Through this support, EU has provided over 150 million ECUs to support ACP countries in their efforts to establish and manage their protected areas. Individual EU countries have also provided additional support to Pas through their own programs and budgets. To help plan its development assistance to protected areas in ACP countries, the EU has benefited from IUCN policy guidance drawn on best practice lessons and project experience of donors and partners in Africa, the Caribbean and Pacific regions [The policy guidance is detailed in a document entitled "Parks for Biodiversity" prepared by the IUCN/WCPA in 1999.]

The Skukuza Action Strategy for Protected Areas in the Afro-Tropical Realm

This Action Strategy was the outcome of the African Region Working Session of the IUCN/WCPA held at Skukuza, in Kruger National Park in October 1994. It identifies the key protected area issues in Africa and presents actions that are required for these critical areas to remain a viable force in the conservation of African biodiversity. The strategy makes the case that the future of Africa's biodiversity and its protected areas is dependent on actions taken by national governments and other stakeholders. The success and sustainability of such actions depends on broad based support, and in many instances on collaboration at regional and international levels. The Strategy is geared towards advancing national, regional and international efforts, in establishing and managing a comprehensive protected area system in sub-Saharan Africa.

The Strategy is structured following the Caracas Action Plan with the following key goals:

- Integration of protected areas into larger planning frameworks;
- Expansion of support for protected areas;
- Strengthening capacity for their management;
- Expansion of international co-operation in finance, development and management of protected areas.

Conclusion

At the start of the new millennium, protected areas on the African continent face increasingly new challenges, the great majority of which are beyond the immediate grasp of managers and decision-makers. The diversity and scale of challenges facing protected areas require a new vision to mobilize and implement solutions to maximize long-term success. The Africa Protected Areas Initiative (APAI) is envisaged as a crucial step towards such a vision, and linked to the WCPA global partnership initiative on Ecosystems, Protected Areas and People. Africa's protected area systems stand to benefit tremendously from these initiatives, and both APAI and EPP will set the stage for an exciting World's Parks Congress in 2003, where lessons, results, experiences and new tools will be presented and shared.

Acknowledgments

This paper benefited tremendously from documents and proposals prepared for the Ecosystems, Protected Areas, and People project and the Pan-African Protected Areas Initiative. We specifically thank Kenton Miller (Chair, WCPA), Lee Thomas (Deputy Chair, WCPA), David Sheppard and Pedro Rosabal (IUCN Program on Protected Areas) for providing core leadership to both initiatives. Many thanks also to Jeffery McNeely (IUCN, Gland) and Eldad Tukahirwa (IUCN, EARO) for contributing in major ways toward developing the various initiatives. Finally, we thank everyone who has contributed ideas to the initiatives through various meetings held over the last year and half.

Wilderness in South Africa, Serving All Communities

The Honorable Valli Moosa
Minister of Environment, South Africa

The last time the World Wilderness Congress (WWC) convened in our country was in 1977, at the first Congress, and things were different then. Things were different because we could not speak then of communities or people and development. So South Africa is therefore proud to host this 7th World Wilderness Congress.

This topic should have been more defined as "wilderness and people," because in this century for development, all what we do should be about the interaction of people and nature, for the continuous protection of our natural resources on the one hand and on the other a commitment to ensure that through sustainable use, people can feed, find work and benefit from such protection.

And these people are found collectively in communities, and as we quest to protect our natural resources and specifically our wilderness areas, we should not lose sight of the fact that as a result of hundreds of years of wilderness habitation our people have become part of the wilderness and without them it is incomplete, and so is our people without the wilderness.

At the 6th WWC held in India, resolutions were passed on how to move forward in advancing the work of protecting our wilderness. We need to ask ourselves therefore how those resolutions have impacted on our communities.

Some of the areas covered in the resolutions were on transparency and the right to information. Can we proudly say that our communities and people have access to information and decision-making as it relates to the legislation we pass and the programs we partake in nature conservation, or are they just bystanders who are relocated each time we declare a natural site "a protected area." If not, then our quest will not be a successful one.

We should deliberately raise the level of their awareness and education and training for wilderness conservation. They have a critical role to play, and have we been able to settle all land disputes with communities without insisting that our governmental views and programs come first.

There is also a need for training in the techniques and science of wilderness management, and others with a specific interest in wilderness conservation, environmental management should no longer be seen as a profession of the elite, our communities should not only to the hard labor, but with the right skills we should find theme in the management of the wilderness areas.

These communities protect and defend the wilderness, and because they don't have the funds to stage massive publicity campaigns, we don't recognize them, and to them mostly the degradation of the wilderness is about being left homeless.

We therefore need to recognize their views and the importance of the impact of their daily lives on the conservation of our protected areas.

For us in South Africa and the region one of our most important achievements in recent years has been the formal establishment under the new World Heritage Conservation Act of the Greater St Lucia Wetland Park in one of our country's most biodiverse yet poorest regions. At the symbolic heart of the Park we have also entrenched a 470km^2 wilderness.

Here Africa's oldest designated wilderness—first proclaimed in 1955—has at last found formal protection of the highest order. At the time of its proclamation and listing as South Africa's first World Heritage Site, we stressed that this Park represents an important new benchmark in the history of south African conservation.

It was not just lip service when we argued that St. Lucia balances a fundamental commitment to conservation with a strong emphasis on responsible development through the Lubombo Spatial Development Initiative. A new dedicated World Heritage Authority has been established to ensure that St. Lucia will be developed for the benefit of the region and the nation.

This is an imperative of the greatest importance. It has enabled a major land claim on the 270km^2 wildernesses to be settled in a manner that retains this wilderness, enhances park management and enables meaningful economic empowerment.

The landmark settlement sets a precedent for other conservation areas of major significance. St Lucia's unique sense of place is sacrosanct. At its core lies a place untrammeled by modernity.

We are also consolidating our transfrontier conservation areas with the full support of communities who rely on the various national parks for employment and as small-scale entrepreneurs for the high tourist turnover in these parks.

Our greatest task, if we are to succeed, therefore should not only be to inform, to educate to consult with our communities on the various environmental management strategies we engage in, but should be on the formation of solid sustainable partnerships with these communities.

Without these partnerships we will then go it alone, and alone we will not succeed.

Why a Wilderness Area?

Richard Cowling

W hy a wilderness area? There are four reasons: first, restoring the land; second, the reintroduction of animals; third, community involvement; and fourth, wilderness itself.

The creation of wilderness areas is the most difficult of these. The difficulties lie in finding land, repairing land, and the "declaration." Other colleagues in this section will deal with finding and repairing land, and I will deal with the declaration of Wilderness Areas.

In South Africa, there are two acts of Parliament which deal with a "Wilderness Area": The Environment Conservation Act 73 of 1989, and the National Forests Act of 1998. The declared objectives in relation to Wilderness Areas are:

To protect largely undisturbed natural areas which serve human physical and spiritual well being. In order to achieve that, a Wilderness Area must be an enduring natural area of sufficient size to retain its natural character. It is an area where little or no persistent evidence of human intrusion is permitted, so that natural processes will take place largely unaffected by human intervention. Cultural resources which may occur in these areas will also be protected. Non-mechanized and strictly controlled access to Wilderness Areas should be stressed. As pristine natural areas, they should be established to ensure that future generations will have an opportunity to seek solitude and understanding in largely undisturbed areas.

As criteria for selection and management it was stipulated that:

An undeveloped area, preferably uninhabited by man and retaining an intrinsically wild appearance and character, capable of being restored to such a condition. It must be of sufficient size to protect the wilderness character and to provide the wilderness experience and be physically and visually separated, preferably by other protected area categories from adjacent areas of development and habitation. Preservation of the natural environment and wilderness character will be the highest management priority. Controlled access for visitors seeking the wilderness experience in a natural environment will be permitted in strict accordance with the natural carrying capacity of the area. It is to be managed by a nationally recognized authority or institution.

If the declaration is made under the Forestry Act of 1998 the Minister has to make the declaration and only if he is of the opinion that it is not already adequately protected in terms of other legislation.

Procedures to be followed include giving notice of the proposal and the invitation of comments; consideration of the comments and objections; notice of the intention must be Gazetted, published in newspapers and aired on radio; and the decision to declare a protected area may not be revoked without the Minister following the same procedure as required for declaration and. Most importantly, the approval by Resolution of Parliament.

Having considered the state route of wilderness designation, The Shamwari Game Reserve and its legal advisors agreed that there is nothing to prevent the owner of private land (which falls within the definition and has as its objectives the same Wilderness Area concept enunciated in the Environment Conservation Act) from granting a servitude over its property. This legal servitude would be placed in favor of an internationally recognized institution, in terms whereof the owner permits the land being utilized in accordance with the principles enunciated by the policy, but without the formality and statutory regulations, delay and bureaucracy involved in seeking formal declaration of protection.

The servitude required no more than an agreement between the landowner and his successors in title, and the Institution, binding them to the specific use and the method of use of the land in question. As with any agreement, it can only be amended or cancelled by consensus between the parties and is enforceable in a Court of Law.

A suitable body of rules—a management plan—can be contractually agreed upon which will govern the use of the land and which would achieve the same result intended by the policy described above insofar as it relates to Wilderness Areas.

The construction of the servitude agreement would be by consultation with an internationally credible institution.

It is with this perspective, and on the occasion of the 7th World Wilderness Congress, that the owner of Shamwari Game Reserve, Adrian Gardiner, proceeded to declare Africa's first Wilderness Area on privately owned land.

Shamwari Wilderness

Model for a Private Wilderness Area

S. Johan Joubert

Due to the lack of legislation for private wilderness areas in South Africa, Shamwari Game Reserve has entered into a legal agreement with the Wilderness Foundation (South Africa), giving them right of servitude to a newly designated wilderness area. Thus the Shamwari wilderness area will be managed as a de facto wilderness area, with the objective to declare it a de jure IUCN class 1b wilderness area once South African legislation recognizes private wilderness areas.

Shamwari Wilderness Area

Shamwari Game Reserve is a privately owned game reserve situated 75 km north east of Port Elizabeth and lies between 33° 24' S 26° 10' E and 33° 32' S 26° 10' E with the median annual rainfall being 420 mm in the south and 530 mm in the north. The vegetation is varied and divided into 15 vegetation units. Introduced game species include large herbivores and predators.

The reserve has been zoned into four zones: Wilderness, Roaded Natural, Rural and Breeding Centers.

The surface of the wilderness area is 2915 ha and it is situated in the northern section of the reserve. Thus 18.1% of the surface area of Shamwari Game Reserve will be managed as wilderness.

Staff Preparation and Training

Prior to declaration, Shamwari wildlife management staff had extensive consultations with members of the Wilderness Foundation, held a wilderness planning session with the assistance of the Wilderness Action Group and attended the

7th World Wilderness Congress Certified Wilderness Training Course. A wilderness management plan was written to set proper guidelines for development as well as management.

Identified FGASA accredited trail rangers with extensive walking experience had received on site training in the Umfolozi Wilderness and will have further on-site training in the Shamwari Wilderness Area.

Pre-Declaration Preparation and Clearing

As a section of the wilderness area consisted of recently acquired stock farms, extensive clearing of fences and old buildings had to be done. Although methods were sensitive to environment, the principles of "minimum" tool had not been followed as this happened prior to declaration.

The major procedures were:

- Erecting of an electrified game fence around the northern section.
- Removal and transportation of all existing stock fences.
- All existing buildings (houses, reservoirs, etc) were demolished and buried on-site.
- A section invaded by encroachers, such as *Elytropappus rhinocerotis* and *Europs* spp, had to be burned.
- Windmills were dismantled and some boreholes will be capped and buried and GPS reading taken.
- All exotic plants, such as *Acacia cyclops, A. saligna, A. mearnsii, Eucalyptes* spp, *Pinus* spp and *Scinus molle* had to be poisoned and cut down.
- Limited erosion reclamation had to be done. A mixture of indigenous grass seed as well as exotic tree brush packing is being used to rehabilitate these areas.
- Existing roads had to be used for pre declaration clearing. Afterwards smaller tracks are left to get overgrown, larger tracks are being brush packed and the odd road ripped and seeded with appropriate indigenous grass seed.
- Some general game are being introduced before dismantling of dividing game fence.
- The game fence between the wilderness area and reserve will be removed as soon as plains game had time to form new home ranges and territories.

Zoning of Wilderness Area

The wilderness area is zoned as follows:

Pristine	113	ha
Primitive	1,935.8	ha
Semi-pristine	269.4	ha
Semi-primitive	596	ha

Although pristine areas are small, it will be expanded as the condition of reha-bilitated primitive areas improve. Semi-primitive non-motorized areas include areas of historic cultivated lands and pastures as well as sites of demolished buildings. The semi-primitive motorized zone is a buffer zone around the entire wilderness area (the buffer between the roaded natural area of the reserve in the south as well as the buffer between perimeter fences in the east, west and north).

Problems Encountered

- Overgrown vehicle tracks were opened due to transport of old fence material out of wilderness area.
- Heavy rains prohibited burning program and transport vehicles left more obvious tracks in the muddy soil.
- Uncontrolled fire burned a section of neighboring land. Section of wilderness that burned was supposed to be burned and had no adverse affects. The terrain of the wilderness is of such a nature that it is difficult to create fire breaks.

Limits of Sophistication (LOS) for Hiking and Camping

A comprehensive guideline for limits of sophistication is laid down in the wilderness management plan. Each of the four zones mentioned will have its own LOS guidelines with pristine areas at the lowest level and semi-primitive motorized at the highest level.

Visitor Utilization and Carrying Capacity

- All visitors to the wilderness area will be led by a recognized trail guide to ensure wilderness ethics are being kept up.
- Visitors will be limited to eight participants on overnight trails and eight participants on day trails, thus a total of sixteen per day.
- Horse trails is a possibility in future, but will be limited and strictly controlled.

Limits of Acceptable Change (LAC)

Naturalness and solitude are qualities of wilderness. As human induced changes will occur, the challenge is to limit and control it to a specific level. The nine interrelated steps to control LAC are set out in the Shamwari Wilderness Management Plan.

Annual Wilderness Audit

All management programs must be adaptive and if LAC is surpassed the relative management program should be altered accordingly. Thus regular monitoring needs to be done. For this purpose an annual audit will be carried out as laid down in the management plan.

Annual Wilderness Closure

The wilderness area will be closed during September each year. September is the month with the highest rainfall, thus the ideal time for early spring recovery of vegetation. During this time, annual game census, annual audit and other management programs will be completed.

Access and Casualty Evacuation Procedures

- There shall be no roads in the wilderness area. No motorized equipment shall be allowed in the wilderness area. Access to the wilderness area will only be on foot and possibly on horseback in future.
- Helicopter and fixed wing flights for census reasons will be above 300 ft. Although the minimum tool principle will always be followed, helicopter landings might be permitted during serious casavac procedures.

Structures

The only structure is the base camp situated in the semi-primitive motorized zone on the northern boundary.

Litter Disposal

All litter will be carried out by hikers. At the base camp a recycle system will be functional.

Management of Fauna and Flora

Although the objective of wilderness management is to let nature take its course as far as possible, a monitoring program for both fauna and flora is essential to ensure the sustainability of the wilderness area. The minimum tool principle will always be used.

Supply of Game Water

In the event of extraordinary drought, water will only be supplied in the wilderness area if monitoring indicated that endangered species are at risk. In this case an appropriate borehole will be uncapped, and connected to a solar panel and submersible pump. This area will be zoned accordingly.

Awareness Program

Shamwari wilderness awareness will be an integral part of Shamwari's marketing campaign. The Shamwari wilderness will be explained to all guests to the reserve. International students that participate in the Shamwari education program will be exposed to the wilderness area.

Conclusion

Shamwari's wilderness area is a long-term project that can only succeed if the highest standards are set and adhered to. As the first privately designated wilderness area in Africa, it will be managed to this highest standard.

The Private Sector Role in Sustaining African Wildlands

Matemela Cyril Ramaphosa

We are fortunate in South Africa to live surrounded by wild beauty. This great continent of ours—Africa—is the last place remaining on earth where significant pieces of our world's original, natural ecosystems still exist.

It is essential that these wildlands continue to survive, if we are to maintain a healthy planet. The importance of the "balance of nature" is something that few people these days would question. We have all heard the wise words attributed to Chief Seattle in the early 19th century: "Whatever happens to the beast, soon happens to the man. All things are connected."

I believe that, in this interconnected world, it is foolishness to think that it is only important to protect our own species, perhaps along with a few other species we think are useful to us. It is the interrelation of all things—the vital "circle of life"—that in the end, makes our life on earth possible.

I am an African and am passionate about Africa. I am passionate about her people, but I also have a personal passion for her wild creatures and wild places.

I take every opportunity to spend time in the African bush. I have a deep love for the Kruger National Park, and spend time there whenever I can, either camping or in its lodges. I remember quite recently, when I went to Skukuza with the Southern African Natural History Unit (SANHU), a wildlife documentary television company in which my company, Johnnic, acquired a majority shareholding in 1995. Two giraffes had died—one accidentally, the other had been killed—and Kruger's predators had come to feast upon the carcasses. I sat spellbound, for several hours, long after night fell, watching nature in action.

When I am in the bush I feel a sense of peace, and of how right it is when all things are in balance. I realize, once more, how important it is that these wild places be preserved, for the benefit of all the generations that will follow our own.

And yet, as Mavuso Msimang, Chief Executive of South African National Parks, has said: "The conservation of South Africa's natural heritage constitutes one of the biggest challenges of our time."

This is true not only for South Africa, but for the entire Southern African region. To conserve the indigenous wildlife, vegetation species and associated cultural assets that lie within the treasury of our region's national parks and wildlands, takes time, effort and funding. Our governments face pressing social concerns—health ... housing ... the welfare and education of the people. It has become increasingly difficult for the public sector to address the issue of conservation needs. It is time for the private sector to step forward without hesitation, and give their assistance.

I once stated, when talking about black empowerment in the New South Africa, that a fundamental change needs to take place within the business community. I said:

"Notions of accountability and proper conduct have largely been anathema in an environment in which poor ethical, social, and even business practices were allowed to take root. It is not just the complexion of South African business that needs to change—it is the entire ethos, culture and approach which needs to be reviewed."

There are businesses in the private sector that have begun to make these fundamental changes. The Johnnic Group is certainly one of them. Outside the arena of conservation, Johnnic, through the Group's corporate social investment program, proves its commitment to social upliftment by investing in the communities in which Johnnic operates. In 2001, our investment was 27 million rand—32% higher than the previous year.

The Johnnic Group has identified education as an important area of focus, and we have dedicated over 50% of our expenditure towards education-related projects. In addition, Johnnic Learning was launched in August 2001—based on the principle of using electronic communications media, especially the Internet—to allow students to learn in a variety of preferred learning styles. Since Johnnic is a focused media, entertainment and telecommunications group, this initiative is fully in keeping with our core business—and it simultaneously contributes to social upliftment.

Johnnic has also been working in association with Compaq Computer, the World Bank, and the SA Government through the Ministry of Social Development, to initiate our flagship project—the Ikageng Community Development Trust—which has as its objective the improvement of the quality of life for disadvantaged communities in Africa.

At the 7th World Wilderness Congress I am proud to officially announce that support for conservation—and conservation education—has been added to the Johnnic Group's corporate social investment programme. And here, I stress the word "social"—for it is Johnnic's view that conservation is, at bottom line, a social obligation—essential for the wholeness, healthiness, and joy that interaction with nature brings to all people.

But the reasons for supporting conservation go beyond social responsibility. Contributing to the preservation of protected wildlands is a sound business move.

Obviously, tourism has always been vital to the South African economy—and eco-tourism in particular, with the Kruger National Park being one of most important attractions in South Africa. It is well known that tourism is one of the biggest money earning businesses of our country. Tourism also contributes significantly to the welfare of South Africa's people—for every eight tourists that visit South Africa, one job is created … for each job that is created, ten people are fed.

Even after the disastrous events of September 11 in America, foreign tourists continue to come to South Africa. Should our wildlands not be preserved, should there be no wild animals left to see, then not just our joy and pride in this wild beauty, but also our economy and our personal livelihoods, will suffer.

It is imperative that the entire private sector begins to truly see the very real need to actively work towards conservation of our wildlands. Neither time nor circumstance is on the side of Southern Africa's natural heritage. The region faces the daunting task of attempting to preserve its precious natural assets, with the full knowledge that the existing funding available to help perform this important duty consistently fails to be adequate. The government has many other concerns on its hands, and the generosity of a few private individuals and of local and international environmental support organizations cannot continue to be solely relied upon. In view of the critical role played by conservation, its long-range importance in ensuring a healthy economy and vibrant businesses, and the joy and benefit it brings to all people, it should be not only our duty, but our pleasure, to assist in every way we can.

Without additional income, the passing of just a few more years could mark the beginning of the end for Southern Africa's natural heritage. And Southern Africa's wildlife and natural environment is a legacy for the whole world … that we hold in our hands.

I challenge other corporate leaders to join Johnnic in leading conservation support into a new era of change for the better: to actively espouse the environmental cause; to incorporate eco-awareness in our corporate training and community outreach; and to be pro-active and innovative in approaches to promoting, protecting and preserving our wildlands and wild animals—not just because of "social responsibility"—but because it makes sound business sense.

The Johnnic Group has heard the cry for help from Southern African conservation and is determined to answer that call. As we are doing with education, so we shall do for conservation—and that is, use Johnnic's own core business as a foundation on which to build a model that earns revenue not only for the good cause of conservation—but also for Johnnic as a business.

Our new "business model" for conservation utilizes our key communications tools—again, the Internet in particular, but also other communications. This new model is a vital conservation and education initiative. It is intended that the Initiative will, through raising significant funds, help protect and preserve Southern Africa's threatened wildlands for generations to come—and simultaneously, via its in-built Education Initiative, ensure that the younger generation takes to heart, as well as to mind, the urgent environmental conservation message.

My Acre of Africa

A New Funding Strategy for African Protected Areas

Gareth Pyne-James

My Acre of Africa (MAA) started as an idea to assist the great national parks we have in South Africa, and I was compelled to make a reality of this idea. Mavuso Msimang, CEO of SA National Parks Board, first encouraged me to do so saying that the conservation of South Africa's natural heritage constitutes one of the biggest challenges of our time. The great philanthropist of our country, Dr. Anton Rupert, has said that conservation without money is merely conversation. What we're trying to do with MAA is turn conservation—with money—into something to really boast about.

The Concept

It starts with a simple, natural, clay or granite brick, and one of the greatest keeps of wildlife in all the world—that wonderful place, the Kruger National Park. We've used Kruger here as an example, to represent Southern Africa's wild and beautiful places.

Importantly, Kruger comprises of 4,692,914 acres of land. This is a number that I will never forget as long as I live. In MAA's plan, each one of those acres will be represented by one brick. (That's an awful lot of bricks!)

The bricks are different colours: there are sand coloured bricks, there are brown bricks, there are dark green granite bricks and dark brown granite bricks. These bricks are going to be sold to the worldwide public priced on a sliding scale—the least expensive being US$49, and the most expensive (the corporate bricks) being $500. Now I can hear the mathematicians already working out how much money this is … it's a lot.

Each brick will have a unique inscription—the name of a person, a family, a club, a school, a business, or an organization—and those bricks will be laid out in a very special place, on the periphery of the Kruger National Park ... a "living," scale-model replica map of the Kruger National Park.

The Living Map

This living map will be approximately one and a half kilometres long, and 800 metres wide. Within this map, the bricks will be laid out in pathways through the natural bushveld.

The pathways correspond to certain major features of the Kruger National Park. For example, the brown bricks represent the road network, the dark green granite bricks are for the rivers and dams, the sand coloured bricks are for the park border, and the brown granite bricks are for the tourist camps and entrance gates. In total, just over 4.6 million bricks will be used to create these pathways.

The different natural vegetation types that occur in the real Kruger Park, will be represented on the map, so that people can walk along the pathways and in the North they can see where Baobab trees grow; in the middle they can see where Mopane trees grow, and so on. It will be a wild botanical garden that people will be able to walk through, experiencing the whole of the Kruger National Park in microcosm, in less than one day.

The Conservation Education Facility

A further feature of this "living map"—a conservation educational facility—has been designed by a young black architect, called Bai Tshetlo, from GAPP Architects. The facility will consist of conservation education resources, including a conservation "station," a school tour center, a cinema, an open-air amphitheater, a craft market, and other features. We hope it is going to be a shining example of what can be done for conservation education in our country.

The Trust

We've heard about the bricks and the money, but who is behind this initiative, and who is going to look after the money raised? Who is going to make sure that the funds are used for the intended purposes? As a result, My Acre of Africa Trust has been created.

We are enormously proud and very honored to have the former president of the Republic of South Africa, Dr. Nelson Mandela, as our Patron-in-Chief.

Because Dr. Mandela is our Patron-in-Chief, he has agreed that we may send out a certificate, bearing his signature, to every single person who buys a brick. So, every person who donates $49 or more, will have their name immortalized in the Kruger National Park, and they will also receive a certificate bearing the signature of Nelson Mandela to frame in their homes.

The Trustees are: South African National Parks Chairman, Mr. Murphy Morobe, chairman of the 7th World Wilderness Congress; South African National Parks Chief Executive, Mr. Mavuso Msimang; Peace Parks Foundation (PPF) Chairman, Dr. Anton Rupert; PPF Director, Advocate Frans Stroebel; Johnnic Holdings Chairman, Mr. Cyril Ramaphosa, and Johnnic Communications Chairman, Mr. Mashudu Ramano. These are the founding Trustees—there will be more.

What Will the Money Be Used For?

We firmly believe that if we do not teach children about the importance of conservation—the children who are the future custodians of our wildlands in this country—then, how can we ever expect them to look after this important natural heritage? So, a lot of the money and the effort is going to go into conservation-related education programs. Unfortunately, many of the children in our sub-continent live in degraded and they never get an opportunity to see a wild animal or wildlands. We need to take these children, and we need to give them the opportunity to do so. We need to ensure that the younger generation takes to heart, as well as to mind, the urgent environmental conservation message. It is important that we teach our children, so that they can look after this legacy long after we are gone. We need to give them first-hand, first-rate, conservation education. Unfortunately, that is something that does not presently exist to any great degree in our country, and we need to do something about it. My Acre of Africa intends to do so. We want all our children to learn to love their cultural and their natural heritage.

We also need to purchase additional land for conservation. South Africa has only 5.6% of its total land area given over to conservation. Minister Valli Moosa has stated the challenge: we need to increase that percentage. So, part of the money that comes into My Acre of Africa will be used by South African National Parks and the Peace Parks Foundation to purchase additional land. There are some beautiful places in this country, incredibly beautiful places, and if we don't protect and preserve them, they will be lost.

Another area that needs a lot of money is wildlife translocation. As you buy more land, so you need to spend money moving animals to that land to populate it. My Acre of Africa will help pay for wildlife translocation.

Wild animal disease research and control is also very important. We have all kinds of man-made problems, and some natural problems which we need to look after. For example, we need to find a cure for, or perhaps something that can stop the spread of, Bovine Tuberculosis in the Kruger National Park, which is seriously affecting the lion population. That requires money and expertise—and My Acre of Africa will hopefully contribute towards this.

In addition, any Peace Park that is linked to a South African National Park will benefit from My Acre of Africa. Dr. Rupert's dream of Africa without fences, re-establishing the ancient migration routes of the animals, is now starting to come to fruition after all his hard work, and My Acre of Africa is very proud to be part of the Peace Parks initiative.

Web Site

www.myacreofafrica.com is up and running. It's a very powerful e-commerce site that has been built by M-Web to transact all the brick purchases—so that people can go onto the site from anywhere in the world and buy their brick for $49, $75, $150 or $500. The internet is a wonderful tool to help make the whole thing happen.

Objective

The enormity of this project is that if we sell 100% of these bricks—and we firmly believe that we will (not overnight, but within the next 3 years)—it will bring US$200 million into this country for conservation. It's also a huge amount of money to bring into the South African economy, which will obviously have benefits. And there are other benefits as well, and has great potential for job creation.

Fund Allocation

The funds will be allocated as follows: 82.5% goes directly to conservation projects and 17.5% of the money comes to My Acre of Africa management company as a management fee. As Cyril Ramaphosa asserts, My Acre of Africa is sponsored by Johnnic, a commercial company. If MAA is successful, Johnnic will see some return of the funding they have put into the project.

They have taken all the risk; they have put in all the seed money to get My Acre of Africa to where it is today; they will continue to pay all the costs out of the management fee. Conservation, however, ends up with 82.5% of the money without any further deductions—this has been agreed by all parties associated with the initiative.

Conservation Education Facility

What is the Conservation Education Facility going to look like?

There's a gateway to the complex, where you can access computerized information about how to find your brick, interactive information about South African National Parks, Peace Parks and other Southern African conservation concerns; and which is also the starting point for My Acre of Africa ranger-guided tours through the Living Map.

There will be a conservation station, which I mentioned earlier—an interactive, educational, entertaining museum-come-exhibit centre for children, and indeed also for adults ... a place where kids, especially, can go and learn. We want them to walk in as little children and walk out as little conservationists.

We'll have a school tour center, because one of the things that we want to do is to have children come and spend a whole day or longer at the education facility. We shall have a facilitating area that will include lecture rooms and catering and other amenities, where we can look after the kids. Overnight accommodation will be provided in the Park for longer stay-over school tours, and children will be able to come to the My Acre of Africa conservation center and have a truly enjoyable learning experience.

There will be a cinema, to give us the opportunity to teach children and adults through the visual medium—100 people seating capacity with both surround-screen, and a conventional big screen.

There will be an open air, boma-style amphitheatre, giving people the opportunity to sit outside and listen to talks by conservationists, and to enjoy African cultural performances and round-the-campfire bush stories—which used at one time to be done in Kruger ... rangers used to sit and talk to the public around the campfire.

There will be a craft market—just one of many areas where the local communities can get involved with the My Acre of Africa project, through the arts and crafts that they produce.

Kruger's heritage sites—places like Thulamela in the north and Albasini down in the south—will also be represented. People will be able to see and learn about these heritage sites without having to actually drive all the way there. This will give visitors to the center a great opportunity to find out about the heritage of the Kruger National Park.

Waterholes are placed so that they are actually outside the My Acre of Africa complex and open to the rest of the Kruger National Park. In time, animals will come down to the waterholes, and people will be able to view wildlife at close range from the safety of the My Acre of Africa complex.

The major topographical features of the Kruger Park will also be replicated to scale on the Living Map, which is a wonderful way for people to get an overview, in miniature, of what the enormous Kruger Park is all about.

Other facilities included in the Complex will be an admin center, first-aid facilities, a shop selling conservation-orientated merchandise, a full restaurant, barbecue and picnic areas, and refreshment outlets. It's a big place—one and a half kilometers long—that people will be walking around, so they will need to be fed and watered, hence the utilities.

We believe that this is going to be a unique experience ... a "Big Five" experience: to taste, to touch, to smell, to hear and to see Africa—in microcosm, all in one day, right next door to the Kruger National Park.

There are great benefits to this whole initiative. Apart from the money that's going to become available to make conservation work, there will be employment opportunities, with over 500 jobs to be created by the project in a part of our country that really needs it. There will also be ongoing generation of income to local communities, because this Complex will bring increased tourism to the area. Obviously, people will also be employed in long-term jobs by the project— so we perceive it bringing a lot of benefit to the local communities.

Conclusion

My Acre of Africa is not, by any stretch of the imagination, the answer to all the problems faced by conservation ... but we think it can help considerably with the task at hand—which is to preserve South Africa's wildlife treasury for generations to come. By taking part in the My Acre of Africa initiative, each one of us can make a positive contribution towards the future of the country's—and the region's—wild heritage.

Wilderness in Namibian Parks

The Honorable P.N. Malima
Minister of Environment, Namibia

Namibia is endowed with an extensive system of game parks and protected areas covering approximately 14% of the country. It is a dry country with a hyper-arid coastal zone. Rainfall ranges from less than 50 mm in the south and west, to 700 mm in the northeast. Only 8% of the country receives more than 500 mm per year, and low and erratic precipitation is typical.

Despite this grim climatic picture, Namibia is a place of immense, contrasting natural beauty. It is environmentally very sensitive due to its unique ecological features, and is home to several endemic and internationally endangered species, such as Hartmann's zebra, black rhino, desert-dwelling elephant, black-faced impala and cheetah, etc.

A wide array of innovative and progressive policy and legislative instruments have been put in place or are under review, to create an enabling environment and an understanding of the fact that effective conservation management and sustainable economic development, are intrinsically linked.

Namibia has also joined the global movement in the quest for managing the environment in a holistic manner by acceding to relevant international treaties and conventions such as the Convention for the Protection of the Ozone Layer, the RAMSAR Convention on Wetlands, the Basle Convention, the Convention on Climatic Change, the 1992 Rio Summit Biodiversity Convention, the Convention to Combat Desertification, and the Convention on International Trade in Endangered Species.

To focus on the topic of wilderness, I would like to quote a statement made by my President some time ago with regard to wilderness.

In his message on the occasion of the Wilderness Management Symposium, held at Waterberg Plateau Park in Namibia in June 1996, his Excellency the President of the Republic of Namibia, Dr. Sam Nujoma, stated that "Declaring an area as a wilderness enclave is the highest form of protection that can be given to a piece of land," and that "this is particularly true when such declaration is translated into law."

His Excellency further stated, "The subject of Wilderness Areas is not about land-grabbing or alienating the land from the people. It is about preserving our natural heritage, about enriching the quality of an outdoor experience, about enhancing the quality of life in general and about broadening our eco-tourism field, respecting our history, our culture and our future. The Wilderness Areas concept introduces a measure of balance in our approach to eco-tourism on one hand, and respect for the environment on the other. We are proud of our growing eco-tourism industry, but we must be careful not to kill the goose that lays the golden egg," but then cautioned that "Wilderness Areas must be relevant to the people, otherwise they will be a useless creation."

Increasingly, my Ministry in particular and the Government in general have realized the importance of Wilderness Areas. Namibia is blessed the wide open spaces and much de facto wilderness still remains both in and outside the Parks, but there is no doubt that this precious resource deserves a special type of protection, because it is diminishing at an alarming rate all over the world. Sadly, in some countries, wilderness is even under threat within the very Parks that are supposed to protect it!

Virtually, all the major parks in Namibia have recently had—or are in the process of having—new management plans drawn up that now make provision for wilderness zones. Up to now under existing legislation, such wilderness areas are administratively managed, but that is about to change, because the final draft of the Bill leading to our new Parks and Wildlife Management Act, includes Wilderness as Category 1, in accordance with the World Conservation Union (IUCN) standards.

We are proud to say that Wilderness legislation will not only pertain to our National Parks, but will also be applicable to registered Conservancies as well, should they meet the criteria and request Category 1 zonation under the new law.

The "Conservancy" program is the Namibian Government's innovative approach to devolving rights and responsibilities over natural resources to communal and freehold farms and citizenry in Namibia, creating a strong link between conservation and rural development. I am pleased to announce that communal and freehold conservancies now cover over 8 million hectares of land in Namibia.

Wilderness is as old as Africa. It is also emerging as one of our most precious and sought-after commodities, not only for the enduring quality of life for our own citizens, but—due to its scarcity now all over the planet—as a Panacea, a healer, to the citizens from all over the world that visit our country. They come from places, where true wildlands don't exist any more. Interestingly enough, they don't only come to visit our lodges and tour the parks in comfortable vehicles: increasingly, there is a desire to experience wild nature at its best, in other words in non-mechanized ways such as on foot, or by camel or horse. And this is best achieved in a wilderness area, as we all know.

Aside from this aspect, we believe that declaring wilderness zones (that are safeguarded at the highest level of government), expresses a true and honest commitment to good land management, and a genuine respect for the creation as it stands without all the trappings of modern technology.

Wilderness is the base, the root, of our culture, heritage and development, and we must preserve as much of what remains as we possibly can. At the national level, Namibia is committed to safeguarding this heritage which we hold in trust for our children.

We are past the stage of arguing over the usefulness or necessity of setting aside wilderness areas: in Namibia it is now seen as a priority to manage large zones within the Parks as Wilderness Areas, and, just as importantly, to have a stated policy and guidelines within all Management Plans, for making them available to our citizens and visitors, such as in the form of Wilderness Trails.

In order to achieve this, my Ministry has already hosted, since 1996, five Basic and four Advanced Wilderness Management Training Courses on an annual basis, for our own staff as well as for NGO's, conservancies and members of the public. Assisted by the Wilderness Action Group of Southern Africa, we have trained over 100 people associated with protected land management in this way.

My Ministry has supported the establishment of a national Namibian Wilderness Association, which was also assisted by The WILD Foundation of the United States, to facilitate wilderness information, involvement, funding and training to all sectors of society.

We have to date also held two Wilderness Information Workshops for members of the public, community leaders, civil servants and the press, and in 1996 Namibia hosted the first major Wilderness Management Symposium on the continent outside of South Africa, attended by over 120 delegates from eight different countries around the world including Africa. In the Waterberg Plateau Park, we have hosted some 1,600 people on over 240 Wilderness Trails, and in due course, we hope to extend this experience to other Parks.

Namibia was represented at the previous (6th) World Wilderness Congress in India. In the Resolutions of that Congress, you expressed your recognition and support for Namibia's endeavors to further the cause of Wilderness, for which I proudly thank you today. Rest assured, my Ministry is more determined than ever to ensure, that within the magnificent Parks of Namibia, Wilderness will be given its due recognition and protected at the highest level possible.

The Sperrgebiet—the Desert Wilderness of Namibia

Trygve G. Cooper

Nearly fourteen percent of the Republic of Namibia has been proclaimed as some form of park or recreation area, and in a country the size of France, but with a human population of only around two million, there are still vast open spaces and relatively unaltered landscapes within this African country. Much of the protected area is contained in the arid Namib Desert, two examples being the Skeleton Coast Park of 16,390 sq. km, and the Namib Naukluft Park extending over 49,768 sq. km.

A great proportion of this area is *de facto* wilderness, and managed administratively as such. Up until now, there has been no provision for legal entrenchment of Wilderness as a specific category, but the situation is about to change, with the impending replacement of the existing Nature Conservation Ordinance by a new Parks and Wildlife Management Act for Namibia. The final draft of the Bill recognizes the six IUCN categories for protected areas, and makes provision for Wilderness under Category 1.

The Sperrgebiet, otherwise known as Diamond Area No. 1, lies in the southern Namib Desert in the southwestern corner of Namibia, on the Atlantic coastline, between the Namib Naukluft Park and the Orange River.

Nearly 300 km long, and up to 100 km wide in places, the Sperrgebiet ("forbidden area") was created as an exclusive no-go buffer zone to the coastal diamond fields immediately after the first precious stones were discovered there in 1908. Diamond recovery is still centered along the southern coastline and parts of the Orange River, but is increasingly moving to offshore operations, and though the scars of nearly a hundred years of mining remain and will take extensive time to recover in places, if at all, the bulk of the 26,000 sq. kms contained within the Sperrgebiet is still a virtually pristine Wilderness. High security measures instituted by NAMDEB Diamond Mining Company— previously known as CDM—in accordance with the requirements of the Halbscheid Agreement and the various Diamond Acts, have ensured a high degree of protection. NAMDEB have acquired ISO 14001 certification, and have shown much commitment in recent times, to managing their operations as environmentally correctly as possible.

Outside of the diamond concessions, the area has been opened up to prospecting for base minerals, but only for a three-year period of exploration. The eighth biggest zinc mine in the world is about to be opened at Skorpion just inside the eastern boundary of the Sperrgebiet in the Rosh Pinah area. This coincides with a recently completed Land Use Plan commissioned by the Government, to explore the best way to make the area available to the public, since a large proportion of the Sperrgebiet was recently removed from exclusive diamond prospecting, and has reverted to the status of unproclaimed State Land.

In the Land Use Plan, due to be deliberated by Cabinet soon, it has been suggested that the Sperrgebiet be proclaimed as a National Park, zoned in accordance with the six IUCN categorizations for protected areas, to be managed and conserved in perpetuity for the benefit of the Namibian people.

We cannot pre-empt the Cabinet decision, but should this become a reality, then large tracts of the Sperrgebiet would be designated Wilderness. The interface of winter rainfall and desert conditions has resulted in a high biodiversity and the evolution of many endemic and rare species of succulents, insects and reptiles. The Sperrgebiet is regarded as one of the world's Top Ten "Biodiversity Hotspots," but to layman and scientist alike, it is really the extreme weather conditions, the breathtaking scenery and pristine landscapes, that leave a lasting impression. The Wilderness qualities of solitude and raw expanse, of awe-inspiring beautiful coastline and offshore bird breeding islands, vast plains and rugged mountains, interspersed with numerous historical, archaeological and palaeantological sites, are almost unequalled on the sub-continent.

Furthermore, the Sperrgebiet borders on the Huns/Ai-Ais Game Park in Namibia, and you will recall that our own Minister of Environment and

Tourism, the Hon. Mr Philemon Malima, recently signed a Memorandum of Understanding with his South African counterpart, Mr. Vali Moosa, beginning the process towards forming a Transfrontier Park with the Richtersveld National Park. We have a similar dream for a Peace Park linking the Skeleton Coast in northern Namibia, with Iona in Angola. You can well imagine where this may lead to, if the Sperrgebiet becomes a National Park: it would enable the three countries—Angola, Namibia and South Africa—to negotiate an unprecedented tri-national, contiguous stretch of the oldest desert in the world as one massive Peace Park / Transfrontier Protected Area. It would stretch from Iona in the north to the Richtersveld in the south, including the Skeleton Coast Park, the Namib Naukluft Park, the West Coast Recreation Area, and the Sperrgebiet.

At the moment we (in the Sperrgebiet) are the vital "missing link," but there is no doubt that Namibia will make the right decision in time. Our Government has instituted one of the strictest environmental management policies on the continent, and under the leadership of an extremely environ-mentally committed Head of State, H.E. Dr. Sam Nujoma, backed by Article 95 of the Constitution which states, inter alia, that "the State shall actively promote and maintain the welfare of the people by adopting policies aimed at the maintenance of ecosystems, essential ecological processes, biological diversity of Namibia. ..." We are confident that the Sperrgebiet will receive the legal status that it deserves in the near future. What is important here is the knowledge that whatever happens, we are committed at all levels of society (and this has been confirmed by numerous public meetings during the Land Use Plan deliberations) to ensure that a major proportion of this stunning, globally important protected landscape is maintained as Wilderness.

Restoring Wildlife and Wilderness in Angola

Wouter van Hoven

Introduction

A twenty-six year long war in Angola is ending—other countries participated, and everybody lost. Once again the innocent and defenseless became the major casualties—the wildlife and the people were the real victims.

Very little of the teeming herds and unique species of wildlife in Angola can be seen today. The Kissama Foundation is now reversing this trend. The Kissama Foundation was formed in order to solicit support for its mission—to rehabilitate the national parks of Angola, to reintroduce wildlife species that have disappeared, to nurture back those species that are on the brink of extinction such as the Giant Sable, to give back to the people of Angola that which a war fuelled by foreign ideologies took away from them.

The Republic of Angola covers a geographical area of about 481,353 square miles (1.247 million square kilometers). It lies on the southwestern coast of Africa and its neighbors include Namibia to the south, Zambia to the east, and Zaire and the Republic of the Congo to the north. Angola's population is estimated at 11.6 million.

The Portuguese arrived in 1583 but colonization really gained momentum in the 20th century with the arrival of 400,000 Portuguese. After a civil war that started in 1961, Angola eventually received independence from Portugal on 11 November 1975 and the MPLA (Movimento Popular de Libertaçao de Angola), led by Agostinho Neto, took power. During the civil war, with the opposing groups respectively backed by the former USSR and Cuba and the USA and South Africa, thousands were killed. The economy suffered severely and many people were left destitute.

José Eduardo dos Santos, born 28 August 1942, took over as President after the death of Neto in September 1979. Although general elections were held in September 1992, UNITA (União National para a Independéncia Total de Angola) did not accept the outcome and remobilized its forces. Since the signing of the Lusaka Protocol in 1994, which became the basis for ending hostilities between the two warring parties, Angola has had greater political stability but the hostilities (to date) are not over.

Angola is now firmly set on the path to build up its economy. The importance of rebuilding the tourism industry and the conservation of natural resources have been recognized as contributors to this endeavor and naturally include the rehabilitation of the National Parks of Angola.

The Kissama Foundation was founded in 1996 by a group of South Africans and Angolans who were concerned about the present state of Angola's National Parks and the conservation of the country's natural resources in general. The Foundation is both legally constituted and registered.

The President of the Republic of Angola, President José Eduardo dos Santos, is the Patron of the Kissama Foundation. Several ministers and generals are serving on the Board of the Foundation, including the Minister of Finance, Joaquim David, the Minister of Environment and Fisheries, Maria de Fatima Jardim, the Minister of Social Integration, Albino Malungo, and the Minister of Tourism, Dr. Jorge A. Valentim. General João Baptiste de Matos, Genl Antonio E. Faceira, General Luis P. Faceira and General C. A. Hendrik Vaal da Silva are some of the other prominent Angolans serving on the Board.

The primary objectives of the Foundation are the rehabilitation of the Quicama National Park as well as the other national parks of Angola. The Quiçama National Park will be receiving first priority.

Researchers from the University of Pretoria's Center for Wildlife Management participated in formulating a viable ecological management plan for the Quiçama National Park. Extensive research conducted over the past five years form the basis for the five-year development plan for the Park. Upon completion, this management plan was presented to President José Eduardo dos Santos at a formal banquet.

Implementing the Management Plan

The Quiçama National Park is situated in the northwestern part of Angola, approximately 70 kilometers from Luanda, the capital of Angola. The Atlantic

Ocean forms the Park's 120-km-long western border, while the perennial Cuanza and Longa rivers constitute the northern and southern borders respectively. The eastern border consists of a belt of dense, tall thicket. Quiçama covers an area of roughly 9,960 square kilometres (1.2 million hectares).

Established as a game reserve in 1938, Quiçama was only proclaimed a National Park on 11 January 1957. A wide variety of habitat types occur such as the flood plain of the Cuanza river, an adjoining low escarpment and a transitional zone of grassland. The interior of the Park includes dense thicket, tree savanna and large open grasslands. This implies a carrying capacity for a potentially wide-ranging spectrum of wildlife.

Due to various factors, such as the war of independence, the 26-year war, widespread and persistent poaching, as well as the over utilization of the herbaceous vegetation, little is left of the once teeming herds that roamed the Park. At this stage the remaining number, if any, of elephant, rhino and buffalo in Angola, are unknown. Dwarf forest buffalo (*Syncerus caffer nannus*), roan antelope, eland, bushbuck, waterbuck, as well as the manatee, marine turtles and tarpon have been sighted in Quiçama but only an extensive game count will provide a reliable estimate. An impressive amount of birdlife, however, still abounds.

The first step in implementing the management plan was to create a secure area of 20,000 ha in the northern part of the park. An electrified game fence was constructed with the help of ex-military soldiers. A number of these soldiers have been trained as game guards and patrol the area on foot, horseback and river patrol boats.

A network of roads has been designed that would function both as tourist game-viewing roads as well as firebreaks. The regular use of such roads cuts down on the cost of maintaining dedicated firebreaks.

Reintroduction of Elephant

A crucial part of the rehabilitation of the Quiçama National Park is the reintroduction of wildlife. Operation Noah's Ark, an extensive project involving the reintroduction of elephant and several other species over the next few years, kicked off in September 2000. The first phase involved the successful reintroduction of two family groups of elephant, 10 kudu and 8 Livingstone eland. The elephants were donated by the North-West Parks & Tourism Board, and captured in the Madikwe Game Reserve.

Figure 1—The chief trunk-holder making sure that the elephants breathe comfortably, as breathing is impossible through the mouth.

In September 2001, a further 16 elephants were relocated in family groups to the park, a donation from the government of Botswana. These elephants were captured in the Tuli Game Reserve, an area with an overpopulation of elephant. 16 zebra, 12 blue wildebeest, 12 ostrich and 4 giraffe were relocated shortly after, all being airlifted by the Illusion 76 cargo airplane.

In the construction of suitable containers it is important to comply with the requirements published annually by the International Air Transport Association (IATA). This information is available from the Director, Traffic Services, 2000 Peel Street, Montreal, Quebec, Canada, H3A 2R4.

In selecting family groups to be captured and relocated, an important aspect is that the absolute maximum shoulder height should be 2.25 m. Standard shipping containers of 6 m in length and 2.5 m in height were used.

Figure 2—Loading a container with elephant into the IL76 cargo airplane.

Figure 3—Trap doors are fitted around the bottom of the container to seal completely, preventing waste products from leaking into the aircraft.

These containers were specifically modified to transport elephant and to be suitable to fit and use on an Illusion 76 Russian Cargo jet (see Figure 2). This type of aircraft was not only chosen because of cost and availability, but also because it needs a relative short runway.

The containers were fitted with a grid steel floor at a height of 25 cm. This allowed all feces and urine to pass through the floor and accumulate underneath the floor. Trap doors were fitted on the outside of the containers all along the bottom 25 cm of the floor (see Figure 3). When closed, these doors sealed in a way that no elephant waste products could escape onto the floor of the aircraft. After the flight, however, these trap doors could be opened all around and waste products removed with water hoses. This also improved the flow of air through the container since the roof hatches can also be opened.

Figure 4—A young elephant in the recovery truck, ready to receive the antidote.

Further modifications to the containers included the removal of the swing doors at both ends and replacing them with sliding doors. With a sliding door, the container can be fitted flush against a larger container, which functions as the recovery container. When the elephants are brought in from the veld they are put into a large container truck where they are fitted with radio collars or measurements are taken before the M5050 anti-dote is administered (see Figure 4). After the elephants are revived they can be regulated to walk from the large container into the aircraft container and remain in family units (see Figure 5).

In order to further regulate movement of elephant in the containers, a set of sliding doors have also been built into the middle of the containers dividing it into two sections of three meter each. In the middle of the containers along its length a set of vertical and horizontal poles were built into each 3 m section of the container. One horizontal pole at a height of 1.3 m and a support pole vertical to the roof in the middle of the 3 m section divided the 6m container into four quarters. This arrangement allowed for four elephants to stand comfortably yet preventing too much movement that could influence the air stability of the aircraft. Juveniles and sucklings can move around freely underneath the horizontal poles as their weight displacement has minimal influence on air stability. Having learnt from experience we would recommend that these dividing poles be fixed in such a way that they can be easily removed if required. We found that when an elephant lies down in the container compartment the poles do in some cases become a severe obstacle in the process of getting up again. In

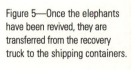

Figure 5—Once the elephants have been revived, they are transferred from the recovery truck to the shipping containers.

one case we had to use a hacksaw to cut the poles out before an elephant could get up again.

The actual selection of the family unit for relocation is done from the helicopter and they are then separated from the main herd and pushed towards a suitable area that is easily accessible for the trucks. Individual elephants are darted from the helicopter with darts containing 3 mg M99 for juveniles of 1.3 to 1.5 m shoulder height, 5 mg M99 for sub-adults up to 2 m and 7 mg M99 for those with a shoulder height of between 2.0 and 2.25 m. The rest of the dart is filled with Azaperone varying between 50 and 150 mg.

Each elephant is numbered with white spray paint, its shoulder height measured, the sexes and age groups determined, the dart wound treated with antibiotics and a long-acting tranquiliser (Trilafon, Sherag) and a short-acting tranquiliser (Haloperidol, Kyron Lab) are injected. Detail on the capture technique for elephant families is described in Du Toit (2001) and the management in smaller areas in Gerai (1999).

The third phase of Operation Noah's Ark will be the most extensive, involving the relocation of 300 elephant and several other wildlife species by ship. The SA Navy has made the SAS Outeniqua, a supply ship, available to carry the animals by sea from Walvis Bay to the Quiçama National Park. Animals will be sourced for relocation from various countries in Southern Africa, especially from areas where an overpopulation of a specific species exist. This operation will hopefully occur in 2003, depending upon a number of factors.

Tourism Development in the Quiçama National Park

The development of tourism facilities in the park has taken off with the restoration of Pousada Càua, one of the original rest camps in the park. Accommodation comprising thatched chalets, which overlook the flood plain of the Cuanza river, have been renovated and are open to tourists. Every unit is self-contained with its own ablution facilities.

A luxury lodge of world-class standards will be built within the foreseeable future at the mouth of the Cuanza River. The lodge will be unique in that it will incorporate both a sea and river front. Activities will include fishing, sunning on the beach, cruises on the river, bird-watching as well as game drives into the Park. This will be a lodge set within unsurpassable surroundings with a myriad of activities to choose from.

An ultra-luxury riverboat, named *Muxima*, has been bought by a private businessman from Luanda and imported from the United States. This boat is now operational as the owner has obtained a concession to operate on the Cuanza River paying a 10% levy on income to the Kissama Foundation.

The Kissama Foundation encourages the private sector to invest into the hospitality industry by building, owning and operating a number of lodges within the park. By arrangement with the Angolan government these concession holders have a 25-year tax holiday, but pay a 10% levy on income to the Kissama Foundation, which again is implemented in the proper management of the park and its wildlife.

Social Integration Program

A comprehensive project of capacity building and integration of local communities into the management of the park and provision of hospitality services is being launched parallel with the wildlife rehabilitation program.

In order to ensure that the park is managed not as an island but in conjunction with the communities that live in and around the park, a link should be fostered between benefits and community initiative in conservation. Community interest primarily is about benefiting from or utilizing natural resources. Emphasis should not only be on protecting wildlife, but also trees, water catchment areas, river banks, springs, dry river beds and other natural phenomena from over-exploitation.

Figure 6—The bishop of Angola blessing the park, its people and its animals with the President of Angola, Jose Eduardo dos Santos, looking on. This was during the official re-opening of the park on 16 December 2000.

There is potential for a partnership between communities and conservationists. Communities will have to protect their environment but at the same time earn from that environment, ideally through alternative use. There is also scope for the formation of a community conservation service, where communities actively and possibly on a semi-formal basis participate in conservation activities.

Community conservation efforts and area management will be linked to create an effective buffer zone through wildlife monitoring by game scouts around the park. Giving people responsibility for managing and protecting resources must go hand in hand with employment opportunities.

The park is viewed in a systemic context—land use master plans will integrate the park and its surrounds as well as those overseeing and using natural resources. This system will ensure sustainable integration over the long term. People displaced by war will be assisted to voluntary return to their places of origin. This assistance will always be such that their standard of living is improved.

A small community, who are not war refugees, live in the eastern border-area of the park. A process has been started whereby they are educated to become active in farming practices. This includes the raising of chickens, pigs, sheep and cattle, as well as vegetables. These products can then be bought by the Kissama Foundation as food rations for both its staff and tourists. Thus, this will become a mutually beneficial undertaking, and save us the trouble and high expense of buying rations in Luanda.

The reintroduction of wildlife and eventual repopulation of the entire park will enable the park to become self-sufficient through ecotourism to the area. People from the local community have been trained to work in the park as game wardens, hospitality staff and educational officers in the camps. With this

Figure 7—A local children's choir dressed in Kissama T-shirts, welcome the arrival of new animals.

integration of the local community, it is guaranteed that the park finds the acceptance it needs. With its proximity to the Angolan capital, Luanda, the Quiçama National Park will also play an important role in conservation education.

To date, 60 previous soldiers, left unemployed by the downscaling of the civil war, have been trained and employed as game guards. These guards also assist with monitoring and surveillance of the wildlife. With further re-introductions additional game guards will become necessary. Already over a hundred people, previously unemployed, are now working for the Kissama Foundation. They, in turn, improve the living conditions of a number of dependents.

Further training of game guards will take place in 2002. They will be trained in ecology, tracking, navigation and safety procedures. They will be crucial in monitoring the park and protection of the wildlife.

The Caua rest camp has been restored and opened to the public. Several members of the local community have been employed and trained as hospitality staff. More camps are planned and a second lodge will also be developed shortly. This will create the opportunity for more employment of the local community in the hospitality industry.

Conservation officers and educational officers from the local community will also be trained to fulfill an educational role in interacting with the public in the rest camps and lodge as well as on guided trips in the park. An educational center will also be established in the park. Daimler-Chrysler have donated two buses for transporting school children to and from Luanda, who might never otherwise experience nature and begin to understand the purpose of conserving these resources.

Conclusion

This operation has been a great team effort and recognition for their support is given to the following organizations:

> Shell Angola; Sonangol; Angolan Airforce; The Humane Society of the United States; The WILD Foundation, USA; TAAG Airlines; Government of Botswana; TAU Lodge, Madikwe Game Reserve; North-West Parks and Tourism Board, South Africa; Synchrony Logistics and Truck Africa; Televilt, Sweden; University of Pretoria, Centre for Wildlife Management; EcoLife Expeditions; and Christopher Osborn for photographs used in this chapter.

The Green Leaf Award 2001

Presented to:
*Angola—A Conservation and
Wilderness Priority*

Acceptance by:
The Honorable Alexandre Duarte Rodriguez

It is with great honor and appreciation that the Government of Angola receives, on behalf of its people, The Green Leaf Award presented by The WILD Foundation and the Executive Committee of the 7th World Wilderness Congress. Indeed, this is the first such international award we have received, and for a country that has been at war for so long, with so much devastation, it means a very great deal. Thank you.

Nature Conservation represents a very important issue in the political agenda of the Angolan Government. Despite the aggressions and other issues faced by the country, this option was addressed through the National Conference on Nature Conservation, held in Luanda in January 1977, whose closing ceremony had as principal speaker the first President of the Republic of Angola, Dr. Antonio Agostinho Neto.

At the independence time in November 1975, the National Conservation System was comprised of six National Parks, one Regional Park, two Strict Natural Reserves and nineteen Forestry Reserves, which represented the different types of biomes and ecosystems from the rain forest in the North to the Namib desert in the south of the country.

Due to the evolution and transformations occurred in the environmental culture from the Stockholm Conference on Human Environment in 1972 to the Rio Conference in 1992 and in view of protecting the richness of the Angolan wildlife, the Government set up the national bodies and became a Party to several international agreements such as the Convention on Biodiversity (CBD), the Convention on Drought and Desertification, and the United Framework Convention on Climate Changes. The option made by our Government to move on the international trend to protect the environment and the wild nature is expressed by the decision of the Angolan Government to further ratify the RAMSAR Convention, the CMS convention on marine turtles and the Memorandum of Abidjan for the marine turtles conservation.

Actually, a complete review and updating of all national legislation related to environmental protection and nature conservation is in process to sustain all the policies and programs evolving in those areas. To compliment those initiatives, the Government is also developing a National Plan for Rehabilitation of the Protected Areas, adjusted to the implementation of the CBD and other related conventions.

To make efficient the policy set up by the Government in environmental protection and nature conservation, the Government promoted a series of contacts with the civilian society represented by NGO's, the international community and other partners such as the Kissama Foundation and the UNDP. At the 7th World Wilderness Congress the Global Environmental Facility (GEF) made possible the financing of US $1,000,000 for the rehabilitation of the protected areas in Angola.

To compliment its efforts and seeking to establish an adequate framework for the implementation of the national plan for protected areas, and to install the technical and scientific capabilities for management and conservation of protected areas, the Government established specific protocols with the Kissama Foundation. This included an intensive and accelerated program for the training and specialization of human resources in those areas with the contribution of the State University Agostinho Neto and the cooperation of other foreign universities and training centers. This program should address within the next several years the lack of skilled personnel on those sectors. International NGO's are also helping us get started in this regard. We were glad to see the involvement of Angolans in the wilderness training program prior to the 7th WWC, sponsored by The WILD Foundation, Wilderness Foundation and the Sierra Club.

On behalf of Angola's Government, I offer sincere appreciation for all acknowledgments and support to our efforts in environment and nature conservation, to the NGOs as well as to the top GEF authority, Dr. Mohamed El-Ashry.

Following our policies for the environment and nature conservation, the new master plan for rehabilitation of the protected areas in Angola is focusing on local communities issues, creating new job opportunities and fighting the poverty which is the main enemy of nature conservation.

To the people of Angola and the Fundaçao
Quiçama for vision and perseverance
on behalf of wilderness and
wildlife in Angola.

Presented to Minister Fatima Jardim
2 November 2001, Port Elizabeth, South Africa

from The WILD Foundation
and the Executive Committee of the 7th WWC

Murphy Morobe	Vance G. Martin	Andrew Muir
Chairman	President	Director
7th WWC	The WILD Foundation	7th WWC

Wilderness—
A Future in Madagascar?

Serge Rajaobelina

√The Current trends

- The importance of Biodiversity
- The Forest Status
- The conservation challenges
- The current strategies

√The Protected Area Network

- The current strategies
- ANGAP
- The future of protected areas

√Venues for Wilderness Areas

- The corridor strategy & Ecoregion

The importance of Biodiversity in Madagascar

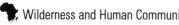

✓ 80% of the fauna and the flora are endemic to Madagascar

✓ 100% of the 34 Malagasy species of Primates are found nowhere else on Earth

✓ 96% of the 4,220 Malagasy species of trees and large shrubs are endemic

✓ 95% of the reptiles and amphibians are endemic to Madagascar

✓ 7 different species of Baobab in Madagascar

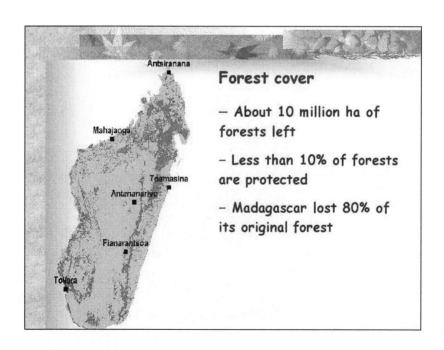

Forest cover

— About 10 million ha of forests left

— Less than 10% of forests are protected

— Madagascar lost 80% of its original forest

Why is conservation a challenge?

Poverty has pushed communities to use more and more the forest as a resource

Living little to accommodate conservation measures benefiting biodiversity.

DEVELOPMENT NEEDS

⇩

SUSTAINABLE NATURAL
RESOURCE MANAGEMENT
FOR MADAGASCAR

⇧

BIOLOGICAL IMPORTANCE
BIOLOGICAL INFORMATION

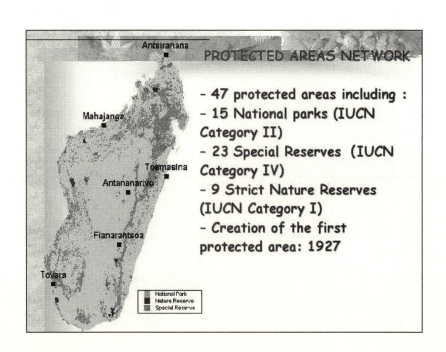

PROTECTED AREAS NETWORK

- 47 protected areas including :
- 15 National parks (IUCN Category II)
- 23 Special Reserves (IUCN Category IV)
- 9 Strict Nature Reserves (IUCN Category I)
- Creation of the first protected area: 1927

Antsiranana

Mahajanga

Toamasina

Antananarivo

Fianarantsoa

Toliara

National Park
Nature Reserve
Special Reserve

Special Reserve

1. Purpose: to protect threaten and endemic species
2. No restrictions in terms of access
3. Limited and controlled land use is permitted by communities living in the buffer areas of the Park

Strict Nature Reserve

1. Purpose: to preserve the environment in its original format
2. Restrictions: not accessible to the public and land use inside the reserve is forbidden

National Parks

1. Purpose: forest set aside for future use upon presentation of a management plan
2. Cover 90% of the forests of Madagascar
3. Little information exists on those forests

Classified Forests

1. Purpose: to educate the public about the environment
2. No restrictions in terms of access
3. Limited and controlled land use is permitted by communities living in the buffer areas of the Park

ANGAP'S MISSION
Association Nationale pour la Gestion des Aires Protegees

To maintain biodiversity in all the protected areas by developing a long-term conservation process that integrates ECOTOURISM development, research, and environmental education-outreach activities by means of promoting an open, dynamic, participatory relationship between local communities, regional authorities, the private sector, and the other organizations.

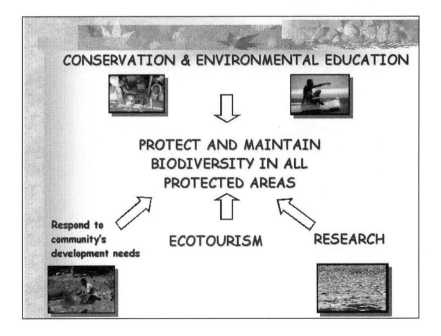

ECOTOURISM

- Numbers of visitors in 1992: 5,928
- Numbers of visitors in 2000: 85,743
- Revenues from Parks fees in 1992: $ 37,000 / 2000: $422,875
- 60% of the visitors are foreigners
- 50% of Park fees revenues to support community work

The future of Protected Areas

Because of the importance of biodiversity, creation of new protected areas is on the way

Increase participation at the local level to manage protected areas

Looking for new ideas to better manage forested areas: wilderness areas?

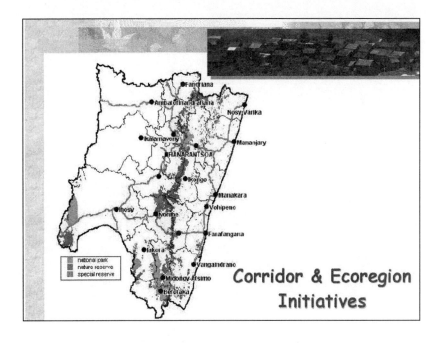

Corridor & Ecoregion Initiatives

We are here to learn

Notes on the Congolese Forest

Marcellin Agnagna

Congo is a Central African country covering 345,000 kilometers, 60% covered by humid tropical forest. The Congolese Forest covers 20 million hectares in three major forestry blocks (zones): Mayombe—1.5 million hectares; Caillu—3.5 million hectares; and the North Congo major zone—15 million hectares. It is part of the great equatorial central African forest, representing the world's second largest humid tropical rain forest after the Amazon. The many scientific expeditions conducted during the last ten years on Central Africa and Congo in particular have proved the immense biological and ecological potential of this forest. Nevertheless, a lot of research and work remains to be done on bio-ecological, socio-cultural, economical and conservation aspects.

The Bio-Ecological Aspect

The tropical Central African forest, by importance and surface area, is the world's second largest after Amazonia. It represents a unique home for many faunistic and floristic species, many still undiscovered.

In Congo, 45 snake species, 2,000 mammal species, and 600 bird species have been identified. We will never know the entire biological potential and richness of the Central African tropical forest, or how many territories remain unexplored and face destruction. Ecologically, the Central African tropical forest is a vital element for humanity, both local and global. It represents the survival for local populations that are highly attached to it. Fresh water originates in the forest. Pygmies and some Bantu clans who have lived and continue to live in it are sustained by the forest, and could not survive without it.

Socio-Cultural Aspects

Central African populations have drawn their essential vital resources from nature, mainly from forest. Through myths and traditions, populations have established principles and traditional rules from natural resources management and have lived in symbiosis with their environment. The concept of rational use is therefore not new to the forest people. Some examples: For some Congolese tribes both in North and South, forest was always under the Chief's Authority; he was responsible for upholding rules and principles of utilization. Some forest areas were strictly protected and access forbidden. There was no need for guards. Through respect of mythic or mythological beliefs conservation and protection principles were practiced. The system was perfectly functioning, as everyone knew his existence was directly linked to the forest. Some animal and plant species were strictly protected by means of those beliefs. For example, the biggest forest trees (Entanolophragma) were the incarnation of main leaders, and some were longevity symbols. A big tree could not be taken without prior authorization of the Chief, or the spirit of a main leader could be destroyed. The same rules were applied to some animals, untouchable and respected for a long time through mythical beliefs. Such is the case for the Bongo antelope. For most of north Congo ethnic groups, the python, the leopard and many other species are also thus protected. This is the reason why some forest areas are still unspoiled after millennia.

The African forest speaks, but have the Pygmies understood it? I answer yes! as they are certainly the most knowledgeable people as far as forest values and benefits are concerned. They knew how to move through the forest from North to South without a compass or a GPS! Unfortunately, all those precious rules have not been respected for the sake of modernity and economic development.

The Economic Aspect

In most Central African countries the forest plays a very important role. Timber and wood industry is one of the most important sources of income. But a question remains regarding the actual profit and real benefit from the country of origin and for the local populations.

In the Congo, over 20 million hectares of forest were given to forestry industry. The remaining 10 million hectares are flooded or are at risk of flood with only a few protected areas. Over 6,500 species are identified, amongst which 150 are exploited as high-quality wood and only 30 are exported to the international market. The timbers are exported untransformed, and transforming industries are very few.

In North Congo, raw or semi-transformed woods are transported from the forest to Cameroon, often escaping from Congolese Forest Administration. Timber poaching is rampant. Timber and wood industries have created over-sized cities in the middle of the forest where thousands of people are living. Those cities are attraction centers with all kinds of commercial activities: household products, poaching, trophies, wild meat, ivory traffic, leopard skin and all sorts of prohibited activities.

Wild meat (bush meat) is the only source of meat for employees, therefore poaching is a major threat to wildlife and in some areas shortage of wild meat is recorded. Forestry resources are over-spoiled in a dramatic way, most parts of the trees are left on the ground or burned on site. Valuable timbers for export are put on the market by foreign private companies paying very little taxes to the local administration.

Are these commercial activities beneficial to the local communities? The answer is very embarrassing and is dependent upon the definition concept of development. If development means the well-being of human African populations at all levels, in the Congo and elsewhere in Central Africa, then forest exploitation contributes to the ruin and to the alienation of forest populations. The Pygmies, who have been living in peace in the forest, are deprived of peace and tranquility due to bulldozers and sawing machines, and soon by AIDS.

Conservation

Forestry policies in Central Africa and in the Congo have mainly been orientated to wood extraction, ignoring the conservation issues in the absence of an example from their colonial heritage. Gently encouraging initiatives are being taken at the political level in the region, such as the implementation of structures working on the biodiversity management: Conference on Central Africa Dense and Human Forest Ecosystems (CFDHAC); the Central African Heads of States Summit in Yaounde, Cameroon (development of Congo river biodiversity); Conference of Central African Ministers in charge of Central African Biodiversity; creation of Trans-border Protected Areas; and the creation of a protected areas network.

Nevertheless, this political issue will have to materialize on the ground by upgrading protected areas, which in many countries are not economically productive even though their potential in biological biodiversity and tourism activities is immense. Many conservation and protected areas projects were initiated in the region under the guidance of the international community (GEF, EU, WWF, WCS, IUCN) but have not yet given concrete results or have a slow start-up. Southern African and South African experiences are therefore most welcome, as they have more success than ours.

Conclusion

There is in Central Africa a real problem regarding management and protection of natural resources. Central African tropical forest is in danger due to the forest industry, and the danger increases daily. It is alarming. In the Congo 4% of total productive forest disappears every year. Even protected areas are in danger. Central African Tropical Forest, one of the last Edens on earth must be saved. Action is needed now!

The international community is being called to help the regional counties to develop and upgrade existing protected areas in order to save the forest. My last message is the following:

Let us save the forest to save humanity!

The Congo Basin Forest—
The Future Is Now

Michael Fay

*[Editor's note: The following is an edited transcript of a
presentation by, and discussion with, Mike Fay.]*

The forest of Central West Africa is well over one million square kilometers.
It's a very big area and until 1985 conservationists had no idea what was
going on there. We knew very little about Gabon and knew almost nothing
about the Central African Republic (CAR), and we still don't know anything
about the Democratic Republic of Congo (DRC). In about 1985, I went there
with Richard Carol and we started a survey of gorillas in the CAR. There was
a report that gorillas were extinct in the CAR, but in fact we found a high
population. In addition, there were good populations of forest elephant and
buffalo, red river hawks and everything else. But logging was already serious
even in the CAR, which is logistically a difficult and expensive place to work.

In 1989, after we had established a Reserve in the CAR, there was a vast
territory to the east, in Congo, about which we knew little. I went there in 1989
for the first time and I met Marcellin Agnagna. He is Congolese, an employee
of the Ministry of Forestry, and was my primary contact for those first few
years. We undertook a big expedition to survey the elephant population
throughout the Northern Congo. We did long walks through the forest, and it
was on one of the first walks that we decided to study the map, locate human
populations, and traverse the forests from one side to another. This was the
basic design that eventually lead to the Mega-Transect, about which I will speak
later. That first walk was a 150-kilometer trek from one end to the other,

recording elephant dung and various other signs of wildlife, humans, and a lot of data on vegetation. We found that in Northern Congo elephant populations were high, as were populations of all other wildlife, especially gorillas. Red river hawks were abundant, and there were six species of duikers, ten species of monkeys, hundreds of species of trees, and gorgeous forest.

"Bai" clearings—open areas within dense jungle—are also fairly abundant in Congo, Gabon, and the CAR. Though many people know the Odzala National Park now, until 1995 people didn't recognize its importance. After we did the elephant survey we started a project and discovered a place called Nouabale-Ndoki. It is now the name of a park, established in 1993, as a result of our three years of work. We found many clearings there, with no sign of human beings. It was a very large forest, completely uninhabited, of about 1.5 million hectares.

If you look at the map, you realize that every bit of Congo has been divided into logging concessions, and right now there are logging companies operating in virtually every single one of those blocks. There are roads to every center in each one of those blocks. Once established, these roads change the forest forever. The area just south of where we created the Nouabale-Ndoki National Park is a typical kind of checker board of exploitation.

But the good news in Congo over the last few years is that we have been able to create new protected areas. We have successfully expanded the Odzala National Park to about one million hectares, established Nouabale-Ndoki, plus conserved a triangle of forest in the south. In 1991 when we started the Nouabale-Ndoki project we had good financing from the World Bank. There was a lot of initiative, a fair amount of money, and a lot of momentum. Many people were talking about saving these forests, having sustainable logging throughout Central Africa by the year 2000, and more such promises.

We established our project in 1991, and by 1993 we had a National Park (Nouaballe-Ndoki) of 400,000 square kilometres and were working with all of the nearby villages. This was facilitated by Marcellin who speaks the Pygmy language. His mother actually came from a village just to the east of Nouabale-Ndoki National Park, and he knows the area and the Pygmys very well.

We quickly discovered that wildlife responded positively to the creation of the national park. Elephants started repopulating the forest because of intense pressure on them in other areas. For example, hunting pressure on elephants was very high. In fact, the village where Marcellin and his mother are from is in one of the central hunting zones for ivory in all northern Congo and exported many thousands of tusks. Added to this pressure is logging. People frequently analyze timber cutting in a very sterile manner, talking sustainability, good practices, about how 100,000 cubic meters and 12,000 hectares come out per year. In fact, when loggers go into the forest it alters the ecosystem in a long term and catastrophic way – not necessarily permanently, but to return to a forest that you would not recognize as having been logged in Central Africa would take at least a thousand years.

Logging companies are systematic. They block off the forest in little parcels, each representing an annual cut of about 15,000 hectares. They cut lines into the forest, in 1,000 X 500 meter grids. They touch at least every single hectare, and they probably touch every 100 square meters in the forest. They kill all the wildlife first to feed the road and logging crews. They build dense road systems, then they take out every single usable tree. They say they only take one tree per hectare, but what they don't say is they take the biggest tree per hectare, one that has a crown of maybe 50 meters in diameter. One hectare is only a hundred by a hundred meters, and when you build a skidder trail to each of those blocks, build a road to get there, and you cut a tree that has a 50 meter diameter crown, the ecosystem suffers a major impact.

We've started making some progress in how the logging companies think about fauna, flora, and the ecosystem. But it's a small start. They still regard the forest resource as one that is there for the taking. They regard ecosystem management as the government's responsibility, not theirs.

In 1996, we finally got an aeroplane in Congo. This plane allowed me to expand beyond foot surveys over Congo and Gabon, to investigate and explore every little place in every river valley, and look at every single clearing throughout those one million square kilometers of forest. I learned two things: the forest was largely empty, and human populations were concentrated mostly along roads. We did an aerial video survey around the mostly large forest blocks, and found that people lived in very low density around them. We were able to document almost every village, using single capture images from one of those surveys.

We discovered amazing places too, where "dinosaur hunters" have gone over the last ten or fifteen years. Marcellin was one of the first to go in as an interpreter with the dinosaur hunters, and to their credit they talked about rhinos in the forest more than dinosaurs. Marcellin really did bring the forest of Congo to a lot of people, not just to me. He was the only person in the entire Ministry of Forestry in Congo that had a strong appreciation of the forest situation, and he pushed very hard for action in Congo. Without Marcellin, nothing that we accomplished would have been possible.

The war started in Brazzaville in 1997 and it was a pretty violent time in Congo. We stayed, the Parks survived, and didn't suffer much. We found the rebel forces just as easy to work as the non-rebel forces, because they were the same men we had always dealt with. Nothing really changed other than all of a sudden, there they were on one side of the political spectrum rather that the other. During that time I decided on the scheme of walking from northern Congo, where we started in 1991, all the way to the Gabonese Coast. I chose the largest uninhabited blocks all the way across the forest, looking at them from a human habitation/human settlement point of view and drew a line through the forest that would take me from the edge of each one of those blocks to the upper center of the lowest human influence, in every single block

During the "Mega Transect," I recorded data on large mammal densities, abundance, diversity, human impacts, and vegetation. For instance, we counted every single tree over 60 centimetres in diameter, 10 meters on either side; transected over 3,000 kilometres. We have a huge data set right now. It was not easy. It was a long walk, and when we started, I didn't think we would make it. When you go into the forest, your body degrades the entire time. You think, "Well I'll make it because we have only ten days left, nine days, eight days," and your body is going down, and all of a sudden you are cured and you recover. If you are going to do that for what you thought would likely be eighteen months without leaving the forest, you don't know what is going to happen to your body. You don't know if it's going to survive or not. In fact, one of the keys is to not wear a shirt, or not to wear pants, just wear little skivvies (going naked would even be better) with some river sandals. It's the best way to travel in the forest. I found after about four months that my body stabilized and I was able to keep on going. I got stronger and stronger but skinnier and skinnier.

When you get deep into the Gabonese Forest, the trees are awesome. In these blocks you walk for about two or three days, and human signs diminish rapidly. You get to zero human impact and then you have a couple of days in a true no-man's land. That's when the forest just kind of opens up. It's as if you go through a gate and you leave the human world completely; you enter into something that is evolving without any influence from human beings at all. It is difficult to describe the feeling and what you observe. An elephant knows, for instance, where the Mohabi tree is. One of the largest in the forest, the Mohabi tree has beautiful fruits the size of a mango, full of oil. Elephants love them. Every single tree in that forest is known and every single tree has a constellation of trails radiating from it. When you think about the elephant infrastructure in those forests it is incredible, because these elephants really do know where every single large Mohabi tree is. As they travel, if they hit a bifurcation in the trail, they know where left goes and where right goes. They've built that infrastructure over thousands of years, directly to trees that are likely a thousand years old.

This was the same way we discovered that gorillas know these "bai" clearings, and that some of the gorillas have knowledge of the human species and some do not. An animal that is naive is curious, inquisitive, and approachable more than other individuals in the group. These "bai" clearings are created by animals, and are the "cities" of that constellation of trails. In this case, all roads lead to "Rome" in the forest. If you hit a trail that is 2 meters wide and it gets wider and wider, you know that it's going to a clearing. The trails leading into a clearing are about 6 meters wide. You could have driven a 40-ton truck down these trails for the last portion.

We crossed many, many rivers on this trip, and getting across would have been impossible without good men. I had many good men and didn't lose anybody on the way. The point men used to look back at me at least a hundred times a day, completely lost, completely disorientated. They had no idea where they were going but they kept on. Babay was the second of two point men who chopped a trail all the way. He chopped all day over 1,500 kilometers to get us from one end of Gabon to the other, certainly the only Pigmy who had ever done that.

Half way through Gabon—that is about twelve months into the trip—we were in a forest called Langwe, at the Congo Waterfall on the Wendo River, certainly one of the most spectacular waterfalls in the African continent and almost completely unknown to the outside world. Langoue, particularly, showed that we still have opportunities in Central Africa, because the logging hadn't reached into this block yet. You could travel three to four weeks without seeing any sign of human beings. We still have time, but it's going fast. Chimpanzees are a good indicator of what's going on out there, and there was only one bad sign of chimpanzee behavior on the entire trip. He was really bizarre: he decided to go on the attack. He just hung out about 5 kilometres from us and kind of chased us many times. That was the only time during the entire trip that we had a negative encounter with wildlife; all the rest was absolutely great.

This long walk, 3,000 kilometres through the forest, has received lots of publicity. What's the result, and what's the meaning of this? Is this just one more of those kinds of crocodile-hunter expeditions—that show on TV? Not at all. We're setting up a website to contain a database. It will have every single item pre-recorded, every single elephant dung pile, every single observation of any monkey species, every video clip that we took of 360 species of vegetation, elephant encounters, or gorilla sightings. We will have a popular website where people can look at the sights and sounds of the trip and will be able to explore all the region. Another website will pick the scientific data set from the database to show every variable in the landscape. Using GIS software, people will be able to virtually fly over the landscape, look at satellite images and topographical maps. We collected data on at least forty different variables consistently for over 3,000 kilometres. People will look at those and really see elephant encounters, or how elephants' dung varied in this block or that or view the human impact. They will be able to query the database on the web. Everyone on earth can essentially look at it or play with various modelling tools that will be available on the site.

We now have a human population dataset for the forest, but are just using a simple 3D model of village locations to help understand human influence. We've broken up the dataset into 5 kilometers transects that can be re-grouped into 1, or even 10, kilometer sets. Elephant dung density varies along a transect and if you put elephant density on top of this 3D model of human influence, then you can see that humans have a very significant impact on elephant locations in a particular forest block. This will be one of thousands of queries, with many combinations of variables performed easily on this website. The GPS track will also be available.

When you look at Gabon on our map there is little evidence of human beings in the forest. If there was a significant human influence you would be able to see the impact. Gabon has no national parks. It has a few reserves and most of those are under funded. In Gabon, the 600,000 hectares of reserves has a budget this year of about $65,000.

When people look at Gabon they think it is covered with forest and is wild, but in fact it is not. The logging companies are ripping through Gabon, cutting primary forest so fast that there probably won't be any left in about another fifteen years. A typical logging road is not a little meandering fun road in the forest;

They are 40-meter wide clear cuts, to get to every single tree in that forest. This causes significant change: canopies essentially disappear. People can talk about sustainability but when you are walking your way through 3,000 kilometres of forest and you hit a place that has been logged, it is devastating. It is completely, one hundred percent devastating. You yell, scream, and cry. You just can't believe the human species is capable of that kind of destruction in exchange for a few bits of lumber. It's just not reasonable.

There is a plan in the process of formulation to create a new national park system in Gabon. Much of that area is going to be logged very soon and some already has been. At this point we have a dream, and the plan doesn't really have much behind it. In 1991, we had good support for the national parks creation in Congo. It was easy, with lots of open areas, and we could choose any 400,000 hectares with nobody living in it. There were no logging companies. The Government said, "It's a great place, we've got six million bucks, we can start up this project." In two years you have a national park that will be part of the landscape for hundreds of years to come. We can already see Nouabale-Ndoki appearing on the satellite images over the last five years. It is different in Gabon, as there are active logging concessions everywhere. We will need the highest authority in the country to approve. We have the bones of a plan...and miracles are possible.

In talking about the result of this Mega Transect, people like the data. The bottom line for me is that data is important, but data doesn't create national parks: people create national parks. Usually very few individuals are responsible for the creation of national parks. We need to act now. The most glaring example of why we need to take action concerns the trip in Langoue, south of those waterfalls, where we discovered a very large clearing, one that had never been seen, and was the first one ever found in Gabon. It was a classic elephant clearing. The trails coming into this clearing are about 4 meters wide, from the forest on all sides. It is as intact an ecosystem as is possible. It is primeval wilderness, with groups of 50–75 elephants at a time, and perhaps 30–40 resident sitatunga.

I was back there recently helping map this place for the reserve. We discovered that gorilla densities are some of the highest in the world. There was a dwarf crocodile just 1 meter from a human. They are great indicators of human impact on an area because they are very easy to kill. In this clearing about every 10 meters along the creek there was a dwarf crocodile. We think this means that this place has never been hunted.

So, consider the logging scenario in Gabon, and consider what we are trying to do: We're trying to put this new little "bai" on the map. The bai and surrounding forest is about 250,000 hectares. It is difficult to find anything larger. Just about ten years ago we could pick an empty block of 400,000 hectares. Today we are down to 250,000, and we've got ten logging concessions within that. It is going fast, very fast.

Another disturbing reality is that international agencies seem to have lost interest in protecting the forests in Central Africa. The amount of money and the ability to find money for forest conservation in Central Africa is dangerously diminished. We don't have money. It has become almost impossible to make a coherent plan and create a national park—even if you could deal with the logging concession problem on the ground. And a logging company can completely obliterate the ecosystem of a forest block essentially in two years.

We've been trying hard for the last six months to raise private funds to create a new national park in Gabon. This has involved talking to the Gabonese government about reverting the logging rights back into the public domain. From my long experience on the ground in Central Africa, and from my own heart, I am certain of one thing. We have a very, very short amount of time left, probably two to three years, to establish any more national parks in Central Africa. The human race needs to understand this, now.

When we arrived in Central African in 1985, nobody knew anything, and we discovered these unbelievable places. Fifteen years later we are at the end of our window of opportunity. We have been able to come up with a couple of million bucks from private individuals to put this place on the map; but we don't have enough money, we certainly don't have enough diplomatic support. These areas are real wilderness. The World Wilderness Congress—that is, every delegate and organization that participates—can make a difference.

[*Editor's note:* Less than one year later at the World Summit on Sustainable Development (Johannesburg, September, 2002), Gabon's President Haji Omar Bongo announced a new national park system for his country composed of 11 new parks and covering more than 10% of Gabon. U.S. Secretary of State Colin Powell announced a major funding commitment to the Congo Basin Initiative. This was a direct result of Mike Fay's work, and that of a small, dedicated team of people. Mike's comment: "President Bongo sees the potential for his country. Others must follow. It's a start."]

The United States and Africa— Conservation Partners

U.S. Member of Congress, E. Clay Shaw

The tragic events of last month and the anthrax attacks near my home district and in Washington have made this time both difficult and auspicious. No less so for Africa. I have had the privilege to travel to Africa multiple times, and in doing so, have become educated as to both the wonders of and the challenges facing that fascinating continent. I have witnessed firsthand Africa's natural glories, having visited some of the most pristine natural areas like the Ndzlama Reserve in South Africa, Etosha National Park in Namibia and the forests of the Ndoki National Park in the Congo. However, it was also on these travels that I became alerted to one of the most serious problems affecting the continent, in particular sub-Saharan Africa: rampant and unsustainable logging.

We in the United States recognize the overwhelming need to protect tropical forests, pristine wilderness and other sensitive natural habitat around the globe, but few are aware of the true extent of the problem. Like every other nation, America has a huge stake in seeing that the stewardship of African natural treasures is taken seriously. If not, Africans will remain impoverished and the world will suffer the consequences of Africa's environmental degradation, including the destruction of its forests and grasslands, and the loss of the elephant, the cheetah, the mountain gorilla and other wonderful species. Africa's loss is our loss and the world's loss.

In an era of concern about ozone depletion, global warming, widespread disease and conflict, long term resources management should be an essential part of U.S. policy. The world's tropical forests are a bountiful source for our medicines, and the cradle of the habitat and wildlife most in need of protection. It is not a stretch to say that if we are not vigilant, and fail to pay attention to what is happening in Africa, our complacence may very well put us one day on the endangered species list ourselves. There is a lesson to be learned as well as a chore to be accomplished.

All told, the United States provided sub-Saharan Africa with just under $2 billion during the recent fiscal year, funding which goes to a variety of extremely worthwhile efforts, including development assistance, child disease programs, AIDS treatment and grants to various non-governmental organizations to conduct humanitarian and environmental programs. But one area in which I believe the wealthiest nation in the world has been derelict is its responsibility to take notice of the widespread destruction of wilderness. Conservation-oriented debt buy backs and debt swap programs on the part of the United States, such as the Tropical Forest Conservation Act, constitute a good start to the effort to leverage American resources to address the problem of wilderness loss. Such programs indicate that American leaders are beginning to hear the alarm that has been going off, as the heavy debt burden of many nations very clearly contributes to the unacceptable exploitation of tropical forests. But failure to pay heed and see the direction in which we are moving in Africa will have serious consequences and will indicate what could happen to the entire globe if we do nothing.

I believe it is time for the United States to adopt a new, more focused approach to the preservation and management of tropical forests, one in which we work more closely with local governments and give them the resources and tools to preserve their great natural assets. We must be creative in the way we address this challenge. We also need to recognize why these lands are disappearing—not necessarily insensitivity to environmental needs, or even the business interests or simple greed of loggers (at least not in total), but practical concerns. The need to provide people with jobs, to promote economic stability, to maintain order—these are needs common to every nation and community around the globe, and in developing policy, we must not lose sight of this simple fact.

The clear challenge is to effectively utilize American resources in Africa, taking into account these needs. With them in mind, I will be soon introducing in the U.S. House of Representatives legislation that would allow for the use of American foreign aid dollars to purchase timber and logging rights abroad. The goal would be to acquire these rights in order to protect the most sensitive and threatened wilderness areas, land that otherwise would fall victim to clearcutting. Once we can be assured there is adequate infrastructure in place on the local level, these rights would be handed over to a host governmental entity to protect these lands in perpetuity. Obviously the challenges beyond the purchase of such rights are many and daunting. The threat of poachers hunting for bushmeat and renegade loggers are but two. Therefore, we cannot address the problem as if in a vacuum, but recognize just how difficult a task this may be.

The principles upon which my legislation will be crafted reflect the theme of the 7th World Wilderness Congress—"Wilderness and Human Communities: The Spirit of the 21st Century," namely:

- reducing the amount of land available for logging immediately and directly;
- understanding the importance of partnerships with local governments, taking into account the fact they better understand local land use policy than the U.S. government;
- keeping the needs of locals in mind (providing sustainable development for indigenous peoples);
- allowing governments and environmental groups to come up with creative, flexible ways to offset the economic losses associated with a decrease in logging;
- redirecting the logging community, thereby recognizing economic realities;
- preserving existing efforts to protect wilderness.

My goal and the goal of those whose support I will seek in promoting this legislation is to increase the wilderness area under protection without legislating winners and losers, without being punitive or capricious. We understand no two states are the same, and vary greatly in terms of geography, economy, and society. We will not punish those nations who are unable to do what others may do. We do not suspend aid to a nation in need of assistance in freeing itself from the grips of warfare, civil unrest, famine, or economic blight.

That being said, we expect those nations with the means available to act responsibly with regard to the evaluation and protection of their untouched or sensitive wilderness. Those nations with the means to tend to their own natural resources must do so.

The United States has a great responsibility, and though the political and logistical challenges of this approach are great, I cannot feel but heartened in my efforts, and committed to the notion that this is absolutely worth fighting for.

Wilderness & Human Communities— United States Federal Agencies

Elizabeth Estill

This chapter is a brief summary of the National Wilderness Preservation System (NWPS) in the United States, how it was established, the Government agencies charged with its management, its incredible diversity, and some of its affects on the nation as a whole, on special interest groups, and on communities located adjacent to designated Wilderness. In this regard, I will touch on the economic effects of Wilderness designation as well as the attitudes and values of people affected by these designations. And I will take a look at the challenge of sustaining Wilderness into the next millennium.

The history of the National Wilderness Preservation System in the United States begins long before its establishment by law. However, that history alone could be the subject of an entire presentation. So, I will just note that, after many attempts and political skirmishes among a number of powerful interest groups, in 1964, protected areas as designated Wilderness in the United States were legislatively established by an act of the United States Congress. And, when President Lyndon B. Johnson signed the Wilderness Act into law on September 3, 1964, many people believed that the long battle for wilderness preservation in the United States had finally been won.

The Wilderness Act establishing the National Wilderness Preservation System is one of the most significant pieces of legislation signed into law in the United States. The Act provides for preserving underdeveloped Federal lands, to retain their primeval character and influence, without permanent improvements or human habitation, so that they may be protected and managed to preserve their natural conditions. The National Wilderness Preservation System was established to secure for the American people of present and future generations the benefits of an enduring resource of Wilderness.

The Act established the following: 3.6 million hectares in 54 areas to be managed to preserve its natural condition; a framework for establishment of additional areas; and requirements that apply to all four of the land managing agencies in the United States. These agencies include the National Park Service, Forest Service, Fish and Wildlife Service, and Bureau of Land Management. The National Park Service manages the bulk of the National Wilderness Preservation System at 41%, followed by the Forest Service at 34%, and the Fish and Wildlife Service at 20%, with the Bureau of Land Management having responsibility for 5% of the System.

In the last 37 years, the National Wilderness Preservation System has grown from 3.6 to 41.6 million hectares—105 million acres—and can be found in 44 of the 50 states in the country. In total area, the NWPS is about the size of Greece, Nicaragua, or Tunisia.

Protected areas in the United States include a number of incredibly diverse ecosystems: From the deserts of the Southwest to the hardwood forests of the Northeast; from the timbered alpine regions of the Northwest to the swamps of the Southeast; from the dunes of the Great Lakes to the Arctic tundra of Alaska. Some of these areas are quite remote, while others are the backyard for small and large communities, and clearly effect and are affected by people.

What is the affect of Wilderness designation on the United States as a whole (the national community)?

One measure is the economic impact of Wilderness designation. In estimating the national value of designated Wilderness:

- The best available estimates of the economic value of a visit to a Wilderness area in the United States show $41.87 per person per day (Loomis, et al, 2000).
- Estimates of total number of visits to areas in the NWPS are 34.7 million, plus or minus 7.8 million (Cordell, et al, 1998).
- Overall recreation value of the NWPS alone = 34.7 million visits x $41.87 = $1.45 billion per year.

• And studies agree that option, existence, bequest and altruism values make up approximately 75% of the total value of Wilderness. Thus, total national value of the NWPS is estimated to be approximately $5.8 billion per year.

The attitudes of people toward Wilderness and the values they hold about Wilderness are other measures of the affect of Wilderness designation. In the United States, we have an excellent tool to measure these affects—the National Survey on Recreation and the Environment conducted under the direction of Dr. Ken Cordell, a senior scientist with the Forest Service. According to the results of this survey, there are several specific reasons people give for being supportive of Wilderness designation. They value protected areas because they protect air quality, water quality, wildlife habitat, and threatened and endangered species; and because protected areas provide people the opportunity to leave a legacy of Wilderness for their children. While there are a number of additional benefits from Wilderness, they did not resonate as strongly with the population surveyed. The least important values of protected areas that respondents identified were to provide recreations opportunities, for spiritual inspiration, for purposes of scientific study, or, interestingly enough, for stimulating income for the tourism industry.

What is the affect of Wilderness designation on people represented by special interest groups (communities of interest)? The United States is a representative democracy. As a result, public land management policy is greatly influenced by special interest groups, both through the non-governmental organizations that represent them and by their representatives in the U.S. Congress.

Nationally, between eight and nine percent of Americans 16 years or older regularly contribute to or participate in organized conservation group activities, including support of wilderness conservation. As an example, the Sierra Club has approximately 700,000 members that are dedicated to adding 40,000 hectares to the NWPS in the next decade. As another example, The Wilderness Society has 200,000 members that are dedicated to increased designation and improved management.

However, other non-local interests frequently oppose Wilderness designation. Examples include off-highway vehicle use, mining, timber, grazing, tourism development, such as ski resorts, water—both user and industry organizations. Each of these interests groups has a great interest in public land management as well as Wilderness designation, and are typically concerned with the restrictions on uses and development associated with Wilderness.

What is the affect of Wilderness designation on adjacent communities (communities of place)? These are the people that are most directly affected by Wilderness designation.

Wilderness designation, by law, protects Wilderness values. And Wilderness designation is frequently described, promoted, and opposed as locking in place the status quo. At the national level and for many special interest groups, this is the case. However, for local communities it is different. For these adjacent communities, Wilderness designation brings change, both real change and the perception of change.

Commonly, over time, Wilderness designation has a positive economic impact on local communities. However, in many cases, these gains are associated with changes that are resented and resisted by these same local communities. Such changes can be linked to the transition these communities often experience when moving from a commodity/extraction based economy, such as those relying on timber and mining, to an economy based on recreation and service. The affects such a change has on the people living in these communities can be significant.

In estimating the positive economic impacts on local communities:

- Research shows an average expenditure per person per day for a Wilderness visitor is approximately $30.31.
- 35 million visits x $30.31 = $1.06 billion Wilderness-related visitor spending per year in local communities.
- With the multiplier effect, local community impacts are estimated to be:
  — $1.41 billion in personal income per year
  — 58,000 jobs
  — $2.24 billion in total value added in local communities
- And local property value increases are estimated to be 13%.

However, despite the economic gains that can be documented, people in local communities have concerns. Their lives and, for some, their livelihoods are impacted significantly as a result of the changes that come with Wilderness designation. This fact is inescapable and needs to be considered fully and acted upon in some manner during the process leading up to designation, and made an important consideration in public land management thereafter. These local communities frequently feel that their concerns and needs are given less weight than national interests; that uses that have been accepted for generations are now restricted; that big government is stepping in and taking away a part of their lives and, frequently, their livelihood; that they are being invaded by "outsiders" that would never have come into their communities without a Wilderness designation, that, as visitors, these "outsiders" can never appreciate the character of the area like the people that live there; and that recreation/service jobs with lower pay are created at the expense of higher paying commodity/resource extraction jobs.

So, although it is clear that a majority of people surveyed nation-wide are supportive of protected areas in the United States, some who's livelihood or lifestyle depends on the natural resource base, directly or indirectly, would rather see development of short-term commodity values such as logging, petroleum and minerals production, or hydropower. Or they want to be able to drive their sport utility vehicles, snowmobiles, or mountain bicycles. Or they want to hang glide, helicopter ski, site and install research equipment, or use the Wilderness in larger groups. These individuals object because these types of activities are expressly prohibited by the Wilderness Act.

So on one hand, the majority of people, although relatively silent, are supportive of Protected Areas in the United States. However, those whose livelihoods or lifestyles depend on the extraction of natural resources are typically not supportive of wilderness and, although the minority, are very vocal and highly influential.

While the majority of people surveyed in the United States support wilderness, they lack an awareness and understanding of what Wilderness means, particularly the scope of activities that are restricted in Wilderness. As a result, it appears that support is best characterized as broad and shallow while opposition is narrow but deep.

So, how do we meet the challenge of sustaining Wilderness into the next millennium and beyond?

The answer is simple and basic—Wilderness is not, and cannot be, everything to everyone. Despite the best efforts of the best interpreters and educators among us, there are those that simply will never understand the importance of Wilderness, or accept that there are values that only Wilderness provides, or appreciate that there are fundamental human needs that are met only by Wilderness. Many of these people are important and influential members of our communities. Their perspectives, beliefs, and concerns cannot be ignored or dismissed—to do so risks the survivability of Wilderness.

We have a saying in the United States, "If you can't beat them, join them." Of course, I am *not* suggesting that we agree with those that oppose existing or new Wilderness. But I do believe that, while we make every effort to educate, interpret, and develop a greater and more widely held appreciation for the vital importance of Wilderness, it is also important to identify and focus on the needs of our communities—our national community, our communities of interest, and our communities of place, particularly our communities located adjacent to designated or proposed Wilderness—and to work closely and cooperatively with these communities to meet their needs. Too many perceive Wilderness as being in conflict with their objectives or standing in the way of meeting their needs. We must reach out to the people in these communities, and pursue and discover alternative means of meeting their genuine needs, while still maintaining the integrity of existing and future Wilderness.

Every day, our Wilderness managers and land management agencies work cooperatively with external individuals, groups, organizations, and governments to manage conflicting demands and uses. As pressure for access and use of our public lands continues to increase, these demands come into ever greater conflict with the limited access and use restrictions of Wilderness. During the last 50-plus years, Wilderness advocacy non-governmental organizations have focused largely and narrowly on campaigns designed to add more land to the NWPS. We now need these non-government organizations to also actively support prudent, responsible, and ecologically sustainable natural resource management, including appropriate access and a diversity of uses on non-Wilderness public lands. For example, not all of the roadless areas of the United States should be or need to be designated Wilderness. Many of these areas are ideally suited to provide alternatives to Wilderness. Support or funding to meet public demand for access to and use of a broad range of public lands will go a long way toward relieving some of these pressures on Wilderness, and, as a result, directly support the sustainability of Wilderness and the National Wilderness Preservation System.

Many special interest groups are promoting either wilderness designation or resource development. As managers, we shouldn't view land management decisions as either/or. Our public lands may not be able to provide all things in the same place, but many uses can be accommodated somewhere. Our challenge is to work with both communities of interests and place to provide as much as we can in ecologically sustainable and socially acceptable ways and places.

Effective communication and coordination – we need much more of both among all communities with an interest in Wilderness; internally and externally, supporters and opponents, and all those in between. As Wilderness managers we are all too frequently caught in the middle between two or more parties that cling obstinately to their respective positions, each unwilling to consider alternatives. As managers of public lands, to effectively fulfill a facilitation role requires a willingness of all parties involved to work with each other. Special interest groups each want more lands reserved for their specific passion. And they tend to be fiercely independent. Getting them to work together and with government agencies may be our greatest challenge.

For many years the four land management agencies in the United States managed public lands quite independently with limited communication or cooperation. I am pleased that our management of the NWPS has been increasingly different than this management approach of the past. We are working closely and cooperatively on an interagency basis to establish a common vision and strategic plan for the NWPS. Notably, working together, we established two interagency organizations, the Arthur Carhart National Wilderness Training Center and the Aldo Leopold Wilderness Research Institute, which support NWPS management through focused training and research programs. We must continue to work across agencies to conduct research about Wilderness, gain an understanding of what the American people value about Wilderness, and share research and understanding through employee training and information and public education.

However, this is only a start. For Wilderness to be sustainable, we must aggressively pursue new alliances with, and increased cooperation among, a diversity of partners from all communities. This means establishing and maintaining relationships with those most interested, both those who support Wilderness designation and those who oppose it. This will require considerable time and a genuine willingness to listen if we really want to understand what peoples' values are and what motivates them. We have to start where people are, not where we wish they were. We must bring interest groups together and collectively build a shared vision, finding common ground and building on it. Additionally, we must connect with both our supporters and our opponents, learning new ways to work together with respect for our shared and different goals. We must understand and appreciate the needs and concerns of others that are different than our own. We must be careful to consider and, wherever possible, address local concerns, and not be swayed too greatly by survey data gathered on a larger scale. We must be persistent and patient, vigilant and sensitive, determined and humble.

If we take this approach, I am convinced that not only will there be a NWPS at the end of the millennium, but that support for Wilderness will deepen among a much wider array of Americans. Most importantly, this support will deepen among the citizens of the United States whose will is carried out by the elected officials that hold so much sway over public lands. In this way, we will increase awareness, understanding, appreciation, and, ultimately, support for the preservation of Wilderness for present and future generations.

The Sierra Club—A Century of Wilderness Activism

Bruce Hamilton

The Origins of Wilderness in the United States

Most Western scholars will say that the idea of permanently protecting wild country as national parks and wilderness areas was born in the United States. After all, that's where the first official national government-designated National Park—Yellowstone—and the first designated national wilderness areas were established.

The very idea of needing to designate and protect wild country through legislation must seem very odd and foreign to most indigenous cultures unfamiliar with nations and national governments. To them, wilderness was just a part of their daily lives—their environment and home—and it required no protection.

The idea of protecting nature from development through government action grew up in the United States because we had a culture clash of immense proportions. Right as the Industrial Revolution was making it possible to exploit wild untamed country at a record pace, an intellectual movement grew up that caught the imagination of the American people and some key influential leaders that nature was something to be revered and preserved rather than tamed and exploited.

By the middle of the 1800s, the United States was a young country with rapidly developing coastal states, and an interior that was mostly remote and undeveloped. The interior lands were bought (such as the Louisiana Purchase) or won in wars (such as the American Southwest). After their annexation, the federal government had in mind handing them over to private use—farming, mining, logging, grazing—as rapidly as possible. There was no thought given to retaining wildlands in public ownership.

When Yellowstone National Park was established in 1872 the primary purpose was to promote the tourism industry for the railroads. While it was recognized as a scenic wonder, the Congress noted that there was no harm in designating the area as a national park and putting it off limits to development because it "had no pecuniary value" and if some profit-making scheme could be devised in the future, "we could always undo the act." Now how's that for a noble conservation vision?

The Role of John Muir and The Sierra Club in Defending Wilderness

But by 1890, a little-known Scottish immigrant with a love of wildness burst on the scene. This self-proclaimed tramp—John Muir—had hiked from the Canadian border to the Gulf of Mexico and throughout the Sierra Nevada in California. An amateur inventor, naturalist, writer and geologist, Muir loved all things wild and could not stand to see them destroyed. He also wore his passion on his sleeve, knew how to find adventure, and had a great gift for words and placing them in key places at key times.

In 1889, at the urging of Robert Underwood Johnson (an editor of *Century Magazine*), Muir undertook a campaign to designate his beloved Yosemite as a National Park. That same year Underwood and Muir discussed establishing some sort of conservation association that Muir would lead.

In 1892, in San Francisco, California, The Sierra Club was founded, with Muir as its first President. He said the idea behind this new club was he was "hoping to do something for wildness and make the mountains glad." Muir all too quickly found out what the Club needed to do for the mountains, for, no sooner had Yosemite become a National Park and it came under threat of dismemberment. Under pressure from timber, livestock, and mining interests, a bill was introduced in Congress to drastically reduce the Park's dimensions.

The bill died in committee, thanks in large part to The Sierra Club and John Muir, but this brief but important battle made it clear that no wild place was safe from development—even the National Parks. As David Brower, the Club's first executive director, was fond of saying no environmental war is ever finally won, though any battle, when lost, is lost forever. Not a very comforting thought, but it is a recipe for full employment of environmentalists—we will never be obsolete.

In his fight to protect wildness Muir knew he had to court people in power and effectively use the media to shape public opinion. He published his writings in the most influential newspapers and magazines of his era—*The New York Tribune, American Journal of Science, Harper's Weekly,* and *Scribner's Monthly.* This brought him great fame so that soon major writers and politicians were seeking out Muir. His most famous encounter was with President Theodore Roosevelt in 1903, when the two tramped around Yosemite and even got caught in a snowstorm. Muir's love of wilderness was contagious as he hoped to "do some forest good in freely talking around the campfire" with the President. Roosevelt called the encounter "the grandest day of my life." Roosevelt's Presidency was a high water mark for land preservation. Through executive action he set aside millions of acres of forest reserves, national monuments, and national wildlife refuges.

By 1900, the moneychangers were back at the doors of the temple, this time trying to flood the Hetch Hetchy Valley in Yosemite National Park to provide water and power for the City of San Francisco. For those of you unfamiliar with Hetch Hetchy, it was a twin to Yosemite Valley, with equally spectacular waterfalls, granite domes, and sheer rock walls. Muir and The Sierra Club waged a campaign for over a decade to stop this desecration of the National Park, but after the 1906 earthquake, when the city burned to the ground and allegedly lacked an adequate water supply to fight the associated fires, the political momentum became too great to stop.

The battle over Hetch Hetchy also clearly delineated a major chasm in conservation philosophy and politics. While John Muir staked out the clear and compelling case for preservation, Gifford Pinchot, a Pennsylvanian schooled in forestry in Europe, was establishing the case for utilitarian management of public lands. The vast forest reserves that Presidents Grover Cleveland and Theodore Roosevelt had established to protect them from timber barons were consolidated in the Agriculture Department under the Forest Service, with Gifford Pinchot as its first chief. To Pinchot, scientific management was essential and nature could not be left to its own devices. Each acre needed to produce "the greatest good for the greatest number in the long run." Pinchot and Muir clashed over Hetch Hetchy and ultimately Pinchot convinced Roosevelt to back the dam.

Muir railed against the dam and invasion of the Park, saying what use was the whole idea of National Parks "inalienable for all time" if Yosemite could be sacrificed? "Dam Hetch Hetchy?" he declared. "As well, dam for water-tanks the people's cathedrals and churches, for no holier temple has ever been consecrated by the heart of man."

President Woodrow Wilson signed into law the bill allowing Hetch Hetchy to be built in 1913. A year later, though the official cause was listed as a lung infection, Muir died and close associates said it was of a broken heart over Yosemite. He was 76.

But the ideals that Muir articulated so well, and the organization that he had built to defend the earth's wild places outlived him. With the inspiration of John Muir, the leadership of Stephen Mather (who became the first National Park Service Director in 1916), and the profit motive of tourist-oriented western railroads, the National Park System expanded rapidly into the 1930s.

Leopold and Marshall and the Evolution of Wilderness

However, as the park system expanded, so did the developments within it. During this period two great wilderness advocates—both Forest Service employees—spoke out in alarm at the growing industrialization of the parks. Aldo Leopold complained in 1921 that "the parks are being networked with roads and trails as rapidly as possible" to promote tourism, and as a result wilderness was being lost. Bob Marshall, his contemporary, wrote in 1937 to the Secretary of Interior Harold Ickes that "the Park Service seems to have forgotten the primitive."

Leopold, while trained as a wildlife manager, was a brilliant and beautiful essayist. His *A Sand County Almanac* is a classic in world conservation literature and wilderness philosophy. In 1935 Leopold wrote: "This country has been swinging the hammer of development so long and so hard that it has forgotten the anvil of wilderness which gave value and significance to its labors. The momentum of our blows is so unprecedented that the remaining remnant of wilderness will be pounded into road-dust long before we find out its values."

Leopold argued against Pinchot's utilitarian philosophy, siding with Muir that some areas needed permanent protection from all development. His advocacy led to the establishment of the Gila Wilderness Area in 1924—the nation's and the world's first official wilderness—though it was just an administrative temporary designation. Leopold's campaign finally caught the attention of the Forest Service's leadership and in 1929 the agency adopted "L-20" regulations, which called for the designation of "primitive areas" on the forests. But the regulations did not strictly prohibit any form of development or use, including logging and road-building, so no primitive area was completely safe and inviolate.

This steady loss of wilderness lead Bob Marshall to remark, "Wilderness is melting away like some last snowbank on some south-facing mountainside during a hot afternoon in June. It is disappearing while most of those who care more for it than anything else in the world are trying desperately to rally and save it."

The steady loss of National Forest wilderness led the Sierra Club and others to continue to campaign for more national parks. In 1938 and 1940, respectively, Olympic National Park and Kings Canyon National Park were established from Forest Service primitive areas. Noted wilderness photographer and Sierra Club leaders Ansel Adams took a portfolio of his wilderness shots back to Washington, D.C., where he showed them to Congress and the Administration to convince them of the need to preserve Kings Canyon. But also fearful that parks could be overdeveloped, they convinced the bills sponsor to designate Kings Canyon a "wilderness park."

Throughout the 1930s the greatest champion of wilderness was Bob Marshall. In his job at the Forest Service he convinced the agency to replace the flexible "L-20" regulations with new "U" regulations, which called for the designation of wilderness areas (over 100,000 acres) and wild areas (under 100,000 acres). And unlike the "L-20" lands, these new "U" designations prohibited logging and road building.

The Wilderness Society and Legislated "Permanent" Wilderness

Marshall, like Muir, also realized that to protect wilderness one needed to also build public support. So he joined with Leopold, Olaus and Mardy Murie, Howard Zahnizer, Dick Leonard, Sigurd Olson, Stewart Brandborg, his two brothers and other visionaries and established The Wilderness Society in 1935.

The Wilderness Society joined forces with The Sierra Club and other conservation groups of the day to continue to fight for protection of wild places. But The Wilderness Society also became the nucleus of the think tank and center of activity devoted to developing the notion of permanent legislated protection for wilderness.

In 1934, Marshall had suggested the need for permanent legislative protection for wilderness. The idea lay dormant after Marshall's premature death in 1939, but resurfaced in 1951 at a Sierra Club National Wilderness Conference where Howard Zahnizer, the Executive Secretary of The Wilderness Society, floated the radical notion in a speech. However, it was not until 1956 that Zahnizer drafted a wilderness bill and had it introduced. And it would be eight years later, in 1964, before the bill would be signed into law following years of intense campaigning by conservation groups to overcome the opposition of miners, loggers, ranchers and other opponents. Surprisingly, the bill ultimately attracted broad bipartisan support and passed the Senate 78-8 and the House 373-1. The lopsided vote was a tribute to Howard Zahnizer and the conservation community who worked tirelessly to address all parties' concerns. Sadly, Zahnizer passed away just four months before the bill was signed into law by President Lyndon Johnson.

The Wilderness Act not only established some Wilderness Areas. It also established a clear unambiguous national policy that to preserve Wilderness for present and future generations was in the public interest. It also established a national standard for wilderness. Wilderness areas were defined as areas "where the earth and its community of life are untrammeled by man"; lands of 5,000 acres or greater "without permanent improvements or human habitation." Logging and use of mechanized equipment was prohibited, but grazing (where established) was allowed to continue and hunting and fishing were allowed.

When the Wilderness Act passed, it designated the first 9,140,000 acres of statutorily protected Wilderness out of the existing national forest system of administratively protected areas. At the insistence of the main opponent of the bill, the new law also required that only Congress would be able to add lands to the system. While this provision was originally viewed as an insurmountable obstacle—after all it had taken eight long years to pass the Wilderness Act—it turned out to be a blessing in disguise. The reason is that this provision reserved a place for the Congress to regularly review agency decisions not to protect areas, and it set up a process whereby citizens could influence the final decision by lobbying Congress.

Another extremely helpful provision, which laid the foundation for the wilderness movement of the last thirty-five years, was the requirement of a ten-year review of an additional 5 million acres of roadless wildland in the National Forests, National Parks, and National Wildlife Refuges. The law also demanded that as the agencies reviewed these lands and prepared recommendations for Congress on their status, they were to consult the public. This provision forced wilderness advocates to build up strong grassroots support for each area, which could then translate into a potent lobbying force when the agency recommendations returned to Congress. So when the agencies came back with greatly scaled-back proposals for additional acreage in wilderness, citizens were ready to have Congress step in and up the ante. This drove the agencies crazy because citizens and Congressional staff were overriding agency recommendations and drawing new larger wilderness boundaries while removing lands from the timber base.

Building a Wilderness Advocacy Citizen Movement

But citizens refused to stop at the 5 million acres of primitive areas mandated by the 10-year review process. If Congress could step in and establish a Wilderness Area and not just follow the agency lead, then why not look at designating some areas that were completely overlooked by the agencies. There were easily 200 million acres of de facto wilderness on the public lands; why should Congress be restricted to only look at the 5 million acres deemed primitive and wild by the agencies?

The first successful citizen-initiated Wilderness proposal was the Lincoln-Scapegoat Wilderness in Montana in 1972. That victory set the stage for a flood of new proposals and new reviews over the next thirty years.

Another extremely significant development was a Sierra Club lawsuit, decided in 1972, which required the Forest Service to prepare a detailed environmental impact statement to evaluate the wilderness potential of each and every roadless area before any development could proceed. This legal victory gave citizens a tool to stop development and organize support for wilderness before an area was destroyed by a bulldozer or a chainsaw. This legal victory ultimately led to two national comprehensive reviews of all roadless lands on the National Forest system and the passage of dozens of Wilderness bills covering millions of acres of wildlands.

Soon every Federal Land Management agency was required by law to review the Wilderness potential of their lands, to involve the public in that review, and to report back to Congress with recommendations. Before the wilderness debate was focused primarily on high alpine National Forest primitive areas with very little development potential, but now there were wilderness reviews on national grasslands, desert lands, National Park backcountry, seashores, and previously logged second-growth forests in the eastern States.

Perhaps the most ingenious stroke of wilderness politics was a provision in the Alaska Native Claims Settlement Act—a law whose primary purpose was to give Alaska native tribes certain ancestral lands and rights—requiring that the Federal Government look at establishing new parks, wildlife refuges, and Wilderness Areas in Alaska and report back to Congress. This provision was championed by Dr. Edgar Wayburn of The Sierra Club, who realized that when the state of Alaska and the natives were carving up 375 million acres of Federal lands in the state, it was important to make sure the public's interest in wild-land preservation was also considered.

In Alaska, for the first time, conservationists had the opportunity to look at establishing wilderness areas that encompassed entire ecosystems and watersheds. In past wilderness disputes in the lower forty-eight states, the debate was over whatever lands had not been developed—all too often just the mountaintops or the canyon bottoms. While these wild remnants were highly scenic, they all too frequently were completely inadequate from the standpoint of protecting biological resources. Key habitat or watershed lands were often unsuitable for consideration as wilderness because they were too heavily developed and no longer met the wilderness criteria.

The battle over, what came to be called the Alaska National Interest Conservation Lands Act took ten years, but when it was finally signed into law by President Jimmy Carter it doubled the size of the Wilderness System, the Park system, and the wildlife refuge system in a single day. The act established 55 million acres of Wilderness, 32 million acres of new National Parks, and 18.5 million acres of new national wildlife refuges. This was the single biggest land conservation victory in U.S. history. All told it established 104.3 million acres of new protected areas in one stroke of the pen.

Today, the National Wilderness Preservation System includes nearly 105,800,000 acres in 644 areas in forty-four states. It includes arctic tundra, tiny islands, high volcanoes, vast desert sand dunes, deep forests, snowcapped peaks, sunny beaches, wild rivers, fjords, lakes, swamps, and sandstone arches. But while this looks like the wilderness campaign is near to complete, in fact, our work has only just begun. There are at least 200 million additional acres of wildlands in need of defenders and deserving full statutory protection.

New Challenges for a New Generation
of Wilderness Advocates

Ecosystem Protection

For the first 100 million acres, with the notable exception of the Alaska Lands Act, wilderness bills have designated undeveloped wildlands without regard for ecosystem boundaries. The Northern Rockies Ecosystem Protection Act is a notable exception. This proposal would increase protection for 20 million acres of wild country in the Northern Rocky Mountains of the United States. In addition to designating 18 million acres of new wilderness, the proposal calls for a National Wildland Recovery System to restore almost 1 million acres where roading, logging, and mining have severely damaged vital ecosystem components such as wildlife corridors. NREPA also establishes special corridor management areas, where development is limited, but not prohibited, allow for biological connectivity between core reserves. This approach is a first for the United States as a legislative proposal, though this approach has been successfully pursued by private land conservancies on a much smaller scale. The leadership that The Wildlands Project is providing in articulating the case for ecosystem protection, and providing the scientific justification to back it up, has been invaluable in this process.

Roadless Area Protection

In the United States, one of the biggest threats to wilderness and wildlife habitat are roads. Roads are built initially to access a timber sale or oil drilling site or stock water pond, but then quickly get taken over by off-road vehicle enthusiasts, hunters, and other motorized users. The roads introduce alien plant and animal species and diseases, destroy habitat for sensitive species, lead to erosion and stream sedimentation, increase fire danger, and pave the way for more development. Roads are the number one cause of water quality degradation on the national forests. On the national forests of the United States there are over 380,000 miles of roads, so that as one looks at a map or flies over most forests they look like a plate of spaghetti with a twisted maze of roads dominating the landscape.

If one looks at the 190 million acres of national forests in the United States, about half are already so crisscrossed with roads, mines, pipelines, clearcuts, and transmission lines that they cannot be considered for wilderness; another 35 million acres of National Forests are already protected as wilderness by Congress. What remains in the balance is 60 million acres of roadless undeveloped National Forest that needs full protection, but is at risk.

After decades of debate over the fate of these lands, in 1999 the Clinton Administration launched a national effort to determine their future. Over 600 local hearings were held and over one million comments in support of full protection were gathered by The Sierra Club and our allies. At the conclusion of the process, Clinton recommended protection for 58.5 million acres—all roadless lands over 5,000 acres in size. Unfortunately, with the election of George W. Bush the new administration has abandoned support for this vital initiative. Now development-oriented states, such as Idaho, are challenging the Clinton Forest Policy in court and the Bush Administration has refused to put up a defense. It will be a huge legal, administrative and legislative struggle over the next few years to keep the Bush Administration and the timber industry from destroying these wild forests.

Desert and Grassland Wilderness

To date, most of the U.S. wilderness debate has been around Wilderness on the National Forests. The fate of wild non-forested deserts, "sky-islands" in the deserts, and grasslands is a wilderness protection chapter yet to be written. While The Sierra Club led a successful campaign to protect the California Desert—the single biggest park and wilderness bill for the lower forty-eight States in our history—the fate of millions of acres of desert and grasslands from North Dakota to Utah is yet to be decided. Citizens are drafting proposals and organizing support for this next generation of wilderness, and we can expect Congressional action over the next two decades.

The National Grasslands pose a special problem and opportunity. Over 99 percent of the native prairie in the Great Plains of the United States has been plowed and fenced. After the dustbowl of the 1930s abandoned farmland that never should have been cultivated was returned to public ownership and managed by the Agriculture Department to restore its native grass cover. Today these National Grasslands offer a chance to establish prairie wilderness, if we can overcome local opposition from entrenched interests, including ranchers and oil companies. These lands also may serve as core areas to restore native wildlife species such as bison, wolves, bighorn sheep, elk, black-footed ferrets and other species that have been driven out of the plains by civilization.

As each of these proposals are coming forward, wilderness advocates are looking not only at what is left that is still wild, but also what is needed for ecosystem protection and restoration and how can we "re-wild" an area to recapture its wilderness qualities.

Alaska Big Wilderness, Round Two

While some would say that the 104 million acres of Alaska that we protected through the Alaska Lands Act in 1980 was the resolution of the debate, conservationists see it as just the first round in a much longer fight. Already in 2001 there is a huge national fight over the fate of the Arctic National Wildlife Refuge, which oil companies and the Bush Administration see as the next big North American oil field, and conservationists regard as America's Serengeti and the biological heart of the North American Arctic Ocean coastal plain. Similarly, the Tongass National Forest in Southeastern Alaska is the United States' largest temperate rainforest, but under intense pressure from the timber industry. There are also tens of million of acres of Bureau of Land Management and Defense Department lands (including the National Petroleum Reserve—Alaska) in Alaska deserving full wilderness protection. It is easy to envision at least an additional 100 million acres of Alaska wilderness being added to the system over the next few decades.

International Wilderness—The Right Sort of Globalization

Wilderness, the creatures that depend on it, and the watercourses that run through it, do not recognize international borders. While there are a small number of complementary preserves, such as Glacier National Park in Montana (USA) and Waterton National Park in Canada, there are many more cases where wild country and ecosystems are fragmented and have competing and contradictory management strategies across international borders. The Yellowstone to Yukon (Y2Y) campaign is an attempt to tie together wilderness management for the entire Northern Rocky Mountains. Similarly, there are attempts to coordinate wilderness management around the Arctic, both on our border with Canada and our boundary with Russia.

Joint wilderness efforts with Mexico are equally important, but complicated by border security and immigration control concerns. As The Sierra Club has promoted wilderness areas along the Mexican border, the Immigration and Naturalization Service and Border Patrol have raised objections, claiming they need to use motorized vehicles, erect fences, employ spotlights, and clear vegetation to keep a secure border. There is also less of a history of wilderness and parks protection in Mexico, and the industrialization of the border factory towns or maquiladoras, fueled by the North American Free Trade Agreement (NAFTA), has led to urbanization, destruction and widespread pollution of border wild areas.

International cooperation will also be essential to help recover endangered species that depend on wilderness habitat that spans international boundaries. Grizzly bears, woodland caribou, Mexican wolves, jaguars, and ocelots are just a few of the species that will benefit from international wilderness cooperation. NAFTA has in many ways been a disaster for working families and the environment—especially along the U.S.–Mexico border. While the countries in North America have been quick to tear down trade barriers—all too frequently leads to environmental degradation—they have been slow in building up and investing in international environmental cooperation to preserve and restore our common continental wild heritage.

Establishing international wilderness complexes along ecosystem boundaries and rewilding those areas that have been degraded, while establishing the necessary international agreements to make this all work as one unified system, will be a major challenge for the future. It will require us to be world citizens.

Conclusion

The wilderness idea is over 100 years old and the U.S. Wilderness system has over 100 million acres preserved in perpetuity—but our work has only just begun. We need modern day John Muirs and Bob Marshalls to carry on where the present generation has left off. While we should be proud of our accomplishments and the wilderness heritage we have secured for present and future generations, if we don't continue to build on this progress we will leave our children a greatly diminished planet. Most wilderness areas are too small to support the full complement of native flora and fauna that should be restored to rewild our wilderness areas. Global warming is predicted to cause major shifts in flora and fauna, which could wipe out ecosystems that have endured for centuries.

A new generation of wilderness advocates can lead the way to establish the next 200 million acres of wilderness, while simultaneously restoring the ecosystems around our existing wilderness areas. This is a future vision that would, as John Muir hoped, "make the mountains glad."

Australia's Wilderness—The Status, The Challenges, The Future

(... A snapshot)

Alec Marr

Australia is an ancient continent, a giant piece of the old super-continent Gondwanaland. When Australia separated from Antarctica around 45 million years ago, it drifted north. It is still drifting north at a rate of approximately 7–9 centimetres per year.

The Australian continent's isolation over this immense period of time has been a major component in the evolution of an exceptional diversity of plants and animals.

Australia is home to unique ecosystems, an extraordinary array of endemic species and, at 50,000 years occupation, the oldest continuous culture on earth. The impact of European settlement, through the use of inappropriate agricultural practices, the introduction of feral animals, sheep and cattle, and the occupation of aboriginal land has been dramatic on our ecology and on indigenous communities.

At the beginning of the 21st century, the challenge for Australian environmentalists is to protect our last wilderness areas, to restore some of the ecological damage done by Europeans since 1788 and to restore some of the cultural damage done to the first Australians.

The Wilderness Society believes we can achieve all these things: but we need a holistic approach to protect our remaining wilderness areas, to restore the ecological flows across our landscapes, and to ensure that significant areas of land are returned to traditional owners or are jointly managed with them.

After years of searching we believe that the best model we have seen, which can meet all these objectives, is an Australian version of the U.S. Wildlands

Project. We believe that this approach is the next logical step for the wilderness movement globally.

Australians are passionate about protecting wilderness. It is not an accident that most of the big environmental battles people outside Australia have heard about have been over wilderness areas. The Franklin River, the Daintree rain-forests and Kakadu are just a few of the hundreds of campaigns that have been fought to protect wilderness areas over the last 70 years. Many wilderness areas have been protected but many more remain under threat.

The wilderness movement in Australia is vibrant. An increasingly sophisti-cated understanding of what is required for nature conservation is being matched by an increasingly diverse approach to campaigning.

Diversity in Australian Wilderness Landscapes

Australia is one of the top twelve mega diverse countries in the world. It has ecosys-tems ranging from Antarctica and the Sub-Antarctic Islands through to some of the tallest forest in the world, alpine regions, savannah woodlands, extraordi-nary tropical landscapes and marine ecosystems.

1. Antarctica and the Sub-Antarctic Islands

Everyone knows that Antarctica is the greatest wilderness left on earth but what many people won't know, is that Australia claims around 40% of the continent. Australia operates three permanent bases on the Antarctic mainland at Casey, Davis and Mawson.

When you think of Australia, it is worth remembering that Australian Government policy has a significant influence over around 6 million hectares of this continent. Overall, the Australian Government is one of the best govern-ments operating in Antarctica. It has just initiated a major campaign to clean up rubbish from our Antarctic bases and is urging other countries to do the same.

Australia also administers three World Heritage-listed sub-Antarctic islands: Heard and McDonald at 369 sq km and Macquarie Island at 128 sq km. Australia is, therefore, a major influence in the Antarctic Treaty.

2. Forested Wilderness

Forests are rare in Australia and rainforests are rarer still. All of Australia's rainforests could fit into one third of our smallest province, Tasmania. Areas of rainforest wilderness are highly valued jewels in the Australian landscape. Our largest rainforest areas, the World Heritage Wet Tropical Rainforests of Far North Queensland, and the cool temperate rainforests of the Tarkine in Tasmania still contain magnificent wilderness areas protecting ancient Gondwanan plant lineages.

Australia's forests are some of the most magnificent, unique and biodiverse in the world. They contain the tallest flowering plants on Earth, more than one twentieth of the world's plants and land animals, and some of the most significant tall temperate old-growth forests remaining globally.

It is the *Eucalyptus regnans*, not the Sequoia, that is the tallest living organism ever recorded on Earth. The oldest living tree on earth is a 10,000-year-old Huon pine on Mount Read in northern Tasmania. And right on the doorstep of Sydney, Australia's most populous city, there survives the recently discovered Gondwanan relic, the Wollemi Pine.

More than half Australia's terrestrial biodiversity is found in the 5% of the Australian continent with forest cover.

3. Arid Wilderness—Water in an Arid Landscape

The vast majority of Australian wilderness (excluding Antarctica) is arid land.

Australia is regarded as being more arid than any other continent apart from Antarctica. Rainfall in much of Australia is unpredictable and varies markedly, not just with the seasons. This, combined with a low mean annual runoff, leads to very high variability in water flow, which produces a large number of intermittent water bodies in arid and semi-arid areas. Areas of moisture in a generally arid continent are vital to many groups, notably birds, and many communities of floral and faunal species are specifically associated with them.

Permanent water bodies are few and far between. For example, the Coongie Lakes of central Australia form an important wetland area with a complex system of claypans, channels, fresh and saline lakes, internal deltas, swamps and flooded meadows, occurring over the floodplains. The diverse aquatic flora and fauna of this area is characterized by spectacular fluctuations in abundance and for its adaptation to an "opportunistic" lifestyle. The lakes support a diverse and often extremely abundant bird population, including 24 species classified as rare or endangered (for example, the freckled duck—one of the ten rarest waterfowl in the world). The lakes also support an exceptional number of zooplankton species as well as rich frog and fish faunas.

4. Tropical Savannah Woodlands

Australia's harsh, highly seasonal climate has produced a distinct landscape of tropical savannas, Australia's northern woodlands. The woodlands stretch in an unbroken line right across northern Australia, and are superficially similar throughout their range. But varying rainfall, soils and fire regimes have produced a range of types—from tall open forests, to the more common open woodlands, through to open grasslands. The dominant trees are mostly eucalypts and the understory is dominated by a range of summer growing grasses. Along rivers and in areas sheltered from fire, small patches of rainforest grow.

Northern Queensland's Cape York Peninsula is a vast 137,000 sq km area of unique wilderness landscapes, including vast savannah woodlands. Recent work on the natural significance of Cape York has noted the region as a "treasure-house of biodiversity", a "living mosaic of interlocking habitats that provide a globally outstanding resource for the in-situ conservation of biodiversity, both for widespread and common species as well as the more localized, rare and endemic biota."

5. Marine Wilderness

Australia has the largest area of coral reefs in the world.

The Great Barrier Reef (GBR) is the largest complex of coral reefs in the world. Ningaloo Reef, in Western Australia, is the largest fringing reef on Earth and is one of the best kept marine wilderness secrets on the planet.

North of Cairns the GBR is high-quality wilderness with the opportunity for high-level protection if the abutting wilderness on Cape York Peninsula is itself properly protected.

Unfortunately, despite Government policy discussion papers on marine wilderness, we are yet to see any formal definition or recognition of the concept.

This snapshot of wilderness diversity in the Australian landscape helps to understand the significance of wilderness protection and restoration for the survival of our highly unusual and endemic flora and fauna.

Australia's Endemism

Australia is not just one of the world's mega-diverse countries. It is rich in endemism. 92% of Australia's vascular plants are endemic. About 83% of Australia's mammals also occur nowhere else, as well as 45% of our birds, 89% of our reptiles and 93% of our frogs (see Table 1).

Table 1: Australia's endemic species and world ranking by families		
	Endemic species	Rank in world
Higher Plants	14,458	5
Non-fish Vertebrates	1,350	1
Mammals	210	1
Birds	355	2
Reptiles	616+	1
Amphibians	169	5

Clearly Australia is home to a unique part of the world's natural heritage, but we still have a long way to go before it has adequate protection.

Australia's Protected Areas

Australia has approximately 61,720,000 ha in its terrestrial protected area system, representing 8.0% of Australia's 7,690,150 sq km continental land mass.

However, over a quarter of the world's countries have a more comprehensive terrestrial protected areas system than Australia.

In the last 25 years, environmental campaigns have protected approximately 10,700,000 ha of Australia's wilderness and wildlands (see Table 2).

Current Condition of the Australian Landscape and Natural Systems

1. Forests and Woodlands

Since European settlement, 213 years ago, half of Australia's forests have been permanently cleared. Now only 5% of the continent has any forest cover at all. Only 8% of the pre-settlement old growth forest remains. Our forests, particularly in the southeastern portion of the continent, are now islands of old growth in a sea of regrowth or clearfelled land (see Figure 1).

Old growth forests on wet fertile soils are now extremely rare and considered by many scientists to be endangered.

More than 6 million hectares of our most productive rainforest ecosystems have been permanently cleared. Now little more than 2 million hectares remain, with much of that highly fragmented and highly threatened. Rainforests now cover just 0.3% of the Australian continent. In some states they are still being

Table 2: Wilderness protected by environmental campaigns over the last 25 years		
Wilderness Area	**Hectares**	**Year(s)**
Western Tasmanian Wilderness	760,000	1982
Wet Tropics World Heritage Area (WHA)	894,000	1988
Snowy River National Park additions (Victoria)	54,100	1988–92
SW Tasmanian Forests WHA additions	600,000	1988–90
Douglas Apsley National Park, Tasmania	16,000	1989
Kakadu Nat Park/WHA Stages 1–3	1,980,400	1972–92
Shark Bay WHA, Western Australia	2,197,300	1991
Victorian Mallee wilderness national parks	918,500	1991–92
Fraser Island WHA, Queensland	181,000	1992
Kangaroo Island wilderness, South Australia	70,000	1993
Shoalwater Bay Conservation Park, Queensland	16,002	1994
East Gippsland forests, Victoria	3,000	1997
Beech Creek forests, Tasmania	4,000	1997
Savage River forests, Tasmania	18,000	1997
Eden forests, SE New South Wales	67,000	1994–98
Australian subantarctic islands WHA	49,685	1998
Wongungarra alpine wilderness, Victoria	13,000	1999
SE Queensland forests	425,000	1999
Wongungarra wilderness, Victoria	13,000	1999
NSW wilderness areas	1,243,927	1987–00
NSW Southern Forests	324,000	2000
Silver Plains wilderness, Cape York Peninsula	307,000	2000
Starcke wilderness, Cape York Peninsula	190,000	1993–00
Stockton Bight, coastal NSW	4,800	2001
SW Western Australian Forests	351,000	1999–01
TOTAL	**10,700,714**	

damaged or destroyed by logging. Exactly 80% of rainforest frogs and 40% of rainforest birds are rare, declining or threatened with extinction.

Over a hundred native animal species that live in forests are listed by State and Commonwealth Governments as threatened with extinction.

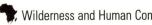

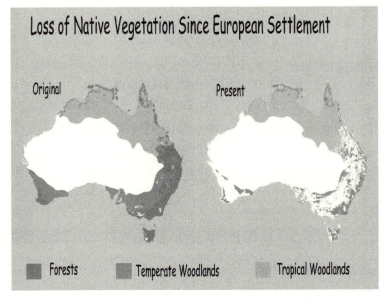

Figure 1—Loss of Native Vegetation Since European Settlement. Forest and woodland cover prior to European settlement (base year 1750) and after 213 years of European settlement.

Very few areas of forested wilderness remain in south-eastern Australia (see Figure 2). Clinging to the very edge of a dry continent, forests coincide with most of Australia's population and our most productive farming land. Unprotected forested wilderness is still subject to intense community campaigns for protection.

Areas of high Wilderness Quality in Australia, from the data of the National Wilderness Inventory (objectively measures the extent to which a location is remote from and undisturbed by the impacts of post-European settlement. Data compilation date 1997.

Unsustainable logging, clearing for plantations, firewood removal and over-grazing threaten much of what is left outside the protected area estate.

The loss of southern temperate woodlands has been extreme. Over 85% have been completely cleared. Old growth woodlands are now extremely rare—less than 100 hectares are left in Victoria, for example—and the condition of the remaining woodlands in southern Australia is poor.

Astoundingly, 530,000 hectares (5,000 sq km) of Australian bush, largely woodland, are still being bulldozed, chained or poisoned each year to "improve" land for agriculture. This makes Australia the fifth worst land-clearing nation on earth.

Broad-scale land-clearing currently represents the single greatest threat to Australia's biodiversity, and is responsible for much of Australia's wide-scale land and water degradation. Destruction of habitat, a direct result of land clearance, is one of the main causes of loss of biodiversity. It is believed that up to 20 bird species, 21 mammal species, and 97 plant species have become extinct in Australia since European settlement. Some of this loss is a direct result of landclearing.

A further 70 bird species are considered to be in danger of extinction as a result of land clearing. Recent work has found that in south-east Queensland between 49% and 56% of regional ecosystems will either be extinct, endangered or vulnerable in the next 100 years if clearing continues. Extinctions due to over-clearing are now widespread and continuing in southern states. Many woodland birds, such as species of Robins, Treecreepers, Owls and Cockatoos, are now regionally extinct or highly threatened and declining in South Australia, Victoria and New South Wales.

By comparison, northern Australia's savannah woodlands are still reasonably intact—less than one percent of the northern woodlands have been cleared. Whilst no species seem to have been completely lost from the region, all is not as stable as it seems. Recent research has shown that at least 16 bird species and some mammal species have declined greatly in range. Interactions between cattle grazing impacts,

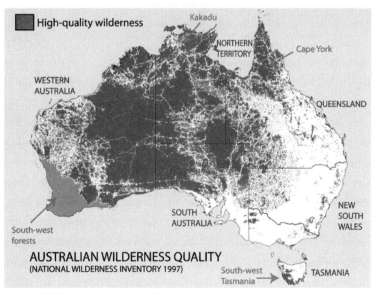

Figure 2—Wilderness Quality in Australia.

altered fire practices and animal populations have not been fully disentangled, but research to date indicates that these factors are involved in the declines in complex ways. Added to this is the great new threat of broad-scale clearing for agriculture and plantations across the north, with the risk that the unsustainable clearing of the southern woodlands will repeat itself in the north.

The combined impacts of loss of wilderness, threats to biodiversity, serious declines in water quality and quantity and losses of productive land to salinity has resulted in a high level of environmental awareness and concern among the Australian public.

Protecting the best of what's left in the Australian landscape and undertaking serious restoration programs are strongly supported by the vast majority of Australians.

Major Environmental Battles

Australians have been fighting for wilderness areas since Myles Dunphy began the National Parks and Primitive Areas Council in 1931. Much has been achieved but much has yet to be done.

The Australian Wilderness Society was founded in 1976 and expanded on already well-proven campaign techniques. Since that time we have worked closely with many other wilderness activists and organisations and have together protected over 10 million hectares (see Table 2).

1. Kakadu—Australia's Largest National Park

Despite massive public support for wilderness protection in Australia it is still necessary to mount major campaigns in their defense.

Nothing illustrates this better than the recent campaign to protect the Kakadu World Heritage site from the Jabiluka Uranium mine. This mine, which was being dug in an enclave within the Kakadu World Heritage site has arguably been the dominant environment controversy in Australia over the last four years. Over 500 people were arrested at the Jabiluka blockade. Tens of thousands marched in rallies and wrote letters to politicians. Eminent Australian scientists challenged the assumptions allowing development of the mine. A major corporate campaign mobilizing company shareholders against the mine was the first of its kind in Australia.

The Wilderness Society also coordinated a huge international NGO-based lobbying effort to have Kakadu inscribed on the list of "World Heritage in

Danger." Through this process the Australian Government suffered massive domestic and international embarrassment, and ended up paying between AUS $5–10 million for their own international lobbying costs.

The Kakadu campaign could not have been so effective without the help of wilderness activists from all around the world. Some of the organizations and people who helped are here at this conference. I would like to take this opportunity to let you know that we are close to success!

The mine has officially been put on hold for at least ten years by its new owner, and recent indications suggest that the company is prepared to "sterilize" the resource and rehabilitate the mine site to a point where it could be incorporated into the Kakadu World Heritage area.

A heartfelt thanks to everyone here who helped!

2. Forests

No other issue has mobilized so many people from so many different walks of life over such a long period of time as the campaign to protect Australia's forests. Many intense campaigns have been won and lost.

Community pressure for forest protection, particularly old growth and wilderness forests is reaching new heights as we face an unprecedented onslaught from woodchipping, clearing for plantations and proposed new industries to burn native forests for electricity generation and charcoal.

Our smallest state, Tasmania, home to many wilderness forests with well-established World Heritage Values, is being cleared and woodchipped at the highest rate in Australia's history. It may seem unbelievable but the Tasmanian Government sanctions the destruction of rainforest wilderness for woodchipping and plantations. Tasmanian logging is the most brutal in Australia. After clear-cutting, and fire bombing, 1080-poison carrots are dropped to ensure a slow death for thousands of native animals each year who otherwise browse on regrowth.

The Australian community has mobilized to protect their forests as never before. New political parties, new professional lobby and campaign groups and rural and city communities alike are working to save the last of their precious "fringe of green."

In Christmas 1999, the Wilderness Society received international publicity for creating the world's tallest Christmas tree in the Styx Valley in Tasmania. Over 10,000 fairylights and a giant cross were used to decorate one of the 80-meter

Eucalyptus Regnans under threat from clear-cutting. Incredibly, *The Guinness' Book of World Records* refused to recognize the World's Tallest Christmas Tree because it wasn't a Spruce! Next thing they will be telling people in the southern hemisphere that they can't celebrate Christmas in summer!

The Styx campaign has also been the catalyst for the launch of the biggest corporate campaign in Australia's history against the Tasmanian woodchip giant Gunns Limited. We are focusing on major bankers, key markets, investment houses, stock market analysts and funds managers. We are also coordinating an ethical shareholders group which will be in a position to call a special meeting of the company on its appalling record of forest destruction early next year.

The success of diverse campaign strategies which mobilize all sectors of the community is best illustrated by the success of the recent "Vote Forests" campaign in Western Australia, where the government was changed largely on the strength of a promise to end the logging of old growth forests. Old growth logging ceased within three days of the election, a successful conclusion to a very long campaign.

The Need for WildCountry

Although protecting our last wilderness areas is fundamental, by itself it won't be enough to stop the extinction of many species and ecosystems in Australia.

As previously mentioned, the Australian continent has a very irregular climate. Eastern Australia's climate fluctuates between drought and flood, due to the effects of El Niño (which brings droughts) and La Niña (which brings floods). Our tropical savannah's are monsoonal and our arid areas have not just low rainfall, but erratic rainfall.

Many species of Australian native wildlife need to move across the landscape for seasonal migrations, many lead a nomadic existence in response to fluctuations in climate (see Figure 3 for a summary of seasonal and nomadic bird migrations).

So, even if we protected all our remaining wilderness areas as they are today, it would only protect a portion of the ecosystems on which many species depend for their long-term survival.

Although, generally speaking, the scale of habitat fragmentation is less in semi-arid and arid areas, European settlement has still brought major impacts through the introduction of feral animals, sheep and cattle.

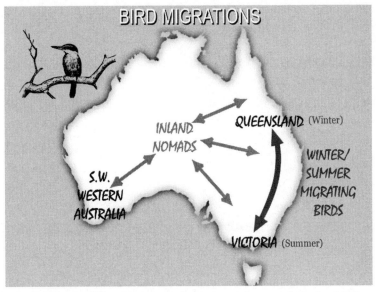

Figure 3—Bird Migrations. Winter/summer migrating species: regular seasonal migration. Inland nomads: move around arid and semi-arid inland Australia, on a more "random" route and timetable, following unpredictable rains and food supplies.

In the arid and semi-arid areas most of the permanent watering points, which function as drought refuges, have been taken over or degraded by cattle or feral animals. Introduced European rabbits change the vegetation as well as out-compete native species for food. Cats and foxes are major predators of native mammals, reptiles, frogs and birds.

In the more temperate southeast of the continent habitat fragmentation has been most dramatic as evidenced by the National Wilderness Inventory maps (see Figures 4 and 5).

Any long-term environmental vision for Australia must encompass the entire continent. It must have protection of wilderness at it's core but also include a rehabilitation plan based on restoring the ability of wildlife to move across the landscape and native plants to migrate in response to long term changes in climatic conditions. Elimination of feral plants and animals, and in many instances the restoration of pre-European fire patterns, will also be crucial.

No long-term environmental vision for Australia will succeed unless it also delivers social justice to aboriginal traditional owners, who were the first land

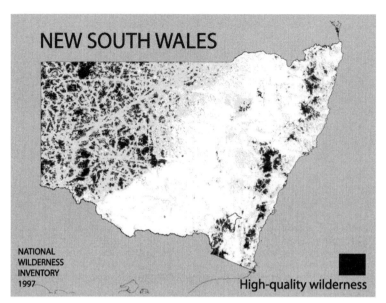

Figure 4—Areas of high Wilderness quality in New South Wales, from the data of the National Wilderness Inventory (objectively measures the extent to which a location is remote from and undisturbed by the impacts of post-European settlement). Data compilation date 1997.

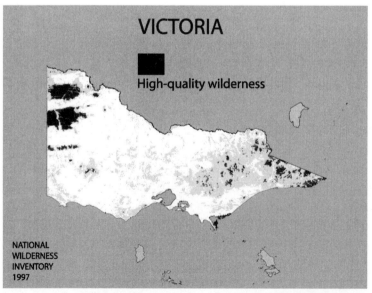

Figure 5—Areas of high Wilderness quality in Victoria, from the data of the National Wilderness Inventory (objectively measures the extent to which a location is remote from and undisturbed by the impacts of post-European settlement). Data compilation date 1997.

managers in Australia and who are again playing an increasing role in land management and conservation.

The Wilderness Society's response to all these needs has been to develop a long-term vision for the Australian continent called WildCountry, which has been inspired by the U.S Wildlands Project.

A primary WildCountry goal is to produce an Australia-wide, comprehensive system of interconnected core protected areas, each surrounded and linked by lands managed under conservation objectives. Eventually every region of the continent would be represented.

In Australia, wilderness also has an important and undervalued indigenous connection. Landscapes that retain their full compliment of natural features and seasonal cycles provide important and ancient signposts to the history and stories of Australia's indigenous people.

As the WildCountry program enshrines protection of our wilderness areas and begins to restore the ecological flows in this ancient landscape, it will also strengthen the indigenous culture which depends on it.

Wilderness will be a foundation stone on which to rebuild a fragmented continental ecology and a battered indigenous culture.

WildCountry in Action—Cape York

Our work on Cape York Peninsula was important in persuading us of the need for a WildCountry approach to conservation. Only by adopting a WildCountry approach will we be able to take maximum advantage of the biggest conservation opportunity in Australia today.

Cape York Peninsula covers 14 million hectares. The Australian Heritage Commission, through the National Wilderness Inventory Project, identified 80% of Cape York as high or very high wilderness quality (see Figure 6).

The range of ecosystems and landscapes include 20% of Australia's remaining tropical rainforests, globally significant tropical savannahs, the most pristine component of the Great Barrier Reef World Heritage Area, open forests, monsoonal wetlands, shrublands, heaths, sedgelands, grasslands, mangroves, seagrass, saltmarsh systems, extensive dune systems and 21 intact wild river catchments.

Approximately 1.4 million hectares of the region is already protected in National Parks. An additional 1.2 million hectares of land has been purchased for conservation purposes. Negotiations are presently taking place to allocate

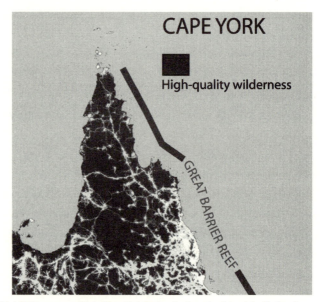

Figure 6—Areas of high Wilderness quality in Cape York Peninsula, from the data of the National Wilderness Inventory (objectively measures the extent to which a location is remote from and undisturbed by the impacts of post-European settlement). Data compilation date 1997.

these lands as protected areas or returned to traditional owners with conservation agreements attached.

Broad-scale land-clearing and horticulture has been confined to the south east corner of the region covering an area of approximately 1,300 hectares. While cattle grazing is extensive over much of the Peninsula, densities are very low with an approximate total herd of 120,000 cattle.

Approximately 10,000 indigenous Australians live within the Cape York region. The history of contact between indigenous and non-indigenous Australians has been punctuated by periods of violence and overt oppression, including the virtual enslavement of east coast communities at the height of the pearling industry in the 19th century and a long period of passive paternalism and assimilation. Over the past twenty-five years, the region has been at the forefront of indigenous rights–based campaigns.

What Has Been Achieved

In 1996, Cape York cattlemen, indigenous groups and conservation groups negotiated the "Cape York Land Use Agreement". The Agreement proposed the resolution of land use issues through negotiation, the creation of a fund to purchase lands of high conservation and spiritual values and assessment of the global and national significance of the Cape's conservation values.

Also in 1996, the Australian Government allocated up to $40 million for protecting Cape York.

In September this year, the Queensland provincial Government formally became a signatory to the Cape York Agreement. In doing so, it committed $3 million to purchase high value properties and created a high level group of senior government ministers to help implement the Agreement.

In October this year, the Queensland Government released a comprehensive assessment of the natural values of Cape York: "The Natural Heritage Significance of Cape York Peninsula." This report, by a group of Australia's leading environmental scientists, concluded that the Cape is "one of the most intact (if not the most intact) relatively protected and accessible, major tracts of tropical monsoonal savanna and rainforest complexes" at a global level.

Figure 7—Earth Charter Principles. The Earth Charter is envisioned to serve as a universal code of conduct, based on fundamental values and principles, which will guide people, communities, organizations and nations towards sustainable living. The Charter therefore will be a globally agreed charter describing a shared ethical framework for promoting sustainable development and environmental protection. It will be developed into a United Nations "soft law," document for ratification by all nations in the General Assembly (proposed for 2002).

In response, the Queensland Government announced its intention to protect fully the Cape's natural values and to ensure that development only occurs if it maintains and protects these values.

The Government has also appointed a panel of eminent scientists to assist with the development of a Cape-wide conservation plan.

Land Ethic

WildCountry is one logical extension of Aldo Leopold's Land Ethic and it puts us well down the path of ethical (and we would argue spiritual) development identified in Roderick Nash's excellent book *The Rights of Nature*.

If we can achieve this, we are well on our way to implementing the first principle of the Earth Charter, which is to "respect and care for the community of life" (Figure 7).

If we can seriously implement the first principle of the Earth Charter, we will be justified in calling ourselves good planetary citizens.

The Wilderness Trail ...
An Example in India

Bittu Sahgal

In India, as in the rest of the world, natural wildernesses are vanishing before the onslaught of commercial ambition. The author points out here that while wild species were the first to suffer the adverse impacts of this loss, forest dwelling human communities have suffered terribly as well.

A full moon was out. Far below me I could see a silver shimmer as a wild river snaked its way through dark hills. It was cold and the nocturnal sounds of the forest floated gently over the night. Distant calls of jackals combined with the closer "chucking" of a nightjar and somewhere behind the rest house owls were about, hunting rodents no doubt. Then, over the relative still of the forest came that magical sound ... a tiger's call

India's Melghat Tiger Reserve is a magical forest. Austere, forbidding and seemingly at peace with itself, Melghat is part of one of the world's most critical tiger breeding habitats, the Satpura ranges.

But all is not well here. In the past five years poaching incidents have risen. Major timber gangs are operating with near impunity and ill-equipped forest guards are simply unequal to the task of fighting people who are often armed with automatic weapons and sophisticated wireless equipment. Yet, thanks to a few dedicated officers, determined NGOs and the support of a world community that wants tigers saved, the battle continues.

Sitting far from tiger forests, in cities and forests across the world, each one of us has a role to play in protecting Melghat, just as we do in preserving all precious wildernesses.

But Why Save the Wilderness?

In and around the many sanctuaries and national parks that I seem to spend my life defending, the sight of people drinking directly from streams and rivers is a common sight, as is food and fuel gathering. A few kilometers downstream of such forests, however, the very same water sources spew disease, death and destruction. What is more, biomass for survival must largely be obtained from heartless markets. Though it is not commonly known, wildlife protection initiatives over the past three decades have turned out to be the best protection enjoyed by true forest-dwelling communities in India who have chosen not to "join the mainstream."

Look around India and you will see that where wildlife and forest laws are not applicable, or enforceable, tribal people, such as the Korkus, Baigas, Bhils, Gonds and Chenchus, have been mercilessly converted into urban migrants, rural labourers and environmental refugees. Robbed of dignity and self-sufficiency they must now negotiate survival with PWD Ministers and apathetic bureaucrats and technocrats. Almost every tribal welfare department in the many states of India, particularly Maharashtra and Madhya Pradesh and the Northeast, has served merely to compound the erosion of tribal cultures. Their attempts to "develop" tribal people have accelerated the loss of identity and have often also caused death and disease to strike remote and vulnerable forest communities. It is in this context that I would like to discuss the issue of environment and human rights.

But first, two bland facts:

1. Apart from biodiversity values, water and food security is the central rationale for the protection of India's (and the world's) wilderness and the waterways they nurture and feed.
2. Wildlife and forest laws in India have protected human forest cultures more effectively than any other tribal welfare initiatives.

"The Forest is the Mother of the River" was the accepted, conventional wisdom of yesterday. But we have forgotten such lessons in our haste to ape the industrial North. If this trend is allowed to proceed unchecked; if we are unable to protect our water sources from plunder by the industrial and intensive agriculture lobbies, India too will be forced to confront a sub-Saharan famine situation a few short years from now. And with such famine will come the violence, which has crippled much of resource-exhausted, World Bank-managed Africa.

Saving wildlife and wild habitats is the only way we can possibly protect our water regimes and thus break out of the cycle of floods and droughts that has us in its grip. For decades, however, a terrible misrepresentation has been doing the rounds in the corridors of power that: "India cannot afford the luxury of protecting its environment." The source of this fiction can readily be laid at the door of the development lobby, which long ago planted the canard that protecting the environment would go against the national objective of "eradicating poverty." Armed with this "master-key," dam builders, miners, timber contractors, chemical manufacturers and a clutch of mega-project profiteers managed to side-sweep opposition to their lethal plans. In search of profits they managed to poison, displace and generally diminish the ecological security of the people of the Indian subcontinent. All this in the name of development. Fortunately, this destruction was arrested at the outer boundaries of over 550 sanctuaries and national parks. But now a wave of "denotifications" threatens to remove their legal mantle. Thus even these relic forests and cultures may now be at the mercy of those seeking to exploit minerals, timber and other commercial resources.

As we approach the much-vaunted 21st century, ordinary people across the globe will need to shed the notion that protecting the environment is a luxury. And planners and policy makers will have to be made to see that the poor are the principal beneficiaries of laws that protect rivers, forests, mountains and coastlines. But even before we force such recognition on policy makers, we need to sit among ourselves—human rights activists and environmentalists—and recognize that the right to clean air, water and safe food is without a shadow of doubt the most fundamental of all human rights.

As of now, this realization is, sadly, conspicuous by its absence. In Jhagadia, Gujarat-India, for instance, organochlorine effluents being dumped in the Narmada have begun to seriously affect the health of millions who risk death, deformity and immune system diseases. Instead of cleaning up their acts, industrialists there use workers as a shield to blackmail society at large, stating in effect that investing in clean technologies and processes will involve retrenchments. This is untrue, but they have managed to get trade unions to tow this line even though the first sufferers of this produce-and-pollute policy is the worker himself.

So ... should the public enjoy the right to clean air and water? Or is this right to be subjugated to the owners' right to profit and/or the workers' right to employment? No one advocates shutting down all industry, but labor union leaders should see that they have proven to be almost as irresponsible as the industrialists themselves on the issue of occupational health.

Somehow, environmentalists and social activists will need to arrive at acceptable positions on issues concerning human rights and environmental protection. And together they will have to force the developed lobby to alter its priority to take these serious concerns on board. They must also recognize that protecting forests has a justification that goes beyond just biodiversity.

Wilderness and Tribals

The root of the holocaust unleashed on tribal India had its origins in the colonization of India by the British, but tribal communities suffered even more after Independence. Of the roughly 60 million *tribal* people in India, 95 percent have already been aborted from their resources and their way of life. Latter-day colonialists in our midst saw no irony in using black laws crafted by the British— *The Land Acquisition and Official Secrets Acts*—to usurp tribal properties and resources. The direct result of this land-grab for minerals, timber and land has assassinated the cultural genius of all but three million tribals. These last few communities (*Chenchus* in Nagarjunasagar, *Korku* in Melghat, *Mannans* in Periyar, *Maria Gonds* in the Indravati Tiger Reserve, *Adis* of Arunachal Pradesh) live in and around the network of sanctuaries and national parks set aside to protect India's biodiversity. Tragically the displacement of tribal communities and the loot of their lands, forests, rivers and ancestral properties continues unabated. However, with a no-forced-displacement policy having been officially placed on record by government bodies, such as the *Indian Board for Wildlife* and *Project Tiger*, forest communities are able to practice their traditional lifestyles in and around the over 550 protected forests set aside for wildlife protection.

There can be no denying however that the Wildlife (Protection) Act 1972 and the Forest (Conservation) Act, 1980, like all other Indian laws, also had their genesis in colonial legislation. Human rights activists never tire of pointing this out at every opportunity. What they do not point out, however, is that the same legislation effectively keeps most market forces at bay, thus allowing nature to be ... nature, and tribals to be ... tribals.

It is not my argument that wildlife and forest laws did not violate many legitimate rights of *tribal* communities. They did. And minor changes in the law that prevents the exploitation of *tribal* communities at the hands of irresponsible and sometimes corrupt forest staff are indeed called for. It is vital, however, that in trying to deliver justice to *tribals*, we do not loosen the provisions of the Acts to the point where Chief Ministers, businessmen and contractors, thus far prevented from consuming wildlife areas, are able to usurp the wealth of wild India. This, after all, is precisely what they have done outside wildlife protection zones. This is how 57 million out of 60 million tribal people were forcibly displaced from their ancestral homes and why they can no longer access natural resources or live a life of dignity as their ancestors once did.

It would also do us well to remember that tribal communities know their forests better than any forest department staff and are therefore able to use hidden forest trails and ancient technologies for survival to access life-support resources. And that wildlife laws kept Chief Ministers, miners and dam builders out of our wildlife reserves. Human rights groups and social activists need to drum up the humility to accept that they have failed to prevent such powerful forces from wiping out tribal cultures. They will also have to admit that in the surviving forests set aside to protect tigers, elephants, deer and birds, a relatively small but significant percentage of scheduled tribes such as the *Adis, Bhils, Baigas, Bhumias, Chenchus, Garos, Korku, Mannans, Maria Gonds, Nagas, Santals,* and *Warlis,* have been able to hold on to many of their ancient traditions. Here they have been able to follow their own genius for survival ... with a dignity denied them elsewhere.

Who Has *Really* Saved the Tribal People of India?

As anthropologists, and ethnographers will themselves confirm, outside the protected area (PA) network, quite apart from the wounds inflicted by economic dominion, tribal communities have actually been irreparably harmed by legions of intellectuals and bureaucrats who saw to it that *tribals* conformed to their own visions of development, language and customs. Thus, as pointed out with anguish by Shalina Mehta, a well-respected anthropologist, (*Continuity and Change in Tribal Society*), *anganwadis* were forced upon *tribal* communities whose elders traditionally looked after the young ... and, using funds from the Indira Vikas Scheme, toilet blocks were built near the living quarters of *tribals* who considered defecation next to where they slept "obnoxious"... and sewing machines were distributed to women in Madhya Pradesh who never in their lives wore stitched clothing. These were the least of the traumas inflicted on forest people across the length and breadth of India. A juggernaut of mines, dams, roads, thermal plants, copper smelters, forestry schemes literally extirpated tribal lands displacing millions and killing lakhs. For all their utterances, not one human rights or social activist group was able to prevent this human tragedy. Without resort to wildlife laws, not even one single 1,000 sq km forest has been saved in the past 50 years by social activists to enable *tribal* communities to sustain their traditional survival techniques and customs.

The most tragic example of such policies was the denotification of one-third of Maharashtra's Melghat Tiger Reserve, allegedly to benefit local tribal communities. The real reason, of course, was to make way for future timber operations.

The modus operandi was clever. Records reveal that the greater Melghat region (4,000 sq. km) had witnessed the death from malnutrition of over 4,000 *Korku* tribal children in a five-year period spanning 1994–1998. But in the same period, *inside* the Melghat Tiger Reserve (1,500 sq. km) the infant mortality rate remained static through the worst drought. This is what I wrote about Melghat in the *Times of India*, Bombay, in October 1993:

> "It is sad to see that politicians are trying to turn the tragedy of starvation deaths in Vidharba to their advantage by asking for the denotification of the Melghat Tiger Reserve. Here is what will follow the denotification: tar roads will quickly replace the dirt tracks, two and three star hotels, luxury farm houses and other such distractions for the rich will be built. A long-standing proposal to construct a major dam across the Tapi River will be pushed through, displacing still more villagers and usurping the forest that feed their children."

This, however, is precisely what happened. Millions of dollars were spent in 1998 on tarring and widening roads that the tribal people would never use as they prefer their own shaded forest paths that get them where they wish to go quicker. Poaching and illegal timber felling. There is talk of hacking down timber in the 500 sq. km denotified area to "provide the Korku people with employment." This charade is being played out in the name of preventing malnutrition! Geographically based in the Chikaldara and Melghat tehsils, the Korku have four distinct endogamous groups namely Mouase, Bawaria, Ruma and Bondya or Bopche (K.S. Singh, *The Scheduled Tribes of India*). According to J. K. Roy the caloric intake of tribes such as the Korku, who are cultivators, is greatly supplemented by food gathering. Mahua flowers, honey, fish and crabs form a significant part of their diet. The communities that lived inside the Tiger Reserve boundary survived pinch periods and their children were saved not on account of any help from human rights activists, or the government. On the contrary, because strict protection had encouraged wild plant species to flourish, they knew how and where to access wild fruit, roots, tubers, vines and leaves.

Now that infrastructure for the commercial exploitation of the forest and its tribal communities has been laid, such safety nets will vanish. Though they acknowledge the fact that communities inside the protected forest were dramatically better off than those outside, the human rights groups who had joined hands with developers in demanding roads have not come forward to prevent illegal timber operations or other commercialisation that affects both the Korku and the tiger.

The Way Forward

There is something in the human psyche that seeks to dominate that which is wild. Whether or not we will find the collective will to resist the impulse cannot be predicted. Clearly, however, under our attention wilderness after wilderness is wilting. Toxics in polar bears. Sharks in decline. Tigers on the verge of extinction. Amphibians in trouble. Cities in disrepair. Wars and malnutrition on the rise.

These are hardly the signs of humanity on the march towards Nirvana. Fortunately, however, all is not lost. Through all the mayhem, all the despair, we can and should rely on the fact that nature is a self-repairing machine. Left to its own devices for long enough, it can restore health to mismanaged wildernesses. It can restore health to ravaged rivers and can help feed the hungry with its ocean and wilderness larders. Species thought to be extinct—such as the Doublebanded Courser, a nocturnal grassland bird in Andhra Pradesh and the Forest Spotted Owlet, from northern Maharashtra—have been rediscovered. Once-dry streams have regenerated, more can follow suit if benign neglect, rather than militant assault on nature becomes the order of the day.

What we need most at this juncture, of course, is to take a step back, contemplate our place in the world … and simply desist from desecrating the wilderness trail.

Seeds, People, and Wildness

Vandana Shiva

How can we really defend wilderness if we keep excluding those who have defended wilderness over thousands of years? The problem of exclusion is our real challenge in terms of wilderness conservation. I think the wild was threatened the day that "bully logic" created the law of the excluded middle. You are either with us or you are our enemy. You are either in a park or a human settlement. You are either cultivated or you are wild. I don't think those are the appropriate or right ways of structuring the world. In fact, it is that middle which is the most exciting place for the conservation of wildness. The wild is not opposite to the cultivated, as so much of the wilderness conservation has been inspired by cultivation and so much of technologic development has taken inspiration from the wild.

Wild is the opposite of the captured; it is the opposite of the controlled. In the wild we experienced diversity. In the captive and controlled we experience monocultures. In the wild everything has multiple functions. In the captive it is controlled to be one-dimensioned, single function. In the wild every species, every being, every organism, is self-organized. In the captive it is externally controlled. Being self-organized, in the wild every being has a capacity to renew itself, and renew its existence for future generations. In the captive, every bit of reproduction of life depends on external inputs. The protection and maintenance of life and vital energy, as Martin von Hildebrand suggests, is the objective of living in the wild.

The production of commercial output, of profits for humans, is not just for human use. We need to acknowledge that the indigenous peoples in the Amazon are able to meet their needs as well as the needs of the habitat. They are not just producing outputs to reach markets irrespective of what it does to the share of the animals or the water spirits and the mountain spirits. The conservation of biodiversity is a built-in outcome of functioning wilderness. Its annihilation is inevitable if both wilderness as well as the non-wilderness areas are managed with a mindset which views the human as the captive, and that which is useful to human species as only being useful enough and improved enough if it is held in captivity.

In the world today, the implications are even more far-reaching for protecting the wild. Within the conservation of cultural diversity there is a built-in security. What we are experiencing today is often described, inappropriately, as "the clash of the civilizations." (I say "inappropriately" because I do not believe it is a clash of civilizations and because it depends on your version of what constitutes civilization—you might remember what Ghandi said when he was asked what he thought of civilization—"Good idea!") I believe what we are experiencing is conflicts of cultures; we are seeing clashes between different groups of religions and ethnicity. We are experiencing ethnicides and genocides in every continent like we have never experienced—the rights of religious foundations, the rights of religious fundamentalism, terrorism, and multiple reactions to terrorism. It is time to reflect on how much we can learn from the wild, how it functions and evolves. To be wild, we have to leave space for other beings and other cultures, and through that create peace.

While I started my ecological journey with the protection of forests in the Himalayas working with the Chipko movement, I have good reason for dedicating my last two years for the defense of wildness within the cultivated. Many years ago the poet Tagore gave a speech that became a very beautiful essay called *Tapovan* (the sacred forest). He was a Nobel Laureate from India who gave back his Nobel Prize because he did not like the way the empire was running the world. He said western civilization is experienced through brick and concrete, where learning is assumed to occur only if it is locked into buildings that are regarded as centers of learning. In India, however, our learning has been from the forest. From the forest we learn that every person, every species, no matter how small, no matter how big, has a place. From the forest we have learnt democracy. In spite of being born in the last century, Tagore built a "forest university." He built where one would learn from nature.

Every alternative year I teach at the Schumacher College, a "green" college in England. It was built by Elmhirst, Tagore's secretary. Tagore encouraged

Elmhirst "to start a forest university in the West," and Elmhirst asked, "Where do I go?" "Go to Devon," said Tagore. "Where in Devon?" enquired Elmhirst, and Tagore replied, "Just find the most beautiful place, because only where there is a place of beauty is nature alive and it is only there that real learning can take place." So many of the good decisions in life are under compulsion from friends. We have links with Schumacher College and have founded a Schumacher College in 2001 on our organic farm in India. At the University of the Seed we learn about earth's citizenship directly from nature!

Why do we need to have learning from within nature? We are increasingly destroying everything aside from an exclusive human notion of wildness. In the process, not only do we threaten other species, we threaten our conditions of survival. I give you a very simple example. In the mountain areas of my region in the Himalayas, agriculture is very diverse. We are able to grow 250 species in every tiny farm of 1 or 2 acres. However, when development comes so does the package of tomato seed. The result? The peasants begin to grow the tomatoes off-season in high altitudes when it is too hot in the plains. Trucks will load those tomatoes up from their doorstep, drive them to Delhi where they are put into containers and shipped off to where ever or whoever has the money to pay for fresh, off-season tomatoes. Growing tomatoes in place of the 250 species means our people are no longer growing food for their families and are no longer providing a food source for local animals. From where do the animals then get their food? They begin to place more and more pressure on the forestry. Our assessments show there is a 300% increase in biomass pressure on forests just by changing the biomass production on farms. One of the very, very basic things about agriculture and its sustainability is the moment you start thinking of agriculture as producing food only for humans, you start denying their share of food to other species that are needed to maintain ecosystems.

The supposed miracle of the green revolution was the creation of dwarf varieties of plants. It assumed that because humans eat grains, that straw is a waste product and only the grain is needed. It ignored the fact that straw is eaten by earthworms and cattle and sometimes used for housing and thatching. So the brilliance of the human mind was applied to starve other species. In the process of starving other species we created desertified soils. Depriving the soil of organic matter ended up spoiling the water retentativity ten times, which created droughts. Even when there were no meteorological droughts and the rainfall was good, the water could no longer be retained by the soil, causing increasing levels of crop failure, increasing famine, and increasing vulnerability. All because humans thought that the food for the earthworm and the thousands of microorganisms was not part of what we were producing.

In the same way we are now reaching a stage where we have stopped seeing the capacity of wildness on our farms—not just in terms of how we think of individual crops, but how we think of the farm. I would love to ban herbicides around the world because I have been very deeply involved in the debate on genetic engineering. Much of genetic engineering involves breeding new seed to generate crops which are resistant to herbicides, so that you can spray more herbicides. Herbicides like Round Up are broad-spectrum herbicides, whose advertising material suggests they are so effective they will kill anything green that comes in contact with it. To me this is Jihad against wildness!

If you move beyond advertising, you get to the science of it. Scientists argue that we have to spray herbicides to generate sufficient agriculture because weeds steal the sunshine. I believe the level of our humanity is seriously lowered if we imagine that our existence on the planet requires that the sun should only send its energy to us. If this happened, can you imagine a planet that would survive? Of course these same scientists would then say that, since we are not efficient enough, we have to depend for our survival on plants that get the most sunshine. First these scientists say that plants don't deserve it—they are stealing the sunshine—then they say plants are stealing it from us. Perhaps their solution is to then put "green genes" for photosynthesis into human beings and just stand us in the sun!

I am not exaggerating when I say that these same techno-scientists wiped out 250 species. Most of them are green, and most of them were rich sources of beta-carotene. Some crops in India—the tamarind, the fenugreek, the drumstick tree—provide 14,000 to 20,000 micrograms of beta-carotene or the Vitamin A equivalent in 100 grams of food. Yet the status quo technicians have decided it does not actually exist and are now genetically engineering rice with Vitamin A. After all that they develop "brilliant" ways of using genes from petunias to make the yellow rice, or "the golden rice" as they call it, to achieve the grand total of just 30 micrograms per 100 grams. You have to eat 3 kgs to get your dose of Vitamin A.

We do a lot of work on biodiversity as the basis of food security. My calculations based on studies on individual farms found that you can very easily, if you conserve wildness on the farm, produce about 20 tons of food per hectare. In contrast, with all the manipulation of the one dimensional plant breeding under modern farming conditions, they get to half a ton per hectare. Under some of the high-input, industrial conditions of rich farmers they might get to 4 tons per hectare, but it is a very inefficient way of producing food because you are using 300 units of input to produce a 100 units of food. If we organize around a wildness principle, our productivity would increase dramatically because we could use five units of input to produce 100 units of food. You can plant a little acorn and it will give you an oak, tree. You can plant a coconut and it will give you a coconut tree. The very embodiment of that diversity is in that tiny seed. It is structured all the way from the beginning that an acorn will not become a coconut. We don't have to hold an acorn and say, "don't become a coconut"—it's got enough intelligence of its own.

Wild seeds are the way this planet has renewed itself and, until recently, the way humanity has grown crops. Now, all the brilliance of humanity is being dedicated to removing the wildness from the seed, and making it captive. These seeds are becoming captive through developing hybrids, which often results in a next generation of seed that is no longer capable of producing a good crop. They are captive also in the sense of being genetically engineered with traits that become a hazard to the ecosystem, for example developing Round Up resistance or having "toxin genes." The third form of captivity is through plant patenting. The argument of these people is that despite the fact that plants naturally reproduce—a form of wildness—lets make it illegal. Let it be turned into a crime to save seed and grow it out for the next generation. Lets turn it into a crime to exchange seed with each other. This is the battle of intellectual property rights in the World Trade Organization (WTO). I believe those battles are about wildness.

We fought the patents on Basmati and on Neem, and these were not mere phenomena. These were not revolutions against invention. They were revolutions against piracy—piracy from nature and piracy from other cultures.

Interestingly, the patenting debate is now surviving in an extremely constrained way. It survives in a very relevant, necessary debate about public health, which is further restricted to AIDS in the African debate. The placing of the pharmaceutical industry against the South African Government was a very important piece in this. It is very interesting that it is the one issue that they are not allowing into the renegotiations.

The ecological and environmental community needs to become active again within the issue of "the illegitimacy of patenting life." The public health community only got into the debate a year ago. Some of us have not been sleeping, but the rest have. What we have is a situation where it seems to be possible for some parts of humanity to say we invented life—we are the owners. The part of life we don't find useful, we have the right to exterminate. And, as competitors we have the right to own specific species and collect fees from everyone that uses them.

I think we need very, very rapidly to be able to consider the wildness in the bees and butterflies that is exterminated when Btcotton and Btcorn is put into our fields. The insects, what they are what they do, are wilderness. We need to see the wildness freely evolving seed stocks. The interruption in the life cycles of seed is the most severe threat that humanity could ever put on the planet. The tragedy is that this thought reached the human mind at all and, even worse, that some corporate and political figures exercise it with the worst forms of brutal power. But let's not stop with seeds and insects. There is also still a wildness in many of our domesticated animals, which we need to recognize and save. The cows that don't go "mad" still have some wildness. Saving them and their wildness will save our sanity!

Restoring Wilderness, Transforming the Individual

The Need for Wilderness Restoration in Scotland

Alan Watson Featherstone

It is estimated that several thousand years ago, before humans had any substantial impact, 70–80% of Scotland's land area was covered in forest. However, several millennia of deforestation meant that by the latter part of the 20th century, the natural forest cover had been reduced to just 2% of the land, and in the Highlands, in the north of the country, the native pinewoods, the boreal component of the Caledonian Forest, comprised just 17,000 hectares (42,000 acres) (Forestry Commission)—a mere 1.1% of their original 1.5 million hectares (3.7 million acres) (McVean & Ratcliffe) (illustrated in Figure 1).

Many factors contributed to this loss, including climatic change when Scotland's climate became cooler and wetter about 4,000 years ago, but the major causes were human ones—clearance of the land for agriculture, utilisation of wood for fuel, house construction and boat building, burning of the forests to eradicate "vermin," such as the wolf, and, in the last 300 years or so, industrial timber exploitation, the introduction of sheep grazing on a massive scale and the rise of so-called "sporting" estates. These are large private land holdings where the main activity is "sport" hunting of red deer (*Cervus elaphus*) stags for the trophy value of their antlers. In the absence of their natural predator the wolf, red deer numbers have increased from 150,000 in the 1950s to over 350,000 today, and together with the estimated 5 million sheep in Scotland, they prevent any natural regeneration of the existing remnants of the original forest (Staines). As a result, these remnants consist of isolated and fragmented patches of old trees—a "geriatric forest," with no new trees growing to replace the old ones as they die. With all the forest's native large mammals (wolf, brown bear, European beaver, lynx, moose and wild boar) long since extirpated from Scotland (the wolf was the last to disappear, when the final individual was shot in 1743) (Ritchie; Darling & Boyd), and with the forest understorey completely overgrazed by the massive herbivore population, the scattered and isolated fragments of the Caledonian Forest (illustrated in Figure 2) have been in a state of terminal decline for over 150 years.

The problems of forest destruction and extinction of species which are now rampant on every continent are nothing new—they've been taking place here in Scotland for several thousand years. However, just as this country has the unenviable record of having been in the forefront of deforestation, so now is the onus on Scotland to help show the way forward with the ecological restoration of highly degraded forest ecosystems.

There is no land in Scotland, which can be called truly wild today, in the primeval sense. The challenge which faces wilderness advocates here now is to engage in major restoration initiatives, so that appropriate areas can have their full complement of biota returned to them, and that natural ecological processes can reassert themselves in due course, free once more from human-induced degradation and "management."

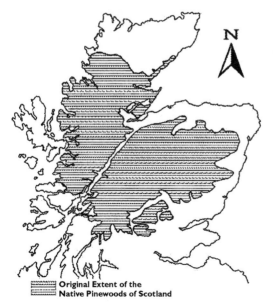

N

Figure 1—Before humans had any substantial impact, 70–80% of Scotland's land area was covered in forest. However, several millennia of deforestation meant that by the latter part of the 20th century, the natural forest cover had been reduced to just 2% of the land, and in the north of the country, the native pinewoods, the boreal component of the Caledonian Forest, comprised just 17,000 hectares (42,000 acres)—a mere 1.1% of their original 1.5 million hectares (3.7 million acres).

Original Extent of the
Native Pinewoods of Scotland

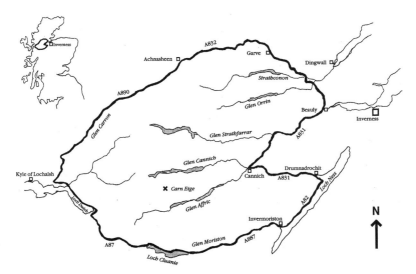

Figure 2—With the forest understorey completely overgrazed by the massive herbivore population, the scattered and isolated fragments of the Caledonian Forest have been in a state of terminal decline for over 150 years.

Restoration of the Caledonian Forest

Scientists first drew attention to the plight of the pinewoods in the late 1950s, and experimental work to help them regenerate was begun in Glen Affric by forester Finlay MacRae, and in some other forest fragments in the 1960s. Deer fences were erected around some of the remnant stands of old trees to exclude grazing animals, and inside these, healthy regeneration of the trees and other vegetation took place, thereby showing that the forest could recover if it was given a chance (Fenton). Public awareness and conservation concern for the forest grew in the 1970s and particularly the 1980s, and the efforts to regenerate the forest increased (Callander). However, these initiatives were generally small in scale and uncoordinated.

In 1986, Trees for Life was founded to help restore the Caledonian Forest to a large, contiguous part of its former range, recognizing that a substantial area of forest would be required to restore the ecosystem to a healthy, self-sustaining natural balance, with its full complement of species, including the top predators. Working initially in Glen Affric, which contains one of the best remnants of the original forest, and the next valley northwards, Glen Cannich, our goal is to expand the forest outwards from these surviving fragments into a remote, virtually unpopulated area of 238,000 hectares (587,000 acres) (illustrated in Figure 3). With a mountainous core, almost no economic activity apart from deer hunting taking place, and no roads cutting right through it, this part of Scotland offers probably the best opportunity in the whole of Britain for restoring a substantial tract of land to a wild and natural ecosystem.

Our work began on a small scale with the erection of deer proof fences around several stands of old trees to facilitate the successful regeneration of naturally occurring tree seedlings. Now, twelve years after the first of those exclosures was erected in partnership with the Forestry Commission (the UK government agency, which owns some of the best old forest remnants such as Glen Affric), young Scots pines are over 3 meters (10 feet) tall, and the sequence of natural restoration of the ecosystem is well under way. Some of the pine saplings flowered for the first time in 1998, and after a two-year maturation period their cones released their seeds in the spring of 2000, thereby moving the regeneration process further forward. Ground vegetation, such as bog myrtle (*Myrica gale*) and creeping lady's tresses orchids, has flourished, and for the first time in over 150 years (and reversing a centuries-long decline) new life is becoming successfully established throughout the 50 hectare (125 acre) extent of the exclosure. Each year, more young trees germinate and grow, and whereas, for example, we only knew of a couple of junipers (*Juniperus communis*) when the fence was erected, there are now several dozen growing healthily.

Figure 3—The goal is to expand the forest outwards from surviving fragments into a remote, virtually unpopulated area of 238,000 hectares (587,000 acres).

Forest Regeneration Area Envisioned by Trees for Life

Existing Remnants of Native Pinewoods

A similar story is unfolding elsewhere in the Affric River watershed in a series of fenced exclosures we've initiated in conjunction with both the Forestry Commission and the National Trust for Scotland, who own 4,000 hectares (10,000 acres) of land in the Affric headwaters. Strategically situated around stands of old trees, either on the periphery of the forest or where a remote group of trees have survived the grazing pressure by virtue of their location in a steep gorge, these exclosures are providing a safe haven for the regeneration of the forest in an otherwise barren and continuously degrading landscape.

In some of the exclosures, where their isolation and lack of an adequate seed source from parent trees mean that natural regeneration would be extremely slow to occur, we have been planting trees as the primary method of forest restoration. The planting is done in a manner that copies the pattern of self-regenerating seedlings elsewhere, with the trees being planted in the soil conditions they naturally occur in, and in groupings that avoid human constructs such as straight lines and regular spacings. The seedlings themselves are grown wherever possible from seed collected from the nearest surviving trees, seeking again to mimic the natural process of regeneration, and also to maintain the geographic variation in genetic diversity within species such as the Scots pine. Since 1991, we've planted more than 428,500 trees in this way, even though our planting, most of which is carried out by volunteers, is done at about one-tenth the rate of commercial planters working on tree plantations. Meanwhile, a larger, but uncounted, number of young trees are regenerating naturally inside the exclosures.

As these young trees grow, they will form discrete patches or "islands" of new forest throughout the watershed. In the years until they reach seed-bearing age, we will be working closely with landowners to promote a substantially increased cull of the red deer (sheep have already been removed from Glen Affric) to get the numbers down to a level at which they are in ecological balance with their habitat once more. Natural regeneration of the trees can then become successful again without the need for further fences, and the forest restoration process should become self-sustaining. At that stage the fences around the existing exclosures can also be dismantled, as they will have fulfilled their current emergency measure function, and the land will be another step closer to a truly wild condition.

Deepening the restoration process

When we began work in the late 1980s, our efforts, and those of most other organizations working to help restore the Caledonian Forest, were concentrated on the Scots pine. As the principal tree in the ecosystem it is a critical species, and by assuring its regeneration, much of the other flora and fauna would also benefit. This focus on the pinewoods resulted in a massive upsurge of public awareness and concern for the forest, and led to a number of very significant developments. In 1994, for example, the Forestry Commission declared 9,000 hectares (22,200 acres) of their land in Glen Affric as a Caledonian Forest Reserve, to be managed primarily for nature conservation. This reversed much of their previous policy for their landholdings there and resulted in hundreds of hectares of non-native trees, which had been planted amongst the old Scots pines of the original forest remnants as a commercial crop, being felled and left to decompose in situ, thereby helping to restore those areas to naturally regenerating native forest.

Trees for Life volunteers carried out some of this work, and we also began the process of removing fencing from areas where the original regeneration experiments had been instigated in the 1960s—the young trees that have successfully grown since then are now large enough that deer can no longer damage them. Thus, reduced numbers of deer are now able to live in balance with the returning forest, and with the Forestry Commission now implementing a much heavier deer cull on their land in Glen Affric, this success should be repeated throughout much of the watershed in the years ahead. More recently, Scottish Natural Heritage (the government conservation agency in Scotland) approved the designation of almost 15,000 hectares (37,000 acres) of Forest Enterprise-managed land in Glen Affric as a National Nature Reserve—this is the highest level of conservation protection currently available for land in Scotland.

Over the years, we have expanded our focus from the Scots pine, and from Glen Affric, to embrace a longer term goal: the restoration of the Caledonian Forest and all its species to a larger, ecologically sustainable area. We've begun work to help the forest recover in several other strategically-sited locations within our target area, and are now working with a number of different landowners. We've also been increasingly focused on other species in the forest ecosystem, and have initiated specific programs of mapping, protection, and propagation for under-represented and threatened trees such as aspen (*Populus tremula*), hazel (*Corylus avellana*), and holly (*Ilex aquifolium*).

Other work focuses on the regeneration and restoration of some of the key components within the forest ecosystem, such as the riparian woodland zone and the tree-line shrub community, both of which have suffered greatly from past deforestation. The restoration of these parts of the ecosystem are a central part of our strategy to reconnect the isolated fragments of the old forest, as healthy riparian zones and montane shrub communities will form the "stepping stones" in the return of the forest to a large contiguous area.

Trees for Life is the main organization in Scotland publicly advocating the return of all our missing mammal species, such as the lynx, wolf, wild boar, European brown bear, moose and beaver. The British government is required, under the terms of the European Union's Habitats and Species Directive, to investigate the feasibility and desirability of reintroducing extirpated species, and Scottish Natural Heritage is planning a trial reintroduction of the European beaver to Argyll in Scotland in 2002 (Scottish Natural Heritage). The possibility for the return of the other species lies further in the future, and in the interim we are helping to restore adequate habitat for them and conducting educational programmes to inform people, and especially schoolchildren, about the true nature of misunderstood species such as the wolf.

Underpinning and complementing our practical work, we've enlisted the involvement of several universities in Scotland and England to carry out research into the ecology of the Caledonian Forest and the effectiveness of our restoration measures. From such research, and the experiences we've accumulated through our practical field work, we've formulated a simple list, "Principles of Ecological Restoration," which guide our work (see Chart 1). Based on the premise that "Nature knows best," most of these will be familiar to anyone involved with restoration work elsewhere, although the final point on the list is perhaps unique to our work.

Arising from our origins in, and continuing relationship with, the spiritual community of Findhorn, we have observed that as we help to restore the Caledonian Forest, the trees and the land respond in a positive way to the amount of human love and care we (and others) bring to our work. This simple observation has profound implications and points the way to another equally important result of our (and others') ecological restoration work—the effect this has on the individuals who take part in the restoration process.

The Transformative Effect of Engaging in Restoration Work

Most of Trees for Life's practical restoration work is carried out by volunteers, who take part in week-long volunteer programs based in the Caledonian Forest remnants. In the last 10 years, over a thousand people of all ages have participated in these work weeks, with many individuals coming back to take part in them year after year. By the end of each week, close-knit groups are forged from the strangers who met at the start of the program, through the transformative effects of working together to achieve positive and practical results for the regeneration of the Caledonian Forest. Statements such as the following are frequently made to us after participants return home: "Being in such an awesome environment with people I consider now to be 'friends for life' has had an effect on my life that cannot be quantified—all I can say is that my soul was set free."

Chart 1—Principles of Ecological Restoration
As developed and used by Trees for Life

1. Mimic nature wherever possible.

2. Work outwards from areas of strength, where the ecosystem is closest to its natural condition.

3. Pay particular attention to "keystone" species—those that are key components of the ecosystem, and on which many other species depend.

4. Utilize pioneer species and natural succession to facilitate the restoration process.

5. Re-create ecological niches where they've been lost.

6. Re-establish ecological linkages—reconnect the threads in the web of life.

7. Control and/or remove introduced species.

8. Remove or mitigate the limiting factors that prevent restoration from taking place naturally.

9. Let nature do most of the work.

10. Love nurtures the life force and spirit of all beings, and is a significant factor in helping to heal the Earth.

Whilst this will be familiar to anyone who has taken groups out into wilderness areas around the world, the act of engaging in restoration brings in another entire dimension to the experience which the participants have. It is Chief Seattle who is reputed to have said that:

> "This we know—the Earth does not belong to man—man belongs to the Earth. This we know. All things are connected like the blood which unites one family. All things are connected. Whatever befalls the Earth—befalls the sons of the Earth. Man did not weave the web of life—he is merely a strand in it. Whatever he does to the web, he does to himself."

This quote has frequently been used by environmentalists and ecologists in the last two decades to illustrate both the interdependence of all life, and the fact that when we damage the planet we actually harm ourselves. However, through our work to help restore the Caledonian Forest, it has become very apparent that the statement is equally valid in a positive sense. Ecological restoration—helping to heal degraded ecosystems—involves reconnecting or reweaving the strands in the web of life (which, in most instances, have been severed by the impact of human activities). However, crucially, the work of restoration is not just something which happens to Nature, separate from, or external to, humans. Taking part in restoration work provides a major opportunity for people to become reintegrated into the web of life again as well—it restores us to our rightful place as an integral, conscious part of the web. Restoration is literally the work that reconnects, at many different levels.

Many of the environmental problems which confront us in the world today arise directly as a result of our separation from the rest of Nature. Restoration, then, offers a way to not only bring the world's ecosystems back into a condition of healthy and dynamic balance, but it also provides a meaningful reconnecting experience for people, by helping to re-establish or deepen some of the most important personal links in our lives. Such links can include:

- Reconnecting with Nature. For those who are separated from Nature through urban living etc. (as the majority of the world's population now are), taking part in practical ecological restoration projects offers a significant opportunity to reconnect in a direct, hands on manner with the natural world.

- Reconnecting with place. Ecological restoration is, of necessity, site specific, and it demands an intimate knowledge of the ecosystem which is to be restored—its component species, ecological processes, seasonal cycles etc. By getting to know a place in this way, restoration practitioners become a conscious inhabitant of their ecosystem or bioregion, in contrast to the disconnection from the land which much of the world's human population experiences today.

- Reconnecting with life. Ecological restoration is focused on nurturing and enhancing life, and as such provides a meaningful opportunity to experience those qualities firsthand. When an individual sees trees growing in a forest as a result of their work, this can nurture and enrich their own life. As regenerative work, restoration offers a potent model for a new culture, in contrast to our present day society, which is in many ways death-oriented, through such things as our chemical assault on nature with herbicides and pesticides, and through the mainstream media's fixation with violence and crime.

- Reconnecting with other people. Working for restoration can bring together disparate people from a wide diversity of backgrounds, with their shared concern for their local part of the planet enabling them to transcend traditional divides and unite in cooperative work at many levels. The relationships between people which are formed thereby are often much more satisfying and long-lasting than those created by, for example, the adversarial nature of conventional political systems or even the campaigning environmental movement.

- Reconnecting with personal, inner power. In our world of 6 billion people today, many live with the belief that they are unable, as a single individual, to make a difference in the world. Engaging in restoration work provides a direct and tangible experience that the Earth responds to human love and care, and that seemingly small actions can have a profound effect on various parts of a regenerating ecosystem. Extending this understanding to the human world can help people gain a sense of their own personal inner power to effect meaningful and positive change in society.

- Reconnecting with healing. As a self-regulating system, the Earth has an inherent ability to heal itself, but in much of the world this healing process is impaired or prevented by human activities. Ecological restoration works with that process of healing, rather than against it, and that quality touches and affects the restoration practitioner, as they become reintegrated into the web of life.
- Reconnecting with hope. Restoration is a science and practice full of hope. Through its nurturing of new or renewed life, it represents a belief that humans can be effective agents for positive as well as negative change to the world's ecosystems. At a time when hope is absent from many expectations for the future, engaging in restoration can stimulate, inspire and strengthen hope in human hearts and minds and can therefore help to pave the way to a culture which is based on hope instead of fear.
- Reconnecting with spirit. In contrast to the world views of most traditional cultures, our industrial consumer society, with its materialistic and mechanistic basis, separates spirituality from Nature and the Earth. It often distances spirituality from direct personal experience as well, and through this "desacralisation" it paves the way for the desecration of Nature which follows. Ecological restoration, on the other hand, through its nurturing of life and through the visible effects of human love and care on Nature, can reawaken in us a reverence and respect for the Spirit within all creation. This, in turn, can lead to a recognition of the importance of allowing areas of the planet to be "self-willed" again, where Nature is given free rein to itself without human interference. Such recognition is essential if wilderness is to continue to exist in our world.

Experiencing some or all of these qualities can have a profound effect on those who engage in restoration work, and participants in the work of Trees for Life have often made major life changes afterwards. For example, some people have left their regular employment, because they realized it was supporting the destruction of nature and ecosystems, and have chosen new careers more aligned with the well-being of the planet.

Restoration, therefore, is work which reconnects humans with the rest of the world, and, as such, it has the potential to form a foundation for a new, or renewed, human culture—one which is based on respect for Nature, and on the needs of other species and of the planet as a whole.

Restoration, with its positive vision of regeneration, points the way to a future of hope for us all. To help translate this into practice, Trees for Life's latest project is promoting the ecological restoration of the world's degraded ecosystems as being the most important task for humanity in the 21st century. We seek to catalyse and help establish a new human culture, in which the central focus of all human endeavours becomes the revitalisation of the Earth. Only through such a shift can the future of all the planet's species, of wildlands and indeed of humanity itself, be guaranteed. Restoration, to help the healing of the planet, is the essential work of the decades ahead.

> "Ecological restoration, allied with the creation of ecosystem-scale wilderness reserves, represents the main hope that the organic quality of wildness may someday be resurrected in human souls and in all life-places on planet Earth."
>
> —*Stephanie Mills*

Wilderness—
Working with Local Communities

Mission Mountains
Tribal Wilderness

Terry Tanner

The striking peaks found in the Mission Mountains of Flathead Nation of Western Montana crown a wilderness range unique in the United States both in majesty and management. Standing more than a mile above the farmlands and towns of the Mission Valley, the western front of the range provides one of the most spectacular valley landscapes in the Rocky Mountain region. But the range is more than a natural wonder. It is the first place in America in which an Indian Nation has matched, and possibly excelled, the Federal Government in dedicating lands managed as a wilderness preserve.

The Confederated Salish and Kootenai Tribes are comprised of descendants of Salish (Flathead), Pend d'Oreille, and Kootenai Indians who traditionally had occupied a 20-million-acre (8.3-million-hectare) area stretching from Central Montana to Eastern Washington and north into Canada. The signing of the Hellgate Treaty of 1855 ceded the vast majority of those ancestral lands to the United States Government in return for the approximately 1.243 million acres (518,000 hectares) now known as the Flathead Indian Reservation. The Treaty agreement only formalized the Tribes' relinquishment of their lands; events long preceding the Hellgate Treaty event had guaranteed this eventual loss.

In the words of then governor of the Washington Territory, Isaac Stevens, the Treaty gave access to "much valuable land and an inexhaustible supply of timber" and enabled "settlers to secure titles to land and thus the growth of towns and villages." The loss of this vast wilderness meant the potential loss of traditional Indian society. Every aspect of the Indian culture, from hunting and food gathering to religious practices, was dependent upon a wilderness setting.

To the Salish, Pend d'Oreille and Kootenai Indians, the Mission Mountains were one part of this wilderness homeland, distinct in its incredible ruggedness and extreme weather but no more wild or primeval than anywhere else. And, like other features of the landscape, the Mission Mountains influenced the culture and economy of the Tribes. The area could be crossed only through certain passes, used for hundreds of years by many different tribal bands and still used today for hunting, fishing, plant gathering, and cultural activities.

The first attempt by the Tribes to officially protect the Mission Range occurred in 1936, during a period of extensive trail construction by the Indian Civilian Conservation Corps in the mountainous areas of the Reservation. The Tribal Council voted to set aside about 100,000 acres (41,666 hectares) of the western slope of the Mission Mountains as an Indian-maintained national park. The Tribes were to retain ownership of the lands but planned to parallel the National Park Service in its administration of the area. The main goals were to encourage Tribal member use of the park with traditional encampments and activities and to provide an economic opportunity for Indian guides to bring visitors into the park. Nothing ever came of the Tribal Council action. Correspondence suggests the idea died in Washington, D.C., in the office of the Commissioner of Indian Affairs, while performing their trust responsibilities for the Flathead Nation.

Ironically, one year later the Mission Range was classified as a roadless area by the same Office of Indian Affairs but the Tribes objected because it was classified without the consent or input of the Tribes and some of the land was determined to be better suited for other uses by the Tribes. The Mission Range Roadless Area was declassified in the Federal Register in 1959.

During the mid-1970s, the Bureau of Indian Affairs' Flathead Agency proposed to log portions of the remaining roadless area on the western front of the Mission Range on behalf of the Tribes. The proposal fueled a renewed interest in preserving the Mission Mountains in a natural state and the Tribal Council decided to set aside approximately 91,778 acres (38,240 hectares) as a Tribal Wilderness in 1979.

This decision came about through the efforts of a number of Tribal individuals and groups. Three greatly respected grandmothers (Yayas) raised the initial protest to the proposed logging and lead the way for other community leaders to organize the Save the Mission Mountains Committee, to stop timber sales proposed for the area. The Committee circulated a petition in 1975 asking the Council to designate a Mission Mountains Primitive in which logging would be banned. Soon after this, the Council seriously began to consider some type of wilderness protection.

Several proposals were advanced, all of which lacked overall management considerations other than logging would be prohibited. A proposal containing the least acreage included only those lands unfeasible for timber harvesting. Advocates of this proposal were concerned about loss of income from reduced commercial timberlands.

Save the Mission Mountains Committee proposed a boundary that came to the base of the mountain range and included private and roaded lands that made it politically not viable. Their interest centered on protecting aesthetic values and preserving the wilderness character of the area, thereby helping to retain some of the cultural and spiritual values important to the Tribes.

In 1976, the Tribal Council, at the recommendation of Thurman Trosper (a Tribal member and retired U.S. Forest Service employee and past president of the Wilderness Society), contracted with the Wilderness Institute of the University of Montana to develop a draft boundary and management proposal for a Mission Mountains Tribal Wilderness Area. Two years later the Institute presented the drafts, which were a compromise of previous proposals, to the Council for review. The Council took no immediate action on the Institute's management proposal and boundary until a year later when they approved the draft boundary and decided to create a new Tribal program to oversee the interim management of the area. This program, called the Wildland Recreation Program, was also charged with developing a wilderness management plan to meet the specific needs and values of the Tribes.

The Program completed the plan in the spring of 1982 and on June 15 the Council voted overwhelmingly to approve Ordinance 79A, The Tribal Wilderness Ordinance, and the Mission Mountains Tribal Wilderness Management Plan. The Council's action was historic. It was the first time that an Indian Tribe had decided on its own accord to protect a sizable portion of its lands as wilderness and provide policy and personnel to fulfill its propose. The first section of the Tribal Wilderness Ordinance states that: "Wilderness has played a paramount role in shaping the character of the people and the culture of the Salish and Kootenai Tribes; it is the essence of traditional Indian religion and has served the Indian people and the culture of the Salish and Kootenai Tribes; it is the essence of traditional Indian religion and has served the Indian people of these Tribes as a place to hunt, as a place to gather medicinal herbs and roots, as a vision seeking ground, as a sanctuary, and in countless other ways for thousands of years. Because maintaining an enduring resource of wilderness is vitally important to the people of the Confederated Salish and Kootenai Tribes and the perpetuation of their culture, there is hereby established a Mission Mountains Tribal Wilderness Area and this Area, described herein, shall be administered to protect and preserve wilderness values."

The Tribal Council continued it's historical precedent by following through with specific management actions to fulfill the wilderness mandate. A Mission Mountain Grizzly Bear Management Plan was written to foster greater care of one of the wilderness's greatest resources. A Mission Mountains Tribal Wilderness Fire Management Plan was developed to facilitate reintroduction of natural fire to the wilderness ecosystem, and a Wilderness Buffer Zone Plan was created to cushion the wilderness from outside influences which may impact it's integrity.

Note: Other special management direction/regulation, primarily for Non-Tribal members only.

1. Use of any Tribal lands or waters by Non-Tribal members requires the purchase of a Tribal conservation license and the appropriate activity stamp (fish, bird hunt, or camp); this is a requirement for use of wilderness lands.
2. A group size limit of 8 persons and 8 head of livestock is in place for wilderness lands.
3. Use of a campsite for longer than 3 consecutive days is prohibited.
4. It is illegal to carry or use a firearm.
5. A spring stock closure helps protect pathways from erosion.
6. A 10,000-acre (4,166-hectare) grizzly bear zone is closed to all human use between July 15 to Oct. 1 of each year to protect critical grizzly bear habitat and maintain visitor safety.
7. Fisheries management is weighted to give special attention to waters containing native West Slope Cutthroat Trout and native Bull Trout.
8. Any commercial use of the Tribal Wilderness is not allowed (no outfitting or guides).

The first Flathead Nation wilderness manager stated: "Wilderness is, to a segment of the Tribal population, vitally important. It is one part of the Indian culture that remains as it was. Preservation then, expresses reverence for the land and its community of life, as well as respect for Indian culture."

Confederated Salish & Kootenai Tribes

The Confederated Salish and Kootenai Tribes are comprised of descendants of Salish (Flathead), Pend d'Oreille, and Kootenai Indians who traditionally had occupied a 20-million-acre (8.3-million-hectare) area stretching from central Montana to eastern Washington and north into Canada. The signing of the Hellgate Treaty of 1855 ceded the vast majority of those ancestral lands to the United States Government in return for the approximately 1.243 million acres (518,000 hectares) now known as the Flathead Indian Reservation. The treaty agreement only formalized the tribes' relinquishment of their lands; events long preceding the Hellgate Treaty event had guaranteed this eventual loss.

In the words of Isaac Stevens, then governor of the Washington Territory, the treaty gave access to "much valuable land and an inexhaustible supply of timber and enabled settlers to secure titles to land and thus the growth of towns and villages. The loss of this vast wilderness meant the potential loss of traditional Indian society. Every aspect of the Indian culture, from hunting and food gathering to religious practices, was dependent upon the surrounding wilderness.

Historical Impacts on Salish and Kootenai Resources

Long before the signing of the Hellgate Treaty of 1855 and the establishment of the Flathead Indian Reservation, the Tribes had begun to experience dramatic changes in lifestyle. Some of the more significant events that influenced the Tribes before the creation of the Reservation are highlighted below.

The Introduction of Horses and Firearms

Tribal life changed dramatically with the introduction of horses and firearms. Salish people first acquired the horse from the Shoshone sometime between 1680 and 1720. The tribes quickly built large herds that became attractive targets for the neighboring Blackfeet who, by the late eighteenth century, had acquired guns. The combination of horses and guns made intertribal warfare more frequent and more deadly.

Disease
Smallpox and other diseases struck the Salish and Kootenai by at least the early 1780s, and during the 1800s waves of diseases repeatedly swept through the area. Some of the elders alive today still remember the last smallpox epidemics of the early twentieth century.

Pressures from Non-Indian Settlements to the East
By the beginning of the nineteenth century, the westward movement of non-Indians and the loss of the great bison herds forced the Salish and Kootenai tribes to concentrate most settlements in Valleys west of the Continental Divide. Nevertheless, both tribes continued to rely heavily on frequent and often large hunting expeditions to traditional territories east of the mountains.

The Arrival of Lewis and Clark
In the early 1800s, Salish Indians assisted Lewis and Clark across the Bitterroot Mountains. One interpretation reported that the explorers mistook the Salish for one of the Chinook Tribes of Oregon and so called them Flatheads, a name still used today.

The Fur Trade
While some individual fur traders preceded Lewis and Clark into the region in the 1790s, the trade began in earnest in the 1810s and 1820s and eventually changed the regions ecological balance. The fur trade was the first inroad of the market system to tribal economies. It had a profound impact on the traditional way of life, as it emphasized the privatization of resources and altered the balance of wildlife resources. It also sped the introduction of European religions.

The Arrival of the Blackrobes
According to Salish oral tradition, a Pend d'Oreilles elder named Shining Shirt, had a vision that told him: "When you grow up there will come men wearing long black dresses. They will teach you about Amotqen, the good spirit who sits on top, and about Emtep, the evil one who sits at the bottom. From them you will learn to live your life on earth." The Bitterroot Salish learned of Jesuit missionaries from a small party of Iroquois Indians who settled among them. Several delegations attempted to travel across the plains to St. Louis to ask the

Jesuits to come to the Bitterroot. One was successful. In 1841, the Jesuits arrived and established the St. Mary's Mission in the Bitterroot Valley. The mission closed in 1850 and remained closed for sixteen years. In 1854, the Jesuits established the St. Ignatius Mission farther north in the lower Flathead River Valley, at the winter camp of the Kalispel and Pend d'Oreilles Tribes.

Some Indian people converted to Christianity, but many Indians refused. Others practiced both native and Catholic teachings. The church, along with discouraging Indians from practicing traditional religion, tried to assimilate the Salish and Kootenai people into a settled, agricultural way of life. Priests and nuns, who actively tried to discourage hunting and harvesting, encouraged the people to take up farming, and sent children to Catholic boarding schools where English was the only language spoken. They punished Indian children for speaking Tribal languages.

The Hellgate Treaty

In July of 1855, Governor Isaac Stevens of Washington Territory, met with the chiefs of the Salish, Pend d'Oreilles and Kootenai near present-day Missoula. Their purpose was to negotiate a treaty between the Tribes and the United States Government. After a long discussion, Stevens presented the assembled Indians with an agreement whereby the Kootenai and Pend d'Oreilles would live on the Jocko Reserve (now called the Flathead Reservation) and the Bitterroot Salish would remain in the Bitterroot Valley until the government surveyed it.

The final treaty stated that, "... if [the Bitterroot Valley should] prove, in the judgment of the President, to be better adapted to the wants of the Flathead tribe than the general (Jocko Reserve) provided for in this treaty, then such portions of it as may be necessary shall be set apart as a separate reservation for the said tribe." The treaty went on to state that "no portion of the Bitter Root Valley [sic], above the Loo-lo Fork [sic], shall be opened to settlement until such examination is had and the decision of the President made known."

In exchange for lands ceded by the Tribes, the federal government promised a cash settlement, as well as medical, agricultural, educational, and vocational services and infrastructure. All of the tribes retained off-Reservation hunting, fishing, gathering and grazing rights and the exclusive use of the Reservation. Later, in October of 1855, the Flathead Nation executed a separate treaty reserving expressly, among other things, the right to hunt and fish in areas east of the Continental Divide.

More than 15 years after the treaty was signed, the United States Government had still not surveyed or examined the land in the Bitterroot Valley. In addition, substantial numbers of non-Indians had settled there in violation of the treaty.

Finally, in 1871, President Grant issued an executive order relocating the Salish to the Jocko Reserve and opening the Bitterroot Valley to non-Indian settlement. Grant sent James Garfield to negotiate the Tribe's removal. The Salish subchiefs Arlee and Joseph consented to the move, but Chief Charlo refused. He and several hundred of his followers remained in the Bitterroot Valley until 1891, when the government forced them to move to the Jocko Reserve under military escort.

Flathead Indian Reservation History

The signing of the Hellgate Treaty and forced relocation of the Tribes brought even greater changes to the traditional Indian way of life. The major periods and events in the history of the Reservation are summarized below.

Early Years

For more than twenty years after the treaty was signed, a series of corrupt government agents did almost nothing to honor the promises of the treaty.

The Ronan Years

Peter Ronan became agent for the Reservation in 1877. He encouraged Indian people to take up farming and oversaw the construction of irrigation ditches in the Jocko Valley. According to his annual reports to the Commissioner of Indian Affairs, the crop output on the Reservation more than quadrupled during his sixteen-year term. The number of horses tripled, and the estimated number of cattle went from 1,100 to 15,010 in 1893 (Trosper).

Most Tribal food production was for subsistence and not for market. Hunting parties were discouraged from leaving the Reservation. Tribal police and courts were established, and troops were deployed from Fort Missoula after the Nez Perce War of 1877. Federal Policy outlawed traditional dances and feasts. During Ronan's tenure, the Jesuits converted the Mission Boys' School to a boarding school, and the Northern Pacific Railway Company built a railroad line across the southwestern portion of the Reservation (Fahey 1974).

The Railroad

The United States Assistant Attorney General came to the Reservation in 1882 to negotiate a price for a railroad right-of-way. Pend d'Oreilles, Salish, and Kootenai leaders voiced concerns about trespass, livestock theft, illegal timber cutting and liquor sales by some non-Indians who traveled through the Reservation. They were also concerned about land loss to depots and rights-of-way. They asked to reacquire the land north of Flathead Lake in exchange for the proposed railroad right-of-way, to protect the resources of the northern part of the Reservation for future generations. Although Attorney General McKammon said he could not negotiate with the Tribes at that time for the land north of the lake, he said, "I will promise to use my influence to get that strip of land for you, and I want you in return to get signatures for this agreement." The Tribes signed the agreement, but the land was never returned. The railroad was completed in 1883. Early on in the negotiations process, Chief Eneas said: "Seven years after that (the Treaty) we learned that the line of the reservation ran across the middle of Flathead Lake. We didn't know that when we signed the treaty. That is the reason we want that country back." (Arthur 1883).

The Allotment Period

In 1887, the United States Congress passed the Dawes Act that called for a survey of all reservation lands in the United States. The act required the federal agent of each reservation to draw up a tribal roll and assign land allotments with the consent of the tribe. The Congress, through its allotment policy, continued the attempt to assimilate Indians into the dominant culture.

The Flathead Allotment Act

Despite continued opposition by the Tribes, the Flathead Allotment Act passed the U.S. Congress in 1904. The Tribes never approved of the allotment program, and in fact submitted petitions and sent delegations to Washington protesting it. Nevertheless the government assigned allotments.

Other Land Reserves

By 1908, the first set of allotments had been completed. The federal government withdrew portions of unallotted lands for missions, government agencies, town sites, and a biological station for the University of Montana.

In addition, the government withdrew approximately 18,524 acres from allotment or sale for the National Bison Range; 45,714 acres for reservoir or power development sites; and 60,843 acres (usually Sections 16 and 36 of each township) for the State of Montana for school purposes.

Non-Indian Settlement

In 1910, a Presidential Proclamation opened "surplus" reservation lands to settlement. Non-Indians settled much of the land in the valleys, including many of the areas where bitterroot, camas and other food and medicinal plants grew. Some homesteaders allowed Indians to continue to harvest plants and berries on their lands, but others forbade it or plowed plants under to make room for crops.

Flathead Irrigation Project

In 1908, Congress authorized construction on the Flathead Irrigation Project. Congress intended the project to serve 150,000 acres of Indian lands (Flathead Allotment Act of 19043). Its design and construction altered the natural flow and course of the streams on the Reservation and destroyed some of the fishery (Smith and Big Crane 1991).

Although the project was justified as primarily serving the interests of Indians, it benefited non-Indians to a far greater degree. Without it, many homesteads would have never made it, and many did fail during the early years when the project was incomplete.

Second Series of Allotments

In 1920, the government began a second series of allotments for those Tribal members born between 1908 and 1920. Many of these allotments were on range or timberland and were not served by the irrigation project.

Federal policy forced the conversion of many allotments to fee status, as opposed to keeping them in trust. As a consequence, many of the tribal members who received allotments in 1908 and in the 1920s lost them to non-Indians because they could not pay taxes or because they owed debts.

The Indian Reorganization Act

The Indian Reorganization Act of 1934 marked the official end of the allotment period. The government encouraged tribes to adopt a model constitution and charter of incorporation that would give them the power to acquire and manage property. This act also gave tribes the authority to define their memberships (a power previously held by the BIA during the allotment period) and to govern themselves by a council of elected tribal officials. The tribes on the Flathead Reservation adopted a constitution and corporate charter in 1935 and were the first tribes in the nation to do so. The action established the official Tribal name of "Confederated Salish and Kootenai Tribes (CSKT) of the Flathead Reservation."

The Termination Era

In 1953, the U.S. Congress considered House Concurrent Resolution 108 that allowed for the abolishment of federal supervision over certain tribes. The "Flathead Tribe of Montana," as listed in the resolution, was never terminated. A number of the tribes that were terminated have been reinstated.

Establishment of the Culture Committees

In 1975, several Tribal members established an initiative to preserve Tribal heritages and spearheaded a cultural program that involved recording Tribal Elders' stories in native languages. The Tribes formed two culture committees to "preserve, protect, perpetuate and promote" the histories and cultures of the Confederated Salish and Kootenai Tribes.

CSKT Wildland Recreation Program

Program Functions

Created in 1980 to provide Tribal wilderness management, the program currently coordinates recreational use and facility development on all Tribal lands. The program also manages the 44D Recreational Permit system. Major areas of program attention are the Tribal Wilderness Area, the South Fork of the Jocko Primitive Area. Flathead Lake and River Corridor, Wilderness Buffer Zone and Blue Bay Campground.

Program Goals

The goals are to protect the recreational resources that are important to the sustenance, cultural enrichment, and economic support of the Tribes, and to promote the conservation, development, and utilization of the recreational resources for the maximum benefit of the Tribes and other recreational users.

Program Objectives

- Intensify management activities in the Mission Mountains Tribal Wilderness Area.
- Implementation of the Wilderness Buffer Zone Plan, Lower Flathead River Corridor Management Plan and Kerr Mitigation objectives.
- Monitor recreation use and develop and maintain related facilities in the Tribal primitive areas. Assist with management plan development.
- Maintain and develop existing recreation facilities and monitor recreation use Reservation wide.
- Assist in fisheries, wildlife, and other natural resource programs' studies and special projects.
- Explore and secure alternative funding and solicit volunteer work for special projects.
- Provide the Tribal Council with management guidelines for recreational resource use.
- Provide the Tribal membership and recreation permittees with a high level of program services.

Program Resource Areas

40+ campgrounds and recreational sites
30+ backcountry trails
91,778 acres of wilderness lands
59,169 acres of South Fork primitive lands
37,020 acres of Lozeau primitive lands
20,000 acres of river corridor
22,833 acres of wilderness buffer zone
9,757 acres of Chief Cliff management area
45 recreation permit vendors
6 recreational outfitters
20,000 (appx.) recreation system users

Indian Self-Determination

The Indian Self-Determination Act of 1976 (Public Law 93-638) allowed tribes to contract with the federal government to manage certain Federal programs. The Confederated Salish and Kootenai Tribes have taken a lead in assuming management responsibility for these programs on the Reservation (Jeanine Padilla, Telephone Interview, 1994). In addition, the Tribes manage 70 Tribal programs and have repurchased more than 245,000 acres of Reservation land since 1944. Because of these successful efforts, the Confederated Salish and Kootenai Tribes have become one of ten tribes nationwide to participate in a Self-Governance Demonstration Project initiated in 1988. In addition, the Tribes are now developing a cultural center to assist the culture committees in their efforts to promote the cultures, languages and histories of the Tribes.

Conservation, Community and Craftwork

Brenda Locke

Early in 2001 The WILD Foundation requested Embocraft Training Trust to set up projects to emphasize the meaning of Wilderness and Heritage sites in Africa, across cultures, perspectives and poverty. We had previously been successful with a number of Craftaid projects in black rural communities and so we agreed.

The complex issues inherent in rural development have always to be taken into account before any project, no matter what it is, can succeed. For the aims of Embocraft to become concrete outcomes, we must deal with all the underlying realities that exist in rural communities. Taking these specific conditions into account we focus on the following principles:

- training in basic craft skills
- storytelling
- the making of a story quilt
- teaching very basic business skills

The resultant program involves upliftment incentives based on teaching income generating skills, plus a storytelling workshop.

Our target groups are mainly rural women where the very high incidence of unemployment and poverty perpetuates the cycle of abuse of women. Many women live in fear as they do not trust their partners and have no rights to question or deny. Giving the women the ability to earn an income strengthens their financial independence and if they are thrown out of the home they have some ability to fend for themselves and their children.

Figure 1—Quilt hanging, from Hibberdene Community, KwaZulu-Natal.

Giving them self-esteem, peer group support and awareness of various potential life threatening issues is a small boost towards independence and their ability to claim their human rights. Many women have formed self-help groups as a result of our projects. These groups have continued to operate. We are currently working to get their groups to form co-operatives that will give them access to various forms of financial assistance and other training.

It is relevant to take a look at the Craftaid program.

Goals of CRAFTAID

To deal with taboo and other unconsidered issues and through skills training to support communities undergoing the devastating effects of disease and poverty.

Objectives

- To raise awareness of the complex issues resulting in the AIDS pandemic and the destruction of the environment
- To provide healing and learning using craft skills and workshop techniques in the making of story quilts
- To provide life skills training to promote upliftment of disadvantaged people in rural areas
- To reinforce the efforts of both men and women to take responsibility for the problems they identify and wish to address
- To utilize group work and peer learning to maximize training
- To provide the means of economic empowerment through skills training that results in saleable products
- To teach the basic tenets of small business to support these income generating opportunities.
- To ensure sustainability of the outcomes of the course through networking with established groups able to provide mentors and assistance both with the participants and with the marketing of products
- To develop Craftaid courses and register all courses within the South African National Qualifications framework

Summary of the CRAFTAID Course
Outline of Craft Skills Taught Over Five Days

- Textile Dyeing—sun dyeing and tie-dyeing

- Textile Printing—block printing using potatoes and polystyrene
- Embroidery—basic stitches
- Resist printing—using flour and water or mealie (maize) meal
- Story squares—pictures drawn, painted and embroidered, using techniques learned (i.e., storytelling using the medium of craft)

Opportunities
- Income generation
- Entrepreneurship development
- Networking with Community Development Fora and other organizations

Our Craftaid courses are followed by a three-day basic business course, provided that funds are available. Entitled "Manage Your Own Small Business" and developed by the Democracy Development Program, it focuses on very basic accounting principles such as costing of raw materials, mark up and profit principles, budgeting and how to use a calculator. The course is highly interactive and a manual in the form of a workbook and stationery used for the course are left with the participants for future use.

For The WILD Foundation project we intended to use methods similar to those mentioned above, employed by the successful Craftaid program. This would help empower communities to take a step forward out of their extreme poverty by training them to produce acceptable craft items such as wall hangings and cushion covers.

Seventeen communities were included in this project, two funded by the Democracy Development program and the balance by The WILD Foundation. British Petroleum provided start up capital for materials and equipment when the course has been completed, in order that communities can continue developing their skills by producing saleable stock until they begin to receive income from their sales. B. P. also provided funding to enable us to get the project off the ground in the Eastern Cape and in the Free State.

Since our emphasis was on a broad range of conservation issues, it was necessary for us to first run the basic Craftaid Program, funded by Care Deutschland, in most of the selected communities where special environmental issues were at stake. Following that, we were able to do the environmental storytelling workshops to bring out the themes we wanted them to express through the craft skills just learned.

Figure 2—Quilt from Mnweni Community, KwaZulu-Natal.

This situation applied in the Eastern Cape and Free State in particular, since the Craftaid workshops had not been introduced in these Provinces. Since we believed it would be of interest and useful for The WILD Foundation it was decided to develop the skills of a community at Paterson, a village between the Addo Elephant Park and Shamwari Game Reserve, to possibly enable delegates to the 7th World Wilderness Congress to visit and speak with participants and see the impact of the program on the community for themselves.

Our rural and peri-urban squatter communities, in particular, are trapped in a cycle of poverty and we discovered very little spiritual association with wilderness. The thought of the need to preserve the often very beautiful environment where they live had not occurred to communities who had been given no environmental education. Several communities had had the benefit of workshops with environmental and conservation officers, prior to our storytelling workshops. These showed much more awareness of their surroundings as possible income generators through properly managed tourism. Some were already working on ideas and plans to attract tourists and their potential income generation to their surroundings.

There were noticeable differences in attitudes to environmental issues where prior education had been given. Our trainers believe that significant impact would be made on rural communities if they were able to participate in a wilderness "trail," or trek, before attending our workshop. In the future, such trails may be provided by the S. A. Wilderness Therapy Institute. We believe that these trails will impact usefully on participants with regard to their creativity since their minds will already be open to many previously unseen—or rather, unobserved—wonders of the environment when they first come into contact with the new creative materials (paints, pigments, dyes, etc.) and are asked to express their ideas.

Community Response to the Project

Very positive feedback came from all the communities that participated in these workshops. Most of the responses from the evaluation exercise at the end of the workshop were similar, and I quote a few of these from the reports:

> "We enjoyed everything—the games, the dancing and singing,
> the painting, the embroidery, learning about the embroidery,
> the patient teaching by the craft facilitators, the appreciation of

their traditional attire, cookery, homes and the way the trainers told them about their own families."

"We learned more about each other, the environment, our mountains (parrots, fish traps, etc.) and what these meant to visitors and tourists and we learned how to take care of our own area—the trees (rivers, paintings, turtles, etc.)."

"We want to teach our children and others about what we have learned and organize meetings with our leaders to tell them what we have discovered and become aware of and to urge our leaders to appoint guards for the environment."

"We liked talking about the environment and realize that we must preserve the things that are disappearing. We want to learn more advanced craft and more about cultural issues— yours as well as ours, and more about tree planting." (Centocow project)

In viewing the beautiful hangings produced, it should be borne in mind that none of the communities we worked with had any previous knowledge of the techniques we taught since they had not learned art and craft at their schools. Most of the people we worked with had very limited education and most were barely literate in Zulu. Their stories were written for them in many cases by our Zulu trainer and then translated into English for the benefit of those who would purchase the hangings. Some of the stories seem to be irrelevant and some appear to be old fables. Many of the stories express the feelings of alienation older members of communities feel from the young who appear to be lacking in discipline. Many of the members of all the communities found it difficult to listen to the others speak and insisted on carrying on side conversations. This situation required some handling by the trainers so that the speakers could be heard. It also seemed difficult for many of them to listen carefully to instruction given by our trainers, indicating that they were unused to participating in workshops. As the workshops progressed this situation generally improved somewhat.

One or two of the resultant hangings comprise stories from more than one community. This is due to many extra participants arriving for the workshop they had heard about by bush telegraph, and travelling long distances to take part. They were not turned away since some had gone to considerable trouble and expense to get to the venue. Our mandate was to produce hangings of a particular size so extra stories were combined with other "surpluses." Where this is the case, the stories are carefully marked on the story sheets attached to the hanging.

Our trainers have found the workshops satisfying and feel that the education and training they have been able to offer is worthwhile. As a result, phase two of this program, in cooperation with The WILD Foundation, will assemble in communities to produce up to 100 wall hangings for display and sale at the World Summit on Sustainable Development in Johannesburg in August–September 2003.

Wilderness Quilt Stories Kosi Bay— Mvuchane Community

Kosi Bay is a World Heritage site situated on the very northeastern border of Kwa Zulu Natal close to the Mozambique border. The Bay is part of a system of four lakes; the farthest one being fresh water and becoming more saline as they get closer to the ocean. Kosi Bay is well known for its fish traps, which are owned by families in the community, and ownership is passed on from generation to generation. Hippopotamus and crocodiles abound around the lakes and there is an abundance of bird life, including the fish eagle whose call is frequently heard echoing across the Bay.

The Kosi Mangrove, which is endemic to this area, is to be found in the Mangrove swamps around the Bay. On the shores of this coastline the endangered leatherback turtle swims thousands of kilometres to lay its eggs, and wonderful, protected snorkelling reefs are home to a variety of sea life. Lala Palms are used in basketry.

The aim of the workshop was the maintenance of a pristine area and an appreciation of all the natural beauty and wildlife that this community have the honor of living with. Fortunately, one of the local Nature Guides was a participant on the workshop and he was able to give the group a very comprehensive description of what he does, why the area should be preserved and what visitors

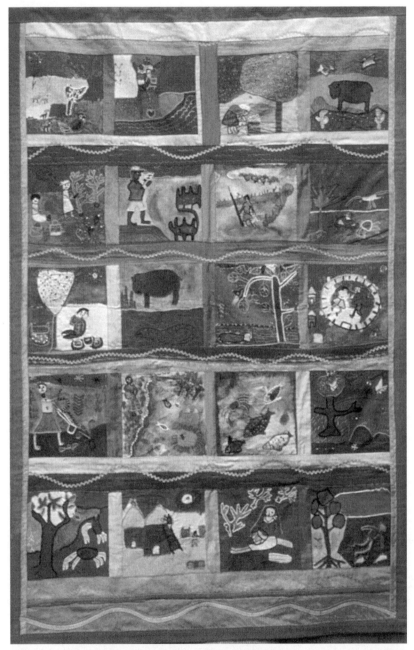

Figure 3—Quilt from the Mvuchane Community, near Kosi Bay, KwaZulu-Natal, on Mozambique border. (please see related stories produced by maker of each square. Squares are numbered starting with #1 from the top left, across to the right, then next row on the left starts with #5, etc)

to the area come to see. Many participants had no idea as to why the turtle should be preserved as they had always looked upon the eggs as a food source. The community lives very close to nature and practice conservation naturally in their fish traps. Everyone participated with great enthusiasm and was very eager to depict their surroundings in their craft work to be sold at the new craft center.

The question asked was, "If you were a visitor to this area what would you like to see?" Enjoy your quilt and your discovery of their answers. Great fun was had by all.

Square No. 1—I would like visitors to see and hear birds at the top of the beautiful trees.

Square No. 2—If I were a visitor to this place I would like to see the turtles and how they lay their eggs.

Square No. 3—In my culture I collect the fruit of the Umdoni tree to make wine for my husband. I put the seeds into a bucket and cover them with water. I leave them for a long time to rot. I bury the wine in the ground because it is cool and leave it there until it is ready. We use the wine for a special ceremony. I love handcrafts.

Square No. 4—What I like about this place is that it has nice trees, which give people different fruit and nice smells. It is very nice because when it is raining there is no mud because it is sandy. When the people of this place build their houses they normally use natural things and only have to buy a few things.

Square No. 5—I would like to see my children learning to make handcrafts and making baskets like me from the lala palms so that they can have a bright future.

Square No. 6—Kosi Bay and its wonders. I have been to the highest viewpoint and gazed at the different lakes and saw the "railway lines" in the water. I asked the guide named Jan how could there be a train in the water. He told me it is not railway lines but fish traps. He took me down to see the fish traps. I have never seen anything like it anywhere else.

Square No. 7—My friend has a fish trap (Utshwayelo) in Kosi Bay. His traps are near the mangrove swamps. On Sundays I go down with him to spear the fish. The traps are built in a special way so that when the fish go in they can't turn to come out. The traps catch only the big fish because they are built so that the little fish can escape. We walk through the water when the tide is going out to spear the fish in the trap. The fish are cleaned on the waters edge and then we thread them onto a strong reed and carry them home for dinner.

Square No. 8—If I were a visitor to this place I would like to see the turtles laying their eggs. I have heard that there are two types of turtles laying their eggs here. I would also like to see the people cooking African food.

Square No. 9—I like my culture and hope that the people will not let it die so that our children will be able to learn about it. We collect the fruit from the Marula tree to make wine. The Marula tree is also used for muti (medicine).

Square No. 10—What I will never forget and what makes me very happy is that the people are very friendly and are not disruptive. This place is very quiet because there are no factories and locations. The people still use their traditional culture. I love to watch the hippos and the crocodiles down at the lake.

Square No. 11—I would like to see the local people practicing their traditions like cooking African food and seeing the sangoma (witch doctor). I love to wander around the indigenous forest seeing and listening to all the different birds singing with their nice voices. I love to go to the bay to see the fish.

Square No. 12—I like my culture and would not like to see it go away. My hope is that my children learn and like their culture like our traditional wedding ceremony.

Square No. 13—What I would like my children to learn is to behave themselves and learn to respect their elders. They should go to school and also know how to plough the fields. In that way they will remember me. I like to plant and grow things especially madumbies.

Square No. 14—I don't think there is a better place than being at the Kosi Bay mouth view site. You feel very special to God to experience that. Moreover, God's love grows even bigger than before seeing the sea, the fish kraals and the different lakes. Even the local history fascinates me, like who owns the fish kraals and where it all started.

Square No. 15—I love to see the ocean and the fish swimming in the reef.

Square No. 16—I like to spend time walking by the sea, on the mountains and in the indigenous forest where I can see the birds and animals.

Square No. 17—If I visited here I would like to see the ocean and to see how they make the fish traps. I would like to go to the top of the mountains where I can see another country like Mozambique. I would like to see all the different trees and listen to the birds singing nicely. I would also like to see the trees called mangroves and see all the things that live there like the crabs.

Square No. 18—I wish that my culture does not die out and that the behavior of the people stays the same. Our place must be good for visitors then we will have work.

Square No. 19—I like living in this place and I would like to see the people making handcrafts and developing themselves so that they can give life to their families. The people of this place have been taught to do handcrafts like making baskets from the lala palm.

Square No. 20—I like Kosi Bay because I like to swim in the ocean and see the fish. I also like to go to the indigenous forest to see all the different birds and flowers.

Empowering and Training Local People

The RARE Center and the Nature Guide Training Program

Jose Alvez

The RARE Center for Tropical Conservation is a U.S.-based international non-profit organization that has been active in twenty-four countries in Latin America, the Caribbean, and the Pacific since 1973. RARE is the acronym for Rare Animal Relief Effort. Initially, during its early years, RARE Center's work primarily encompassed single-species conservation projects.

RARE Center's mission is to protect wildlands of globally significant biological diversity by empowering local people to benefit from their preservation. Focusing on providing education and economic opportunities, it pursues this mission by working in partnership with rural communities, NGOs, local government, and other local stakeholders to develop and replicate locally managed conservation strategies.

The Nature Guide Training Program (NGTP) was developed through a unique collaboration with Latin American protected area managers, local tour operators, and WorldTeach—a Harvard University-based volunteer organization. The NGTP falls under the Ecotourism and Community Development Program (ECDP) of the RARE Center, which "helps local people plan, manage and benefit from sustainable ecotourism development."

The first NGTP was launched in Costa Rica in 1994. RARE Center has since collaborated with dozens of tour operators, NGOs, and government agencies to provide courses in Mexico's Southern Baja Peninsula and Yucatan Peninsula, the Mexican state of Chiapas, and the North Coast of Honduras. Future courses are anticipated in Indonesia and throughout Central America.

Background to the
South African Nature Guide Training Program

In an effort to assist with ecotourism jobs creation in the rural communities neighboring the Namaqua, West Coast, and Augrabies Falls National Parks, RARE Center implemented a Nature Guide Training Program (NGTP) in collaboration with South African National Parks (SANParks) for the year 2001. The training program helps rural adults participate in and benefit from ecotourism by providing course students, with little formal education, the basic skills needed to work as nature guides, community-based tour operators, and other related jobs.

A Focus on Namaqualand

The newly created Namaqua National Park, officially declared on August 4, 1999, is a world-class tourism destination, with great potential to be a generator of sustainable employment for local residents.

Situated near the Namibian border in the Northern Cape Province, the park is located in a semi-desert biome known as the Succulent Karoo, which is an internationally recognized biodiversity hotspot. It is home to the world's richest concentration of succulent plants and is also famous for its spectacular display of vivid spring wildflowers. Encompassing 55,000 hectares, Namaqua National Park has the untapped potential to attract ecotourists throughout the year with its stark natural beauty, remoteness, bird-life, reptiles, and plants.

The South African government has identified tourism as an important factor in the long-term economic prosperity of Namaqualand. The provincial tourism department has had an active campaign promoting tourism through extensive marketing, and an estimated 100,000 tourists travel to the region each year. Roughly 65 percent of visitors are from other parts of the country, while 35 percent are foreign tourists. However, despite the tremendous ecological attractions and this significant volume of tourists, the regional unemployment rate hovers at approximately 60 percent, and local incomes are very low.

The reasons communities are not benefiting from tourism stem from the lack of local involvement and limited local capacity. With low educational levels—most residents have not completed junior high school—there is a very limited pool of job skills necessary to fuel a local tourism industry. Residents who have found employment work on farms or in mines and lack transferable skills. Language is also a barrier as most residents speak only Afrikaans, while the majority of visitors speak English.

Initially, when the RARE-SANParks partnership was discussed, the Namaqua National Park and its local communities were identified as the sole recipients of the NGTP in view of the region's under-developed tourism potential. Subsequently, however, due to the poor short-term employment opportunities of the Namaqualand region it was decided to maximize the opportunities inherent in the program and include Augrabies Falls and West Coast National Parks and their communities. The following student-guide quota per park was structured: Namaqua (7); Augrabies Falls (5); and West Coast (4).

Description of the Program

The NGTP curriculum is based on a state-of-the-art training methodology in which students live and study with their teachers in an isolated, English language-only environment. During the three-month course, students receive more than 1,000 hours of practical experience, equal to more than a year at a U.S. university. The curriculum covers conversational English, local natural and cultural history, interpretation and guiding skills, and basic tour planning and marketing. Curriculum and teaching materials are adapted to the specific needs of each country or region.

The program utilizes proven experiential learning techniques so that students acquire skills by actually using and developing them, rather than by simply studying them. Throughout the course, students design and lead tours, give oral presentations, design signs, collaborate to solve problems, and carry out role-plays. As the programs in Costa Rica, Mexico, and Honduras have shown, this hands-on approach encourages students, who might otherwise be hindered by self-consciousness, to become enthusiastic and active learners.

Results of Past Programs

- More than 180 rural adults have been trained through twelve courses in Costa Rica, Mexico's Southern Baja Peninsula and Yucatan Peninsula, and Honduras.
- Graduates' monthly salaries have increased by an average of 92%.

- To date, it is estimated that program graduates from the first 11 courses (half of these graduated within the last two years) have already generated additional revenue of more than $1 million (not including revenue from related, non-guiding services).

- In Baja California Sur, 65% of graduates have found employment as nature guides and another 18% are working or studying in conservation or ecotourism-related fields. Seventy percent have initiated or participated in community environmental education programs, and many others have started other local conservation projects.

- In Honduras, the majority of graduates have joined the staffs of the NGOs that manage protected areas. They are working as nature guides, educators, or public use coordinators.

The South African Nature Guide Training Program (NGTP-SA) Framework

(1) Goals

The overall goals of the NGTP-SA are:

- To train 16 residents of communities neighboring Namaqua, Augrabies Falls, and West Coast National Parks to be nature guides, environmental educators, and community tour operators.

- To introduce a set of nature guide training educational materials designed specifically for the ecosystems and cultural aspects of the course training sites.

- To offer follow-up support and technical assistance in community-based nature tourism and environmental education projects developed by the course graduates.

- To increase community awareness of the biological and economic importance of the surrounding natural resources.

- To develop, in each of the students, professional skills and personality traits that enrich and empower these individuals for better integrating with the local eco-tourism industry.

- To facilitate the acquisition of employment for each of the course graduates within the local eco-tourism industry.

- To increase the monthly earnings of the course graduates through local eco-tourism work.

(2) Orientation and Program Set-Up

A first priority was to establish an office and home for the core staff (Program Manager, Training Coordinators (2) and Natural History Coordinator) with the basic infrastructure in a town that would be most strategically located from which to administer the program in all three sites (National Parks) chosen for the course. Kamieskroon, a small town in the Namaqualand region of the Northern Cape Province, which is situated on the outskirts of the Namaqua National Park, proved to hold these qualities. Namaqua National Park is approximately equidistant (around 500km from each) of the two other collaborating parks and hence this region held a central position from which to operate the program.

The initial phase involved training the core staff in their various roles by two senior RARE Center staff, the ECDP Assistant Director and the Mexico NGTP Regional Director. As part of the staff preparation procedures, each staff member had to become familiar with relevant sections (to her or his terms of reference) of the NGTP Manual. This very comprehensive five-volume work is a compilation of background information, instructions and guidelines (supplied with past course examples) on how to set-up, manage, implement, evaluate and generally run a Nature Guide Training Program based on previous courses' experiences and tested methodologies.

The next phase had the two Training Coordinators (TC) prepare and train a group of North American volunteers for their course teaching roles in English, Interpretation and Assessment. The volunteers (to be referred as teachers in this document) offered their services through the World Teach program of Harvard University.

The program staff for course orientation purposes visited all three course-training sites and meetings were held with the parks' collaborators as a means to establish a relationship between the two partner organizations.

The NHC had the main responsibility of producing a natural history document, the *Guides Guide*, relevant to the three biomes/ecosystems of the areas where the course took place as well as additional chapters pertaining to general conservation and ecology. Unlike past courses due to the high English literacy level of the course candidates, as determined prior to the start of course, it was decided not to translate the *Guides Guide* into the area's mother tongue, Afrikaans, in the South African case.

During these initial two months the Program Manager and the program's collaborators in each park (Park Manager and Social Ecologist) *identified and pre-selected individuals* (through local advertising) from the respective communities of each park. These likely course candidates were invited to attend the *Student Selection Workshop*, which took place at each of the three parks.

Additionally, a Vision Workshop, organized by RARE-SA and held between all three collaborating parks (represented by their Social Ecologists, Park Managers and any other relevant and interested authorities) took place in Kamieskroon. This workshop had the main function of developing a working framework whereby the goals of the SANParks/NGTP-SA partnership could be met.

(3) Description of the Student Selection Process

The course was advertised in the form of pamphlets amongst the communities of the three collaborating national parks. This task was mainly achieved by the services of the parks' social ecology unit and in Namaqualand by the park manager and the Program Manager.

Pre-selection meetings were convened in order to enlighten interested candidates on the contents of the course and provide further information on the student selection workshop that would follow days ahead. Additionally, each interested candidate would be asked to fill an Application Form that was structured to determine whether the person held the pre-requisite qualities for acceptance. These personal criteria were:

- Age (18–35)
- Resident in the area
- Level of interest and experience in local community and conservation work
- Reasons for wanting to attend the course
- A high school level of literacy (in both South African primary national languages, English and Afrikaans)

In this manner a preliminary screening process was put in place.

On the day of the Student Selection Workshop a series of interviews, an oral and written comprehension test and a storytelling presentation was asked of each candidate. The two interviews and the storytelling components were conducted in Afrikaans to create a comfortable communication environment for the candidate (all the candidates held a preference for Afrikaans in light of it being the primary spoken language of the three community areas).

The two comprehension tests were handled in English as a means to allow the Training Coordinators and two Teachers (all four were North American) to interact with the candidates and assess their level of English in preparation for how to modify the Latin American English curriculum to the South African setting. The examiners consisted of NGTP and park staff.

As with all NGTP's, sixteen students were originally selected for the course. However, one candidate from the West Coast NP area resigned from the program during Site 2 of the course.

Four alternates (students with borderline selection results) were accepted into the program in place of successful selection candidates. The latter cancelled their places on the course due to having decided to accept some other career opportunity.

Three selections took place on different days for each of the park areas. Once the results were analyzed a series of discussion meetings amongst the staff would follow to assess the list of chosen course candidates. The selection result, based on the five tests would not always determine who would be selected, as priority was placed not only on test achievement but also on providing a unique opportunity to an individual with special interests in nature guiding. The latter could not always be determined by simply looking at the results.

In contrast with previous NGTP's, the candidates on this course had no relationship with a sponsor organization or supervisory institution, which in previous programs would contribute financially towards the student's course costs. Furthermore, except for four of the students (see table below) the NGTP-SA students had no connection with a conservation body and most were unemployed or held unpaid positions within their communities at the time of the course.

(4) Information of Course Participants

Neighboring National Park	Number of Candidate Students	Employment Status (at start of course) and Description of Activities
Namaqua National Park	7 Candidates	• Six unemployed • One is a nursery school teacher *Of the unemployed:* • One is a police reserve officer • The other live under family support systems, acquire temporary work where available and practice farming.

continued next page

continued from previous page

Neighboring National Park	Number of Candidate Students	Employment Status (at start of course) and Description of Activities
Augrabies Falls National Park	5 Candidates	• Four unemployed • One is a Field Ranger at Augrabies Falls National Park *Of the unemployed:* • One is a community farmer and the Treasurer for the Riemvasmaak Community Development Trust. • One is a community framer and an Honorary Ranger of SANParks. • One works for the local council • One runs a tuck-shop
West Coast National Park	3 Candidates	• One unemployed who lives with the parents • Two work as Junior Assistants for the West Coast Fossil Park

(5) Program Schedule

Pre-Selection of Course Candidates	by 23 April

Student Selection Workshop
   • Namaqua National Park
   • Augrabies Falls National Park
   • West Coast National Park
	
	02 May
	07 May
	10 May

Vision Workshop (in Kamieskroon)	04 May

Start of Course
   Course Sites
   • Augrabies Falls NP
      Waterfall Bushcamp
Course break
   • West Coast NP
      Geelbek Environmental Centre
Course break
   • Namaqua NP
      Kookfontein Eco-tourism Camp
      *Kamieskroon Hotel
      Skilpad Environmental Resource Centre
      Student Graduation
	21 May
	
	21 May–12 June
	13–17 June
	
	18 June–11 July
	11–15 July
	
	16 July–24 July
	24 July–02 August
	02 August–11 August
	11 August

continued next page

continued from previous page

* The course stay at the Kamieskroon Hotel was an unforeseen contingency situation that developed due to poor weather in Kookfontein and temporary inadequate facilities at Skilpad.
Course Follow-up (by Training Coordinators and Volunteers)   20 August–20 September
Post Course Follow-up (by NGTP-SA Program Manager & Park collaborators)   October 2001–Feb 2002

(6) The Course

The NGTP-SA course adopted a similar approach to previous NGTPs where students were immersed in an intensive three-month training course with the following main curricula: (1) English language, (2) Natural History (general and applied ecology), (3) Interpretation (guiding skills) and (4) Tourism Services (a new module to the NGTP).

In distinct contrast to Latin American programs, however, the English part of the training was given very limited attention due to the fact that, in South Africa, English is one of the official languages taught at school. Nevertheless the English-only rule was still enforced where English was the only language spoken both in and outside of class. Hence, the English immersion aspect of the NGTP course philosophy was still very seriously entrenched in an effort to develop bilingual nature guides.

A great emphasis was placed on outdoor instruction both for the natural history and interpretation components of the course.

In order to spark the students' interest and motivation the start of classes often included a fun activity with an educational slot such as Bird of the Day (guessing exercise) and Word of the Day (a challenging term for the group). Warm-up exercises were used in developing team dynamics and spirit. These activities as well as campfire and after-hours entertainment were organized by student groups. Everyone was given numerous opportunities for developing inherent leadership qualities.

Student Assessment exercises incorporated Baseline tests (the same test completed twice—at the start and end of course) in English, Natural History and Interpretation. Additionally, weekly evaluations were done, which tested the week's natural history and interpretation materials covered to date.

English baseline levels were evaluated using the ACTFL (American Council on the Teaching of Foreign Languages) system, a well-recognized tool, which is developed to measure the level of a candidate's communication skills.

Once a week each student would give a prepared tour to the staff and peers. These tours would test the student on the Interpretation curriculum (based on the "Twenty Characteristics of a Good Guide," see page 204), which ultimately assesses the student's overall competency in field guiding.

With each successive week the tours would increase in time, having started as a 10-minute tour and at the end of the course the practice tours were of over an hour in length.

The South African NGTP opened the way for the inclusion of a new component to the syllabus, the Tourism Services module. This was partly due to less importance being placed in teaching English with a resulting available time for developing a practical entrepreneurial module where students were taught the business skills for designing itinerary packages based on what their areas can offer in eco-tourism.

In an effort to diversify and expand on the content of the course curriculum, guest speakers (of various expertises in natural and cultural history) as well as field trips were included in the program.

(7) Description of the Course Curricula
(A) English
In previous NGTPs an English workbook and dialogue tape would form the basis for the English curriculum. Based on the high English levels of this program's students (compared to the Latin American programs), a decision was made to omit the use of this tool.

The main challenge in the English area turned out to be something that had not been anticipated—the constant use by a number of students of incorrect tenses and conjugations. They generally knew what was correct but had used the incorrect grammar for so long, during their lives, that to change into the correct mind-set in adulthood made it almost impossible. The RARE/WorldTeach methodology is based on the "Communicative Approach" which holds that effective communication is the goal, not perfect grammar. In this light, all of the students came in with perfectly acceptable, understandable English.

However, when beginning a course, one always strives to make improvements. So, a decision had to be made about whether to follow the communicative approach and allow the students to speak freely in English with periodic lapses of bad grammar and focus instead on other guiding needs. The alternative would have been to give attention to grammar, knowing that there was a risk that insisting upon correct grammar would make the students who were already extremely self-conscious of their English even more hesitant to use it. Eventually it was decided that it was more important for the students to express themselves freely than to have every sentence correctly spoken. In some classes verb tenses were taught, and grammar was corrected in certain circumstances but this was not a focus of this program.

(B) Natural History

The reason for the Natural History Curriculum was to educate the guides on all aspects of Natural History, with particular relation to the course sites. These included: Geology, Climatology, Botany, Zoology (invertebrates and all major vertebrate groups), Ecology, Astronomy and general knowledge on Conservation (history, institutions, practices, etc.).

The goals of the Natural History curriculum were to ensure that during the three-month course period, and during follow-up, the guides were taught sufficient information on the above subjects to enable them to:

- Easily use the relevant field-guide books to access information on their own
- Answer simple questions about any of these subjects
- Interrelate any of these subjects

Most initial lessons about the various animal groups were "the parts of the…" lessons, in order to label the important parts of animals in question. This enabled the students to fully utilize whichever guidebook they happened to use. This initial lesson would also include characteristics of the animal group, (i.e., what makes this animal different from all the other animals?).

Existing lesson plans (based on the Latin American model) had to be altered, as the English proficiency of the NGTP-SA students was higher than that of the Spanish speaking counterparts. This resulted in a shortened lesson time as it was found that the students were able to quickly grasp the lesson themes. Thus it was decided to combine several lesson-plans together. Initially the students were slow to absorb the class material. Eventually during the second week of the Site 1 (Augrabies Falls National Park) they were so avid for new information it was difficult to keep up with their thirst for knowledge. Consequently, to maintain a teaching and learning momentum it was decided to combine lesson-plans. For example, lizards and frogs were combined into one lesson for 4 hours, instead of two separate lessons of 4 hours each.

(C) Birding Curriculum

A birding curriculum was taught outside the context of the Natural History classes and mainly involved morning bird identification walks and specific classes on bird biology related to the "bird watching" field.

As an incentive to create an interest in bird watching amongst our students, a Birding Competition was held for the duration of Site 2 (West Coast National Park). The top three birders were awarded prizes and certificates on the last night of this course site. It was very noticeable how certain individuals had a natural appreciation and acuteness for the bird watching activity while others would find it a constant challenge.

(D) Interpretation

The pre-existing proficiency in English allowed students to surpass the usual accumulation of ecological facts and information to focus more on interrelationships in nature.

In previous NGTPs, the interpretation curriculum comprised solely of the Twenty Guide Characteristics (see table on the next page).

For this program, however, the curriculum was expanded into a more all-encompassing exercise in critical thinking. "*Interpretation*" for this program was defined as: *"The ability to unite the public with the environment through an intimate knowledge of the environment, enhanced communication skills, and a focus on the interrelationships that exist within nature."*

A more detailed explanation of the three aspects of the curriculum are discussed below:

Using Guide Characteristics as Tools of Communication

Students learned the RARE Center's "Twenty Characteristics of a Good Guide" as the standards of effective communication techniques with the public in a

A "GOOD GUIDE"

1. Speaks Loudly and Clearly
2. Uses Non-Verbal Communication; Smiles; Makes eye contact; Body language
3. Acts Professionally; Greets tourists; Is punctual and courteous; Is honest; says "I don't know"; Dresses well
4. Prepares in Advance; Knows about site; Community Inventory; Researches; Practices
5. Provides Necessary Information for Tourists; Informs visitors of the location, time, and length of tour; Informs visitors what they will need to bring and wear; Informs visitors of park rules and special considerations
6. Knows the Audience; Learns about visitors in between stops; Uses visitor info to make examples more personal
7. Helps Tourists learn by Themselves; Asks questions; Uses Guided Discovery
8. Uses the Senses
9. Has a Message for Every Presentation; Simple full sentence message; Catchy title indicating the message
10. Prepares a Structure for Presentation; Uses an introduction, stops, and a conclusion; Writes an outline; Chooses between stationary presentation and tours
11. Is a Nature Detective
12. Suggests a Relevant Conservation Action; Explains environmental and conservation problems; Suggests an action that tourists can undertake to help protect the area; Offers information relevant to general conservation issues; Helps visitors to care for the site during their visit
13. Manages the Group; Makes sure everyone can see and hear well; Chooses comfortable locations for stops; Assures visitors safe passage
14. Makes the Presentation Dynamic; Games/Activities; Demonstrations; Uses props
15. Has a POW; Introduces message with a gripping interpretive illustration
16. Uses Interesting Language; Delivers information with descriptive language such as Natural History Stories; Uses Guided Imagery
17. Makes Smooth Transitions between Stops; Asks questions or provides an activity to maintain tourist interest between stops; Builds suspense at end of stops; Takes advantage of Teachable Moments
18. Carries Appropriate Equipment
19. Evaluates the Tour; Asks visitors questions at the end...check for learning; Does a self-evaluation; Gives the brief tourist survey to visitors
20. Follows Up with Visitors; Sends visitors answers to questions; Sends "thank you" solicitation letters to some visitors; Organizes conservation actions with visitors that help guide's protected area; Works with parks in developing follow-up actions with visitors

guiding environment. Examples of these characteristics were: always prepare in advance; manage the group effectively; provide tourists with all necessary information; suggest a relevant conservation action tourists can do at home; and always make the presentation dynamic. This list of characteristics facilitated the communication between the guide and the public to experience the environment in new and exciting ways.

Forging an Intimate Knowledge of the Environment

Students were encouraged to personally develop a relationship with nature regardless of their prior knowledge or experience. The goal was to encourage curiosity and discovery and not allow students to feel discouraged by the overwhelming amount of facts and information to which they were being exposed. Opportunities for individual connections with nature could consist of admiring the beautiful scenery, discovering a previously unfamiliar species, or exploring new landscapes through extended physical activities. Once the students forged an intimate connection with their environment, they began working on ways to facilitate this phenomenon in others. They started by identifying ways in which they could assist the public in making their own personal connection with the environment.

Identifying Interrelationships in the Environment

This is inevitably the quintessential aim of guide training with regards to this curriculum's definition of interpretation. Essentially, the goal is to be able to interpret what is happening in the environment for visitors. This includes an explanation of disjointed environmental clues and observations as well as the inter-relatedness between those clues that might otherwise be unknown to the public. A guide should enlighten the public to sights previously overlooked. They should also explore possible explanations for nature's mysteries, and expose the tourists to new ways of looking at their surroundings. Guides should ideally inter-relate clues from their surroundings to communicate a story to visitors. Such environmental clues may include signs of approaching weather, rock formations, animal tracks, or particular plant diversity. It is the role of the guide to explain the inter-relationship between these clues and relate it to the visitor. Visitors also develop a personal understanding of these relationships through the help of the guide.

Class Design

The curriculum used various means to facilitate the students' personal interaction with nature. With vast amounts of facts being covered in the Natural History curriculum, the Interpretation classes provided an opportunity for students to break away from the traditional classroom setting and spend valuable time in the field. Students regularly faced open-ended questions that required critical thinking skills.

To some it was a new concept that in interpretation there were not always correct or incorrect answers. Classes began with simple associations. They were asked to link certain plants and animals with other familiar objects. Students were asked, "What does this remind you of?" Or, "What does it feel like?" Exercises consisted of sensory tours such as a Blind Walk where students were blindfolded and led along a trail where they utilized the remaining four senses to experience their environment. Other classes involved students interpreting objects for one another, encouraged to be as creative as possible. Next, students learned how to make information more relevant to visitors. This included "painting a visual picture" for tourists with descriptive language. It also included stating facts and statistics in more colorful and creative means that were more relevant to visitors. For example, a guide might say, "The giraffe stands 3.5 meters at the shoulders … that means that two of you ladies standing on top of one another would only just come up to the giraffe's back." Students were also taught how to make presentations more interactive for tourists. By including the tourists and allowing them to get a more hands on experience, visitors internalize and retain more of the information they are presented with.

Scavenger Hunts

A very popular part of the curriculum included more of an adventure, discovery element in which students were required to use their interpretation skills in the field to complete certain tasks.

A series of Scavenger Hunts that increased in complexity were created as the course went on. Students were divided into teams and embarked for most of the day before returning to camp to present their results.

The first scavenger hunt consisted of finding items in the field that corresponded to interpretive descriptions on a list.

The second scavenger hunt included students receiving riddles depicting a particular location in all of Augrabies Waterval Bush Camp covering many kilometers in the process. Students were to work together to figure out which location the riddle referred to given the environmental clues, and hike there to receive the next clue.

At West Coast National Park, students were split into two teams, and sent on a 16-kilometer hike. They had to answer a range of difficult interpretive questions corresponding to various sites along the trail. An example of an interpretive question is, "Why are there so many broken white mussel shells on the beach when these shells are strong enough to stand up to raging surf year after year?" A possible answer is that the seagulls pick up the mussels, fly high above the beach, and then drop them on the hard sand attempting to break them open and prey upon the flesh inside.

The final scavenger hunt involved a mapping exercise at the Kookfontein Eco-tourism camp where students were broken up into four teams and each set out in one of the cardinal directions to map their own interpretive exploration. The students shared their maps with others so that they may follow their lead and experience some of the extraordinary sights surrounding our eco-tourist camp.

(8) Follow-up
Course Follow-up

For the one-month following the course, back in their communities, the students were assisted by the program's volunteers and training coordinators in their potential integration within the tourism markets of their areas and neighboring park.

The students were encouraged to develop realistic tour itineraries, guided trails, environmental education programs, marketing tools and eco-tourism business plans based on their respective interests and local opportunities.

Additionally, the Natural History Coordinator moved between the three community areas and gave classes to the students in preparation for the FGASA (Field Guides Association of Southern Africa) Level 1 exam. RARE Center registered each student with FGASA as a means to open the way to a professional guiding career for each of the students. Although not yet enforced, the South African tourism legislation stipulates that anyone guiding must be accredited by a nationally recognized system, such as FGASA. FGASA Level 1 is the elementary entrance into the professional field guiding industry of South Africa.

Post Course Follow-up (October 2001–February 2002)

During this time the Program Manager will be the sole staff member of the program and will be responsible to continue to fill the role as intermediate/interface between the students and the parks. During these five months, periodic visits will be made to the collaborating parks and meetings will be held with the graduate guides as a means to measure their developments and facilitate their further developments.

Program Results

(1) Course Results—Assessments for the 15 Course Students

English Assessment

English assessment happened twice, once at the start and once at the end of course. The same test was administered and the results analyzed using the ACTFL system.

English Baseline Test Scores for start and end of course. Numbers of students in brackets.

Start of course ACTFL Score	End of course ACTFL score
5 (3)	7 (1)
6 (8)	8 (6)
7 (4)	8.5 (2)
	9 (6)
Average 6	**Average 8.5**
(Intermediate High) 9 (6)	**(Advanced Mid-High)**

ACTFL SCORING			
Level	Name	Level	Name
1	Novice Low	6	Intermediate High
2	Novice Mid	7	Advanced Low
3	Novice High	8	Advanced Mid
4	Intermediate Low	9	Advanced High
5	Intermediate Mid	10	Superior

All the students finished within the ACTFL advanced level and as the average shows, most finished at the advanced mid or high level.

Natural History Assessment

The Baseline Natural History test was done on the first day of course to test the students' background knowledge in this discipline.

As reflected in the results below, the students came into the course with very little background knowledge in Natural History. The average score for this test at the start of course was 18%. The same baseline test was then administered on the last day of course, "End of Course," to test the students' progress. The average score was 72%.

The Improvement result reflects the candidate's increase in Natural History knowledge between the start of the course (when the baseline test was done) and the end of the course. Hence, it shows a mere jump in improvement. The candidate's overall natural history performance during the course, however, was tested in the weekly natural history knowledge tests, which tested the curriculum matter taught over the past week.

Natural History range of percentage scores for Baseline tests (BL), Improvement BL results (between start and end of course) and Weekly tests. Numbers of students are shown in brackets.

Start of Course BL	End of Course BL	Improvement in BL	Weekly NH Test (Average)
5–25% (12)	45–60% (1)	100–300% (6)	60–75% (5)
20–50% (3)	60–75% (8)	400–700% (9)	75–100 (10)
	75–90% (6)		
Average 18%	**Average 72%**	**Approx. Average 400%**	**Average 81%**

Although not shown in this table, those who entered with higher levels of knowledge show smaller improvements but better performance (weekly tests) and those who come in with lower knowledge levels show much higher improvement but not overall performance.

The aim of the natural history evaluation was to give a weekly assessment test for each of the ten weeks, however, due to the rescheduling of classes and unforeseen logistical challenges, it was not possible to conduct a test per week. Seven tests were given in all, and in these tests all of the Natural History material taught was covered.

Interpretation Assessment

The Interpretation curriculum was based on developing in each of the students the "Twenty Characteristics of a Good Guide" (see page 204). These were progressively taught and concurrently tested (during the Tour testing sessions) on a weekly basis. As new characteristics were taught so the practice tours increased in length.

The assessment tool for testing the Characteristics of a Good Guide was used for both the Start and End of Course Baseline Interpretation assessment.

The average for all 15 students was 20% and 84% for the start and end respectively.

The average of all the students' scores for both baseline tests as well as the weekly assessments was 69%.

As for the Natural History assessment scores an improvement percentage score (between the baseline scores at the start and end of course) was calculated to give a student's percentage of improvement. Seven students improved by a margin of between 100–400% while 8 students improved by a margin of between 500–800%. The average margin of improvement was 400%.

Range of percentage scores in Interpretation Baseline (BL) at start and end of course and the Final Average. Numbers of student are shown in brackets.

Start of Course BL	End of Course BL	Improvement in BL	*Final Average
8–20% (9)	75–85% (9)	100–400% (7)	50–65% (6)
21–40% (6)	86–98% (6)	500–800% (8)	66–85% (9)
	75–90% (6)		
Start of Course BL	**End of Course BL**	**Improvement in BL**	***Final Average**
Average 20%	**Average 84%**	**Approx. Average 400%**	**Average 69%**

*This average includes the results of the weekly Tours in conjunction with both the baseline tests results.

(2) Post Course Results

Eco-Tourism Opportunities

Primarily, RARE Center measures the success of a NGTP based on two criteria:

1. Post course student employment in the field of eco-tourism guiding and conservation.
2. Increased student income derived from an eco-tourism or field guiding related field.

Both these criteria have only been achieved in a very limited way, to date.

The following factors have contributed towards this scenario:

1. Most of the course participants were unemployed at the start of the course (see page 198, Information of Course Participants).
2. Except for the three already employed candidates, there was no work guarantee in place for any of the other course graduates.
3. Minimal conservation experience in the course students. Practically all the students had neither experience in field guiding or in a conservation-related field prior to the course.
4. In the Namaqualand region, in particular, from where seven of the course graduates originate, the eco-tourism industry is restricted to the wildflower season over the two months of spring.

(3) Prospects

The following field guiding and eco-tourism opportunities exist for the graduate guides:

- Possibility of work with the neighboring national park and private game reserves.
- Involvement in the tourism developments of their areas through the local government authorities.
- The three graduate guides already employed in a conservation-related field can expand their activities to include field guiding.
- Initiation of their own eco-tourism enterprise.

Lessons Learned and Recommendations

Overall it is felt that the Nature Guide Training Program is an extremely valuable tool in the training of under-advantaged individuals as field guides from communities neighboring any class of protected area. Testimony to this was the unanimous praise the students had for the course almost throughout its full three months of operation and most definitely on graduation day.

However, certain factors based on the experiences of this particular course should be taken into account and are recommended for future courses:

- For the application of the course in English speaking countries, a revised English curriculum needs to be devised.
- A greater level of student accountability and responsibility should be demanded from each course candidate. As in Latin American programs a system should be put in place whereby a student has to be answerable to an organized structure such as a sponsoring NGO, community-based forum, protected area management, etc.
- In this way a greater student commitment to the course is generated and the future chance for employment improved for the graduate guide.
- Accreditation of the course offered by the NGTP with the necessary South African guiding authorities under the Department of Environment Affairs and Tourism.

Local community trainees in Nature Guide Training, Namaqualand, South Africa.

Wilderness and Traditional Peoples of the Amazon

Martin Von Hildebrand

We all want to contribute to the conservation of the environment, of the rainforest. We come with different experiences and perspectives, and that is very important. The diversity in our points of view contributes enormously to creating an environmentally sustainable society. Many different people have important contributions to make to this process, particularly people from cultures that are different from our western culture. Many of these cultures are as ancient as—if not older than—our culture. All of these traditional people must contribute their considerable knowledge to this process. As an example, let's explore the Amazon Rainforest, my experience there, the cosmology of the people, and what is currently happening in the Colombian Amazon.

The Colombian Amazon is 400,000 kilometres in size, which represents 8% of the Amazon Basin. This northwest part of the Amazon Basin is the most naturally and culturally bio-diverse, with the least outside interference. It is a mix of legally recognized indigenous territories with collective property rights, rainforest that is uninhabited, and about 5 million hectares that has been declared National Parks. (These parks are not directly threatened; they have very few people in the area, and do not demand a great deal of care in the sense of protecting them. There is no pressure on them, as long as the parks do not overlap with indigenous territories, inhabited by people.)

There are no roads or towns here. You can only access this part of the Amazon by river. When one flies over this area, one has the overwhelming sense of its remoteness. You imagine that if you might have to land in the middle of the forest you would be completely lost. And yet one does not realize that people live under this dense canopy. There are people thinking. There are a lot of intellectual processes going on that have to do with the environment and with the modern world.

The forest is not flat: there are mountains and rock formations in the area. Although the forest has this tremendous canopy—it gives you the impression of being very humid, which it is—it does not mean that the land is fertile. The soil is poor quality and very acidic. If you cut down the forest, the rain dissolves and washes away the nutrients. The forest is very slow in recuperating; it takes three or four years for the land to begin recovering, but the forest only recuperates in 10, 15, 20 years, depending on the area. Significantly, if you keep an area open for 10 years it will take 100 years to recuperate.

The Amazon rain forest contrasts with the wilderness in Africa. Whereas east and southern Africa has herds of game and large animals, the Amazonian rainforest has very few large animals (the biggest animal is the jaguar) and there are practically no herds. Instead, there is great diversity of individual species of trees and animals.

We have found vestiges of civilization here in the Amazon, with rock cave dwellings that go back to about 10,000 years. Within an area of the size of England, there are 60,000 inhabitants, with 55 different ethnic groups and languages. Some of the groups constitute 6,000 people, but most groups include 150, 200 or 300 people. Although there might be a one-day travel distance between one group and another, each group maintains a diversity and identity in language and culture. People living here use certain elements from the western

culture (i.e., metal tools and clothes), but they still maintain their language and traditions. They live fundamentally according to their traditional way of life. The people from communities here travel by river and often travel on foot around the falls. They make their own canoes. Ritual dance in the dry season is associated with cultivated foods. The spirits of the river come and dance with human beings, and give them food for harvest.

People live in large communal houses made up of one single space. You might find 50 or 60 people living in the house—an extended family of several nuclear families with parents, their sons and wives, a married woman from another ethnic group, etc. Around these houses is a garden and these houses are often a day's distance one from another.

In spite of the abundance of the plants and of the forest itself in the Amazon, one has an exhaustible amount of nutrients or food to live off in the immediate surrounds. In the forest, there are large areas of rocks and water, and the earth is not that fertile. People that live in the forest—and the animals that live in the forest—have to go and look for their food and spend quite a bit of time doing this. It is not that easy to find a place for a communal house. You need a good place for gardens, you have to have good fishing places and good hunting opportunities. If one lives in the forest one does not have an inexhaustible amount of nutrients or food to live off. What the forest has to offer is limited. Resources are defined by the different biological and environmental aspects because the territories of each ethnic group are limited. Beyond each group's territory are other ethnic groups. They cannot access those territories without having conflicts, without asking special permission.

The amount of nutrients in these areas is limited not only for human beings who live there, but also the animals. Animals have to live and the people there are very aware of this. People talk about "faku"—vital energy—that is precious and limited. Each group of animals and human beings have to have a basic quality of water to be able to survive. They need a basic amount of energy to survive. To be able to guarantee this source of energy, they believe that the animals, the plants, and the human beings have god in spirit. This spirit god will guarantee that their group will have enough vital energy to be able to survive.

At the origin of life for this world, animals and human beings were close to the sea. Where the rivers run into the sea, where the sun rises in the east, there was a large communal house. The spirit of the jaguar brought eggs to this house. Vital energy was born from these eggs. This energy of life travelled beneath the water of the rivers, and started emerging in different parts of the forest. In the different places of the forest they came forth as animals and sometimes as human beings. When they came forth as animals they became the guardian spirits of that area and of the animals that would later inhabit that area. So they would be in charge of seeing that that area would have enough vital energy to be able to survive. Those that appeared on the rivers became human beings, and grew into the different ethnic groups. In the places where they were born they had an intimate spiritual relation, an energetic relation, with their environment because they belonged in that place and that is the place of which they must take care.

Consequently, when an indigenous person walks in the forest he is not walking through an open forest area, but a free area. The moment he leaves the territory where he has his house and his garden area—which might be an hour distance walking around his house—he moves into somebody else's territories; territories or areas that have what they would say their own administrators or caretakers, and he must ask permission to use anything in those territories. He must request to use the trees or to hunt an animal because there is somebody responsible for them. And so, when they walk through the forest, the forest is completely inhabited by these beings—which from their point of view are also humans in the sense that they come from the same vital energy as we do. All humans and spirit come from this vital energy, "faku," which can also be translated into the word "salt" because it is an energy that is intelligent, creates life, and has a "primary order" in it. It is not just simple energy; it is energy that creates energy, that structures, and that gives life.

So as they walk through the forest and they want to use the forest, they have to ask permission. What does this mean—to ask permission? This is something that the headman does, or possibly the medicine man. The medicine man—who of course transcends our concept of western medicine—or the headman are highly trained in many practices, temporal and spiritual. They concentrate and enter into contact with the guardian spirits of the animals of the forest.

When all children are born their thought is taken back to the origin of life—to the place where the sun rises and to the place of the primary ancestors. Here will be defined what they will be—trained as headman, administrators, chanters for their communal house, or just simply as wood gatherers. Whatever activity, everybody has a function in society. From the moment of birth each person begins to be trained, to learn certain stories and to keep a very strict diet. Any amount of "energy" will give them strength and allow them to reproduce. If they use too much energy they become "contaminated"—that is, they may look like human beings but they have become the energy of the animals. In that case, the spirit of the animals, seeing their own energy in the people, will pull back their energy and the people will become sick.

The cause of illness is also understood in the context of abuse of the forest. When too much energy is taken from the forest, the animals hunt people with illnesses in the same way that people hunt animals. There is a current exchange of reciprocity. When the people ask permission, they offer community. Within ritual they dance and they enter into sacred spaces; they move into fundamental energy again just as, originally, they came up the river to come into contact with that energy. In that contact, they relate directly to the animals and they can send back that energy to them. Whatever they eat or drink will go back into the animals. It is in these rituals, held every time the seasons change, that the head-man will put food restrictions and sexual restrictions upon the group. He tells them how they must live for the next season. The seasons depend on when the fruit is harvested. There can be 14/16 seasons, depending on the culture, in a year when someone falls ill.

An individual illness is an indicator that something has gone wrong with the environment, with relation to the environment or relations within society. So, when someone falls ill the headman gets the community together and immediately analyses the source. He goes through the mythology, through the models of understanding the environment, puts food and sexual restrictions on these people, and then tries to cure the individual. If the individual dies it is understandable because he or she is releasing the energy that has been over-accumulated in the community. Therefore, illness of the individual is an indicator that society and the relationship with the environment has gone wrong and order needs to be restored. A lot of the headman's work, together with that of the chanters and the rituals, is to establish and maintain this balance of nature.

Now, we might say that all this is fine and this is what these people do traditionally but how does that affect us? What has this got to do with Colombia today or even with South Africa? Well, it has to do with indigenous people retaining 210,000 sq. km of rainforest. They own this collectively in an inalienable way. They own the natural resources and the right to administer these territories. This is similar to a municipality and in this sense they can, from a western, administrative and political point of view administer their territory like a municipality. In this sense the headman is even referred to as the chairman. They can have agreements with the rest of government and they can receive funds, etc. They can decide how the national resources are to be handled, in joint responsibility with the rest of the state. They are not totally independent, but they can do it according to their tradition and knowledge.

Seventy percent of all the forest in Colombia is in the hands of the indigenous people. If we looked at the whole Amazon Basin, 15–20% of the Amazon Basin is in the hands of the indigenous people. This is a way to ultimately protect the environment because indigenous people depend so directly on natural resources. They will not let other people come in and take the resources because this is their life source. Just as we want to have a bank account to send our children to the best

universities, they want to have a genetic banker, a biological bank. They want a forest bank. They want a place for their children to live and to grow up in. So they are directly committed to the protection of the rainforest, they are spiritually committed with the rain forest and they see themselves as part of the rain forest. They do not see themselves as owners, even if the state has recognized that they own this land. From their point of view, the land belongs to the birds, to the animals, to the water and to them. They are part of it, it does not belong to them. They belong to the land as much as all the animals and all the other species belong to the land. But in western terms, they understand they must have a piece of paper to say "this is mine, please do not trespass." Their knowledge has developed over 10,000 years. They have an intimate relationship with the environment and they have proved that they can preserve this environment because 10,000 years later the forest is there. What is important, I think, is it is not pristine forest. It is a landscape that has modified as a result of people living there. But this landscape has been kept by them and is based on many, many century's knowledge that they have developed. In this sense, what they are doing now—and I mentioned beneath this canopy there is a lot of intellectual work going on, not only from a traditional point of view—is articulating with the western world.

They are developing systems of education based on their traditional knowledge and their understanding of the forest, but articulating with the West. They are finding in traditional knowledge, and in the forest, the laws of chemistry, the laws of physics and the laws of mathematics. Yet from their point of view, without having to imitate or follow our way directly, they can understand the relations with the forest the way we see it. They are articulating the fundamental process of education based on their identity and their knowledge, but they are bringing in western knowledge through literacy and health needs.

This is an extremely long and difficult process because nobody has the answer—it has to be built. We have to construct it. It will take years to look for new paths where the two cultures can articulate and be built into something that will maintain their identity in the forest and yet allow them to have a dignified life to access the western world. I can see the same thing being done for health, for education, for government and for environmental management because there are obviously elements from our culture that are useful. It is valuable for them to understand westernized laws and at the same time to look for alternative economic projects—processes that will enable them to access the markets, but without spoiling the environment. This is extremely important. When the people have something to defend, when the people have the responsibility, when they have a chance to manage the forest and have an income then they will resist others' ways of exploiting the forest. They will be resistant to oil companies, they will resist mining, because they have something to defend not only from a traditional point of view but also from western point of view. So it is fundamental that the land be recognized, that the laws recognize these people who can run these territories. It is important that they build an alternative themselves. It is not something we can do from outside because we would be empowering our own models again. So there is a tremendous process of analysis that is going into this community as it is being built.

Although we talk about culture when we talk with them, sometimes we believe that the culture is disappearing or changing or there is a loss of culture. They will say "no it is not being lost." The culture is there, it is like the seed that lies in the ground for years and years and then sprouts again. The culture is both external expression—the way we live—but it is also internal, within the people. There is a fundamental internal element of culture in our deep feeling, our relationship to other people and our relationship to the environment. As long as we can keep that deep feeling we will have culture. Cultures change constantly and bring you enemies. Even if one thinks that the culture has disappeared, deep down it is there. They believe in that and live by it.

It is a question of enabling the preservers of an indigenous culture to endure—to run their own territories, to enable their own decisions, to run their own lives and to be taken seriously not only in a political administrative sense, but to recognize their knowledge as valid. It is not only western knowledge, not only scientific knowledge that is valid. We must understand other ways of seeing the world. We cannot say that we can do justice to the animals and the environment unless we do justice to these people; to all these different cultures who have been excluded in the name of progress that have been excluded in the name of science, and sometimes excluded in the name of wilderness.

Wilderness means something different in this setting than it does in our developed, technological world. For the wilderness movement to have true value it must take this other reality into account, allow it to grow and evolve, and learn from it as it will learn from us.

Involving Communities
in Protected Area Management

Local Boards in KwaZulu-Natal

Khulani Mkhize

Ezemvelo KZN Wildlife is a parastatal biodiversity conservation service in the KwaZulu-Natal province of South Africa. It was formed in 1998 out of two conservation organizations, the Natal Parks Board (NPB) and the KwaZulu Department of Nature Conservation (DNC) established during the apartheid era. The former was the conservation service of the "white" Natal province and the latter the service run by the "homeland" government of KwaZulu.

Ezemvelo KZN Wildlife has a specific policy to involve neighboring communities in the nature conservation activities of their local protected areas. Against the backdrop of a significant socio-political transformation in South Africa, that policy emphasizes the development and role of Local Boards. These are statutory bodies, constituted to represent the concerns and interests of neighboring communities and other stakeholders in the management of protected areas. Although there have been important successes, the Local Board initiative is still very fragile (as may be expected in a complex and ever-changing political environment) and the future of the Local Boards remains largely dependent on policies and resource allocation decisions that are outside the control of Ezemvelo KZN Wildlife. The "story" of the Local Boards has involved both success and difficulty, and the lessons thus-far learned will contribute to addressing the ongoing challenge of involving resource poor communities in nature conservation in less-developed regions and countries.

Nature Conservation in KwaZulu-Natal: A Brief History

People have inhabited the area known as the province of KwaZulu-Natal for at least 5,000 years. The first inhabitants, the San, lived as hunter-gatherers and signs of their occupation can still be seen in the rock paintings scattered throughout the province, but most notably in the Ukuhlamba-Drakensberg mountain range. Iron-age farmers and pastoralists, from whom the Nguni people (which include the modern amaZulu) are descended, migrated from the great lakes region of East Africa and had already been living in the area for about 1,000 years by the time the Portuguese navigator Vasco da Gama sailed around the coast on Christmas day 1747. He named the lush green land that he saw, "Natal" to commemorate the birth of Christ.

The domestication of cattle was an important component of the cultures of the emerging Nguni kingdoms. But the impact of the on wildlife was limited as the human settlements were restricted to areas free from Nagana (Trypanosomiasis), an indigenous disease of domestic livestock and humans which is harbored by wildlife and transmitted by the tsetse fly. However, as in other parts of Africa, the shifting cultivation that formed part of the Nguni livelihood strategy was accomplished through the widespread practice of "slash and burn." Large amounts of timber were also needed for smelting furnaces for these iron-age farmers. As a result of the farming and smelting activities, the open woodland and grassland that is found in large parts of KwaZulu-Natal may have displaced what was once indigenous forests and closed woodlands. This probably had greater impact on the biodiversity of the region than the hunting that was practiced to supplement their livelihoods.

Although hunting probably had a negligible impact on the wildlife of the area, the amaKhosi (chiefs) of the various Nguni clans introduced the first conservation laws of the region as early as the beginning of the 19th century. During his rule from 1819 to 1828, King Shaka (who had welded the Nguni clans into a powerful Zulu nation) kept a tight control on hunting, decreeing that certain animal "trophies" such as leopard skins, lion claws and crane feathers, could be worn only by royalty. He also set aside an area at the confluence of the Black and White Umfolozi Rivers, in what is now the Umfolozi-Hluhluwe Park, for ceremonial hunts.

The coexistence of people and wildlife was severely disrupted after the death of Shaka. Port Natal (now Durban), established by the British in 1824, grew rapidly into a thriving trading center for wildlife products such as ivory, rhino horn and buffalo hides. Mpande, the Zulu King who succeeded Shaka, benefited from the wildlife trade and therefore encouraged the killing of elephant, rhino, buffalo, kudu and other antelope. Antelope and especially buffalo (together with domestic cattle) were further decimated by an epidemic of rinderpest toward the end of the century. Goodman (2002) estimates that as much as 80% of these species died during the epidemic. But, of all the species, it was rhino that were the most threatened; they had virtually become extinct by the time the first "game reserves" were established in Natal in 1895. As in the rest of sub-Saharan Africa, it was European "big game" hunters who campaigned for the establishment of these "game reserves" and the protection of large mammal species.

Adams and Hulme argue that the hunting of large mammals as a sport was interwoven with the European colonization of Africa (and other parts of the world).

> As colonial territories enacted laws restricting or banning hunting, Africans who hunted for the pot or for trade were reclassified ... as "poachers." Conservation legislation set aside areas of land, and certain quarry species, for European hunters. Most contemporary government conservation departments in sub-Saharan Africa have their origins in agencies established to defend hunting reserves and suppress "poaching." [Adams, 2001 #295]

The first game reserves to be established in what is now South Africa were the Pongola Reserve (1894) in the old Zuid-Afrikaanse Republiek and four reserves in the then British Colony of Natal, viz., the Umfolozi Junction Reserve, Hluhluwe Valley Reserve, the Mdletshe Reserve and the St. Lucia Reserve (all in 1897). The latter is now part of the Greater St. Lucia Wetland Park, a World Heritage site. The Giant's Castle Game Reserve, now part of the Ukuhlamba-Drakenberg World Heritage site followed in 1903 and in 1912 (the year that the former British colonies and Boer republics came together to form the modern South African state) the Mkhuze Game Reserve was proclaimed. In the succeeding 80 years more than 70 reserves and parks were added to these by proclamation in either the Natal, KwaZulu or national assemblies.

Additionally, the first Wilderness Area in Africa—proclaimed as such and with an appropriately differentiated management plan—was created in the Umfolozi Game Reserve in 1958. Still managed as such, this 25,000 hectares is regarded as the spiritual home of the modern wilderness movement in Africa. In adherence to management guidelines for Wilderness Areas, the "wilderness trail" (a walking safari) was initiated in the Umfolozi as an alternative to game viewing by automobile (which until that time was only way in which visitors could were legally allowed to view wildlife). Subsequently, these "trails" have become a popular "ultimate experience" in game reserves and national parks throughout South Africa and across most of the continent.

The protected area system proved effective in allowing populations of wildlife to recover and prosper. However, outside these areas the populations continued to be drastically reduced by concession hunters and farmers. In addition, a major factor that impacted on the wildlife diversity during the first half of the 20th century came about as a result of attempts to rid the area of Nagana, the cattle disease borne by the tsetse fly.

In spite of the dangers that Nagana posed to domestic cattle, soldiers returning from the First World War were allocated land for cattle ranching adjacent to the Umfolozi, Hluhluwe and Mkhuze Reserves. Within a very short space of time cattle were dying of Nagana. Lead by the white commercial farmers a concerted campaign was launched by the South African government to eradicate tsetse flies. This Nagana campaign, which extended from 1917 until 1950, aimed to kill off certain species, which are known carriers of the tsetse fly, and to deproclaim the Umfolozi, Hluhluwe and Mkhuze Reserves. Goodman et.al. report that "in 1917 alone 25,000 wildebeest were shot in an effort to eradicate the disease." Ian Player, in his recent book *Zululand Wilderness: Shadow and Soul,* vividly describes the slaughtering of animals, which went way beyond the need to eradicate the wild animal hosts of the tsetse fly:

> In 1921 one game drive went into the heart of the Mfolozi
> game reserve, and everything that moved was shot, including
> some white rhino. All predators were killed on sight. The leopard
> survived because it was able to take cover in the rougher areas
> of the reserve. The lions were helpless and were exterminated,
> although a few were said to survive in the Mpila area.

The campaigns to eradicate herbivores and the later aerial spraying of DDT achieved the objective of eradicating tsetse fly. But in the process, the

Nagana campaign had a severe impact on the biodiversity both inside and outside the protected areas of that north-western region of what is now known as
KwaZulu-Natal.

In virtually all the protected areas of KwaZulu-Natal, the Zulu people who
were the original inhabitants of parts of these areas were moved off to make way
for the reserves, in the belief that wildlife and people cannot coexist. This
approach to conservation, characterized by Wells as the "fences and fines"
approach [Wells, 1992 #415], dominated conservation thinking throughout
the colonial period. In post-independence Africa, government conservation
bodies levels of participation in the management of protected areas gradually
increased from "passive participation," which were little more than public relations exercises, through to "interactive participation" in the 1990s in which
local people participate in the formation of action plans for protected areas

Unlike the rest of Africa, South Africa has a unique colonial history: formal
independence from the imperial power (Britain) was won in 1912, but this was
replaced by an "internal colonialism" in which whites retained political power.
Because of the racial discrimination practiced during the apartheid era, state
and parastatal conservation bodies (such as the Natal Parks Board) were not
permitted to involve black people in policy setting or management; but, in
those areas of the country designated as "homelands" (such as KwaZulu) this
was not the case. As a result the policy trajectories of the Natal Parks Board
(NPB) and the Department of Nature Conservation (DNC) of KwaZulu differed
with regard to the involvement of neighboring communities.

Strategies and Structures for
Community Conservation in KwaZulu-Natal

Despite the differences in the legal frameworks within which the two organizations operated, both the NPB and DNC realized independently that the "fences
and fines" approach was unsustainable. Because of the high levels of poverty of
the communities on the borders of the protected areas managed by both organizations, the cost of patrolling park borders with increasingly hostile neighbors
was becoming untenable. Perhaps, even more importantly, the emerging realization that the bulk of the indigenous biodiversity of the province lies outside
of the protected areas has convinced role players of the importance of engaging
the people of the province in conservation.

Back in 1982, long before the new South African constitution and the election of the first democratic government, the KwaZulu Bureau of Natural Resources (forerunner to the DNC) had realized that conservation had to accommodate the needs of rural communities. This realization later developed into a "Policy of Sharing," which established the principle of encouraging rural communities to use the natural resources within the game reserves and proclaimed lands through the use of traditional means of harvesting. Under this policy, reeds have been harvested from some of the reserves under its control (e.g., the Tembe Elephant Reserve and Amatikhulu Reserve). The most significant harvesting activity took place in the Khosi Bay Coastal Forest Reserve, which, because of the rare swamp forests, was declared a wetland of international importance under the RAMSAR Convention, and is now part of the Greater St. Lucia Wetland Park, a World Heritage Site. Fish harvesting is also a traditional practice at Khosi Bay.

The harvesting component of the policy continues to benefit communities, although fish harvesting is a cause for some concern. Much more contentious is another component of the policy: sharing tourist revenue from the reserves. This became a significant stumbling block to the effective operation of two of the Local Boards and will be discussed in the next section.

Ever since the mid-1960s the extension services of the Natal Parks Board had promoted the sustainable use of indigenous flora and fauna amongst commercial farmers (who, because of definition under apartheid legislation, were "white") but the NPB was slower in recognizing the needs of local non-white people. Only in 1991 did it formally take account of neighboring communities by implementing a "Neighbor Relations Policy." This policy aimed to encourage neighbor participation in reserve management and planning, foster the economic and social development of neighboring communities and enhance the environmental awareness of protected area neighbors.

Wide-ranging strategies were developed to implement the policy. These included the provision of controlled free access, wildlife resource harvesting programs, the discussion of boundary and land issues and—arguably the most radical of all—the encouragement of neighbor participation in the management of protected areas. The latter was to be accomplished through formal Neighbor Liaison Forums to be implemented by the officers-in-charge of the protected areas. However, as a broad generalization, the agenda of these forums was around community development issues rather than the management of protected areas. In some cases the officers-in-charge attempted to involve community representatives in the management of parks by inviting them to attend annual management meetings but, in practice, the involvement of the community representatives amounted to receiving information about management actions. This amounted to little more than "passive participation," the first level in Pimbert and Pretty's typology of local community participation in park management. There were some forums which could be characterized as being "consultative" or even "functional" on Pimbert & Pretty's scale, but such situations came about as a result of the people involved: highly motivated officers-in-charge and charismatic traditional and community leaders.

Local Boards: Issues and Successes

With the emergence of a new democratic state in South Africa in 1994, a process was set in motion that caused far-reaching changes in the public institutions responsible for the conservation of indigenous biodiversity. The new democratic constitution divided South Africa into nine provinces, one of which was KwaZulu-Natal, comprising the "white" governed province of Natal and the "homeland" of KwaZulu. After the first democratic elections (1994) the new provincial government of KwaZulu-Natal set about amalgamating the two conservation bodies. In 1997, the provincial parliament passed the KwaZulu-Natal Nature Conservation Management Act, which established a province-wide nature conservation service, the KwaZulu-Natal Nature Conservation Service (NCS), which later traded under the name, Ezemvelo KZN Wildlife (EKW) and which is governed by a publicly accountable board, the KwaZulu-Natal Nature Conservation Board (hereinafter referred to simply as the "Board"). This act also established publicly accountable Local Boards for each of the protected areas. The idea of such local boards had in fact emerged from a landmark "Parks and People" symposium in 1995 convened by the Wildlife and Environment Society of South Africa (WESSA).

Since 1997, the neighbor relations strategy of the new conservation service has been based on three legs: the Local Boards, funding for community development projects out of the Community Levy (a fund built up from the levies charged to visitors to the parks) and sustainable harvesting of flora and fauna from protected areas. Although all three are interlinked, it is to the first of the three that we give attention here.

The Local Boards are sectorally represented (tribal authorities, regional councils, business sector, formal agriculture, non-government organizations) and are given far-reaching responsibility under the act. They are tasked with compiling management plans (subject to the approval of the Board) for the protected area(s) for which they were established and the monitoring of these plans. Inter alia the management plans are expected to promote the development needs of protected area neighbors, promote conservation education and determine local policies with regard to resource protection and management and ecotourism.

Successes

Given that the idea of Local Boards was only mooted in 1995 and that they were only officially inaugurated a few years later, some remarkable successes can be claimed for this initiative (although their development has been uneven).

The statutory recognition of neighbor involvement in the compilation of management plans is a radical departure from the previous practice of liaison forums where the participation of neighbors was dependent on the enthusiasm of the protected area management for establishing meaningful relationships with local people. However, it should be noted that where such relationships had been established the task of setting up working Local Boards was made easier.

Members of Local Boards have been empowered through skills workshops and through the experience of participating in the meetings of the Local Boards. In the words of an EKW officer of involved in the Local Board of the Coastal Forest Reserve, "Local Board members have learnt to exercise their rights. They are no longer prepared to be rubber stamps to decisions made by the organization and this is good for the organization."

In many cases where local people were suspicious of and antagonistic towards Ezemvelo KZN Wildlife, relationships of trust have been built up. However, this is dependent on EKW officials showing that they have acted on decisions taken at Local Board meetings. Where trust has been built up, issues are being dealt with rationally rather than emotionally.

Problems and Issues

In the process of establishing operational Local Boards a number of problems have emerged, some of which are yet to be satisfactorily resolved. The main problems have centered on finances. These problems threatened to derail the Local Boards even before they became functional.

From the very beginning, members of Local Boards demanded to be paid as members. However, the Board felt that they should only be compensated for actual expenses in attending Local Board meetings. Proceedings were held up for some time as a result of this dispute and some members of one of the Local Boards went so far as to refuse to participate in any meetings until they were paid. The matter was finally resolved by offering members compensation for expenses plus payment for attendance of meetings.

Arguably the most difficult issue for the Local Boards of the Coastal Forest and the Tembe-Ndumo reserves was the share of the tourism revenue that the tribal authorities felt was due to them. The former DNC "Policy of Sharing" included an agreement that 25% of gross tourist revenue would be given to the tribal authorities, which was revoked by the newly established Board because they felt that this policy was not sustainable. The tribal authorities were angered at the revoking of this policy. Instead the neighboring communities were only entitled to 90% of the Community Levy for development projects, which is substantially less than the 25% of gross revenue as in all the reserves under control of the Board. There were two issues here: the considerable difference in the size of the allocation and the recipient of the funds—community development projects rather than the Tribal Authorities. The matter was only finally resolved through the intervention of two provincial cabinet ministers.

Other problems have been encountered but none of them so serious that they have jeopardized the functioning of the Local Boards. These revolve round the extent of Local Board jurisdiction and representation. Despite being a major concrete achievement of the neighbor relations policy of the Board the following example illustrates the dilemma around the extent of the jurisdiction of the Local Boards.

An initiative was taken by ten amaKhosi (local chiefs) bordering on the Hluhluwe-Umfolozi Reserve. Together with the protected area management they developed a project to invest R750000 from the Community Levy fund to the development of a new tourist lodge in the reserve and in so doing become shareholders of the lodge. This is an interesting venture, being the first of its kind in South Africa and is a significant achievement of the neighbor relations strategy of EKW. However, the allocation of funds from the Community Levy for community projects, without the involvement of a Local Board in the decision-making, is a process is felt by some EKW officials to undermine the role of Local Boards as a link between the local communities and EKW.

A second case that illustrates this issue of the extent of the jurisdiction of Local Boards was the introduction of lions into Tembe by Ezemvelo KZN Wildlife. This was done with the consent of the amaKhosi. The reason for the introduction was to attract tourists into the area. However, the Local Board was not consulted and voiced their concern over this decision, even though the amaKhosi were represented on the Local Board. Some members were concerned that because local people were harvesting reeds in Tembe, under a controlled harvesting program, the lives of those people would be jeopardized by the introduction of lions. In terms of the Act it is clear that the Local Board should have been involved in this decision, but the practice established by the old DNC has been to consult only the amaKhosi. Is the power of the amaKhosi to be usurped by the Local Boards?

Conclusion

Formal conservation agencies in South Africa are indeed going through a process of transformation. Protected areas were previously regarded as elitist areas where black people were excluded either by apartheid legislation or financial incapability.

Given that these protected areas are often surrounded by impoverished rural communities and in many areas an increasingly degraded natural environment, the protected areas and the management thereof have to move into a new paradigm, that of catalyzing the socio-economic upliftment of the people living adjacent to these parks. This is a tremendous challenge and one that requires urgent attention, both from the professional conservationist and public at large. The formation of Local Boards and their success will play a significant role in meeting this challenge. Thankfully, the need to protect the splendid biodiversity of KwaZulu-Natal is well understood and generally accepted by the people of KZN. This will also play a significant role as we meet the pressing challenges ahead of us.

Wilderness and Community in Taku River Tlingit Traditional Territory, Northern British Columbia, Canada

Kim Heinemeyer[1], Rick Tingey[1],
Doug Milek[1], Susan Carlick[2], Bruce Baizel[1],
Dennis Sizemore[1] and Richard Jeo[1]

Introduction

Community-based conservation and land management has the potential to provide a stable and locally supported management structure for natural resources. With a foundation built on science-based knowledge and a decision-based framework, this management structure has the capacity to achieve conservation while providing for the economic stability of the resident human communities. The Taku River Tlingit First Nation (TRTFN) of northwestern British Columbia (BC) is working to re-establish themselves as the primary land manager of their traditional territory. This assertion of stewardship is being pursued through treaty negotiations with the BC and Canadian governments, the development of a territorial land plan, enhanced leadership in resource management, and legal challenges to resource development that threatens the long-term ecological health of their traditional lands, as well as their cultural sustainability.

At the core of Taku River Tlingit traditional territory is the Taku River watershed (see Map 1). This watershed encompasses approximately 4.5 million

[1]Round River Conservation Studies
[2]Taku River Tlingit First Nation

acres in northwestern British Columbia and southeastern Alaska, representing the fifth largest watershed in British Columbia that drains into the Pacific Ocean. The Taku currently has no official protected status, despite being the largest unroaded wilderness watershed on the North American western shore. The TRTFN have used and managed this landscape for thousands of years, harvesting from its abundant fisheries and wildlife resources. Today, Taku River Tlingit people continue to rely on this watershed and its surrounding lands for a variety of resources and cultural needs.

To better understand the ecological requirements and limitations of their traditional territory as it faces development pressures and proposed uses, the TRTFN is working with Round River Conservation Studies (RRCS) to complete a Conservation Area Design (CAD) to form a basis and framework for a territorial land plan. The CAD will provide large-scale guidelines on the ecological limits and resiliencies inherent within the territory, thereby providing a basis for the TRTFN to make sound management decisions.

In this paper, we present the framework and progress of our collaboration towards sustainable conservation for the lands of the TRTFN. We hope this work can lead to the preservation of both the ecological and wilderness values

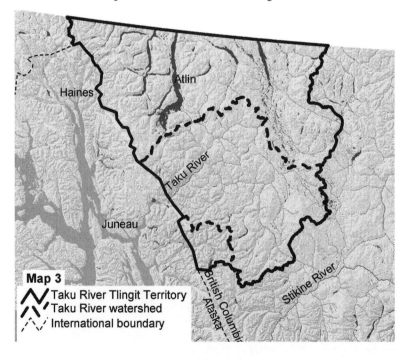

and the human communities of the region. Additionally, we believe that this work can provide a framework for similar initiatives elsewhere.

Ecological Context

The Taku River watershed includes six ecosections that range from the Coastal Boundary Ranges ecosection to the interior boreal Teslin Basin ecosection (see Map 2). The coastal regions support western hemlock, Sitka spruce and subalpine fir, while interior habitats transition through subalpine fir, lodgepole pine, white spruce and black spruce depending upon elevation and aspect. The floodplains throughout the watershed support vast expanses of black cottonwood, poplar, red-osier dogwood, Sitka alder and various willow species. Alpine regions transition into mountain heather, willow and scrub birch. The topography has been carved by glaciation and vast icefields dominate the highest elevations. This complex landscape allows for the diverse ecology that the Taku basin supports.

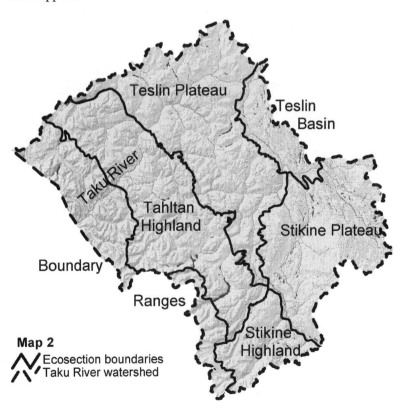

Map 2
Ecosection boundaries
Taku River watershed

The river basin boasts of large runs of five species of salmon: coho, Chinook, sockeye, chum, and pink, as well as steelhead, bull trout, cutthroat trout, and Dolly Varden. The salmon are a keystone species in this system, and are foundational to supporting the Taku's grizzly bear population. Additionally, the watershed supports black bears, wolverines, wolves, marten, and fisher—all predators that utilize to varying degrees the abundant marine protein source provided by the salmon. Abundant ungulate populations, moose, mountain goat, stone sheep and mountain caribou also support this diverse predator community.

The Taku watershed supports several other rare, sensitive, threatened or endangered species and habitats (see Table 1) listed by the British Columbia provincial government as endangered (red-listed) or vulnerable (blue-listed). Also present are Trumpeter swans and bald eagles along the floodplains and wetlands, as well as large numbers of migrating waterfowl, neotropical migrant song birds, and a variety of smaller mammals and amphibians. Rare habitats present in the watershed include vast expanses of cottonwood-red-osier dogwood and several Sitka spruce habitats.

Human History and Relationships

The 10–12 million-acre traditional territory of the Taku River Tlingit people is centered upon the 4.5 million-acre Taku River watershed. For centuries, the Taku River Tlingit have been the stewards for this territory, and its animals, fish and plants. Taku River Tlingit people named the Taku River and still today they strongly identify themselves with this life-sustaining river.

Today, while every Taku River Tlingit household operates in a cash economy, the traditional land use activities of hunting, trapping and gathering remain an important feature in Tlingit economic and social life. For example, consumption of "country food" (hunted, fished or gathered) averaged nearly 300 kg. per household in the mid-1990s.

For the Taku River Tlingit, responsible stewardship requires the exercise of their leadership in all aspects of caring for their lands. Tlingit social wellbeing and sustainable livelihood are viewed as inseparable from the health of the lands and waters and from the decisions about how people live on and use these lands.

Since the early 1990s, the TRTFN has been working on a land protection plan for its traditional territory. Early efforts resulted in evaluations of several

Table 1—Rare, threatened or endangered birds and mammals found or potentially found within the Taku River Tlingit traditional territory. Information based on Redfern Resources, Ltd. (1997).

Species	B.C.[1]	COSEWIC[2]	Global[3]	Presence[4]
BIRDS				
Trumpeter Swan (*Cygnus buccinator*)	B	V	G4	C
Oldsquaw (*Clangula hyemalis*)	B		G5	U
Bald Eagle (*Haliaeetus leucocephalus*)	B		G4	C
Peale's Peregrine Falcon (*Falco peregrinus pealei*)	B	V	G4	R
Anatum Peregrine Falcon (*Falco peregrinus anatum*)	R	E	G4	R
Gyrefalcon (*Falco rusticolus*)	B		G5	C
Lesser Golden Plover (*Pluvialis dominica*)	B		G5	R
Wandering Tattler (*Heteroscelus incanus*)	B		G5	R
Hudsonian Godwit (*Limosa haemastica*)	B		G4	R
Short-billed Dowitcher (*Limnodromus griseus*)	B		G5	R
Red-necked Phalarope (*Phalaropus lobatus*)	B		G5	C
Short-eared Owl (*Asio flameus*)	B		G5	C
Smiths' Longspur (*Calcarius pictus*)	B			R
MAMMALS				
Tundra Shrew (*Sorex tundrensis*)	R		G5	R
Alaska Meadow Jumping Mouse (*Zapus hudsonius alascensis*)	B			U
Wolverine (*Gulo gulo luscus*)	B	V	G4	C
Fisher (*Martes pennanti*)	B		G5	C
Glacier Bear (*Ursus americanus emmonsii*)	B			U
Grizzly Bear (*Ursus arctos*)	B	V	G4	C
Dall Sheep (*Ovis dalli dalli*)	R		G5	C
Stone Sheep (*Ovis dalli stonei*)	B		G5	C

[1]BC:	B = Blue List (vulnerable or "at risk"; not yet endangered or threatened) R = Red List (endangered, threatened or being considered for red-listed status)
[2]COSEWIC:	Committee on the Status of Endangered Wildlife in Canada V = Vulnerable; E = Endangered
[3]Global:	Nature Conservancy Ranking G4 = Frequent to common; G5 = Common to very common
[4]Presence in Area	C = Confirmed presence; R = Rare or unconfirmed presence U = Unlikely and unconfirmed presence

sub-watersheds and recommendations for documentation and incorporation of Taku River Tlingit traditional ecological knowledge into the planning efforts.

In part, these land protection efforts were a response to a proposed cyanide leach gold mine proposal on the lower Taku River. A Vancouver-based mining company has proposed to reopen this mine, which originally operated in the 1950s. While barging was used to move the ore down the river to Juneau, Alaska in the 1950s, this transportation option has been deemed financially unviable by the present mining proponent. The current transportation option is the construction of a 160-km (99-mile) access road through the Taku River watershed. In 1998, after a review under the Environmental Assessment Act of British Columbia, the project was approved by the provincial government. The approval was controversial because of concerns that the mine could cause extensive damage to fish and wildlife habitat, and have potentially severe impacts on the land-based economy and social system of the TRTFN. The Taku River Tlingit, the Alaskan state government, and several national and international conservation groups argued the project should not be allowed to proceed until the outstanding issues had been adequately addressed.

In 1999, the TRTFN filed a lawsuit in the British Columbia courts challenging the permit approval and arguing a number of issues, including that there were procedural shortcomings within the review process and that the provincial government failed to respect Tlingit aboriginal title to hunting and fishing habitat that is protected under the *Canadian Constitution Act* and Supreme Court of Canada decisions. In the summer of 2000, the court handed down a decision which validated the procedural concerns expressed by the TRTFN and the mining certificate was revoked. The provincial government chose to appeal the revocation, but again the court decided in favor of the Taku River Tlingit on the grounds that the TRTFN had not been properly consulted, especially in the absence of a recognized land plan and ongoing treaty negotiations. The provincial government has again appealed, and the case will be heard in the Canada Supreme Court in 2003.

A Conservation Area Design for the Traditional Territory

In 1999, Round River Conservation Studies began preparatory work on a Conservation Area Design for the traditional territory of the TRTFN. A Conservation Area Design (CAD) provides a science-based framework for identifying and prioritizing areas for sustainable conservation, based upon biological values, threats, and opportunities for implementation. As such, it provides a mechanism for identifying biological limits and standards for proposed resource development and human activity within specific sub-area or watersheds of the area covered by the CAD. This broad-scale approach moves away from disjointed and fragmented efforts at conservation planning that prevail in most locations.

A CAD should incorporate the best existing knowledge and planning for a region, in light of well accepted theories of conservation biology, including an emphasis on landscape and biological integrity, connectivity, long term viability and the precautionary principle. A fundamental basis for a CAD is the utilization of a set of focal species, selected for their ecological requirements, status, vulnerability, and social importance in the region. Additionally, a CAD incorporates key ecological and landscape processes that are integral to maintaining the long term integrity of a region, including disturbance regimes such as fire and flooding, as well as natural succession, climatic conditions, and ecological interactions. Other key analytic tools used in CAD development are representation analyses and vulnerability assessments to ensure that all ecological communities have received appropriate conservation consideration and protection.

In 1999, RRCS and TRTFN began to collect the information and data that will be needed to complete a CAD for the TRTFN traditional territory. Because of the remoteness of the region, little federal or provincial government investment in research or monitoring of the natural resources has been done. The exception to this is work being done by the provincial government and the proponent for the gold mine to support the reopening of the mine and construction of the 160-km access road. Unfortunately, much of these data have been withheld by the provincial government and not made available to the TRTFN for their land planning and CAD work. We are using the traditional and indigenous ecological knowledge of the Taku River Tlingit as a key information source on the wildlife and habitat values of their traditional territory. We have also implemented several field research projects to build information and monitoring data on key wildlife species. Thus, we have taken an approach which uses both standard scientific methods of understanding the ecological values of the region and the Taku River Tlingit's own ecological knowledge of their territory. We believe these complimentary knowledge sources will provide the most robust and complete basis for a CAD and land use planning.

The Collection and Use of
Traditional and Indigenous Ecological Knowledge (TIEK)

Taku River Tlingit elders, through their ancestors, have provided the current generation with traditional knowledge of how to care for the territory. This knowledge and
responsibility originates from countless generations of *using, managing, and living
respectfully* in the territory. Additionally, current knowledge of TRTFN hunters and
gatherers on wildlife habitat relations, current distribution and population trends are
extensive, as hunting and gathering remain integral parts of Tlingit life. In order to
ensure that this knowledge informs all decisions about how people relate responsibly
to this land, Taku River Tlingit leadership have strongly supported integration of
traditional and indigenous ecological knowledge into the CAD. Consequently the
collection of the ecological knowledge of TRTFN members has been widely
supported and we have received excellent cooperation from interviewees.

Beginning in the fall of 2000, TRTFN and RRCS staff began to interview
TRTFN elders and hunters to document their traditional and indigenous
knowledge and their experiences with a broad suite of the key focal species
being used in the CAD. These key species include grizzly bear, black bear, wolf,
wolverine, marten, moose, caribou, stone sheep, mountain goat, and the five
species of salmon (chinook, sockeye, coho, pink, and chum). We developed a
standardized set of questions that moved the interviews through the basic ecology of each species, traditional and current uses of the species, and traditional
and current management of the species. The interviews were taped, and work
with maps was encouraged as interviewees discussed historic and current distributions and the key areas or habitats needed by each species.

This TIEK database provides key information for the development of the
Conservation Area Design. From the interviews, a set of maps has been jointly
developed which depict the distribution of each key focal species within the
TRT traditional territory (for an example, see Map 3). In addition, we are using
the verbal descriptions of key or critical habitats to develop spatial models in a GIS
platform. These models will predict key habitats for each species across the study
area. During the summer 2003, we will take TRT elders and hunters into the field
to assist us with ground-truthing the results of these mapping and modeling
efforts. Similar to TIEK research efforts elsewhere, these ground-truthing efforts
and consultation with TRT membership will provide refinements to the map and
model products, and subsequently, to the overall CAD.

Ecological Research and Monitoring

We have also initiated an integrated set of research projects to collect baseline information on key focal species in the region, and to establish long term monitoring protocols for these populations. Our work has focused on those species for which we have the least information, including grizzly bear, other rare carnivores (e.g., wolverine, lynx), trumpeter swans, and amphibians. All of our work uses non-invasive techniques to collect the data for developing indices of population extent, relative abundance, and habitat use.

One of the core research projects is a population study on the grizzly bear population of the Taku River valley. We are using non-intrusive sampling of individuals through the collection of hair samples at numerous sampling stations throughout the region (see Map 4). From these hair samples, we can obtain a unique DNA fingerprint for each individual bear, as well as its sex. This work will not only provide baseline information on the present bear population in the watershed, but will also provide an excellent methodology for long term monitoring of the grizzly bear population. This sampling technique also collects hair from black bears, allowing us to simultaneously monitor black bears in the area.

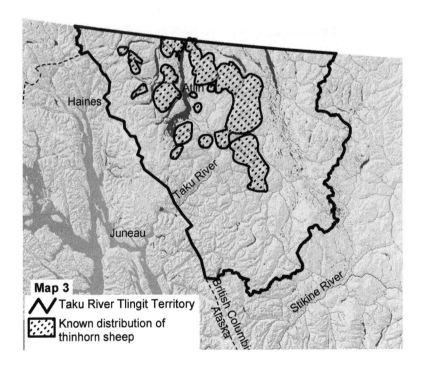

Map 3
Taku River Tlingit Territory
Known distribution of thinhorn sheep

Our other field work includes establishment of linear transects during the winter season, along which we document the presence of wolverine, lynx, marten, wolf, caribou, moose and smaller prey species through track surveys. These transects provide information on the relative abundance and the habitats used by each species. Over time, these track surveys will allow us to monitor changes in the populations of these species. We have also instigated productivity monitoring on the trumpeter swans that use the Taku, documenting the location of nesting pairs as well as the number of offspring produced each year. In addition, our amphibian surveys in the Taku River watershed represent the first coordinated effort to document and evaluate the amphibian populations of the area.

In addition to the terrestrial wildlife research projects, the TRTFN has been active in collecting and incorporating information on fisheries within their territory. Ongoing projects in this area include mapping spawning habitats for the key salmon species in the Taku River watershed and research on the ecology and populations of the numerous freshwater fish species in the larger lakes of the territory. TRTFN has membership at the Pacific Salmon Treaty table, the international governing board that determines harvest limits and levels

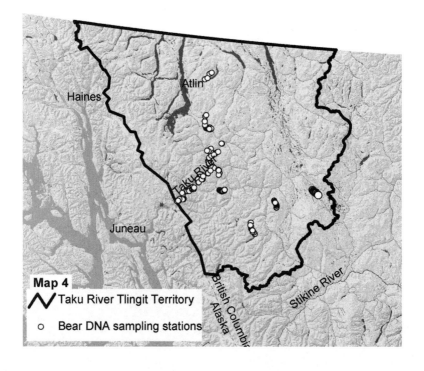

Map 4

/\/ Taku River Tlingit Territory

o   Bear DNA sampling stations

for transboundary fisheries, including the Taku salmon. In addition, the TRTFN has recently agreed to serve as the lead agency in an intergovernmental watershed planning effort for the Taku River.

Capacity-Building

Central to the TIEK and ecological research and monitoring has been a strong emphasis on capacity-building for the TRTFN in the areas of wildlife management, cultural revival, and sustainable economic development programs. Development of the CAD has provided a number of opportunities including expansion and advancement of the existing TRTFN Geographic Information Systems (GIS) office, housed under the Land and Resources Department. An additional GIS technician has been added to the staff, the existing computer and software facilities are being upgraded, and advanced training is being provided to the GIS technicians. Additionally, TRTFN members have been actively involved in the field research and monitoring programs associated with the CAD and the wildlife monitoring programs. TRTFN members have been hired as wildlife technicians throughout the project, and shorter term ecological field training has been provided to other members of the First Nation.

Next Steps

Employing a prepared question set, interviews of TRTFN members are being conducted and community workshops are being held during 2002 and 2003 to obtained Tlingit land values. Once completed, the results from these interviews and workshops will be combined with the CAD to form the basis for completing the TRTFN Land Plan. The development of an economic development strategy is also underway, which coincides with the CAD and the land plan efforts. Discussions of various economic projects between the TRTFN, RRCS and other organizations that may provide seed funding for sustainable development have begun. Potential projects include guide and outfitting, a smoked salmon processing plant, and possible tourism development projects.

Discussion

During the past century, terrestrial wildlife management authority has been vested in the province of British Columbia. However, both treaty negotiations with First Nations and Canadian court cases have explicitly sanctioned shifts to shared authority, or co-management, regimes. The combination of western science and community ecological knowledge has been used to design a number of wildlife co-management regimes in Canada and represents one of the strongest bases for developing and implementing effective wildlife conservation efforts. The exact contours of specific co-management regimes remain contingent upon the ecological knowledge, science, politics and economics that surround individual negotiations. Nevertheless, the precedent is there to negotiate a wildlife management regime that is reflective of both Taku River Tlingit values and the principles of conservation biology.

Since 1992, the Provincial government has undertaken a program to complete strategic land use plans throughout British Columbia. Land use plans have now been completed for eighteen areas of the province; however, planning has not yet been initiated for six areas, including the Atlin-Taku area. In addition, Provincial planning efforts have not well represented the interests of First Nations, and they have largely favored large scale extractive industries over conservation and sustainable economic developments. The low priority the provincial government places on First Nation interests, conservation and sustainable resource management has created the need for the TRTFN to take the lead in coordinating and overseeing land planning for their traditional territory.

From the perspective of the Taku River Tlingit, their elders' wisdom has taught them, and western scientific knowledge has confirmed, that they must understand clearly how the land and its natural processes work before they can consider an activity that may cause long term or widespread disruption. The Taku River Tlingit view monitoring of wildlife populations and careful land planning as crucial parts of their actions as stewards to choose, in an informed way, appropriate development activities. With its track record of fisheries management expertise, the increasing capacity for terrestrial wildlife management, the development of a community-based land plan and a sustainable economic development strategy, the TRTFN is demonstrating the will and ability to oversee the management of resources within their traditional territory. They are taking the steps necessary to ensure that they have a solid foundation of knowledge with which to make land use decisions that are sustainable for both their people and the natural resources upon which they depend.

Community-based conservation is an ideal many strive for, yet few achieve. In the traditional territory of the Taku River Tlingit, this ideal has the potential to become reality through the innovative work and partnerships that the TRTFN has invested in. Key to the success of the TRTFN has been the support they have received from a variety of outside entities, including scientific and conservation organizations and foundations. While Round River Conservation Studies plays a role in the development of the science-based land plan for the TRTFN traditional territory, this partnership would not have succeeded without the support of several other organizations and foundations. Success under this approach requires cooperative and innovative relationships between the key local partners, conservation organizations, and organizations willing to invest their resources over the medium and long term.

TRTFN and RRCS wish to acknowledge the following foundations for their financial support of this work: the Brainerd Foundation, Bullitt Foundation, Endswell Foundation, Kongsgaard-Goldman Foundation, David and Lucile Packard Foundation, Paul Allen Forest Protection Foundation, Rockefeller Brothers Fund, Tides Foundation, Weeden Foundation, and the Wilburforce Foundation.

Wilderness
and Tourism

Wilderness and the Issue of Sustainability— The Role of Tourism

Michael Sweatman

When we talk about "wilderness" in America, South Africa, or in other countries where the term has been "officially recognized," we are referring generally to areas that have been set aside as Wilderness, either by law or by custom. These areas are protected; they are seen as sacrosanct and, usually, nobody lives there. Activities are limited to the least obtrusive.

In most of Africa and other less-developed parts of this earth, the term wilderness per se is less well understood, for there is scant legal protection, and activities in areas that might otherwise "qualify" become "tainted" by too much human activity. Sometimes, we refer to these areas as "wildlands," because they do not fit neatly into our carefully defined wilderness box!

Wilderness or wildlands: we are referring to large areas of land that may be designated as parks or reserves or game management areas; they may be land occupied by tribal people and communities, and they will usually be inhabited by wildlife, protected or otherwise.

When a World Wilderness Congress is held in a developing nation, it must be primarily concerned with these latter values.

Let's not get hung up on definitions. The problem is the same everywhere. Land that remains unmolested in which habitat and wildlife can survive is diminishing inexorably due to unsustainable uses. Burgeoning populations in some areas lead to over-utilization of natural resources. This utilization may take the form of any of those activities associated with livelihood, including subsistence agriculture, domestic grazing, felling of trees, hunting—legal or illegal, and other activities that lead to the degeneration of the natural resource base. Unless alternative uses can be introduced that, at the same time, are both economic and sustainable, these practices will continue unabated, and the resource base and everything that lives on it will continue to suffer.

One of the most significant economic alternatives is tourism. Tourism has been identified as an important, economic use that can influence more sustainable utilization of resources. Although tourism can be overly burdensome on the habitat as well—through overuse and unwise use—the development of low-impact tourism in many areas could furnish a timely and effective provider of economic value.

It is already happening! All over Africa (especially in the southern and eastern regions) local tourist destinations have been developed around a local conservation agenda. In Namibia, for instance, there are several examples:

- At Purros, where revenues earned from low-impact tourism provide the local Himba and Herero people with an economic alternative to poaching;
- At Susuwe in Caprivi, where a new lodge through economic benefits paid to them provides a buffer between the Mayuni people on the one side of the Kwando river and the newly proclaimed Bwabwata National Park on the other;
- At Huab Lodge, which lies beside a river valley that has been rehabilitated and that provides passage for the desert elephant during seasonal migrations, and which helps to keep track of these elephants while they roam on private farms;
- At Wolwedans, where tourism facilities have been developed to sustain the economic case for preserving land reclaimed from farms previously denuded of grasslands and wildlife through unsustainable grazing and hunting;
- At Damaraland Camp, where a local tribe has been assisted by tour operators and others to provide a sustainable lifestyle based on tourism that ensures protection of the desert elephant and rhino in the area.

But tourism does not provide all the answers. In parks like Amboseli and Masai Mara, there is an abundance of tourism—verging on the overuse—which, in itself can lead to depletion of the natural resource base. Whereas it can be argued that this tourism, in addition to providing much needed foreign exchange to the host country, has provided an economic alternative to over-grazing of the land by cattle, still the wildlife in these parts is not safe, and poaching for the bush meat trade is rampant.

So, yes, tourism can be a critical contributor to sustainable development. The problem is that much of it is concentrated in small areas (the hot spots!) where too much of a good thing can be harmful. At the same time, the lodges that lie off-the-beaten-track—very often the very lodges that contribute most to local conservation agendas—are left to languish by the tourism industry because they cannot compete on an economic basis.

The challenge will be to identify marketing mechanisms and dramatically increase the numbers of tourists over time, many of whom can visit these wonderful locations and enjoy for themselves a true conservation experience.

Sustainable Tourism in Practice

Wilderness Safaris Maputaland
(Ndumu and Rocktail Bay)

Malcolm McCulloch and Clive Poultney

Wilderness Safaris, especially in Maputaland, South Africa, has developed a generic model consisting of a partnership between the private sector, the community and conservation authority, both in the lodge owning and lodge operating companies. Ndumu and Rocktail Lodges, as part of Wilderness Safaris Maputaland, were one of six international case studies appraising the way in which this type of approach unlocks opportunities for the poor who live in the vicinity of lodges in wilderness areas.

African Renewal—Restoration of the Wildlife Resource and Community Benefit from Wild Resources

Conservation and the proceeds of conservation, such as tourism, are intimately tied to the well being of the natural resource base and the people who use the natural resources. Thus in order for tourism to prosper, local livelihoods need to prosper. As has been widely documented many indigenous communities have been displaced by the proclamation of conservation areas.

We have attempted to redress this historical imbalance and have tried to restore a balance by having the conservation authority and the community as partners.

Wilderness Safaris—Maputaland (WSM)

WSM is predicated on the restoration of conservation and culture where community and culture has been divorced from wildlife and conservation for many years. Both the community living adjacent to conservation areas in which the lodges are located and the conservation authority who have jurisdiction over the proclaimed conservation area, the Kwa Zulu Natal Wildlife Services (KZN Wildlife), have shares in the lodge owning and lodge operating companies.

Community Development Trusts have been established for as the recipient bodies for share dividends and development in Mqobela and Kwa Mpukane ward near Rocktail Bay and with the Mathenjwa Tribal Authority around the Ndumu Game Reserve.

Besides a share holding partnership, WS is attempting to increase benefit to those communities who participate through the integration of cultural, community and heritage activities and excursions into the wilderness experience.

From this arrangement it becomes evident that the private sector can be instrumental in reconciling community and conservation interests by creating a common interest. A sustainable tourism operation in wilderness areas is reliant on the cooperation of both communities and conservation. If cooperation can be converted into a partnership of which there are many permutations, it is more likely that the business as well as the wild area in which it is located will be sustained.

Impact

The impact of the arrangement has been positive but limited. For example, at Ndumu on the SA Mozambique Border, the WS lodge on Banzi Pan is a 16 bed lodge with 21 local employees. The population in the immediate vicinity of the park is 21,789 people and thus the impact is limited. In terms of the proximate population only 1% of the population is employed at the small exclusive lodge. The upside is that salaries on average are double the annual income of homesteads in the region (average homestead income R 6,000-00 on the South Africa side and half that on the Mozambique side of the border). The average homestead consists of over 6 people and thus over 120 people are supported through WS permanent wage earners.

Even at Rocktail Bay where the population is much smaller (1,566 people), the impact besides wages to 29 local employees in a 20 bed lodge equates to R 2.20 per person per annum. Obviously, however, the aggregate impact from collective income is greater in supporting community projects such as in school facilities, bursaries and other investments and developments made by the Mqobela community.

To improve the positive impact, WSM has decided to re-arrange the share-holding to allow a quicker return for the community and conservation authority through increasing shares in the lodge owning company.

Beside dividends from the core business community excursions such as sangoma safaris, eco cultural safaris with Safariness on the Phongolo Floodplain and at Kosi Bay have been integrated into the range of activities offered by WSM. This is both to WSM's benefit in increasing the product range and to communities benefit as an additional source of revenue. As reported in the "Pro Poor" Tourism Resport, this has had substantial impact on individual families but needs to be done on a regional basis in order for more local entrepreneurs and community projects to benefit.

Regarding security of the premises and area, local community based polic-ing forums are remunerated for their work by the Rocktail Lodge in the Coastal Forest Reserve and this has worked most effectively in providing for the safety of guests.

The overall impact on wild areas, as a result, is that communities are begin-ning to benefit from the wilderness area, and it is therefore in their interest to manage the environment on a sustainable basis.

However, in order to maximize the impact there is a need to go to scale where wild areas are planned more holistically in terms of their economic return.

For Example

Ndumu—Tembe Wildlife Complex—A rationalization and economic manage-ment plan of the existing facilities and the expansion of those facilities we believe will result in a larger benefit to both communities and conservation increasing revenue and reorganizing revenue streams for both as well as making it more profitable for the tour operators. This would also be a significant stim-ulus in bringing the TFCA's such as the one incorporating the Ndumu Game Reserve, the Tembe and the Maputo Elephant Parks in Mozambique on line.

In order to go to scale there is a need to link with regional programs in order to reconcile community needs with use of resources in wildlife areas. One such program is the Lubombo WaterWays program which has been established to support economically and ecologically sustainable projects along the Phongolo, Usuthu and Maputo Rivers. Part of the program is to reconcile var-ious resource use options, such as agriculture and tourism, through scheduling equitable and efficient flood discharges from the fifth largest dam in RSA, Pongolapoort Dam, which effects the entire waterway. A second task is to zone different forms of development in a complimentary manner, where chemical input for agriculture will not leach into the natural system and destroy the ecological system that sustains local livelihoods and tourism enterprise.

In the Coastal Forest Reserve where Rocktail Bay Lodge is situated, a resource management and development plan has been launched with the community partners with the aim of linking in with the Greater St. Lucia Wetland Park Heritage Authority on a co-management of resources program. Here, Wilderness Safaris also works jointly on projects such as the turtle research program with the KZN Wildlife, where it contributes funding to the research program in return is allowed to take guests to see the leatherback and loggerhead turtles laying eggs or the hatchlings emerge and make for the ocean. This is a straightforward example of all parties benefiting, where conservation benefits through research, the operator benefits from taking guests to see the turtles and the community benefit by employment on the program in doing the research and monitoring.

Conclusion

Tourism is a complex and fickle industry where the operator has to contend with market segments, competitive products in various parts of the globe and compete with other countries as a long haul destination.

Africa's draw card is the wilderness and the human heritage and livelihoods that have survived from the wilderness. Just as tourism has to be sustained without continual imports of capital and maintaining a skills base through appropriation of revenue from tourism rather than through external input—the sustainability of tourism in wild areas is contingent on renewable use of the resource base where the skills base is developed from the proceeds of sustainable use of the resource base.

CASE STUDY
Wilderness Safaris, Maputaland, South Africa
Rocktail Bay and Ndumu Lodge

This is a case study of a commercial company entering into a contractual relationship with a community and the state conservation agency to develop up-market tourist lodges. In addition, Wilderness Safaris (WS) is taking initiatives relating to local employment, local service provision and the development of complementary community-based initiatives.

WS is a large, well-established Southern African tour operator that caters to the luxury end of the market. It has a number of lodges and camps across Southern Africa and at a number of these it is involved in some form of partnership or revenue sharing agreement with local communities. This case study looks at two lodges run by WS in Maputaland in the South African province of KwaZulu Natal—Rocktail Bay, which opened in 1992 and Ndumu, which opened in 1995.

Ownership and management of the lodges is vested in two companies—a "lodge owning company" in which the conservation agency, a commercial bank and the community have stakes; and a "lodge operating company" in which the conservation agency, the community and WS are partners (although not equal). Despite this tri-partite equity structure the community has received little in the way of financial dividends for the community so far, because neither lodge has yet turned a profit. Increased occupancy at the lodges is required to make them profitable, but this requires development of the destination as a whole and diversification of the product. It is noted that support of the conservation authority is needed for further infrastructural and product development, but that the conservation agency seems reluctant to sanction this due to concerns about the likely impact on the conservation status of the area.

Progress has been mixed on the other elements of WS's PPT initiative. The local employment strategy has resulted in a high proportion of jobs going to local people rather than ex-pats. Considerable training and skills transfer has taken place and staff turnover is low. Local provision of services has occurred to a certain extent with WS utilising local security and taxi services, and joint planning and implementation of new complementary products has started with cultural visits to a traditional healer (Sangoma). However, growth of local businesses associated with the lodges has been slow, and the case study notes "untapped potential" for local supply of services and products. A consultant has been brought in to help WS work with the community to develop products, but it is felt that a third party is needed to organize, coordinate, develop and train for this since these activities are outside the mandate, and capacity, of one private sector operator.

The case study illustrates three key challenges to such a private sector-community initiative:

- Success is somewhat out of the control of the central actors, being dependent on others players and on the health of tourism in the wider region;
- The initiative needs to be incorporated within a larger PPT program involving other stakeholders to maximize potential;
- Many communities have overly high expectations of involvement in tourism—both in terms of the levels and rates of returns and also the roles and responsibilities of their private sector partners.

Key Obstacles in Implementing Pro-Poor Tourism Strategies	
Case study	**Challenges and obstacles**
Wilderness Safaris, South Africa	• Excessive expectations of the company among community • Lack of conservation authority co-operation for tourism development • Area not taken off as a tourism destination • Lodges still making a loss • To take advantage of enterprise opportunities needs external support
Tropic Ecological Adventures, Ecuador	• Low visitor numbers—diminishes community enthusiasm • Less profitable operation—has to be cross-subsidised within the company • Limited community capacity to understand tourism, meet needs and standards
St. Lucia Heritage Tourism Programme	• Takes time for benefits to appear • Collaborative community management not successful: complex arrangements and weak institutions • Doors are hard to open: difficult for small operators to enter established tourism • Vision not shared by all
SNV, Humia District, Nepal	• Location—"hard trek" route, small market, restricted tourist routes • Lack of supplementary products. • Economic elites in Kathmandu are strong: little access for new entrepreneurs and informal sector. • Difficulties of the remote region—staffing, management, logistics, political instability
SDI and CPPP, South Africa	• Uncertainty over land rights and the reform process—causes delays, reduces competitiveness • Communities' dependence on outside expertise • Benefits are slow, small relative to dense population • High transaction costs of PPT
NACOBTA, Namibia	• Vast training needs and large distances to cover with limited resources • Lack of commercial expertise within NACOBTA; need to work across NGO, community and corporate cultures • Government failure to follow up new policies—unfulfilled promises • Policy influence requires massive effort for limited return • Slow progress of land tenure reform
UCOTA, Uganda	• Low tourism numbers to Uganda • Lack of funding

Wildland Plants and Medicines

Learning from Others—Traditional Plants and Healing

Traditional Dr. Pontso Patience Koloko

My work with the Traditional Healing Association involves learning from others, especially how indigenous people with their indigenous knowledge can collaborate and build up trust with other stakeholders to further the sustainable, ongoing use of medicinal plants. Natural remedies build healthy communities, but promoting the use of remedies is not enough; we also must promote their sustainable harvesting and use. That we will achieve by bringing the awareness, trainings, workshops, meetings and conferences to the people at the grass roots level.

Any commitment we make to local peoples must be fulfilled. This must not be the time of unfulfilled promises, of simply taking and leaving. This has happened too much, we have seen it, but we hesitated to speak out. We feared losing the information we have, and losing our business.

Trust is the key. If we have this, it is wise and easy to contact each other for help. There must be a communication between all stakeholders in the field of traditional medicine. Committees and a working group will promote the sustainable use of biodiversity by identifying novel opportunities for growing and using herbs. These will include the indigenous traditional technologies as well as western technologies. In order to realize the potential benefits we need first to define these technologies and to make sure that the relevant intellectual properties are accommodated in the legal system.

Indigenous people need to be helped to promote their knowledge through capacity building and skills training, in order to be empowered. They have long been marginalized and now need to know how important they are with their

CHAIN OF GOOD HEALTH

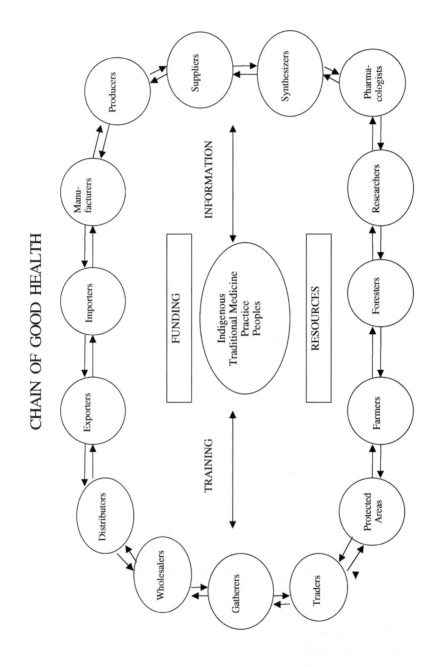

indigenous knowledge. They need to pass their knowledge to others, and books need to be written in their language and given back to them. For example, the book *A–Z Self Help Approach to Good Health: Practical Reference to Drug-free Remedies Using Vitamins and Minerals*, by James F. Balch, M.D. and Phyllis A. Balch, needs to be translated and given back to the communities. There are many other such books.

Land is needed to grow medicinal plants, for they are getting too scarce in the wild. This is a serious issue. I suggest that growing of medicinal plants be done at all levels, local to national, to reach all people including those who are far from the natural or protected areas. Nobody cares about local people, yet they have their traditional knowledge of how to use those indigenous plants, and understand the importance of not over-harvesting. We have the methods to grow and use the plants, and to exchange knowledge. We need help with capacity, encouragement, and empowerment, to understand the way forward and the solutions to how we can protect such useful remedies for use by our grandchildren, and for the plants not to disappear forever. For example, one practical but very important thing is for specialists to write the plants' names both in botanic language and also in the language that the communities understand.

Now is the time we include local women. They play a major role in the community with their indigenous knowledge, where clinics and hospitals are few and far, and they have many health skills. So they need to be promoted and well-trained to fit with the times.

Tourism projects are needed. Women can share the information while taking tourists on guided plant walks. A booklet with this information can be compiled and sold to tourists, and be written in all languages for fundraising. With all their knowledge the local people need to be empowered to sell to the tourist, to export their natural products and to be listed in the Directory of Companies in the Botanical Products Industry List.

We need to have the same vision of what we want to see in the future, giving each stage a time with monitoring and evaluation. We must look to what we want to achieve and who will benefit when we reach our goal.

Phyto Nova
and Wildland Plants—
An Approach to HIV/AIDS

Ben-Erik van Wyck

Wildland Plant Approach:

- Addressing serious unmet public health needs, including African wasting diseases.

- Affordable health care from the most profound African traditional medicinal plants.

- Sustainable harvesting by turning rare wild plants into crop plants.

- Alleviation of poverty by job creation, especially in rural areas.

Wildland Plant Approach
The Plants:

- *Sutherlandia frutescens* (**cancer bush**)—tablets used as profound tonic (also ingredient of a gel used for a wide range of skin conditions).

- *Warburgia salutaris* (**pepperbark tree**)—tablets used as natural antibiotic against oral and oesophageal thrush.

- *Siphonochilus aethiopicus* (**African ginger**)—tablets used as multi-purpose anti-inflammatory.

The Plants:

Sutherlandia frutescens subsp. *microphylla* (cancer bush).

The Plants:

Warburgia salutaris
(pepperbark tree).

Siphonochilus aethiopicus
(African ginger).

Sustainability and Conservation

Wild-Harvesting of Rare Plants
Is Not Sustainable:

• *Sutherlandia* (cancer bush)—selected chemical variety has
been developed into a crop plant: now grown in four different
localities in South Africa.

• *Warburgia* (pepperbark tree)—nearly extinct in the wild.
Trees grown from cutting; leaves are used, not the bark.

• *Siphonochilus* (African ginger)—nearly extinct in the wild.
Plants are grown from divided rhizomes and from tissue
culture.

Sustainability and Conservation

T. Dr Credo Mutwa—a director of Phyto Nova (Pty) Ltd, and T. Dr Virginia Rathele in one of the first commercial stands of Phyto Nova's selection of *Sutherlandia*.

Wildland Plant Approach

Two levels of product development:

- **Social responsibility**—to make product available to people at minimal cost.

- **Inter-African trade**—to develop informal markets in South Africa and other African countries (mainly Uganda and Kenia).

Sutherlandia—Clinical anecdotes

• **Strong convergent anecdotes**—doctors, traditional doctors, nurses, homoeopath s, and the lay pub lic.

• In patients with full -blown AIDS, *Sutherlandia* tablets **clearlyand dramatically improve the mood and appetite and energy levels of patients.**

• **About 50% of patients**(AIDS WHO stage 4) **gain weight over a three to six month period, typically 5–10 kg (up to 15 k g).** The condition of the remaining 50% seems to stabilize.

Zandile Mtetwa, an AIDS patient treated with *Sutherlandia* tablets

1 March 2000　　　**15 kg weight gain**　　　**6 September 2000**

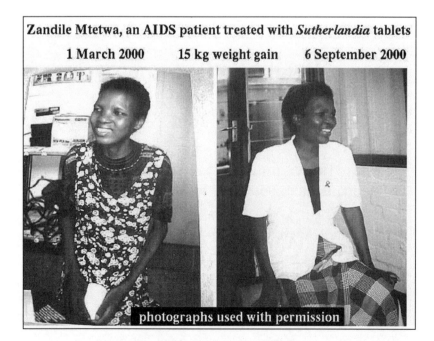

photographs used with permission

Sutherlandia—Clinical anecdotes

• Numerous reports of increases in CD4 counts and decreases in viral loads after treatment with *Sutherlandia* (typically a 50% improvement).

• No claim is being made that *Sutherlandia* is a cure for AIDS but there is growing and compelling evidence that *Sutherlandia* could enhance the quality (and possibly the duration) of life of AIDS patients mainly by counteracting the muscle-wasting (cachexia) effect of AIDS.

Sutherlandia – a first effective anti-cachexia medicine???

Historical uses and recent observations suggest profound activity against wasting diseases:

- improves appetite and digestion

- traditional use against tuberculosis, cancer and now AIDS

CLINICAL TRIALS URGENTLY NEEDED!!

Sutherlandia—a first effective anti-cachexia medicine???

Recently, permission has been granted by the Ethics Committee of the Medicial Research Council of South Africa to conduct an Open Label, clinical, pilot study with 39 AIDS patients (WHO stage 3) to investigate the safety, efficacy and optimal dose of *Sutherlandia*.

Sutherlandia—Advantages of the Wildland Plant Approach:

- **Safety** (very long history of use).

- **Clear evidence of a direct effect on wasting and quality of life.**

- **Affordable**—already treating many people for **less than two dollars per person per month.**

- **Proven sustainable harvesting** (already grown as a new crop plant in four different localities in South Africa.

ACKNOWLEDGEMENTS

The following colleagues and friends are thanked
for their contribution to the information presented
in this lecture and for inspiring collaboration over
many years:

Dr. Carl Albrecht
Dr. Nigel Gericke
Ms. Anne Hutchings
T. Dr. Credo Mutwa
T. Dr Isaac Mayeng
T. Dr. Virginia Rathele
Prof Fanie van Heerden

SCIENTIFIC AND TECHNICAL INFORMATION

A brief overview of *Sutherlandia:*

Current and Historical Uses
Central Nervous System

Has been used to support mental and emotional stress, incl. irritability, anxiety and depression.

Widows of slain Zulu warriors used *Sutherlandia* as a tranquillizer during the mourning period.

The Sotho name Motlepelo means "bringing back the heart" meaning that the plant is a traditional treatment for emotional shock and stress.

Current and Historical Uses
Central Nervous System (continued):

Warriors returning from battle would drink *Sutherlandia* "to take the war out".

The ancient Zulu name *Insiswa* means "the one which dispels darkness" alluding to its anti-depressant effect, and powerful tonic effects.

The present Zulu name *Unwele* means "hair"—alluding to the fact that the plant stops people "pulling out their hair" with distress.

Current and Historical Uses
Respiratory

Used to good effect in the 1918 influenza pandemic, and is traditionally believed to shorten the duration and severity of the illness.

Traditionally used in both the prevention and treatment of the symptoms of asthma.

Sutherlandia has been traditionally used for centuries to treat the symptoms of TB, including wasting, and bronchitis. Historically used to treat unspecified wasting diseases.

Current and Historical Uses
Gastrointestinal

Sutherlandia has been used to treat symptoms of "heartburn", reflux oesophagitis, gastritis and peptic ulceration. Herbalists in Cape Town say that *Sutherlandia* is for "nerves and ulcers".

Sutherlandia was historically used to treat diarrhea and dysentery, and it was used as a supportive remedy for liver conditions. It is slightly purgative at higher doses and has been used as a gentle remedy for constipation.

Current and Historical Uses

Urogenital tract

Sutherlandia was used to treat urinary tract infections, including gonorrhea, and cystitis.

Diabetes

Sutherlandia is widely used to this day by Cape herbalists to treat "blood sugar".

Current and Historical Uses

Musculo-skeletal

Sutherlandia has been used to treat gout, rheumatoid arthritis and osteo-arthritis.

Cancer

To this day *Sutherlandia* is used as a traditional treatment to improve the quality of life in patients with malignant tumors.

Smith, A. 1895. *A contribution to the South African materia medica*, 3nd edition. Lovedale, South Africa.

page 62: "preparation of leaves as tonic";

page 66: "pinch of leaves in boiling water taken twice or thrice a day for extreme weakness and sinking at the stomach";

page 86: "blood purifier";

page 116 & 117: "leaf decoction for dysenteric diarrhoea".

page 188 & 189: "curing of malignant tumors, cancerous in appearance; also used as blood purifier and tonic … to delay the progress of true cancer and much prolonged life".

Watt, J.M. & Breyer-Brandwijk, M.G. 1962. *The Medicinal and Poisonous Plants of Southern and Eastern Africa*, 2nd ed. Livingstone, London.

page 649: "Infusions or decoctions of the leaf and bark are used for influenza, stomach complaints, intestinal complaints, internal cancers, uterine troubles, liver diseases, rheumatism, inflammations, haemorrhoids, dropsy, backache and as a tonic; infusions are taken in amenorrhoea, as blood tonic and as cancer prophylactic; powdered leaf in syrup is used to treat cough; weak infusions taken before meals seem to act as a bitter tonic to improve appetite and digestion; may cause sweating, may be slightly purgative and may be emetic if too strong."

pinitol

Known anti-diabetic agent (Narayanan, 1987)

US Patent (Ostlund, 1996) suggests clinical application in treating the wasting in cancer and AIDS patients

L-canavanine (a non-protein amino acid)

Documented antiviral, anti-bacterial, antifungal and anticancer activities.

Patented anticancer effects (Crooks, 1994; Swaffar, 1995).

Patented antiviral activity, including against influenza virus and retroviruses (Green, 1988).

COOH
|
H₂N—C—H
|
CH₂CH₂ONHCNH₂
‖
NH

L-canavanine (continued)

Selective inhibitor of inducible nitric oxide synthase—possible application in the treatment of septic shock and chronic inflammation (Anfossi, et al., 1999; Levy et al., 1999).

SUTHERLANDIA FLAVONOIDS

Sutherlandia species and populations produce at least six unidentified flavonoids in high yield.

Some populations (e.g. the commercial type) has high concentrations of two flavonols.

The flavonoids may possibly explain the anti-inflammatory activity of Sutherlandia and other effects (possibly a bio-available form of a quercetin-like molecule?).

SUTHERLANDIA TRITERPENOIDS

Sutherlandia species and populations are highly variable in triterpenoid glycosides.

Limited variation WITHIN populations.

Partially identified compounds SU1 and SU2 of great scientific interest (further work in progress).

SU1 and SU2 are structurally related to terpenoids of *Astragalus* (a tonic in Chinese medicine).

References

Anfossi, G. *et al.* 1999. Modulation of human platelet function by L-canavanine: differential effects of low and high concentrations. *Gen Pharmacol.* 32, 321-328.

Crooks, P.A. and Rosenthal, G.A. (Filed Dec 5, 1994) Use of L-canavanine as a chemotherapeutic agent for the treatment of pancreatic cancer. United States Patent 5,552,440.

Green. M.H. (Filed Jan 25, 1988) Method of treating viral infections with amino acid analogs. United States Patent 5,110,600.

Levy, B. *et al.* 1999. Beneficial effects of L-canavanine, a selective inhibitor of inducible nitric oxide synthase, on lactate metabolism and muscle high energy phosphates during endotoxic shock in rats. *Shock* 11, 98-103.

References (continued)

Narayanan, *et al.* (1987) Pinitol—A New Anti-Diabetic compound From the Leaves of *Bougainvillea Spectabilis*. *Current Science* 56(3), 139-141.

Ostlund, R.E and Sherman, W.R. (Filed March 4, 1996). Pinitol and derivatives thereof for the treatment of metabolic disorders. US Patent 5,8827,896.

Swaffar, D.S. *et al.* (August 1995) Combination therapy with 5-fluorouracil and L-canavanine: in-vitro and in-vivo studies. *Anticancer Drugs*, 6(4), 586-93.

More details can be found on wwwsutherlandia.org

Wildlands, Indigenous Knowledge, Modern Illness

A Personal Comment

Gerard B. Bailly

Medicinal plants exist in wildlands, waiting to be used. In indigenous communities, traditional "science" is alive and well, and has been used for millennia to alleviate suffering. The herbalists, sangomas, and others of different names but the same knowledge are the keepers of this tradition.

In modern illness lies the issue! Cultural prejudices and economical conflicts are difficult to solve. Let us take, together, another route, one that simply focuses on what is given within nature and intact, indigenous communities:

- In traditional medicine, respect of tradition means wisdom and wisdom is a rare human quality;
- In medicinal plants, plant is the core concept. Plants, in this case, are primarily nutrients and it happens those have medicinal properties.

So medicinal plants can be considered natural tonics, adaptogenic food supplements, boosters of vital biological functions, resembling multi vitamins and minerals, chemically driven complexes sold by millions over the counter in Europe and the United States with one major difference: their highly favorable ratio in cost effectiveness. They could not only revolutionize medicine, but they are also affordable. And let us not forget: 80% of the African population use medicinal plants and consult traditional healers. For a large part of human

278

population, poor physical, mental and spiritual health is primarily related to denutrition, malnutrition and poor hygiene ... not always to lack of medicines.

This is relevant at different levels for the whole of humanity regardless of continent, country and culture. Poor education and ignorance exist everywhere. Ignorance is a very powerful economic and social weapon. Ignorance does not only mean lack of education, but also lack of exposure to the truth. A person, a family, a society, a world that mainly relies on false or truncated or historically modified values is ignorant.

Since I resigned from my clinical research activities seven years ago, this 7th World Wilderness Congress is the first time as far as I am concerned that knowledge and experience from both African traditional medicine and medicinal plants will be shared with a large, positive, attentive and committed audience representing an active part of humanity from the five continents. My vision for medicinal plants can be summarized simply:

1. If strongly protected
2. If thoroughly researched
3. If correctly cultivated
4. If properly produced
5. If appropriately transformed
6. If widely distributed

Then:

7. African medicinal plants and the indigenous knowledge attached to them will transform into an important sustainable development tool for Africa to the benefit of Africans for the management and fight against modern illness.

Of the eight new HIV contaminations that occur every minute worldwide, seven of them are in Africa. Let us make sure that there will be enough young girls and boys, our descendants, in three generations to appreciate and admire the results of all efforts made to save and protect wilderness.

Medicinal plants are an integral part of the world bio-diversity. Those must be saved, rescued and protected with the same vigilance and tenacity applied to other biological components of our planet.

Africa has given and continues to give to the world its gold, diamonds, oil, strategic minerals and precious and valuable trees, rhino horns, elephant tusks ... the list is too long, but I must add as well millions of men, women, children. Africans are faced with an important question at this time. Are you willing to give more, to give to the world—with no promise of return—the medicinal plants from your wildlands and your immense indigenous knowledge in traditional medicine?

Wilderness and Wildlands—

New Protected Area Concepts

The Upper Zambezi "Four Corners" Transboundary Initiative

Tourism, Ecology and Community

Simon Metcalfe, David Sumba, Nesbert Samu and Henry Mwima

African Wildlife Foundation's Concept of Wilderness Management

The African Wildlife Foundation (AWF) is an international NGO established 40 years ago whose mission is "working with people to keep wildlife in Africa." The Foundation has two core approaches to wilderness management: (1) landscape level conservation—its "African Heartlands" program and (2) Livelihoods impact—its Conservation Service Centers program. These approaches are synergistic in application.

The African Heartlands Program

AWF conceives a "Heartland" as a landscape of exceptional wildlife and natural value extending across land tenure categories—state, private and community lands. A heartland is large enough to sustain natural processes, such as migrations, and the cluster of heartlands AWF works with are representative of many of the ecological zones of Africa. A heartland may be in one or straddle two or more countries. AWF uses specific criteria in selecting these landscapes—ecological, biological, social and feasibility.

How does AWF work in these heartlands? It has collaborated with The Nature Conservancy in developing a Site Conservation Planning process. Using this participatory planning tool stakeholders identify conservation targets and

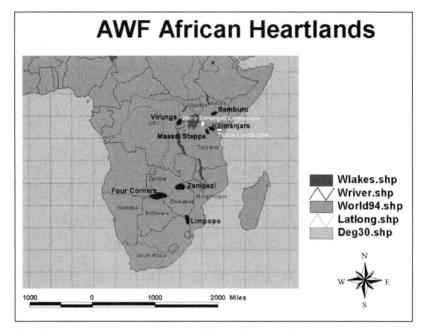

AWF African Heartlands

Legend:
- Wlakes.shp
- Wriver.shp
- World94.shp
- Latlong.shp
- Deg30.shp

develop partnerships overtime to address threats and conserve targets (e.g., species, communities and natural processes). In the "Four Corners" transboundary area the following targets have been identified: wetlands; river systems; wildlife migratory corridors; woodland grassland mosaic; native fish; species assemblages; declining or threatened species; representative woodlands.

Success is measured by (1) monitoring the reduction of identified threats to targets; (2) the improvement in selected species; (3) economic success of the parts and the whole; (4) essential land units being incorporated into the heartland and; (5) the quality of partnerships in the heartland.

AWF has targeted seven heartlands at present:

1. Samburu (Kenya)
2. Kilimanjaro (Kenya/ Tanzania)
3. Maasai Steppe (Tanzania)
4. Virunga (Uganda, Rwanda, Congo)
5. "Four Corners"—Upper Zambezi (Botswana, Namibia, Zambia, Zimbabwe)
6. Lower Zambezi (Mozambique, Zambia, Zimbabwe)
7. Limpopo (Mozambique, South Africa, Zimbabwe)

The Conservation Service Centers Program

The CSCs are small multidisciplinary teams of professionals, located in strategic locations and armed with a "menu" of tools and services. The CSCs prepare, broker and sustain conservation business ventures and positive economic and conservation impact. The CSCs clients are heartlands, communities, private sector, public sector and local government.

AWF presently has four CSCs which are located in Nairobi (Kenya), Arusha (Tanzania), Victoria Falls (Zimbabwe) and White River (South Africa). These locations allow for rapid deployment of staff and linkages with the tourism sector where it is operational. The multi-disciplinary team typically has a customer-orientated manager, an ecologist/ land use planner, community mobilization staff, a business planner, a lawyer and access to part-time staff or consultants.

The menu of tools and services include:

- Information and awareness raising
- Participatory business options planning
- Marketing and feasibility studies for community, public, private partnerships
- Partnership opportunities, options identification
- Training and capacity building for communities
- Legal services (e.g., contract, negotiation)
- Monitoring and evaluation
- Fund management and community endowments

Success of CSC operations is measured by assessing threat abatement in an AWF Heartland. For example, leveraging conservation as a land use in a critical wildlife corridor through a community/private sector partnership. Success is also assessed by a specific contribution to one of AWF's species themes— predators, essence of Africa, disease, endangered species and, human/wildlife conflict. Finally, real market returns on wildlife enterprise that will sustain the efforts of landholders. Examples of CSC deals include:

- ConsCorp Africa and Ololosokwan village, Tanzania. Lease of village land for camp. Benefits to village—$30,000 (year 1). 25,000 ha conserved includes Serengeti wildebeest migration route.

- Kimana Sanctuary, Kenya. Negotiating for a private sector use of community sanctuary. Potential benefits to community $15,000. 6,000 ha of Kilimanjaro heartland will be conserved.

Expected results of AWF's approach:

- Space for wildlife;
- Livelihoods for local people; and
- Sustainable opportunities for landholders and the tourism industry.

The Okavango, Upper Zambezi Transboundary Area

The Okavango–Upper Zambezi area involves five countries (Angola, Botswana, Namibia, Zambia and Zimbabwe) and covers an area of some 260,000 square kilometers. In conservation terms it is anchored in several protected areas including the Moremi, Chobe, Hwange, Zambezi and Kafue National Parks as well as the Okavango wetland and Zambezi River. The area combines vast community lands interspersed between the protected areas. It is an area of major wildlife and tourism importance and features the highest elephant population (140,000+) in the world as well as the world famous Victoria Falls. The area receives some 350,000 tourists a year with an optimal capacity for over three million. (Development Bank of Southern Africa, 1999).

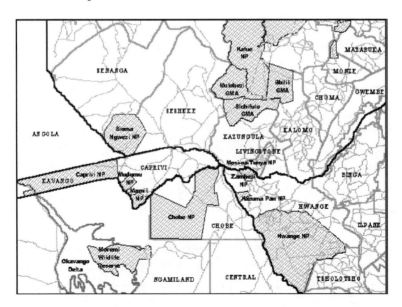

The Southern African Development Community protocols for wildlife and law enforcement, tourism, water, fisheries, trade, tourism and environment potentially provide an enabling framework for operationalizing regional integration.

The Four Corners Transboundary Natural Resources Management Area Initiative

The "Four Corners" TBNRMA Initiative is an activity supported by USAID's Regional Center for Southern Africa under its strategic objective supporting "increased cooperation in the management of shared natural resources." The activity is being implemented by the African Wildlife Foundation with partners, including the four governments and their community, public and private sector stakeholders. The focus of the activity is on shared watercourses, migratory wildlife, and critical ecosystems. Improved cooperation in managing shared resources is intended to lead to improved livelihoods (reduced poverty).

The activity expects increased cooperation to be manifested through: (1) the adoption of viable practices for sustainable management of shared natural resources; (2) the enactment of policies, protocols and agreements; (3) organizations and institutions capable of effective regional intervention; and (4) improved ecological monitoring systems for decision-making.

What is meant by increased cooperation is more public and private entities (communities, institutions, NGOs, businesses) working together effectively to manage shared natural resources and greater operational linkages and collective responsibility among NRM authorities in the region. Viable practices are the core prerequisite for making sustainable improvements in the environment. Harmonized policies, laws, institutions and regulatory environment will ensure that such practices can be adapted to different settings. Organizations and institutions involved in this process should become more effective in the region in promoting the adoption of viable practices. Finally, ecological monitoring of the region will inform policy making, providing feedback about the viability of management practices and assist organizations to make effective interventions in the region.

The Transboundary Discourse

There are several emerging definitions that attempt to describe recent transboundary conservation and development activities in southern Africa. "Peace Parks" have been promoted as an initiative of the Peace Parks Foundation with currency in South Africa. The use of Transfrontier or Transboundary Conservation Areas (TFCA and TBCA) is promoted by the World Bank's support in Mozambique to the Gaza, Kruger, Gonarezhou initiative and others. The World Bank defines TFCA's as "relatively large areas that straddle frontiers (boundaries) between two or more countries and cover large-scale natural systems encompassing one or more protected areas" (World Bank 1996). TFCA's tend to be grounded on protected areas on national boundaries and use the parks to leverage conservation goals in neighboring states. The conservation goal is justified by the economic objective of developing substantial borderland tourism destinations. In South Africa the idea of the TFCA was incorporated into the regional planning approach known as Spatial Development planning where core infrastructure investments are made to leverage development by unlocking potential in "borderland" areas.

USAID, who have invested substantially in Community Based Natural Resources Management (CBNRM) in southern Africa commissioned a study on the issue and now promote the use of Transboundary Natural Resources Management (TBNRM). TBNRM attempts to de-emphasize the necessity of linking protected areas. The USAID study defined a TBNRMA as "an area in which cooperation to manage natural resources occurs across boundaries" and the process of TBNRM as "any process across boundaries that facilitates or improves the management of natural resources (to the benefit of all parties in the area)." The emphasis here is on the process, not the geographic area. Hence, if it serves the function of TBNRM, then it is a TBNRM Area. A TBNRMA exists as soon as there is any sort of TBNRM activity represented by some sort of institution, be it contract, protocol, management plan, or communication forum (formal or informal).

The discourse on these initiatives is important as partie's perceptions vary and these narratives must play out in the transboundary policy arena until a trusting relationship can develop. After a decade of devolution from the old "fortress" conservation approach toward a more community-based approach the ideological divide is contrasted once more through transboundary initiatives. Governments and the private sector can enter these regional debates more readily than local communities who tend to be constrained within national local government structures and do not have authority to create transboundary associations.

Although the "Four Corners" TBNRMA is to some extent being pushed by donor funding, what it is and what it could become remains an issue for the participating countries and their national stakeholders (public, private, community and NGO). AWF has no mandate to promote any particular transboundary vision such as a mega-park, but merely has an obligation to serve the landscape and its stakeholders guided by principles of economic efficiency, socio-economic equity and ecological sustainability.

AWF's Approach to the "Four Corners" TBNRMA

AWF has to link its two-program approach of landscape-level conservation and livelihood improvement through Conservation Service Centers with both the expectations of the donor and those of its clients, the countries and their stakeholder constituencies. In order to meet the core result expected of USAID "viable practices for sustainable management of shared natural resources adopted," AWF has developed four activity specific result areas dealt with in detail below.

Improved Management of Specific TBNRMA Sites

This activity result area is the core conservation thrust of the project and guides the other three result areas by providing the vision for the transboundary ecological landscape.

- First, the AWF activity seeks to secure habitat by joint management activities. The key instrument at this point is the establishment of natural resource management (NRM) agreements between partners. These may be between governments, communities or merely between fishing camps either side of the Zambezi River, undertaking to manage shared habitat, secure migratory corridors, regulate commercial river use or co-manage wetlands and fisheries.

- Second, the "Four Corners" activity intends to support partners to agree on and ultimately establish joint management supported by working groups that may be site-specific (Chobe River, Hwange/Chobe connectivity) or thematic (wetlands, elephant migratory corridors, fences, disease).

- Third, habitat will be defined through agreed conservation targets developed through participatory planning. AWF, with support for The Nature Conservancy, has facilitated both a participatory scoping exercise and a meeting of scientists to establish the targets and their status. The "Four Corners" TBNRMA activity will help develop management strategies to abate threats and improve status of the targets.

Four Corners Environmental Targets and Status		
Conservation target	**Threat status**	**Status of target**
Wetlands	Very High	Good
River systems	High	Good
Wildlife migration corridors	High	Poor
Woodland Grassland Mosaic	High	Fair
Native Fish	Low	Good
Species assemblages	Very High	Fair
Declining or threatened species	Very High	Poor
Representative woodlands	Very High	Fair

The activity will focus on securing wildlife migratory corridors. Ten corridors have been identified, some terrestrial and some aquatic between the four countries. Prominent species using these corridors are elephant, zebra and wildebeest. Use agreements between landholders (state and community), wildlife authorities within and between countries will be the initial management approach, building on cooperation and shared vision toward collaborative management approaches. In addition, the project will support putting shared monitoring systems in place to track and measure impact of conservation strategies on the targets and assess if their status is improving.

Conservation Business Partnerships
Developed and Improved

Whereas the first activity result sets the stage for the conservation goal of the TBNRMA, the second addresses livelihoods and the reduction of poverty in the landscape. Improving livelihoods is a development goal and also a conservation strategy. Landscape level conservation in the "Four Corners" area is largely about reconciliating the land use relationship between the protected areas and the community areas that connect them. The communities in this area have, in the main, been introduced to CBNRM over the last decade. Many have received devolved wildlife use rights and formed "common property" resource management regimes for the natural resources and the costs and benefits that flow through them.

AWF's strategy focuses on leveraging conservation as a land use in community areas through the development of viable natural resource-based businesses. Obvious areas of environmental degradation, fragmentation and disturbance relate to human/wildlife conflicts over pastoral and cropping lands and access to riverine resources (alluvial soils, water, fishing, forage) will be targeted.

The activity aims to develop diverse and sustainable business ventures (community, public, private partnerships—CPPs) and has set a target of five strategic ventures in the first year. Inherent in the concept of CPP partnerships is the idea of trade off between the core values of the respective groups. It is assumed that protected area wildlife authorities are primarily motivated by a conservation goal while communities are driven by a development goal. The relationship between the park and the community as landholding stakeholders could be mutual if both parties give a little of what the other party desires. Thus parks can help communities' position themselves for development and empower them with access rights in order that they can secure equitable deals with the private sector. In return communities can recognize wildlife authorities concerns for biodiversity, wildlife corridors and dispersal areas and sustainable use. Parks and communities are neighbors and partners in a landscape level approach and this relationship is elaborated when taken to a transboundary level.

In themselves communities are motivated by the concept of TBNRMAs as long as they address their needs for social and economic integration. This was the situation prior to the nation–state and communities across the region yearn for the "hard edge" of living on the border to soften in a positive way. The activity also seeks to help improve marketing the of CPP enterprises to further improve livelihoods of communities through increased benefits from conservation ventures from rents, incomes, environmental, cultural and technical goods and services. The overall thrust of this result activity is to increase incentives to conserve resources and abating the threats identified in the conservation result.

Policy and institutional environment

Political power in the world today is mainly centralized in the authority systems of the nation–state. The phenomenon of globalization, particularly in its economic dimension, is a driving force in the development of regional political and economic constellations. In Southern Africa, especially in relation to intersectoral cooperation, the Southern African Development Community (SADC) is the key regional policy arena. An outstanding challenge involves the set of problems related to intersectoral coordination at regional level. For example, SADC has agreements on wildlife, fishing, forestry, water and tourism but in a TBNRMA all these must be coordinated. How can this be achieved? What are the roles of central government sectors, local government structures, communities and the private sector and how do they cooperate within and between countries in a TBNRMA?

The "Four Corners" activity aims to facilitate the development of an intergovernmental process for the TBNRMA. So far, senior officials and now some permanent secretaries of the Ministries of Environment and Tourism have started meeting. Once the civil servants can agree on a first tier framework agreement, Ministers are expected to endorse and mandate the process.

There are few examples of TBNRMA institutional arrangements at present but they provide some important contrasts.

- The Gazaland, Kruger, Gonarezhou TFCA now called The Great Limpopo Transfrontier Park has been dominated by intergovernment cooperation through National Parks and Wildlife Authorities in Ministries of Environment and Tourism. The participation of civic regional stakeholders has not been very active or structured as yet.

- The Zimbabwe, Mozambique, Zambia (ZIMOZA) initiative in the Lower Zambezi area, by contrast has evolved out of the CBNRM program's in the area and collaboration with local government structures with NGO facilitation. This arrangement has yet to be formalized at interstate level when it will be interesting to see where influence rests in the proposed three tier structure—local, technical and ministerial TBNRM committees.

TBNRMAs challenge institutions to coordinate multi-stakeholders (community, public, private) and multi-tiers (local, national, regional). The "Four Corners" activity has a strategy for this but is still working on the official mandates for legitimating the strategy. The plan is to support a functional TBNRMA multi-stakeholder steering committee with representation arising from national forums. Thus the four countries would each have a "Four Corners" TBNRMA forum that would prioritize and account for its participation in the TBNRMA.

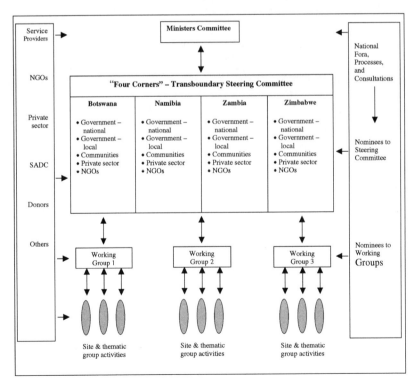

Diagram of Proposed Four Corners Transboundary Institutional Arrangements

Formal undertakings—policy, legal and institutional—needed in transboundary initiatives take time to process and can have high transaction costs. Less formal cooperation should not stultify while the formal framework evolves. Formal transboundary processes should concentrate on adding value to national approaches and not costs. If the costs are too high the added value leveraged through initiatives will diminish. Cooperative agreements may work when the opportunity to grasp efficiencies through harmonization of management strategies is seized.

Transboundary initiatives, through their very formality, may alienate rural communities, who struggle to actively participate in such high level arenas. The project will support communities to associate at national and transboundary level to ensure their voices are heard. It will do this through partnerships between national with NGOs and CBO associations. The transboundary canvas too big for any single agency. Just as alliances between governments and communities are necessary so are coalitions between service providing agencies, focused on specific countries, transboundary sites or specialized themes (e.g., CBNRM management, businesses, monitoring, capacity-building, etc.).

TBNRMA Information Dissemination

Active participation by all stakeholders requires that they have equal access to relevant information and knowledge of new developments. Lessons learned on viable practices must be shared between TBNRM partners. Information on conservation and development enterprise should be shared, contrasted and compared so that "best practices" have the chance to rise to the fore. Finally, shared monitoring and evaluation systems must become functional in order to track and document the TBNRMA process. Most knowledge of the transboundary landscape (ecological, cultural, and economic) is captured in national information systems and an opportunity exists to share existing information and relating it to a regional area (e.g., GIS data). While the project can use new information technologies (Internet) to share information it has to remember that this may increase knowledge disparities with communities. Efficient approaches must be used to reach rural communities.

Challenges to the "Four Corners" TBNRMA Initiative

The desire and will to move toward regional integration through TBNRMAs and other initiatives cannot be taken for granted. It needs leaders and "champions" who can express a vision and bring stakeholders into a process to realize it. Regional agreements are the "turf" of governments, but NGOs can promote and serve legitimate stakeholder parties that want to be involved.

Changes in the political climate of the region can occur suddenly. Whereas the conflict in Angola has lasted decades the semi-collapse of tourism in Zimbabwe and as a consequence in the region was largely unexpected.

Countries may have different policies and may organize their sectors in different ministries, which makes collaboration difficult. For example, some governments place wildlife agencies within tourism and/or environment ministries, others may not. Fisheries may be in the agricultural ministry. Who takes the lead? Is multi-sector coordination viable or do the transaction costs militate against it?

Perceptions of the task at hand vary. Wildlife conservation has a strong public appeal with some constituencies but governments want economic development through regional integration and development of "Four Corners" as a mega-tourism destination. To achieve that an enabling environment has to be established for the tourism industry (local, regional and global) to invest. Will the conservation constituency be able to get ahead of the investment process and guide it toward sustainable development approaches?

Will the policy arena is open for popular participation at the bottom, the middle and the top? Already, perceptions are expressed that transboundary initiatives are being pushed by a wildlife and tourism constituency that tends to be "white" and "foreign" and threatens to alienate both the public and community sectors. Another perception is that the public sector elite will collaborate with the national, regional and global private sector to alienate customary rights and reduce communities to mere laborers. These are powerful stakes and the management of conflict and the process of consensus building are very challenging.

Is it all worthwhile? The most unifying vision at present would appear to be the opportunity to leverage efficient, "green" and "fair" economic growth through the development of regional tourist destinations founded on sustainable natural resource management. Provided the private sector can make efficient investments that consolidate ecologically approaches that are fair in socioeconomic and political terms, then there is a great opportunity. The alternative is to negate the chance and remain with large parks surrounded by smallholders. Subsistence systems of agriculture, pastoralism and natural resource use are the present basis of social security for millions of people in these areas. They cannot be easily engineered and any TBNRMA that has a chance of working must positively relate to the local livelihood strategies in a way that does not risk what little security already exists.

Conclusion

The opportunities for TBNRM in the "Four Corners" exist but a lot depends on how popular perceptions and participation are managed and whether cooperation can produce an enabling environment with a strong new set of economic incentives. The "Four Corners" initiative funded by USAID and implemented by AWF is a time limited activity. It is not the only "show in town" and several other initiatives exist that are related. What finally transpires will depend on the governments and their stakeholders. AWF as an agency has a long-term commitment to its mission of working with people to keep the wildlife in the Upper Zambezi.

Peace Parks Foundation—
An Overview

Willem Van Riet

*[Editor's Note—This is an edited transcript
of a presentation and discussion]*

The Peace Parks Foundation (PPF) supports Government Departments in linking parks together across national borders. We support the National Park Board systems and the Departments of Environmental Affairs in many countries. Because we are not bound by national borders ourselves, we are the catalyst. In a sense, we make the Transfrontier Conservation Areas (TFCA) happen. Borders are incredible chasms between people, and of course they are like a Berlin Wall to wildlife.

The Peace Parks Foundation works across Southern Africa. For example, in South Africa's Richtersveldt we are currently bringing the local community into the workings of the national park. We use their languages and their culture. For example, the prayer opening of the most recent meeting was in the Lama language. The Lama language is ancient and is part of a culture of that landscape so it will be utilized in the development of this transfrontier conservation area (TFCA).

Besides the Richtensveldt, we are working on six areas. Of the six, the Kalahari-Gemsbok is actually functioning. The two Parks Boards—South Africa and Botswana—are running the Kalahari now as the first real TFCA.

The one drawing most of the attention now is the Kruger National Park, Gonarezhou (Zimbabwe) and the Gaza Province Development (Mozambique), one million hectares of wildland between the Elephant and the Limpopo River. Since this area is so huge, let's examine it more closely as the main topic of discussion.

This TFCA is now called the Great Limpopo Transfrontier Park. The big region on the Mozambique side is largely empty of people because the ancient sea used to break against the Limpopo Mountains, and therefore the whole landscape is covered in sedimentary deposits. The soils, coupled with the extremely low rainfall, make it a hard place for people to live. It is very difficult to live off the land with rainfall between 300–400 mm per year, so the communities in the area are located on the alluvium, next to the rivers.

How does one handle an area like this? How do you protect this de facto wilderness? I am a fanatical wilderness person, because I understand and have experienced how wilderness can change people and help society. But we will only protect wilderness if we do it as part of land use planning, and the land use planning in that region is based on allowing the communities to live on the alluvium area, tap into the resources that we are protecting in the wilderness, and use those resources in multiple ways.

The central and most interesting part of this area is 500,000 hectares of sandvelt wilderness. The land use plan has a community resources zone in which the people will all stay, and there are other zones such as a tourist zone next to Kruger. But you really need to see the area, and not just maps—it is magnificent. From the junction of the Limpopo and the Oliphant River one looks upon the incredible vastness of the Mozambique plains. This is where the Mozambican authorities are developing Coudada 16 as a National Park, part of that is the gigantic flood plan that was flooded a few years ago. Further up the Limpopo River is a landscape you have all read about in the book. Wild Africa Rivers, with communities dotted in small villages next to the river itself. Further up, as you head to Kruger Park, there is a gorge in the Limpopo River that has the biggest concentration of crocodiles you will ever see. The crocodiles in this region are so numerous they look like flies on a sandbank. It is a completely unapproachable landscape, only accessible by flying in. Sometimes the helicopters disturb the crocodiles. It is really an amazing wildlife feature that so far nobody has actually been able to see except the Rangers in Kruger. And just a bit farther along from this is the famous fence between South Africa and Mozambique that our Minister Valli Moosa will lift so that the old migration route can be functional again.

It is a truly wild landscape. The ability to survive on the sandvelt is tough because there is no surface water, no surface drainage, and rainfall is extremely low. However, there is a big lake on the Oliphant River, built a long time ago and meant for irrigation, which is probably the biggest source of water and potential tourist development in the whole land use plan. There is only one size-able village in the area with large numbers of extremely friendly people ready to assist wherever needed. Currently a German funding agency is supporting the economic development of this part of the program. Our aim is that the whole process is driven by the actual people of the landscape. Even the villages in the sand forest area will be included in the planning process, with obvious benefits of job creation and economic opportunities. With Kruger Park now outsourcing all their tourism facilities, we also hope more tourism opportunities are shared with the local people, so they become partners in the development.

In October (2001) our Minister Vallli Moosa and our previous President Mr. Mandela released some of the first elephants on the Mozambique side. This actually keeps Kruger from having to cull one thousand elephants. This reloca-tion was quite an emotional experience but also a reality exercise. The fantastic part of the story is we watched the two groups from Kruger meeting a small group existing in Mozambique. Similarly, in the beginning of this last century the hunters had killed all the elephants in the low veldt. There were no elephants in Kruger and 15 elephants walked across the Lubombo Mountain from the Chenqwexi River into Kruger Park and now 100 years later we are relocating 27 elephants back from Kruger into this region. All the elephants have been collared and are tracked four times a day to see how they fit in the landscape, how they interact with communities and their crops. This event had real conservation power in it.

Finally, I close by saying that this work with the communities, currently funded by various donor organizations, was not conducted by educated white people who went out to the communities. We trained the communities to do the work themselves, and they are currently working in the region. The land use planning will only be done when we get feedback from them, and they actual-ly will do the planning. They will decide if they want fences, if they want to relocate, if they want job opportunities, if they want to share in the business opportunities. The Companies to be set up will be partnered by the people in that region. It is their land, their opportunity.

The Necessity of
Changing What Is Possible

*Implementing Large-Scale
Wildlands Protection*

David Johns

The challenges we face as conservationists are enormous. When uncon-
strained by democratic norms, laws, and institutions, we conservationists
are often the targets of the powerful. The conservation movement is in the debt
of those who waged that long and costly struggle against apartheid not only for
recent South African conservation achievements, but also for South African
democracy.

Since the events of September 11, 2001, voices have been heard saying that
in a world of violence, inequality, and evil, conservation is not a priority, wilderness is not important.

Such voices are wrong.

Two decades ago, Erich Fromm, Alice Miller and Scott Peck wrote that evil
is about murder, about non-biologically necessary killing. Such murder is
pervasive, but evil is about more than just corporeal murder. It is also about
murder of the spirit; it is about imposing control on living things: to render
them convenient, pliable, dependent; to destroy spontaneity; to diminish
unpredictability.

Paul Shepard told us that institutionalized evil finds its roots in our
attempts to control nature. In our efforts to control nature we separate ourselves
from it and do great damage to ourselves, making evil and a host of other
maladies more likely.

The wild stands as the antidote to control. At the 3rd World Wilderness Conference, the poet Jay Vest reminded us that the word "wilderness" comes from the old English and the Indo-European words that mean, literally, "will-of-the-land or self-willed land": land that is not dominated. Wild animals, wild water, and wild lands are free from control.

Let us remember that love and control are opposites. To connect with wilderness is to be nurtured: it is to connect with our sanity; it is to connect with our deepest selves. It is seawater that flows in our veins—and some other things flow in seawater as well these days, and they are toxic.

The wild is our true home. We were born on the savannas of East Africa. If we lose wilderness, we lose ourselves. We believe that to protect the wild we must protect those things that make a place wild: unencumbered ecological processes and biodiversity. We must especially focus on wide-ranging species and top predators because they are not only the most threatened by our activities, but because if we protect them so much else is protected. Thus, large-scale wildlands conservation is essential.

In addition to the biological and ethical reasons for large scale wildlands protection, there are also important human reasons. First, we need self-willed lands and waters because we are poor ecosystem dominants. The cultural and

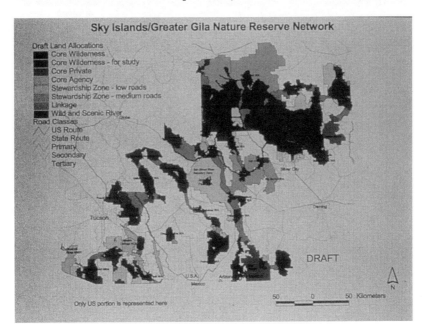

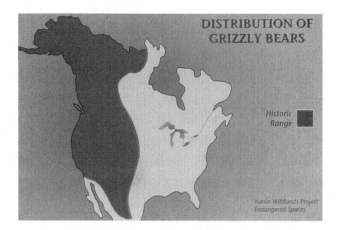

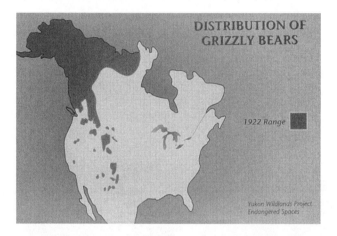

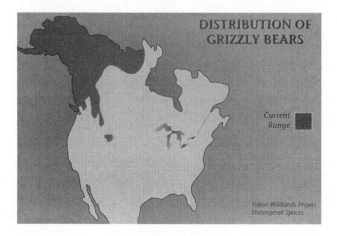

behavioral plasticity that permits us to adapt to any ecosystem on earth by developing technology and changing our social organization, also allows us to impoverish and destroy ecosystems.

The hierarchical nature of virtually all extant human societies insulates decision makers from the ecologically destructive consequences of their decisions. As a species we are easily blind to the long-term ecological deterioration we cause.

The social dynamic of growth that generates ever more people and ever higher levels of consumption, while not intractable, admits to no easy solution. It has deep temporal roots. Over 2,500 years ago, the Greek historian Thucydides quoted this description of the Athenians:

> "(They) are addicted to innovation. They are daring beyond their judgment. They toil on … with little opportunity for enjoying, being ever engaged in getting. They were born into the world to take no rest, and to give none to others."

This Athenian mind-set dominates the world today. Not because we all subscribe to it but because we have allowed it to become deeply institutionalized. The roots, of course, are even deeper. We have been implicated in extinctions for at least 15,000 years and perhaps for as long as 40,000 years.

Secondly, large-scale conservation is essential because small-scale conservation relies excessively on intensive human management. Our institutions are simply too frail and comparatively short-lived to be relied on as the main conservation tool. Finally, nature is simply too complex for us to manage. To substitute our brains for evolutionary processes is to invite disaster.

So, what is our role in conservation? What can we do? To protect what we love, what we need, we must protect continental systems of connected wildlands. We must designate protected areas and connections not on the basis of civilizations' leftovers, but on the biological needs of key species and on what it takes to ensure fully functional ecosystems of all types. For North America we believe that 25% of the landscape should be strictly protected, with another 25% in some sort of lesser protection.

Critics sometimes say we are utopian and that our goals are impossible to realize. But politics is not just about the art of the possible, as it is said to be: politics is also about the art of changing what's possible. Many said that the fall of apartheid or the fall of the Berlin Wall could not be accomplished short of war. Both are gone.

Creation of a conservation vision and plan can, in and of itself, change the public debate. We will never protect and restore the natural world just by responding to threats. We need a positive vision of what a healthy world would look like. This vision can inspire society and must guide our actions. Without such a vision we cannot hope to set the agenda. When the great U.S. civil rights leader Martin Luther King, Jr. came to Washington, D.C., in 1963 he did not proclaim, "I have a strategic plan." He said he had a dream, and called on America to fulfill it.

We start conservation planning by identifying wounds in the landscape: habitat loss and fragmentation, species decline and loss, invasion of exotics, pollution, and others. We then develop, in consultation with scientists, activists, indigenous groups, agencies, landowners and others, action steps that must be implemented to heal these wounds. We also identify the institutions, public and private, that have the authority to make the needed decisions. A political gap analysis is undertaken to identify which action steps are being addressed by NGOs and which ones are not. Action steps are also prioritized and resources dedicated on that basis.

It is useful to think of a conservation plan as the picture on the front of a jigsaw puzzle box. That picture is the vision as a whole. As with a puzzle, the vision is achieved piece by a piece or a few pieces at a time. This is achieved not by one group, but by many. The great new challenge is how to coordinate activity among the diverse groups of NGOs that drive the process. This coordination function is the main implementation role of the Wildlands Project itself.

The conservation planning process is deliberately iterative. Early rough cuts can be used to guide action until the plan is formally completed. In some sense, plans are never completed and must be adaptive.

Many of the tools we utilize to implement action steps are not new. We rely on legislation and agency action to expand existing protected areas and to create new ones. Wilderness designation offers the strictest protection, but park status, wildlife refuge status, and other tools are also used. Examples of large-scale protection include the Muskwa-Kechika in British Columbia, the California Desert Protection Act, a recent proposal to protect public and private lands adjacent to Waterton Park that will ensure linkages to the Jasper-Banff complex to the north and Cebadillas in northern Chihuahua.

Lands do not need to be pristine or near pristine to be included in protection proposals or even wilderness proposals. Almost all lands and waters have been damaged to some degree, and the total of even lightly degraded lands and waters would not constitute a large enough base for conservation: restoration is critical.

Implementation also includes changes in management regimes across the landscape. Pluie the wolf traveled hundreds of miles across thirty-five jurisdictions over two years: in some jurisdictions she was safe; in others not. She was legally shot in Alberta. Management regimes must not only be the right ones, but must be coordinated across jurisdictions to be effective.

Connectivity is vital, as the history of the grizzly shows. From a pre-European distribution essentially consisting of western North America, the grizzly's distribution was reduced in the United States by persecution and habitat destruction, to a number of islands by the 1920s. Even the wildest and remotest of these islands, isolated and small, could not sustain the great bears; not even Yellowstone National Park can sustain its population of grizzlies without connections. The Yellowstone to Yukon Conservation Initiative is proposing connections north from Yellowstone Park to Glacier-Waterton, and northwest to central Idaho's Bob Marshall-River-of-No-Return wilderness complex.

These important connections rely on both public and private lands. We work directly with private landowners; and we work to change land-use and tax laws to support private conservation. Too many current laws discourage it, by subsidizing extraction and other harmful practices.

Can this work in a crowded landscape? Yes. Florida is a populous and rapidly growing state—one of the fastest growing areas in North America. An early wildlands-type plan, undertaken by Reed Noss, first Science Director of The Wildlands Project, was based in large part on the needs of top carnivores. This plan was refined by agencies and NGO scientists and adopted by the state. Even with $6 billion in funding not all needed land can be acquired. In addition to land acquisition the state is therefore using the land-use planning and permit process to steer development away from biologically important areas. It appears to be working.

Success hinges on much more than comprehensive conservation planning, sound strategy and the mobilization of conservationists and close allies. It depends on fashioning a broad chorus of organized interests in support of particular proposals. We are fashioning new coalitions with progressive business and labor organizations, with Native groups, with religious groups and civic leaders.

Bruce Babbitt, after his appointment as U.S. Secretary of the Interior, told conservationists: "Don't expect me to do the right thing, make me do the right thing." Political leaders, facing enormous pressure from development interests, need something to hang their hat on even if they want to do the right thing. We must provide it. Brock Evans once said that success depends on endless pressure endlessly applied. But it also has to be *enough* pressure.

We are a species that can make choices about the habitat we use. Other species do not have that luxury. We can choose to continue on the path of conquest and control and sink further into biological ruin. Or we can choose, with generosity of spirit and truly informed self-interest, to embrace the wild—by helping it to heal, and by letting it be.

KwaZulu-Natal—
Proposed Mzinyathi Community
Conservation and Wilderness Area

Maurice MacKenzie

On the eastern seaboard of South Africa lies the land of the Zulu people. The Zulu people are famous for their legendary bravery coupled to superb physiques and enormous stamina. Their country begins at the hot sub-tropical coast and climbs up the five escarpments to the Drakensberg massif at 11,000 feet. It is the most watered of all the nine provinces of South Africa and no fewer than five major rivers drain from the Drakensberg.

An area exists on one of the major tributaries to the mighty Thukela River ("the frightening one"). The Buffalo or Mzinyathi River has an enormous catchment spreading over most of the savannah country below the Drakensberg and away to the East to the watershed with the Mfolozi River, and then joins the Thukela some 90 miles from the sea. The particular area is the stretch of river from Isandlwana to the confluence with the Thukela. Isandlwana, the sphinx-like mountain rising from the plain, is the site of the famous battlefield where in 1879 the Zulu army with spears and shields defeated the mighty British invasion forces with their cannon and deadly Martini-Henry muskets. The Buffalo River, or as the Zulu's know it uMzinyathi, was the boundary between colonial white Natal and Zululand. The tribes that inhabit this area today are direct descendants of those who lived though the times of invasion and final humiliating defeat. They are fiercely independent and protective of their rugged and mostly inaccessible terrain.

The WILD Foundation of the United States provided support for an in-depth study of this area to determine if it could eventually be a Community Conservation area, including a wilderness area.

The corridor covering the winding Buffalo River extends to some 8 kilometers on both banks and 45 kilometers downstream, and can be classified as "wild, rugged, mostly unspoiled, undeveloped and remote from known civilization." It is very sparsely populated by isolated family homesteads, called muzi's by the Zulu, reached only by winding and at times precipitous footpaths. Scientifically, the vegetation is classified as thick valley bushveld of mostly acacia species with highland open grassveld. The rainfall is low at 60 to 72 cm per annum, rising to 132 cm on the mountaintops. The heat units are high with a mean annual temperature of 16 degrees C. The topography is as mountainous with deep ravines and towering cliffs from an altitude of 1,850 meters down to 460 meters in the valley bottom. Some canyons never see the sun as they are slanted to the south. Unique plant forms grow in this eternal shade.

The current land use systems are cattle grazing with minimum areas being tilled. Marijuana is grown secretly and is one of the few income earners available to these hardy, deprived people. The area is extremely depressed economically, and existence is maintained by repatriated wages from the industrialized centers of the port of Durban and Johannesburg, where the menfolk are employed. Some very young children, three and four years old, have never seen a white person.

The social and tribal systems existing are a remnant of the past and with little or no incentive to develop economically. This is largely because of the migration out of the community, along transport routes, of the menfolk to find work, and of starving families into local towns. The result is rapid and continuing depopulation of this area. Where many years ago there was once a well-populated rural community based on subsistence farming and livestock, there is now an area largely devoid of people. The social-economic-political cycles have combined with the natural cycle, and wild nature is returning.

In the new and democratic South Africa, the wise use of natural resources with involvement by local communities, is a viable option for development. To this end, recent provincial legislation supports the formation of Community Conservation Areas where the community has ownership and a shared equity in the area and its enterprises, along with donor funding. The low cost of infrastructure in the creation of a tourist destination—when compared to the costs and negative impacts of heavy industrialization—makes this option the obvious form of land use.

One of the main principles that framed this study was to not raise local expectations. This was difficult because so much discussion is always required on any matter in these rural communities, whether the issue at stake is large or small. It is imperative to involve and inform people, and listen to their history, hopes, complaints and ideas—it is their land, their future. Because this process is the bedrock upon which any future development can be truly successful, and in an area where few if any other options are available, it is sometimes impossible not to raise expectations. This is a serious challenge inherent in this sort of study. During this process, the tribal leaders (amaKosi) have all been consulted closely and support the initiative, as if it occurs it can only improve the lifestyles of their subjects and possibly bring some of the menfolk back from their urban workplaces.

Significant challenges were identified, however. It is a very remote area, with perennial issues of violence and pockets of criminality. Social stability is dependent more on local tribal authority rather than effective policing. Four or five tribal districts are included in the study area, and one of them located centrally in the area is without an iNkosi, or traditional leader. It is being run by the indunas, or subchiefs of smaller wards within the district. They have a serious problem with commercially driven cattle rustling—with the stolen cattle quickly butchered and trucked to the townships for sale—and their people are intimidated by these criminals. Zululand is beautiful, but can be a rough neighborhood.

Another factor, with both positive and negative impact, is the sheer remoteness of this area. It will draw a certain type of tourist representing a small profile of the overall tourist market. To mitigate this is the relative proximity of other areas of cultural and historical significance. One could foresee an excellent combination of eco-cultural tourism, given the funding, time and marketing.

A very preliminary business model has been formulated. With a minimum of initial capital expenditure, a start can be made on a fenced game reserve, stocked with compatible species. The gradual development of tourist-oriented, unique selling factors, such as authentic Zulu living experiences within the boundaries of the game reserve, as well as luxury lodges on the boundaries, could follow. Management of the whole entity could be done by an entity comprised of KZN Wildlife (the provincial nature conservation service), full representation from all the four different tribal areas that cover the river from Isandlwana to the Thukela, and relevant, participating NGOs and the private sector. Potential sources of revenue, depending on the eventual management plan, could include hunters, tourists on horseback, curio manufacturers, backpackers and the river rafters, and cultural tourists.

Perhaps most important of all is the availability of some real wilderness, the actual extent of which has as yet to be measured, but is substantial enough to warrant an intensive scientific evaluation. This unusual conglomeration of land types, qualities and features—should it hopefully be eventually incorporated as a Community Conservation Area—needs to be protected by buffer zones surrounding the game reserve and wilderness area. This core wilderness area could serve as the nucleus of the Community Conservation Area, and also possibly resuscitate the true value of this whole region.

As mentioned earlier, additional attractions to this area is its historical and archeological significance. Though no mega or charismatic fauna still exist within the area, existing wildlife includes the remnant of eagles, falcons, migrant species and abundant plant life. Past experience elsewhere confirms that reintroduced, indigenous wildlife will quickly readapt and thrive, given appropriate protection is provided. Thus could occur a successful combination of both ecological and cultural tourism.

The suggested development techniques should include minimum soil disturbance and negative visual impact. Wherever possible and depending on the wishes of the people themselves, it is imperative to include tribes people and their homes, ancestors graves and livestock. Significant management issues would need to be addressed, such as the role of exclusionary zones, potential inclusion of predators, and so on. This principle has been tried and implemented successfully in East Africa, but cognizance is required of cultural differences and local anomalies. The over-arching principle, of course, is the full concurrence on all significant issues by the tribal equity holders.

The whole system of Community Conservation Areas in South Africa is receiving close attention and will soon fall under a specific sub department of the KZN Department of Environmental Affairs. The funding of these areas will however not be rated higher that those departments which are dealing with huge backlogs (i.e., Health, Education and Welfare). Therefore, donor funding and participation of the private sector are essential to start the process.

Given the difficulties inherent in a project such as this, each step needs to be carefully considered, with the human factor the significant part of the equation. The reward, however, could be the greatest of all—a priceless wilderness replenished and thriving, in the process of which occurs the upliftment of local and impoverished people, and the enhancement of the pride and dignity of the Zulu people.

Wilderness, Wildlands and Wildlife

Wilderness from an Elephant's Point of View

Iain Douglas-Hamilton

The African wilderness, for me, is epitomized by elephants, so let us consider wilderness from an elephant's point of view. Elephants need a great deal of space. So from an elephant's point of view, the more wilderness the better. At present, where elephants do well in Africa there is much habitat to support them, and so a host of other species is surviving along with them. In this sense, elephants are an indicator of the welfare of the wilderness. Despite serious episodes of decrease over the last thirty years in their range north of the Zambezi, elephants still occur in abundance in huge and often remote wildland areas in Africa, and are still believed to have a total range of over 5 million square kilometers. Much of this is defined by hearsay, the maps are out of date, and as human population increases people build new roads and open up land used by elephants. More and more of this elephant range will be thrown into doubt. Nevertheless, elephants are still found in all but five countries out of the forty-three countries south of the Sahara, and are believed to have gone extinct in only two in the last thirty years—Mauritania and Burundi. They live in some of the most beautiful wildernesses; deserts, forests, savannahs, mangrove swamps and high altitude moorland. Despite all the killing for ivory that has taken place over the last thirty years, elephants have great powers of renewal and several major populations in African savannahs are now recovering from their losses of the 1970s and 1980s.

It is an axiom of conservation that a balance needs to be found between the needs of man and the needs of wildlife which must include the protection of natural habitats and wilderness areas. National parks and protected areas are priority needs. However, preserving habitat is not enough to guarantee the future of wildlife. Ultimately, man is the chief ecological determinant, and over-use of wildlife through unregulated trade and poaching of animals for meat, skins and other products can remove wildlife even where the habitats are still intact.

In the case of the elephant this was particularly marked at the time of the 1st World Wilderness Congress in 1977 when the ivory trade was uncontrolled and rampant in most of the continent, apart from some countries in Southern Africa. The price of ivory had gone up by ten times between the 1960s and the 1970s. In Kenya, where the problem was first identified, it was believed that half the elephants had been lost to ivory poachers by the mid-1970s, an estimated drop from 180,000 down to 60,000—and it was to get worse, with Kenya's elephants descending to about 20,000, before the situation got better.

Fears for the elephants' future led to a continental concern. I was engaged in the first pan-African elephant survey, sponsored by IUCN, the New York Zoological Society (now World Conservation Society) and the WWF. This survey was just two years old at the time of the 1st Wilderness Congress, and in collaboration with many other scientists I helped compile the first continental figures of elephant numbers country by country. Scientists and conservationists all over the continent began to pool figures on elephant numbers and trends from all the regions of Africa. We were also asking whether or not the ivory trade had the will or the ability to regulate itself? Don't forget that was over twenty-five years ago.

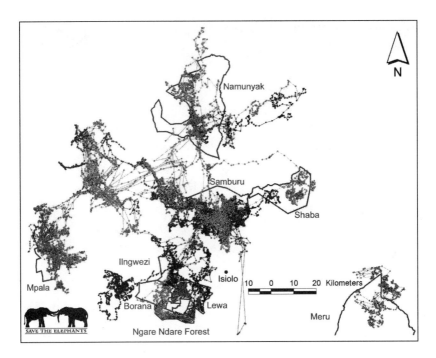

The survey lasted for four years, and was succeeded by other surveys in the 1980s. The ivory poaching in Kenya spread to Northern Tanzania and to other countries across Africa. Some like Chad, Somalia, and Central African Empire had been tranquil when the survey began but soon the elephants were subjected to a rapid increase in poaching.

In the overview I found that West Africa had only fragmented populations. There were a few transfrontier populations including one in the Gourma area of Mali, where elephants move across boundaries, but by and large dense human populations surrounded the few pockets of West African elephants. One population still lived up in Mauritania but it has since gone extinct. West African elephant habitats were under tremendous pressure from the human populations. In Ivory Coast we found intensive logging and we were informed that along the tracks cut by the bush meat hunters radiated into the forests often cleaning out almost all edible species. This problem has grown to even greater proportions and is epidemic today.

In Central Africa I visited Gabon with vast untouched forest where elephants were still abundant, but in the rest of Central Africa, especially in Zaire, the ivory trade was reputedly even more out of control than it was in Kenya. In essence it seemed the resource was being mined and any kind of sustainable use was remote from the minds of ivory traders. The idea of killing off their own livelihood didn't seem to signify.

It was only in Southern Africa that elephants were secure in the 1970s and 1980s, and several populations were believed to be expanding in Botswana, South Africa and Zimbabwe, and they have continued to do so until today.

The best places for elephants were in the Selous Game Reserve in Tanzania where I estimated over 100,000 elephants from an aerial survey in 1975 and where there was little trace of poaching. However, within one decade this changed. The Selous number was halved by ivory poachers and the carcass ratio shot up. I also found, in the Ruaha-Rungwa Complex in Tanzania some 40,000 elephants in 1977, which later were to decline to 10,000. In Tsavo, Kenya's greatest national park, elephants fell from over 40,000 in 1970 to just over 6,000 by 1988.

Early 1980 I came to Uganda for the second time. The national parks, Queen Elizabeth and Murchison Falls had been some of the most famous elephant parks in Africa. Here I witnessed the greatest proportional destruction of elephants I had yet seen. Dead elephants lay like fallen leaves along the trails. Out of the 8,000 elephants that had been living south of the Nile in Murchison Falls National Park, there was only one herd left of 160 survivors huddled together in a terrified mass. I witnessed and photographed whole elephant families shot down, with empty cases from automatic rifles littering the ground. These scenes colored my views. I feared then that this situation was indicative of what was happening to elephants in most of Africa. Ivory was legal all this time and all attempts to regulate the trade had failed.

By 1980 as the continental survey came to the end of its first iteration I had already concluded that there was no will or ability within the ivory trade to regulate itself. The Wilderness Congress in 1977 had sounded the first alarm internationally about the serious threat to elephants from the ivory trade. However, it was not until 1989 that any united international action was taken. At the eleventh hour the politicians of East Africa woke up to the impending near total loss of their elephants. In Kenya 12 tons of ivory was burnt in a huge bonfire to put it beyond the reach of the trade. In the same year the nations of the world introduced a total ivory trade ban through the CITES convention. Finally the situation of the elephants began to turn around.

In East Africa it was possible to monitor the improvement, especially in Tanzania, Kenya and Uganda. In the decade of the 1990s the Tsavo elephant population showed a steady increase. Since the ivory ban they have increased by 50% in ten years. This has been matched by similar increases elsewhere in East Africa. The forest populations of West and Central Africa are impossible to monitor for trends, but in Southern Africa the trend as before has been steadily upwards.

From the first beginnings, the monitoring of elephants has improved. Ever since the mid-1970s there has been a group of volunteer scientists called the African Elephant Specialist Group, working under the auspices of IUCN, that has compiled figures on elephants. Today, this group is very active with a network of scientists. Information on elephant status is sent to a well-organized computerized data base where a geographical information systems analyst compiles elephant figures and produces beautiful maps of the elephant range.

The maps of the African Elephant Database show the ranges of elephants in the different regions of Africa. All the information is carefully graded and estimates of elephant numbers are sorted into definite, probable, possible and speculative categories. Some major changes have occurred since the specialist group first started its work. At present Southern Africa has nearly the same number of elephants of the rest of Africa put together. Yet thirty years ago it was the other way round when East Africa had the largest proportion. Knowing the history we are forced to realize that the numbers in themselves were no protection for elephants in East Africa.

Now in places like Botswana there are the same high densities that we once enjoyed in East Africa in the 1960s. These regional differences in elephant status have led to different attitudes to elephant management and the ivory trade. It has also led to a different perception of the threats to elephant survival, East African nations being much more circumspect about resuming an ivory trade. The hardest paradox to explain is that despite the overall decline of elephants in Africa, there is increase, even overpopulation, for an important minority.

As memories fade of the elephant slaughter, the movement grows to relax the total ivory ban. It is therefore ever more important that the monitoring of elephants should be improved so that a sensitive system is put in place that will be capable of giving an early warning if changes should be induced by renewed ivory trading. Fortunately, such a system is being set in place by the CITES treaty, which goes by the name of MIKE or Monitoring of the Illegal Killing of Elephants. This is based on selected sites across Africa.

Elephants in the wilderness are mercifully unaware of historical changes. From their point of view they still need to find food and water, avoid danger and find or avoid other elephants. In Kenya, we are trying to understand the elephant's point of view, by following their movements in great detail. Save the Elephants in collaboration with the Kenya Wildlife Service has initiated an advanced radio-tracking program. We hope to understand from this how elephants make decisions and what they need to secure their future.

Our core area is a superb undeveloped wilderness in Northern Kenya. It is also a MIKE site. The highest point is Mt. Kenya where the snows fall and melt. The water percolates through the montane forests until it runs through farmlands down to lower forests. The rivers flow north and turn through the Samburu national reserve and other private and public protected areas. It is one of the most exciting areas in Africa because it has a rare combination of land uses. Local pastoralists, the Samburu and Maasai, have set up their own privately owned sanctuaries with lodges, with the help of large scale ranchers in the south who themselves have turned their properties into wildlife conservancies. Within this complex elephant domain, there are also long-established National Reserves like Samburu were we are based, and Meru National Park nearby. In between is no man's land disputed between different ethnic groups. So the elephants are confronted with a mosaic of land uses, some safe, others dangerous to them.

Across this vast expanse, we pinpoint elephants' positions every hour using GPS radio collars programmed to store the fixes in the collar. We then relay the information up to our aircraft that flies by. On the map, we are able to plot out the elephants movements as they move from one protected area to another. The elephants make intelligent use of all this diversity. Their core areas are in the protected areas, where we find areas of intensive use we call hotspots. Each distinct segment of elephant range is linked by thin corridors to the next, and we have found that elephant's streak down these corridors to get from one place to another. They behave as if they are aware of danger zones often crossing them rapidly by night. The more elephants we track the more we realize how interlinked all the land units are by a network of elephant trails.

Our moving maps show how the elephants traverse the landscape. Each little dot is an elephant being tracked with a GPS radio and it is possible to see how they are attracted to fresh green grass where the rains have recently fallen. We have also tracked transfrontier movements of bulls from the Amboseli National Park in Kenya across the border into the West Kilimanjaro area of Tanzania. Interestingly, these bulls spend 90% of their time outside the Park. One bull, in a heightened state of sexuality known as musth, paced up and down in the protected area at high speed. After a month or so he decided to make a reconnaissance across the border from Kenya into Tanzania where he found an area of woodland, superior to that of Amboseli. After investigating the other side, he returned to the Park, resumed chasing the females and then finally moved back to Tanzania where he took up residence for the next four months. This transfrontier movement was important to this bull to reach his bull holding area where better food would enable him to grow strong in preparation for competing with other males for females.

Our technique of GPS elephant tracking is clearly relevant to the establishment of the new transfrontier parks elsewhere in Africa. Similar elephant tracking programs would reveal the key routes and allow conservation planners to link up vital segments of elephant range into balanced ecosystems.

Finally radio-tracking has shown us how elephants and people cohabit in the Samburu ecosystem in Kenya. It has highlighted the importance of maintaining the traditional tolerance between these pastoral people and the elephants that has endured for centuries.

The importance of education for local people as a means for getting them to maintain the wilderness and the animals that live there, cannot be overestimated.

We are fortunate to live in an area where people are used to living with elephants. The Samburu along with the elephants are the well-diggers in the dry season when the rivers dry up. You may often see a Samburu who is waiting to get to his well that is occupied by elephants. Samburu people have an elaborate wildlife lore and many folktales about elephants. I believe that Samburu culture will provide a solid basis for a new conservation ethic in our area based on local values.

At our research center at Save the Elephants our senior research technician, David Daballan, explains radio collars to local children. Ultimately it is these children and others who will decide the fate of the elephant. They watch wildlife films with a Samburu commentary we provide. They love watching films on big cats, a subject very close to the hearts of the Samburu.

The 1st Wilderness Congress was a landmark in alerting the world about what the ivory trade was doing to Africa's elephants. The movement to safeguard elephants from excessive ivory trading grew out of it and was effective in bringing the worst excesses of killing elephants for ivory to a close. The issue is continuously debated at CITES, but the overall situation vis-à-vis the ivory trade is better for elephants now than it was in the past.

On the other hand, loss of habitat and conflict with human beings continue. Habitat protection, community programs, and turning human elephant conflict into human elephant co-habitation are crucial keys for the future.

The World Wilderness Congress needs to continue in its traditional commitment to elephants, and be a landmark in establishing the importance of linking wilderness areas by means of corridors. Our radio-tracking has shown how elephants use corridors to link important segments of their ecosystem. The plan to join Kruger with parts of Mozambique and Gona Rhe Zhou National Park in Zimbabwe is a heartening example of what can be done by reuniting an elephant range that was long ago sundered. There is a little time left in which corridors can be secured, but the ecological and political arguments have been made. If elephants can show the best routes to conservation planners then once again the elephant will prove to be a keystone species.

Cheetah, Wildlands and Human Needs—Working Together

Laurie Marker and Matti Nghikembua

The concept of wilderness describes areas of a rugged and untamed nature, perceived to be free from human exploitation. The establishment of specific Wilderness Areas has historically been concentrated in areas of scenic value with low economic potential, and therefore many of these areas have little value for satisfying basic human needs or are often too small for conserving biodiversity.

In the developing world, even designated wildlands may not be safe in the future and will shrink as humans develop, alter and dominate natural areas. Human population is growing exponentially and natural resources are being exploited for satisfying basic human needs; establishment and sustainability of wilderness is often in conflict with maintaining basic human needs that are essential for living. Today, over 800 million people don't have enough food to eat, water quality remains poor and much of the world does not have adequate housing, health care or education. The failure to meet these basic human needs has often resulted in over-exploitation of natural resources, and political, social and economic pressure to develop existing wilderness areas.

In addition to human needs, wilderness areas often are not able to meet wildlife's needs. Often wilderness areas are limited in size and too isolated to protect viable populations of species, especially wide-ranging carnivores such as the cheetah. We suggest that the development of wilderness areas should be defined using both biological and social criteria, and, as such, wilderness areas could enhance biodiversity conservation efforts while considering the needs of local residents.

Developing methods to address these issues represents a challenge for wilderness, human rights and conservation advocates. Integrating wilderness, biodiversity conservation and social needs will require a systematic approach and will need to take into account the management of protected areas, Wilderness Areas and non-protected areas. Large, wide-ranging carnivores, such as the cheetah, provide an ideal focal species for designing a model that would integrate wilderness areas with human needs.

Namibia

Namibia is a large arid nation (2.7% of Africa) with a relatively small human population (1.6 million). Much of the countries' biodiversity is found outside of protected areas and wilderness areas, which currently represent 12% of the country.

Most of Namibia's protected areas are found in extremely arid habitats that have very little economic value, and very few productive savannah areas are represented in the protected area network. Consequently, much of Namibia's biodiversity is found outside of protected areas or wilderness areas. This is where farming practices, both subsistence and commercial, are taking place, resulting in conflict with natural resource management.

Creation of wilderness areas in productive habitats in developing countries conflicts with efforts to meet basic human needs. In developing countries where resources can be severely limited, rapid expansion of human population (e.g., 3% annual increase in Namibia) poses a threat to natural resources and makes designating new wilderness areas a challenge. The economy of developing countries, such as Namibia, depends on natural resources such as fish, agricultural land, water and scenic wilderness.

The dependency on natural resources in developing countries has economic and environmental costs. For example, the consumptive use of resources on which most rural populations depend may be limited within wilderness boundaries as a result of management policies and limited natural resources. In addition, utilization of available resources is often restricted to local people, because of access to use, accessibility of area and inherent low productivity of Wilderness Areas (e.g., deserts and mountains). These factors, therefore, result in reduced social and economic benefits, which form the basis of fundamental human needs.

Failure to meet basic human needs and to recognize stewardship of people and natural resources can alienate conservation efforts. A result of such action could lead to the loss of suitable habitat for endangered species, conflicts with human interest, accelerated rate of extinction, and overexploitation of natural resources.

Biodiversity conservation in non-protected and non-wilderness areas must be managed to meet both human and wildlife needs, which will alleviate some pressure on the existing protected area network. Balancing human and wildlife needs is difficult, especially since human needs are often overestimated while wildlife needs are difficult to measure.

Over exploitation in many countries has resulted in local extinctions of many species, including the cheetah. There has been a shift of needs that could have been sustainably satisfied by maintaining a healthy ecosystem. The shift of human needs include: human population explosion resulting in loss of habitats and species, less diverse ecosystems that can support species, overgrazing and mono culture systems in agriculture, poverty in most areas due to non-sustainable lands and over exploitation of all natural resources in developed lands, culture erosion—i.e., American Indians and Bushman lived one with the earth providing food, health, and shelter through sustainable use of their lands and differentiating between real needs and perceived needs.

Human needs are expected to grow, resulting in decreasing resources. Therefore, critical issues for the future need to include today:

- How do we decide which human uses are compatible with conservation?
- How do we define sustainable human needs?

One approach is to use a surrogate species to indicate the status or health of existing ecosystems. Large carnivores have been shown to exert top-down forces and play a regulatory role in ecosystems. Large carnivores are also susceptible to local extinction due to human causes, and can serve as an umbrella species because protecting enough area for viable populations of large carnivores will necessarily protect additional wildlife species. We suggest that the cheetah is an ideal species to direct and focus conservation efforts in Namibia and other parts of Africa. Cheetah have large home ranges and were once found throughout much of sub-Saharan Africa. Through the use of this species as an umbrella species, much of the cheetahs range could be re-established while meeting the needs of people and again developing healthy ecosystems.

Cheetah Conservation:
Learning to Live with Predators and Livestock

Cheetah are listed on Appendix I of the Convention on International Trade in Endangered Species, and classified as vulnerable or endangered by the World Conservation Union (IUCN). With a world population of less than 15,000 animals, most cheetah populations are small and fragmented, and found outside of protected areas. Namibia supports the largest free-ranging cheetah population of the world (approximately 3,000 animals), of which 90% are found on the north-central commercial farmlands. Conflict with livestock and wildlife farming exist between cheetah and farmers. This conflict is primarily economically oriented, as farmers perceive cheetah as competitors and a threat to their livestock. These extensive commercial farmlands average 8,000 ha in size and, although non-wilderness by definition, support nearly 70% of the countries populations of ungulate species that provide a prey base for the cheetah. The farming practices are mixed with livestock (mostly cattle) and free-ranging wildlife.

Through research conducted by the Cheetah Conservation Fund during the past decade, Namibian farmers have found that they can live with cheetahs on their lands if simple livestock management techniques are utilized along with practicing sustainable wildlife management. Nomadic herders have found similar methods in Kenya and Tanzania.

Conservancies to Benefit Wilderness

In Namibia one of the new developments of land and wildlife management practices, Conservancies, has great potential for meeting the needs for people, wildlife and wilderness. Conservancies consist of adjacent farms joining together in broad units and developing management strategies sensitive to their farmland ecosystem as a whole. Conservancies provide an alternative to managing game on an individual farm basis while promoting conservation through sustainable utilization. The advantage of conservancy areas over fenced game farms is that wildlife is free-ranging and can thus migrate out of an area if climatic or environmental conditions decrease the habitat suitability for the species. Also, this form of management promotes bio-diversity including cheetahs and other predators. Besides sustainable use, conservancies consider protection, maintenance, rehabilitation, restoration, enhancement of ecosystems and eco-tourism.

Within conservancies, wilderness areas can also be created, thus expanding the goals of wilderness to private lands. An example of this includes two areas within the Waterberg Conservancy. The Waterberg Conservancy surrounds Namibia's Waterberg Plateau Park. The national park known for its rare and endangered species also has the first proclaimed Wilderness Areas in Namibia. Two Wilderness Areas have been proposed within the conservancy, one on the Farm Osonanga, boarding the wilderness area of the Waterberg Plateau Park, and another area on a neighboring farm, Utsig. A similar development has recently taken place in South Africa.

Wilderness and human needs can be met through the development of conservancies that support mixed wildlife, including predators like cheetahs and livestock systems, and promote healthy ecosystems. This balance between human and wildlife needs, although difficult to determine and measure, is critical for the survival of the cheetah, and its habitat. We believe that representative biodiversity, and the persistence of species and ecological processes, as well as considering the needs of local residents are important for conservation to be successful. Through the development of conservancies, which support mixed management systems, a healthy ecosystem can maintain human needs while supporting conservation. In this manner, conservation areas continue to produce services (people and science based) and resources important for satisfying basic human needs as well as the needs of wildlife.

Creative Management for the Future

For conservation efforts to be successful, non-wilderness should be managed to benefit human and wildlife. Successful biodiversity conservation efforts in Namibia have considered sustainable methods of resource utilization, through a combination of research, monitoring, education and community-based outreach programs.

For many of these programs and ideas to work more resources are needed for basic education and training in the form of community conservation capacity building. Increased resources are needed to enhance education from just getting children into school to, teaching environmental education. Environmental education should be a part of all age groups and all curriculums. And in developing nations, resource management and integrated agriculture and wildlife management should be one of the most important courses taught.

Conclusion

The conservation of endangered species and their habitats remains a challenge. The survival of these species can only be realized once necessary strategies for mutual human–wildlife coexistence are developed and implemented on a broad scale.

Today, most of the areas where cheetahs once were found do not have healthy ecosystems and human's needs are not being met. By using the cheetah as a flagship species the health of an ecosystem could be monitored. We believe that understanding how wilderness areas and cheetahs could satisfy multiple needs through a new perspective on land management, would strengthen the conservation of wilderness conservation in Namibia and other developing countries.

This paper recognizes the role and contribution of wilderness area management as an important conservation tool. We believe that as the population growth of most of our developing nations increases so will the combined needs and expectations for a higher living standard and this will cause unprecedented pressure on natural resources. The Namibian response may be an example for other developing countries of Africa. The utilization of natural resources will continue, but we need to consider critical issues such as how to define and decide on sustainable human needs, and which can be compatible with conservation.

We are faced with a clear question. Do we allow our resources to shrink in the 21st century, or can we envision a way that our resource can expand through creative conservation?

Wildlands Network Design

The Role of Top Carnivores in the Regulation of Ecosystem Structure and Diversity

Michael E. Soulé

Designing networks of wild lands is an essential component of any strategy to arrest the global extinction crisis. But connectivity per se does little good unless linkages are planned for particular focal species—usually wideranging carnivores and their prey. In turn carnivores are essential for maintaining the long-term diversity of most ecosystems. Any regional conservation strategy, therefore, must consider the needs of large carnivores and other keystone species and processes. Moreover, the symbolic presence of carnivores in few places, such as in a fraction of national parks, is not an effective conservation strategy. Carnivores should occur throughout as much of their original range as biologically possible and socially tolerable, and should occur in ecologically effective numbers. In this regard, conservation planners must strive to be ecocentric, whereas campaigners and activists need to consider human attitudes and how best to change them where necessary.

Conservation and the wilderness movement began with an emphasis on the most monumental and scenic landscapes—its grandest vistas and most impressive creatures. As the 20th century unfolded, however, and as the science of ecology developed, conservation biologists recognized another conservation imperative: the need to protect less spectacular but biologically richer habitats such as tropical forests, and temperate marshes and prairies. The legacy of these two great traditions is our national parks, wildlife refuges, nature reserves, and wilderness areas. Yet these wonderful jewels are rare, covering only about 5 percent of the land area worldwide.

During the last 40 years, we saw the emergence of three bodies of evidence that have supported larger reserves and greater connectivity. The first is from descriptive biogeography, the major element being the species-area curve—the larger the patch, the more species it contains. The second argument is based on the spatial and temporal distributions of diversity-enhancing disturbances such as fire and flood; the larger the area, the more the spatial and temporal distributions of disturbance events and amplitudes approach historic levels, so that less management is required. The third argument is based on demographic and genetic considerations for vulnerable species, namely that population viability is proportional to population size; hence wide-ranging or rare species require big spaces lest they become locally extirpated or ecologically ineffective.

But these arguments have not slowed the death of nature. As a new millennium commences, we witness accelerated conversion of wildlands to croplands, pastures, tree plantations, and sprawling cities. And the invention of new land-scouring technologies advances yearly, facilitating mechanized exploitation of natural resources, including fresh water, forage, timber, coal, natural gas, and other resources. On top of this we bear helpless witness to the quiet invasion of alien species. All this threatens to extinguish as many as half the earth's plant and animal species. If these trends continue, wilderness will not persist into the 22nd century.

In spite of this swelling calamity, some conservationists and wilderness advocates still think in traditional categories. An implicit premise of much of our work is that biotic diversity can persist in isolated habitat reserves. Although the long-term instability of island-like wildlands remnants is recognized by ecologists, it is virtually unchallenged as a matter of policy and implementation. The evidence that isolated reserves—a category that includes some of the largest national parks in the United States—gradually lose native species, especially large mammals and carnivores, is overwhelming. Such gradual degradation can only accelerate as human activity and development increase on surrounding lands.

The elements of the solution are known: bigness and connectivity, but implementation of such a program is just beginning. We comfort ourselves with the wishful assertion that the "matrix" of semi-developed lands between reserves can sustain ecological processes including animal migrations and dispersal. But an inexorable tide of exotic species, edge effects, and increasing human disturbance and encroachment is slowly drowning our fragmented patchwork of mostly small wildlands.

Larger reserves and better connectivity constitute the foundation for any meaningful program of wilderness protection or nature conservation on a regional or continental scale, and the needed transformation in conservation is still possible in many parts of the world, including those with decreasing human populations such as parts of Europe and North America. The major elements of this new view of nature protection include: (1) recognition of top-down regulation in ecosystems and the need for large core areas and regional wildlife linkages; (2) the need for ecological restoration on unprecedented scales; and (3) a critique of fashionable alternatives such as sustainable development.

The scientific argument for extensive networks of wildlands emphasizes the roles of keystone species. In North America the emphasis is the ecological roles of large carnivores. There is increasing evidence that functional wildlands networks require keystone species, particularly large carnivores, to stabilize prey and smaller predators and to help maintain ecological diversity and resilience. And if large carnivores are essential, then connected landscapes are the most natural way of achieving effective conservation. As discussed below, there is increasing evidence of top-down ecological regulation by carnivores in a variety of ecosystems. Similar arguments can be made for other critical species and processes.

Other considerations buttress the case for carnivore protection and restoration. Conservation on a scale that restores or sustains native top carnivores is an end in itself, for aesthetic, spiritual, and ethical reasons, irrespective of scientific justification. For example, many environmental ethicists and conservationists argue that society is obligated to redress policies that nearly cleansed the United States of animal competitors, such as grizzly bears, mountain lions, bobcats, coyotes, and wolves, for the benefit of livestock owners during the 20th century. Moreover, many conservationists argue that a defining characteristic of wilderness is the presence of powerful predators.

Top-down Regulation

The architecture of viable regional conservation networks must, in most parts of North America, at least reflect the needs of keystone species, meaning those strongly interacting species whose influence is out of proportion to their own. Whether top predators play keystone roles in terrestrial ecosystems has long been a contentious issue, although such roles have been unequivocally demonstrated in aquatic and marine.

The paucity of controlled comparisons has made it difficult to evaluate whether terrestrial carnivores are keystone species. People have eliminated large carnivores from many land areas around the world and still persecute the survivors. Even in regions where they still persist, carnivores are notoriously difficult to observe, and thus little studied. Furthermore, indirect effects caused by their presence or absence may take decades to appear, particularly for terrestrial vegetational changes. For all these reasons it is not surprising that even as recently as 1996, a literature review concluded that "trophic cascades and top-down community regulation as envisioned by trophic-level theories are relatively uncommon in nature."

Yet, mounting evidence contradicts that conclusion. Numerous empirical studies support the view that predation is a key process that regulates the numbers of both herbivores and "mesopredators" and thereby stabilizes the trophic structure of many terrestrial ecosystems. One type of evidence derives from uncontrolled manipulations, such as the introduction or removal of predators or their prey. In an oft-repeated scenario, early seafarers released sheep, goats, pigs, rabbits, horses, cattle, caribou, and other grazing animals onto predator-free islands, both oceanic and continental. The almost universal result was the devastation of native vegetation, a top-down effect that seldom occurs in the presence of top predators. The implication is that predators normally regulate herbivores on mainlands. But an alternative explanation is possible: island plants that evolved in the absence of herbivores might be unusually vulnerable when grazers are introduced, though this explanation is not as relevant on continental islands where there has been insufficient time for the loss of plant defenses.

One can look for prima facie evidence of top-down interactions in the many mainland ecosystems around the globe where humans have eliminated wolves, bears, lions, tigers, and other carnivores. Except in protected areas such as national parks, however, a keystone role for carnivores is masked by human hunting or large-scale replacement of native herbivores with livestock. Yet, in parts of suburban and rural North America, the extirpation of large carnivores, in combination with limitations on hunting, appears to have caused dramatic changes in mammal and plant populations. In the absence of wolves and cougars, for instance, deer, opossums, raccoons, feral cats, beavers and other mammals have become notoriously abundant to the point of becoming serious threats to agriculture and nuisances in many. In some eastern U.S. forests, overbrowsing of acorns and tree seedlings by white-tailed deer is clearly altering the pattern of tree regeneration and threatening some endangered. Overbrowsing by ungulates, both native and exotic, is so widespread in the United States that wildflowers are disappearing, even in some of the most carefully protected old-growth forests, such as the Heart's Content grove in Pennsylvania. Where wolves were extirpated from national parks in the United States and no hunting is allowed, overbrowsing by ungulates has led to a decline in bio-diversity.

An overabundance of raccoons, opossums, house cats, foxes, skunks, and other small to mid-sized predators in the absence of dominant carnivores is a phenomenon known as mesopredator release. The indirect or ripple effects of this phenomenon go far beyond an urban nuisance factor. Mesopredator release has been blamed for declines in or losses of gamebirds, songbirds, and other small vertebrates across a wide range of North American ecosystems, including grasslands, arid scrub, and eastern deciduous forest.

One of the classic examples of a carnivore-mediated keystone effect has been the recovery of the native sea otter from near extinction along the Pacific Coast of North America and the otters' subsequent predation on sea urchin populations. Grazing urchins, in the absence of control by otters, had stripped kelp forests and turned vast stretches of coastal waters into "urchin barrens." The resurgence of otters reduced urchin numbers and allowed a recovery of kelp forests and their associated invertebrate, fish and sea bird fauna. This trophic cascade was recently confirmed when killer whales again reduced sea otter populations by about 90 percent.

Other dramatic effects, including the collapse of native fauna, have accompanied the introduction of alien predators into numerous aquatic and terrestrial ecosystems around the globe: Nile perch in Africa's Lake Victoria, sea lamprey in the Great Lakes, mongooses onto several tropical islands, the brown tree snake onto Guam, and foxes into boreal and Arctic regions.

Bolstering the impressions derived from uncontrolled invasions and introductions, are results from studies in tropical forests. In the neotropics, for instance, one of us (JT) has compared a relatively pristine site, Cocha Cashu Biological Station in Peru's Manu National Park, with Barro Colorado Island in Panama, isolated from the mainland by construction of the Panama Canal more than 80 years ago. Although the two sites are similar in climate and original fauna, Barro Colorado Island, due to its small size, lost its top predators—

jaguar, puma, and harpy eagle—half a century ago. Today, the island harbors markedly greater abundances of mammal species, such as agoutis, coatimundis, sloths, and howler monkeys, than Cocha Cashu where predators occur at undiminished natural abundance. The contrast has been interpreted as signaling the absence of top-down control on Barro Colorado Island, although even in this case alternative explanations have been suggested.

A more tightly controlled comparison of predator-free and predator-containing landmasses is currently underway in and around Lago Guri, Venezuela, where hundreds of forested hilltops have been isolated by the impounded waters of an enormous hydroelectric reservoir. Within eight years after the water reached its final stage in 1986, 75 to 90 percent of the vertebrate species found in the same forest type on the nearby mainland had disappeared from islands less than 15 hectares in area. Currently, a majority of the vertebrate species that persist on these islands have increased by at least an order of magnitude over mainland levels, a result consistent with release from top-down control.

Ongoing studies indicate that strong destabilizing forces have been unleashed by the hyper-abundance of persistent animals on Lago Guri Islands. Among the species showing pronounced hyper-abundance are seed predators (small rodents) and herbivores (howler monkeys, common iguanas, and leaf-cutter ants). Elevated levels of seed predation and folivory attributable to these species have markedly suppressed the reproduction of canopy trees in a manner consistent with a top-down trophic cascade.

In a final example, a series of fenced enclosures was constructed nearly a decade ago in the southern Yukon, Canada, to ascertain the effects of various treatments on snowshoe hare populations. Results so far show that hares continue to follow the classic ten-year cycle of peak and decline, but on average, hare density doubles under partial predator exclusion, triples with food supplementation, and is eleven times greater with both food supplements and protection from terrestrial (but not avian), showing that bottom-up and top-down processes are likely to interact.

Taken together, the results from aquatic, marine, and terrestrial ecosystems at many latitudes strongly suggest that top predators play a major regulatory role in many ecosystems. The precautionary principle compels us to apply such inferences to the design and management of protected areas.

There may be a variety of situations in nature, of course, in which consumers or consumer populations are not controlled by predation. Prior to the late Pleistocene overkill of large mammals in Australia and North and South, for instance, most of the Earth's ecosystems contained mega-herbivore species whose adult members, like today's elephants, were too large to be killed by the largest predators. Herbivore-plant interactions must have dominated these ecosystems, assuming that Pleistocene as well as modern mega-herbivores exert top-down controls on vegetation. For some smaller herbivores (e.g., wildebeest, caribou, bison) herd-forming, migratory behavior effectively limits the impact of predators on herd numbers, leaving a significant regulatory role for plant productivity.

Neither mega-herbivores nor large herds of migratory ungulates occupy much of the Earth's terrestrial habitats today, however, making these types of ecological regulation little more than Pleistocene relics. Therefore, given the preponderance of evidence that top carnivores play a major role in maintaining the diversity in many of today's truncated terrestrial ecosystems, the preservation or reintroduction of viable populations of large carnivores must rank high in conservation programs for the new millennium.

Regional Connectivity

Assuming that top-down regulation is a critical ecological phenomenon in many ecosystems, it is essential to define the conditions which support robust populations of large top carnivores. Big and secure areas are obviously necessary, but not sufficient. Indeed, isolated core areas, regardless of their size, are rarely if ever big enough to provide for long-term demographic and genetic viability of these animals. Therefore, a vital element of this program is the maintenance or restoration of the population dynamics, interchange, and migrations.

The restoration of historical disturbance regimes across landscapes is also essential. Because many abiotic forces, including hurricanes and wildfires, are uncontrollable, wildlands networks must be are large enough and appropriately configured to assure that no single disturbance event can eliminate most of a certain habitat type such as old-growth forest, prevent recolonization of sites from which particular species have been extirpated, or permanently perturb interactions among trophic levels.

Although it has proven difficult to demonstrate with rigor that any specific small-scale landscape linkage increases the movement of target animal species, the available evidence suggests that, overall, promoting the movement of individuals between habitat fragments can increase the persistence of populations and local survival of species. Species differ in how they "see" and use a degraded or fragmented landscape, and so solutions for connectivity must differ with the setting and the species. When designing landscape linkages, therefore, a crucial first step is identifying the target species the link is intended to benefit. In many regions, reconnecting isolated core protected areas may be necessary just to achieve the bigness required to maintain ecological diversity and resilience. On a larger scale, inter-regional linkages, such as those envisioned by the Yellowstone to Yukon project, are needed to accommodate gene flow and dispersal of grizzly bears and other wide-ranging species between the northern Rocky Mountains in the United States and northern Canada. Landscape linkages on that scale also offer the best hope for insuring the persistence of species in the face of predicted climate change.

Restoration

Core protected areas, as mentioned earlier, are vital elements in regional reserve networks. Some current national parks, wilderness areas, and other protected lands qualify as cores, but many others do not. A distinguishing feature of core areas is the absence of motorized access—ideally, road-lessness—a characteristic that will serve the needs of space-demanding and persecution-sensitive species, that will facilitate the return of a more natural disturbance regime, and that will minimize invasions by exotic plants and animals.

It does not follow, however, that core areas must be pristine at the time of selection to qualify for protection as cores. One of the more controversial tenets of regional conservation programs is that most core areas will require restoration of some kind, and some will require active management in perpetuity. The irony is that many lands have been so poorly managed for so long that it will take decades or longer to achieve a system of protected areas in which natural fire regimes, water flows, predator-prey interactions, and other ecological processes prevail. This situation will not please those grassroots conservation activists who oppose "hands-on" management.

Another problematic aspect of this conclusion is that the restoration that will be required in many regions to reconstitute the full array of native species, habitats, and processes represents a novel endeavor on a fundamentally different and grander scale than any past efforts in ecological restoration. In fact, the design and restoration of viable regional networks of nature reserves will require no less than a revolution in restoration ecology.

The required restoration paradigm must focus on large-scale, top-down processes. This program is in sharp contrast to the methodological traditions in restoration ecology, which are modest in scale and ambition, and are oriented toward plants and bottom-up processes. Restoration ecology to date has relied largely on empirical tools developed to achieve specific effects on local, often devastated, sites such as the reestablishment of green plant cover over mine tailings or the reclamation of degraded or filled wetlands and tidal marshes. Further, the tools developed in such local projects have not been studied in controlled, replicated experiments. Partly as a consequence, the field of restoration ecology has evolved relatively slowly despite recognition of its vital importance to conservation. For example, it cannot yet provide a set of models and tools that assures restoration of a full range of native species and ecosystems.

While restoration needs will vary from one region to the next, three key factors must be addressed: control of invasive exotic species, reintroduction or recovery of native species, and provision for the re-establishment of natural processes and disturbances. Removal or partial control of aggressive exotic species is vital to restoration because of the well-documented ability of invasive plants, animals, fungi, and microbes to disrupt ecological communities through indirect as well as direct interactions. The restoration of native species, especially keystone species, restores top-down regulatory processes. Effective restoration also requires encouraging or actively restoring periodic natural disturbances, such as fires and floods, which have proven necessary for maintaining the integrity of ecological communities.

Few previous restoration efforts have dealt with the complex interplay of these three elements that shape ecological communities and species population dynamics. Rather, the most commonly used restoration method has been introduction of one or more plant species (not always natives) in an attempt to mimic or speed up succession. The conscious manipulation of three elements constitutes a new marriage of conservation biology and restoration ecology.

The Human Surround

Another land-use element that may be required to maintain biological diversity is buffer zones, multiple-use areas that can serve as habitat for some species and insulate core reserves from intensive human activities. A compelling argument for buffer zones is that it is impossible to secure enough public land to protect all of biodiversity. In the United States and elsewhere, the majority of rare and endangered species do not exist within nature reserves, and many ecosystems are not well represented in reserves.

On the other hand, buffer zones may do more harm than good for wildlands, depending on the nature and interactions of the stakeholders—both human and non-human. For example, intensive agriculture or dense housing developments seldom make good neighbors for cores because proximity of humans and wildlife can lead to harmful interchanges in both directions. Native ungulates, primates, and other species can be a serious nuisance amid crops. Exotic species, including diseases of domestic animals, can pass into native ecosystems and populations. Native predators may prey on livestock or human beings and be put at risk by roads. Frequently, a "hard edge" in the form of a fence or barrier may serve nature and society better than a buffer zone, depending on the kinds and intensities of human activity outside the protected area.

In all cases, though, attention to the culture, economy, and expectations of local people is essential for long-term success of biodiversity preservation in lands surrounding reserves. Landowners, public land managers, elected officials, and conservation organizations must all cooperate, a difficult task given their often disparate goals. It must be recognized also that the nature of buffer zones and their inhabitants can change over time. Buffer zones are by nature dynamic, and their conservation values will vary with the density of the human populations and the nature and intensity of human activities. Managing these areas effectively will always require tact and patience.

Implementing the New Conservation Program

The principles espoused here—regional and continental networks of wildlands containing the full array of native species including large carnivores—while biologically justified, will not be welcomed by all sectors of society. Notwithstanding the documented long-range economic and social benefits of such a continental restoration of wilderness and biodiversity, energetic resistance from pro-development exponents is predictable, even if based on groundless fears.

Alternatives exist, and are being tried, but they are not adequate to prevent a major crisis for biodiversity and nature. One such approach, here loosely referred to as "sustainability," became prominent following the report of the Brundtland Commission and has sought to harmonize human economic ambition with nature protection. These strategies go by various names: sustainable development, integrated conservation and development, community-based conservation, ecosystem management, and sustainable forest management. It is most unfortunate that such development-based programs have been represented as alternatives to strict nature protection. In fact, the ascendance of the notion of sustainable development has slowed efforts to increase the size and number of strictly protected areas worldwide, and sustainable development projects do more harm than good for nature and wildness.

Underlying the emphasis on sustainable development is the assumption that non-industrialized communities currently use resources sustainably and will continue to do so. This premise, however, ignores the recent changes in these communities due to the adoption of western technologies and because of rapid population growth. Moreover, retrospective evaluations of sustainable development projects show that most have achieved neither sustainability nor conservation.

Another tactic for protecting biodiversity on a sufficient scale has been the setting of target percentages for protection by nations or by international conservation organizations. For instance, a guideline endorsed by many conservation groups worldwide is the call for protection of 10 to 12 percent of each nation's total land area, a target acknowledged to be based more on political expediency rather than on scientific principles. But because current conservation targets are not based on science, they could actually exacerbate the problem. Popularization of such numbers may lead the public to believe that adequate steps are being taken to prevent the predicted mass extinction, where, in fact, science-based percentages are usually much greater. Where such targets have been adopted, such as in some provinces in Canada, the political process has often subverted the biologically based goals by emphasizing the protection of unproductive lands that are already well represented in the system of protected.

A central concept of the new program for conservation described above is that large, interconnected core protected areas are critical elements in regional wildland networks and, in these areas, the needs of large carnivores, other keystone species, and large-scale natural processes, such as fire, must be given priority over capital-intensive, economic activity. Fortunately, it appears that nature protection benefits local communities materially and spiritually more in the long run than most economic development schemes that ultimately destroy environmental values and erode the communal bonds that bind people to the land and to each other.

The program proposed here complements existing currents in the conservation movement. The elaboration of this program by the fields of conservation biology and restoration ecology can help us implement effective measures to maintain critical species, ecosystems, and landscape connectivity before the human enterprise overtakes all.

[Note: Much of this essay is based on M.E. Soulé and J. Terborgh. 1999. Protecting nature at regional and continental scales: A conservation biology program for the new millennium. BioScience 49: 809–817.]

Wilderness—

Integrating People, Perspective and Place

Communicating Wilderness—
Informing, Inspiring, Empowering

M. A. Partha Sarathy

There is a story about a great scientist, in fact, a candidate for the Nobel Prize who was walking around with a microscope firmly glued to his eye. He was brilliant, and seemed fully satisfied with what he had been seeing through the microscope, following which he made notes and produced very profound documents. These great findings were truly important, but what was missing was the fact that nothing was done to organize communication of his findings to those who needed it, and to those who should be provoked to take advantage of it, in one way or the other.

When I first joined the Board of IUCN—the International Union for Conservation of Nature—in Switzerland, my interest was in the Species Survival Commission, and the National Parks Commission, both of which were in the area of "Protection of Wildlife, Nature and Natural Resources." It did not take me long to discover that unless we placed a very important element into the work of IUCN in the area of education and communication, we were probably wasting our time and our money. This is what made me take a keen interest in the commission that addressed education. Soon, I discovered that education had a connotation of being an academic exercise and one that did not connect in the outreach. I therefore added communication to education and named my Commission "the Commission on Education and Communication," which it is now today. It is at this point that IUCN itself, which surprisingly had no communication division at all, woke up, and put one in place. To me, reaching out to people with the message of "Wilderness" is of acute importance. It should be the tool with which we inform, inspire, motivate and empower.

341

Let me pause for a moment here to speak of the key role that film and television are playing and will continue to play, with which people and wilderness can be brought closer together in a manner in which wilderness is seen in all its manifestations, understood, and becomes a motivator of mankind, to respect, protect and preserve. The International Film Festival simultaneous with this Congress was put together by my organization, the International Nature Film and Television Festivals Organization, which runs festivals around the world as a public service. My mission in life is to help people come closer to Nature in a way in which they understand its value while celebrating its splendor and benevolence, and feel a responsibility to protect it for future generations. That is why the theme of the Festival here in South Africa, which has a great gift of wilderness, should be "Wilderness, the gift and the challenges." After all, wilderness on this planet is indeed a gift to us all, but it is not a free gift! A challenge comes with this gift—the challenge to all humankind to be worthy of this gift.

Wilderness, as such, is a somewhat ephemeral concept. It has an academic flavor, but it is the same wilderness—areas of the planet untouched by human intervention—that is the *lifeline* of man's survival and prosperity on this planet.

Wilderness has a very wide dimension of benefits. It is wilderness that orchestrates the climate of the planet. It is wilderness that orchestrates agricultural plenty. It is wilderness that produces the healing touch to man when his health suffers from illness. It is wilderness that also generates great poetry, great literature and great intellectual expression. The great saints and thinkers of India, if not the world, have invariably received their inspiration from wilderness. Wilderness is indeed a mine of gold which spreads across this planet. But this gold mine has been exploited, leaving dust here and there. We need to communicate the values of wilderness. We need to inform, inspire, motivate and empower mankind so that he understands that it has in its midst a gold mine called "wilderness" which needs protection.

Today, thankfully, we have a wide variety of communication tools available to us. Apart from satellite-served Internet and e-mail, there are the other traditional ways which are more relevant, more practical and more applicable to many parts of the world. At a conference I organized at IUCN called "Communicating Conservation and Sustainable Development," we invited a variety of communicators—the printed world, radio, television, cinema and then the traditional ways. A great descendant of a princely family of Africa told us that the way his people communicated was through the drum. He brought a drum and played his messages of conservation. It was incredible to see that this drum, with its various rhythms and frequencies that he played on it—intended to speak its own language from mountain to distant mountain—the message of conservation. And then, there was this young student from the United States who talked about the way she put salt in the coffee being given to her teachers in their lounge, to remind them that they were using non-degradable cups. That was her way of communicating her message. We also had an American Indian who brought a big inflatable whale in her baggage, inflated it, and taught children on the wonders of the sea.

Understanding wilderness in today's context is going to be among the greatest challenges of the new millennium. By this, I do not mean bringing tourists to wildlife, encouraging more tourism lodges, building more zoos, safari parks and so forth. Indeed, they too have a place among the civilizations on this planet. But what I have in mind is wilderness—that pristine presence on this planet, its body, its spirit and the fragrance of its presence—that's what I mean—as one that needs to be brought to people.

Let me go back for a moment to our ancient mythological classic—the *Ramayana*. *Rama* is considered to be among the most dignified, distinguished and gracious presences among our deities. It is the story of *Rama* that is contained in our *Rayamyana*. *Ramayana* is also the story of the war against good and evil, the deity *Rama* representing good.

What is significant in the *Ramayana* is that two young princes—*Rama* and his brother *Lakshmana*—were both sent by their father *King Dasharatha* to the forest, to wilderness, for receiving their education. Their entire impressionable years under a Guru (teacher) were spent in the midst of wilderness. In his teachings to *Rama* and *Lakshmana*, the Guru constantly took advantage of the wilderness surrounding them, emphasizing the value of wilderness, the benevolence of wilderness, the magnificence of wilderness, the magnificence of interrelationship between one entity and another in wilderness and the understanding of the ultimate design that is called "Wilderness."

We need to understand, model, and communicate the inherent design of wilderness. During the 5th World Wilderness Congress, in Tromso, Norway, chaired by the distinguished scientist of Kon-tiki fame, Thor Heyerdah, I remarked that wilderness gives its feeling to even those who do not know it;

that it has no design; that it cannot be considered chaos; and is indeed not chaos. "Wilderness is not chaos and chaos is not wilderness," I said. "It is our own lack of understanding of the grand design of wilderness and its precious values to all life on Earth that makes some of us think it is a chaotic assembly of plants, animals, fish, reptiles, birds, etc."

The concept of "bringing wilderness to people and people to wilderness" is not as easy as one would think. The biggest hurdle will be man's inability or weakness where it concerns leaving anything alone. If a tourist sees a beautiful tree with a magnificent flower on it, he is tempted to pluck a leaf or a flower, or both. It is then probably taken home, put into a beautiful cut-glass vase and allowed to die there. Have we not seen hundreds of tigers in their pristine glory in the forest killed, skinned, made into dead replicas stuffed with straw, plaster of paris and glued, stared at us with their glass eyes—and shown off in the drawing rooms of the rich? Have we not seen the legs of great elephants chopped off after they are killed, stuffed, varnished and made into beautiful peg tables and placed in the drawing rooms of the fashionable?

Wilderness is something that man has often only exploited. What is required, rather, is the identification of wilderness as a human need, to be recognized and respected with a sense of awe—as an important "lifeline" for man's survival on Earth. The idea that wilderness alone can produce mother species which can produce other species—both plant, animal, bird, insect and reptile—which can benefit man's life on Earth, should be spread among the human race—the young, the old, the rural, the urban.

Just one example. A distinguished Indian scientist rediscovered wild rice in a part of South India. This wild rice was identified as the mother of all rice—a gene that needed to be preserved and protected so that all the rice-eating people on this planet, who amount to over a billion people, could be ensured of their staple food.

I have often pondered over bamboo—that glossy skinned hollow stick emerging from earth with a few thin leaves. This bamboo is used as construction material, for making furniture, and what else—just a utility. If one stops to think, this bamboo is nothing other than one of the several precious grasses on earth, the lowly grass upon which we trample, the sugarcane which produces sugar, the reed which is considered to be sacred in many parts of the world—and the bamboo are all grasses. Take grass itself. A grassy land is considered wasteland by many modern cultures. "Dig it up. It is barren land. Plant trees, better still build on this land," says the modern developer. But grasslands are a precious manifestation on earth, a manifestation of precious wilderness on this earth. They clothe the earth while being sponges which, while soaking the rain into its bowels protects it from the harshness, while also nourishing a great array of organisms that are necessary and useful to life on this planet.

I therefore submit that wilderness awareness and its many facets needs to be re-invoked in every form. In our ancient language, Sanskrit, there is a word called "Aranyakam." This does not mean wildlife or nature or environment. It means "of the wild." That is wilderness. The many facets and values that wilderness brings to mankind, keep on increasing as one understands more and more of the gracious benevolence and fascinating presence of wilderness on this planet.

It is our duty to bring out all these facets to the human presence on this planet, so that man and wilderness need not have distance between them, but a close relationship, and respect for each other. Unfortunately, man has achieved a dominant, if not a dictatorial, role wherever it concerns his approach and attitude towards Nature, wildlife and wilderness. Such a relationship is one-sided. We must remember that if this leads to wilderness being assaulted unreasonably, it responds with wrath. How often have we not seen the wrath of Nature when man provokes it beyond tolerance? Unthinking building of large dams to collect huge quantities of water to serve mankind—causing floods, earthquakes, avalanches, typhoons and tornadoes. How often have we not seen Nature's wrath manifested in these ugly episodes?

Against this background, the good news is that communicating the message of "Wilderness" offers us a variety of means. I have already referred to some. In addition, the planet is now virtually "under attack" by the electronic highways and byways that supply instant information and instant access.

Thus, we need only to invoke among the citizens of this planet, of different languages, cultures, colors and geographies, the idea of communicating wilderness to inform, inspire, motivate and empower. With the wide variety of tools in our hands, we can and should use all means of communication to strive to make our beautiful, bountiful planet smile again, contented, productive and protective.

Wilderness and Ubuntu

David Rothenberg

There is no wilderness without people. To a trekker who wants no one but himself in his favorite wild place, or a biologist most concerned with saving enough land to preserve biodiversity, this may sound like social constructivist provocation, but I can assure you I mean it. I'll say it again: there is no wilderness without people. We humans place this category "wilderness" upon the land, and the minute we draw a line around it our presence is felt.

I used to think the moment we call out "wilderness!" was a moment of loss, where the unnamed and unknown lost out to our ruling as much as we struggled to save the important place through names, regulations, politics, and education. We still need to celebrate the irrevocable mystery of nature, but I no longer see it as a tragedy to find people in the wilds. We have been there for thousands of years, and all over the world, many cultures have been far closer to the rhythms of nature than those of us who come from afar with our goals and pronouncements, our fear of the other and the certainty that we are right.

I was honored to perform at the 7th World Wilderness Congress with the great Xhosa guitarist Ray Phiri, famous for his band Stimela and his work with Paul Simon across the globe. The last time Ray was in the same hall in which the 7th WWC was held, fifteen thousand fans were clamoring to get in to hear his protest songs against apartheid. The police ran him out of town and told him never to return or he might not get out alive. Today things are different, and he was at the 7th WWC to proclaim in music his support for the culture and nature of this beautiful country.

A respected presenter at the 7th WWC, promoting the value of private wilderness parks in South Africa, used the catchy slogan that "conservation without money is just conversation." This sounds nice, but it gives the rich the usual pat on the back without respecting enough the fact that the real work of preserving nature requires that we listen to people who live in the places to which we go, and which we love and value. We are not explorers who "discover" the beauty of wild places previously ignored. People who live in the midst of wildness for generations have insights we must gently learn and uphold. Ian Player has emphasized this for years. We need to talk to those who know the lay of the land. Conservation without conversation is imperialism: just another attempt from outsiders to tell Africa what's best for them. Africa is the wildest, toughest, most exciting and brightest continent with its mixture of hundreds of cultures and thousands of wild creatures and landscapes found nowhere else. We come here to learn and to save, not to impose.

And we are all in this together. I think of what Desmond Tutu has spoken of as ubuntu, a Zulu word for the idea that a person becomes human through other persons, in Zulu: "*umuntu ngumuntu ngabantu.*" We realize our goals only by bringing everyone else along with us, and we cannot tolerate anyone being sacrificed along the way—"when one goes down, we all goes down," the bishop is fond of saying. It is a bit like the Buddhist notion of the bodhisattva who is unable to take that last leap away from our world to enlightenment, because to do so honestly means having to take everyone else with you. The bodhisattva stays in this world and continues to help everyone else on their path upward. Or Arne Naess's deep ecology idea of self-realization, where we cannot realize our own goals without realizing nature is an intrinsic part of our selves, and we cannot let it suffer and decay as we unfold our identity in the living world. As Tutu continues, we reach our full humanity only when we are "caught up in the bundle of life. To be is to participate, to belong."

As much as we might imagine that we best experience the wilderness as solitary wanderers, no one ever saves a wild place alone. The journey towards solid preservation requires listening, cooperation, and the building of consensus (among many different kinds of people) that the wild deserves consideration and respect from all of us. When one wilderness goes down we all go down. When one wild place is protected, our individual and total humanity gets stronger. It must not be a question of human culture vs. wilderness, with one side having to win the struggle, but of human culture enhanced by its ability to value wilderness as part of development, and the flourishing of wildness through human attention and respect.

This cooperation between different views of how nature should be used is not going to be easy, but it is essential. The World Wilderness Congress has now convened in India and Africa after several rounds in the North, and if anything we should have learned by now that the places of greatest biodiversity and beauty are also those with the greatest diversity of human populations. Wildness in the South is also of course greatly endangered, because there are fewer regulations and less control of how human development is proceeding. Governments are less stable, there is less money available for the protection of nature. The problems are immense, but they can be solved.

As a philosopher I am quite impressed with the idea of ubuntu as a collaborative kind of compassion that learns from the experience of thousands of years of different groups trying to work out their differences and get along. It is a far more useful and powerful concept than the original, individually based-notion of Self-realization from Hindu religion, and expanded by depth psychology into the central notion of the deep ecology philosophy that binds humanity and nature together. Our human selves are expanded by letting nature flourish, that's what Arne Naess is trying to say. But ubuntu decentralizes human individual success further, by saying "I become fully human only if you are fully human." Any oppression in the world makes me less human, makes me suffer as a result. Expand that view to include the natural world and you will have a powerful, uniquely African environmental philosophy that can help to change the world. On this continent, compassion for humanity leads easily into compassion for nature, once we get beyond the familiar opposition of humanity vs. nature.

Africa is full of case studies that show much disagreement on the implementation of such a nice idea. David Western has written on how the creation of the Amoboseli Reserve in the Kenyan savannah was possible only through the active initiative of the local Maasai, who preserve the natural environment as they preserve their own culture and show how humanity and nature thrive together through the practice of ancient wild pastoral traditions. John Terborgh criticized Western's approach in the pages of *The New York Review of Books* with the view that while native-run reserves might be a nice idea, what really works is top-down management, legal muscle, and a park agency with real power to enforce the protection of nature against the local populations' tendency to exhaust the land and poach the wildlife. According to him, we can't rely upon voluntary compliance. Both conservationists have a point, but in practice,

Western's tendency to involve local people and figure out how to gain their trust and specific local knowledge is less confrontational, less imperialistic, and far more effective in the long run.

Wilderness will simply not succeed as a global concept if it appears as yet another imposed vision from the rich countries upon the poor countries. Why should you listen to us if we have been so wrong in the past? This time we must all work together with a new spirit of shared compassion. When our wild places go down, we all go down. When the wild returns, we are only more human together.

The 6th World Wilderness Congress was in India in 1998, the 7th in South Africa in 2001. It has been two years since we were there. How has the protection of wilderness fared in the meantime? As fortunes have been made and lost, terrorism pushed to the fore in global consciousness, the importance of wild places has only increased as much as they may have faded from the headlines. Widespread American fear, of lost invincibility, of hidden enemies, of flagging markets, has allowed the Bush administration to quietly remove much of the protective laws his predecessors worked so hard to set in place in sunnier times. They've pulled the wool over the public's eyes while cowardly shirking all opportunity to ask the people whether or not we care about the wilderness. This is probably because of their greatest fear on the issue: that most Americans, both liberal and conservative, believe that there is something sacred and patriotically American about support for wilderness, and if the government actually asked us what we wanted, they would find their own greedy, destructive plans in direct opposition to the desires of the people they are supposed to represent. There is an easy lesson here for the wide world of conservation: no laws of preservation are absolute. We need to be constantly vigilant in watching what we believe needs perfection. And the more we recognize that the saving of the wild helps to further all our humanity, the more it will become a consensus issue, not a special interest that will need to fight for attention like all other special interests.

The explosion of access to information that has spread across the globe in the last few years seems at first to take us away from nature and into a virtual world gazed at through glowing computer screens. It is said that someone surfing the Internet can absorb in a few hours more information than a person in the pre-industrial age absorbed in a lifetime. And yet do we know more about our home places, our ecosystems, the plants and animals in whose midst we live? Probably not, because the environment has become more idea than necessity. And yet, when it comes to the facts of wilderness, it is easier than ever for the curious to be informed. We can get the information with lightning speed, if we know what we want and where to look for it.

So in a way there is no excuse not to know what's happening to the natural world. There is no excuse not to share the tragedy with everyone who we know, and to band together to do something about it. We need wilderness to unfold our shared humanity. With its astonishing diversity of peoples and animals, Africa is the most important place to spread this vision. Let's get started.

Reclaiming Our Wild Nature—
From Ecological Ideas to
Ecological Identity

John Seed

At the Rainforest Information Center we have worked since 1979 for the protection of the rainforests and other wild places. In order to do so, we have necessarily had to address the legitimate aspirations of the indigenous and other local peoples for some kind of sustainable, benign, economic development.

But, though such projects are of the greatest importance, I believe that we must simultaneously address the failure of modern humans to understand who we really are and the nature of our relationship with our environment, with nature. As Paul Ehrlich said, we are "sawing off the branch that we are sitting on."

Unless society comes to understand that the wilderness is not just "scenery," not just an eco-tourism business opportunity or a place for recreation, but the very fabric from which our own lives and those of future humanity is woven, I'm afraid that all our conservation "victories" will be far from sufficient and also short-lived.

As long as the dominant paradigm of thinking that rules the world is based on an arrogant fantasy of human beings as the center of the universe, we may have to buy time for the wilderness by finding ways to make it justify its existence in financial terms.

Unless we use the precious time that we buy to work with all urgency to find out how we can change this deluded underlying consciousness, then I believe that whatever we are able to "save" at this time, will necessarily be lost in the near future to the pressures of population, greed and technological arrogance. Unless we can re-ignite the spiritual connection that all primal peoples, including our own ancestors had with nature, I doubt that economic justifications will do the job; as Economics is itself tainted by this false anthropocentric consciousness. If we look at the fundamentals of Economics, we find that the Earth has no value until humans add their intelligence and their labor, is just dirt until we "develop" it into something. Trees have no value until they are cut down and turned into lumber or pulp. If we accept these terms (as Michael Soulé pointed out), how will we ever assign enough economic value to wilderness to protect the vast expanses necessary for the continuation of speciation of large mammals, birds and reptiles? Anything less than that merely creates the illusion of conservation, tiny after-images of the dying world which brought us forth and which linger for a brief moment before being swallowed by the sixth great mass extinction presently consuming our world.

I will first give an example of how we at the Rainforest Information Center have protected wildlands through an economic development project, then an example of a restoration project which attempts to draw together the ecological and the spiritual, and finally I will try to address the question of the revolution in consciousness without which no long-term solution is possible.

In 1982, the Rainforest Information Center (RIC) began working with Australia's closest neighbors, the Solomon Islands and Papua New Guinea (PNG)—among the poorest countries in the world. It soon became apparent that rainforests in these countries could not be protected without addressing the legitimate aspirations of the traditional landowners for economic development. Unless benign, sustainable economic alternatives could be created, the forests would surely be destroyed by industrial logging and mining interests.

We observed that some communities in PNG had been able to get hold of a small portable sawmill—the Wokabout Sawmill (WS)—and we noticed that the multi-national loggers were unable to get a foothold amongst these peoples because they had a means of exploiting their own timber resources and could get a much higher price for the sawn timber that they produced than the loggers were offering for the raw logs.

In 1990, funded by the Australian government aid agency AusAID, RIC conducted an ecological audit of WSs and found that, as we had suspected, even the worst operated WS was less environmentally destructive than the best of the large industrial logging operations. When accompanied by sound forest management, WSs were among the best tools in the world for sensitive harvesting of trees.

In 1991, funded by the Australian Council of Churches, we made our first intervention using WSs. The Zia tribe in Morobe province PNG were about to sign a contract with a large logging company which would have allowed the clearfelling of about 100,000 acres of virgin rainforest. The company was so confident that their negotiations would succeed that they had already built a wharf and fuel dump.

Instead, the Zia signed a contract with RIC and the local non-government organization Village Development Trust (VDT). This contract stated that VDT/RIC would provide the Zia with three WSs and training in ecological forest management (including sawmilling, log utilization with minimum waste, tree felling techniques and safety, sawmill mechanics and maintenance as well as nursery and reforestation techniques).

In exchange, the Zia agreed to allow no logging or mining companies onto their land, to abide by the eco-forestry management plan drawn up by VDT/RIC and to equitably share all proceeds from the sale of timber throughout the whole community. The sawn timber could be sold for $300 per cubic meter and more, compared to the $2 per cubic meter that they would have received for the raw logs that would have been shipped to Japan. The management plan allows careful logging on 1,000 acres (about 20 acres per year over a 50-year rotation) leaving 99% of the land for traditional pursuits and off limits to industrial uses.

In 1992, RIC conducted further WS interventions funded by AusAID in Madang Province. RIC also funded landowner awareness patrols and conferences conducted by VDT and other national NGOs which spread the news about this new mode of sustainable development, updated the WS training manual and translated it into Tok Pisin, and raised funds to buy a boat to get the ecotimber to Lae.

In 1995, funded by the Australian Government Department of the Environment, RIC produced a 60-minute video documentary (with both English and Tok Pisin versions) about industrial logging in PNG and the eco-forestry alternative.

A long, long time ago in India, at the dawn of time, the trinity of great Gods was meeting. Vishnu and Brahma remonstrated with the Supreme Lord Shiva begging Him to stop dazzling them with His unbearable effulgence. His appearance as a column of light stretching from infinity to infinity dazzled them beyond endurance. In His compassion, Shiva relented and henceforth manifested as a mountain named Arunachala rising grand from the plains of Tamil Nadu in Southern India.

Some eleven or twelve centuries ago, the beginnings of a large temple were constructed at the base of Arunachala-Shiva by and for the many pilgrims and devotees who flocked there. Over the centuries it grew and grew, with massive stone walls enclosing many acres of temple grounds and places of worship. By the time that the teenage God-intoxicated Ramana arrived there early this century, many pilgrims were drawn there from all over India. Later he was celebrated far and wide as Ramana Maharshi, one of the great Hindu sages of the 20th century, yet he would always claim that it was the mountain that was enlightened rather than he. Stories are still told of his love and respect for monkeys, peacocks, cows and trees. "It is this Arunachala Hill which grants liberation by the mere contemplation of it as the Ocean of Grace," Sri Ramana had said.

It was in 1987 that I had received the letter from Apeetha Arunagiri, an Australian nun residing in the Sri Ramana Ashram at the foot of Arunachala. She wrote that when Ramana had arrived there, the holy mountain was clothed in lush forest and one might even meet a tiger walking on its flanks. Now little grew there but thorns and goats. Terrible erosion trenched Shiva's sides and torrents of mud attended each monsoon. She had heard about our work for the forests, could we please help her to re-clothe the sacred mountain? It seemed a fantastic opportunity for a project that could demonstrate that there is no separation between the spiritual and ecological dimensions of life.

Two RIC volunteers, John Button and Heather Bache spent the next seven years organizing the rehabilitation of Arunachala, traveling from time to time to Holland or Taiwan to earn money to allow them to continue in this work. With the help of two grants from AusAID, the space between the inner and outer walls of the vast 23-acre temple complex was transformed from a wasteland into the largest tree nursery in the south of India. Hundreds of illiterate Tamil people have been trained in re-afforestation skills—tree identification, seed collection, nursery techniques, watershed management, erosion control, sustainable energy systems, etc., and Shiva's robes are slowly, painstakingly being rewoven as is the ancient tradition that always recognized nature as Divine. Using only native trees with seeds from local sources, Shiva's green robe has started shimmering in the breeze once more.

However, for every forest we are able to protect, a hundred disappear and unless we can address the psychological disease that afflicts modern humans these good works will surely come to naught. According to the British scientist

James Lovelock, the way we relate to nature is as if the brain were to decide that it was the most important organ in the body and started mining the liver. Surely such an attitude indicates a profound psychological problem!

Deep Ecology is the name of a new philosophy of nature which sees the root of our environmental crisis in anthropocentrism, human centeredness. Within the anthropocentric worldview man is seen as the crown of creation, the measure of all being. According to the dominant strand of the Judeo-Christian tradition, only man has been created in God's image, only man has a soul, everything in the world is merely resources for man's use and pleasure.

This world view has permeated every aspect of modern human thinking. Why, only a few centuries ago astronomers were being burnt at the stake for daring to suggest that the Earth was not the center of the solar system. All of the institutions of our society are founded on the premise of human supremacy. The very language we speak conspires to support the illusion of separation between humans and the environment. Even to think of it as "the environment" tries to turn "it" into an object, something separate from ourselves. Yet the fact that this is an illusion can be demonstrated very simply. All we need to do is hold our breaths for five minutes while we ask ourselves whether the air is part of the environment or part of ourselves. Likewise the soil and the water are cycling through us constantly, there is no "out there," it's all in here.

Thomas Berry says that the Cenozoic Era is over. The great age which began with the demise of the dinosaurs 65 million years ago is finished and now our choice is between the ecozoic and the technozoic. The former refers to the shining vision of humanity awakening to who we really are, just one tiny blossom on the tree of life we realize that we cannot possibly flourish at the expense of the tree on which we grow. The technozoic refers to more of the same, business as usual, infinite economic growth, infinite justice for the armaments industry; attempting technical fixes for the most glaring environmental problems and perhaps we will genetically engineer our children to tolerate increased levels of cadmium and radioactivity, co-pilots of an impoverished shattered spaceship Earth, steering it proudly into the brave new world of the future.

As well as protecting biodiversity and rehabilitating degraded landscapes, we also need to transform the consciousness of modern humanity that has so thoroughly conquered the world, conquered nature. But how? Arne Naess, the Emeritus Professor of Philosophy from Oslo University who coined the term "deep ecology" says that ecological *ideas* are not enough, we need an ecological *identity*, an ecological *self*. Clearly, one way that we can develop this ecological self is by spending time in wilderness as attested to by the very existence of this Congress.

Professor Naess is himself a great wilderness advocate and activist, yet he felt that we also need "community therapies" to develop our ecological identity. I co-authored a book with Arne Naess and others that describes one such community therapy, The Council of All Beings, (*Thinking Like a Mountain, Towards a Council of All Beings*, New Society Publishers, 1986).

However, I no longer think of such processes as therapies for the following reason: in the late 1980s I had the privilege to witness a ceremony in a Hopi community on top of a mesa in the U.S. Southwest. This village, I was informed, had been continuously inhabited for longer than any other settlement in the Americas. Their ceremony was just like The Council of All Beings though the masks and costumes were more splendid and the drumming more confident. I realized that they had been performing this and other such ceremonies for thousands of years and therapies weren't supposed to take that long! Even psychoanalysis should be complete after a few years.

As I explored this further, I realized that all indigenous and primal communities have, at the very heart of their culture, such ceremonies and rituals whereby the human community remembers our interdependence with the larger Earth community and thereby nourishes that interdependence. From this it follows that therapy is not the right metaphor to describe what is going on and that for modern people to unearth our ecological identity we must re-establish the kinds of rituals and ceremonies whereby all peoples have ensured that the human community did not drift away into socially constructed fantasy realms but remained rooted in the Earth.

Even hunter-gatherer communities whose daily lives are embedded in the wilderness, nonetheless maintain these ceremonies. This suggests that, as important as the wilderness experience certainly is, it may not be enough to fulfill our need for reconnection and ensure that we remember who we really are under the veneer of "civilization." Besides, there is so little wilderness left that if six billion modern, de-natured people were to try and find their vision and source there, we'd be in worse trouble than we are now.

The Islamic Approach

Preserving Paradise
Through Religious Values of Nature

Hafiz Nazeem Goolam

The root of our contemporary ecological crisis is a mindset which disregards the Lordship, Sovereignty, Power, Control and Will of God in the universe. The human being's self-perception is that he/she is freed from any transcendental authority or higher moral order and thus may act towards natural resources in a utilitarian or selfish manner.

In Islam, nature is God's handiwork which contains His bounties meant for human use and enjoyment within the limits set by Divine Law. Nature is therefore not a resource without an owner for God is the Owner of nature. The *Qur'an* contains numerous verses (*ayat*) which reassert this idea that the universe is Allah's creation and that His Dominion over all that is created is absolute. For example:

> "To God belongs the dominion of the heavens and the earth
> And God has power over all things."
> > *Surah Ali-Imran* (The Family of Imran),
> > chapter 3, verse 189

And again:

> "Unto God belongs all that is in the heavens and all
> That is on earth."
> > *Surah Al Rum* (The Romans),
> > chapter 30, verse 26

The *Qur'an* declares that the creation of the universe, of nature and of the human being is purposive or teleological and that these are signs (*ayat*) of God's Existence, Power, Wisdom and Purpose. It states:

> "Behold! In the creations of the heaven and the earth, and the
> Alternation of night and day, there are indeed signs for
> All who are endowed with insight."
>
> *Surah Ali Imran*, chapter 3, verse 190

And again,

> "And in the succession of night and day, and in the means
> Of subsistence which God sends down from the skies,
> Thereby giving life to the earth after it had been lifeless
> And in the change of the winds: These are signs
> For people who use their intellect."
>
> *Al Jathiyah* (The Kneeling Down) chapter 45, verse 5

In the Islamic worldview the universe, the earth and their contents are made subservient to the human being. But not in the sense that the human being can do with it what she/he likes. Rather, the position of the human being is one of trusteeship (*khilafah*) and this position carries with it great moral responsibility. As the trustee of God on earth, the human being is responsible for treating the environment with care, love and respect and responsible for ensuring that the planet's natural resources are used in a judicious manner so that future generations will benefit from God's bounties. Again, the *Qur'an* speaks:

> "O mankind! Worship your Sustainer, who has created you
> And those who lived before you, so that you may remain
> Remain conscious of your duty towards Him
> Who has made the earth a resting place for you and
> The sky a canopy, and has sent down water from the sky
> And thereby brought forth fruits for your sustenance."
>
> *Al Baqarah* (The Heifer) chapter 2, verse 21–22.

In order to fulfill God's trust in relation to both the environment and the community, the human being must abide by those values and principles of life and living which lie at the very core of God's eternal message to humanity. What this means is that mercy, love and compassion should guide the human being in his/her interaction with the environment and the community. She should hold in check greed and avarice and that all too human tendency to pursue selfish interests to the detriment of her fellow human beings. A moderate lifestyle which reflects balance and equilibrium is the most cherished of the Islamic worldview.

This leads to the question: what is the purpose of the human being on earth, what is the purpose of life? One cannot discuss this question in any detail in this paper. Suffice it to say that in the context of the environment and of nature the Islamic worldview postulates that the life of the human being is subject to perpetual test by God regarding the human being's behavior towards and utilization of all God-given, natural resources (both material and non-material). Are there, then, any principles or values in terms of which the human being should be guided in his/her utilization of the planet's natural resources?

One—perhaps it is the essence—of the fundamental principles of Islam is Balance or *Meezan*. This idea, applied to environmental ethics, requires, an equilibrium between material progress or economic development on the one hand, and the protection and conservation of the environment on the other. In the words of Harith bin Khelef, the chief mufti of Zanzibar, "the need of our religion is to put human beings and other organisms in good order, or balance. If we don't, then there will be mischief and disaster on our planet." Indeed, the fall of nations and kingdoms is, from an Islamic viewpoint, a consequence of the human being's ingratitude to God. An example is the parable of an ungrateful nation, the kingdom of Sheba in south-western Arabia. In the *Qu'anic* chapter, appropriately entitled *Saba* or Sheba, we find the following:

> "Indeed in the beauty of their homeland the people of Sheba had
> Evidence of God's Grace—two vast expanses of gardens saying
> 'Eat of what your Sustainer has provided for you, and render Thanks
> unto Him: a land most goodly, a Sustainer Much-Forgiving.'
>
> But they turned away from Us, and so We let loose upon the
> A flood that overwhelmed the dams and transformed their two
> Vast expanses of gardens into gardens yielding bitter fruits
> Tamarisks and a few lote-trees."
>
> Verses 15–19; see also *Al Nahl* (Bees),
> chapter 16, verses 112–113

The Islamic worldview, through the principle or idea of *Meezan* (Balance) establishes an equilibrium between economic development and environmental protection. However, the practical implementation of this idea has declined within the Islamic world. What are the reasons for this decline? Very briefly, five reasons could be outlined. These are:

1. Ossification within religious civilizations which very often creates a situation whereby the underlying values and true spirit are forgotten or set aside and, instead, static laws and antiquated practices are projected as the defining characteristics of a particular faith.

2. The dominant pervasive power and influence of Western secular civilization in the contemporary world. The secularization of society, which has its roots in the European Renaissance, reached its peak in the twentieth century with the acceptance that religion is a private matter and has nothing to do with issues in the public realm, including the community's relationship with the environment.

3. The rise of a secular worldview has seen the dramatic expansion of a global economy which emphasizes the maximization of profits, the penetration of markets and the attainment of high growth rates with little attention being accorded to balanced development and ethical values.

4. Many of the elites in the South who are either the direct products of colonial education or the indirect products of neo-colonial cultural and media indoctrination possess meager knowledge of what their religious philosophies say about the environment or about the human being's role as God's trustee on earth, or about the nexus between God (the Creator), the natural environment and human values. As a result, many planners, public administrators, academics, professionals, teachers and journalists are in no position to address wilderness, environment and development from a religious or spiritual perspective.

5. Even if there are groups capable of articulating the religious worldview, there is no guarantee that they will rise to the defense of the environment or espouse the cause of balanced development, especially if their own interests or others associated with them are involved. For vested interests linked to wealth, power and status have always subverted sublime values and altruistic ideals. That is why, in today's world, the greatest threat to

the practice of harmonious relations with the environment is the demon of self-serving interest appearing in some or other guise.

Indeed, the degradation of the environment is the result of the human being's disregard of God's Guidance on the Management of His Resources. I believe that there lies within a God-centered worldview an indisputable strength. This is why there should and must be a concerted effort to educate society on the significance of a God-centered worldview, not just for the sake of the environment or for the sake of balanced development but, more importantly, for the sake of the future of humanity itself.

What is urgently and desperately required in our world is a paradigm shift from a materialistic, secular worldview to an integrated, transcendental worldview, a worldview which all religions postulate.

See Hassan MK "World-View Orientation and Ethics: A Muslim Perspective," paper delivered at International Conference on Development, Ethics and Environment, Kuala Lumpur, 1995.

This paradigm implies, *inter alia*, that:

1. Human and natural resources are God-given bounties (ni'mah) and constitutive of the Divine Trust (amanah) held by the human being.
2. The concept of accountability is not confined to public accountability or accountability to human superiors but is extended to include answerability to God.
3. The idea that Allah is the True Owner and Manager of His Resources liberates the human mind from the false sense of autonomy or dominion over the earth's natural resources.

As the late Dag Hammarskjold once couched it:

> "On the bookshelf of life God is a useful work of reference,
> Always at hand but seldom consulted."

Future Cities and the Fate of Wilderness—Balance by Design

Kirstin Miller

The way we build has a profound impact on the way we live. For the first time in human history, the majority of us live in cities. The impact of urban development on ecological systems—from the local to the global—is already gigantic and rapidly growing worse. As we enter what some have called the "Urban" century, the damage now stretches from "paving paradise" to changing the climate of an entire planet.

The physical arrangement of our cities, towns and villages creates systems that organize resources and apply technologies, solidly shaping our civilization and how we interface with each other and the environment. Today, we are primarily focused on building human habitats that must be accessed and traversed by use of the automobile. Understanding that we have design choices, while reinforcing positive trends and exercising ecological rebuilding tools specifically created for solving these serious problems, offers enormous hope, not only for slowing biological destruction but for actually reversing the pattern and, by design and implementation, augmenting biodiversity and creating more wilderness habitat. The foundation for such solutions is in the realization that city structure itself is as necessary to a stable, healthy world for society and nature as is the foundation of a house for its own long-term integrity. This paper explains why this is the case, and guides steps into a future with substantially reshaped city infrastructure and much more wilderness than could otherwise be possible.

A System Out of Balance

It is increasingly clear that the way we currently build and live is out of balance with the living systems that sustain life on Earth. The National Wildlife Federation recently released the first ever quantitative assessment of the causes of species imperilment in California. The study found that outranking all other factors, sprawl now imperils 188 of the 286 California species listed as threatened or endangered under the federal Endangered Species Act—or 66 percent of the state's listed species. The report concludes that the conventional view that species endangerment in the Unites States is a problem most closely associated with natural resource extraction on broad landscapes far removed from metropolitan areas is no longer valid. Additionally, many of the other causes of California species imperilment depend on sprawl. For example, the loss and fragmentation of habitat and the severing of migratory corridors for wildlife caused by road construction to service ever-expanding residential subdivisions are perhaps the most obvious instances of causes of species imperilment that depend on sprawl.

"Sprawl development" is an essentially Western but increasingly global method of city building. In essence, sprawl is a two-dimensional blanket of low buildings linked by a complex network of roads, highways and streets. As populations rise, sprawl spreads quickly outward and even the most carefully planned greenbelt interventions often fail to stop its momentum. One or two roads or highways easily bridge preserved open spaces and the blanket of concrete and asphalt "leap frogs" over strips of open space and rolls onward, paving over farmland and wildlife habitat.

Until recently, the impact of the physical form and function of contemporary cities upon the global climate system, biosphere, energy situation and the overall health of human beings has been seriously under-appreciated. Recognition of this monumental challenge, however, is growing. The United Nations has organized programs and conferences on sustainable development and human settlements since the early 1900s. The Sierra Club made its "Challenge to Sprawl Campaign" a top national priority last year. European Union nations, including The Netherlands and Germany, now aim for a major restructuring in their development patterns.

Within the broader historical context of city building, the contemporary city built for the automobile is a fairly new development. As Murdoch University professors Peter Newman and Jeffrey Kenworthy point out in their book *Sustainability and Cities: Overcoming Automobile Dependence*, the first cities were Walking Cities. Between 7,000 and 10,000 years ago, these pedestrian communities were settled in the Middle East. They were based on walking distances, destinations that could be reached on foot in half an hour on average, and rarely were they more than 5 km across. The half an hour formula has continued to be an end point in how much time most people are willing to spend traveling each way to and from their destinations. In the 1860s, the Transit City began to expand the Walking City of the past. New forms of transportation enabled the city to accommodate more people at reduced densities while keeping to the half hour average accessibility maxim with transit technology: train, trams and streetcars. These cities stretched out to 20 or 30 km.

After WWII, the automobile became the transportation technology that shaped the city. It became possible to build in any direction and out as far as 50 km and still keep to the half-hour comfort zone formula. In the resulting Automobile City, it was not necessary for developers to provide more than basic power and water services, and the phenomenon of automobile dependence became a feature of urban life: not so much a choice as a necessity. Today, many cities have sprawled far enough to make even car commuting an inconvenience.

Waking up to the reality of the dysfunctional city—one which drains natural resources, threatens species, contributes to CO_2 build-up, global warming and generally negatively impacts our human health and well-being—makes many of us wonder if there is a solution to the enormous environmental problems facing us today. Can we really live in balance with the biosphere? "Sustainability" is a term that is currently widespread and is being applied in a variety of ways to our patterns of living. Jeff Kenworthy and Peter Newman define a sustainable city as a city that improves, not harms, the environment. I think we can all agree that this definition is a good one. The question is how do we get there from here?

In 1992's Earth Summit in Rio de Janeiro, sustainability was presented as an agenda to simultaneously solve the global environmental problem and to facilitate the economic development of the poor, particularly those in the third world. Four policies derived from the 1987 Brundtland Report (the UN's report from the World Commission on Environment and Development) were adopted into the 1992 Earth Summit recommendations as the fundamental approaches to global sustainability. Summarized, they are:

1. The elimination of poverty, especially in the Third World, is necessary not just on human grounds but as an environmental issue.

2. The First World must reduce its consumption of resources and projection of wastes. (The average American consumes natural resources at a rate 50 times that of the average Indian.)

3. Global cooperation on environmental issues is no longer a soft option. Hazardous wastes, greenhouse gasses, CFCs and the loss of biological diversity are examples of environmental problems that will not be solved if some nations decide to hide from the necessary changes.

4. Change toward sustainability can occur only with community-based approaches that take local culture seriously.

Local Solutions

Our Berkeley, California,–based nonprofit organization, Ecocity Builders, is attempting to do just that—make a major restructuring change on a local level. We are working within the community to build a breakthrough ecological demonstration project that could act like DNA and spread to other cities around the world. Our position is that unless we start from the foundation of the city and work up, we can't build a whole system that functions in balance with nature. That means looking at basic land use and slowly rebuilding into compact pedestrian oriented centers linked by transit. Demonstration projects can show this gradual reshaping of the city on ecological principals, leading to more compact, diverse centers with restoration of nature and agriculture in areas now automobile dependent.

Our Heart of the City ecological demonstration project is a reflection of future holistic views and growth for urban civilization. Rebuilding on the Heart of the City model, current accepted detriments to public health, safety and welfare will be diminished and eventually eliminated. The city can begin shifting away from dangerous, noisy, polluting and disharmonious automobile infrastructure towards pedestrian, transit friendly, environmentally sound and healthy business fueled by market economics through transfer of development rights initiatives and ecologically healthy practices, policies and ordinances.

Specifically, the Berkeley Heart of the City Project will feature a lively pedestrian environment and public plaza with housing, nature, businesses and cultural amenities, built according to ecological design principles. The project will also facilitate communication and cooperation between business and the community, help individuals take responsibility for their built environment, and demonstrate ecologically progressive programs, such as transfer of development rights and the restoration of natural features within the urban core.

Ecocity Builders' overall mission is to explore ways to restructure the built environment into a creative and healthy system that can function in balance with the local bioregion and biosphere of the planet. Ecocity theory and practice is largely the innovation of Richard Register, Founding President of Ecocity Builders, who has convened major local, national and international conferences on the subject and is a world leader in ecological city building theory, design and implementation. He was written two books: *Ecocity Berkeley, Building Cities for a Healthy Future* and *Village Wisdom/Future Cities*. His soon to be released *Ecocities* will be the definitive resource on the topic.

Ecocity Theory and Design

An ecocity, says Register, is like a compost box. Imagine a city that builds soils and maintains biodiversity and you're talking about an ecologically healthy city. A more specific functional description of an ecocity would basically be a city for pedestrians—a city built for people instead of machines.

The task at hand is certainly formidable, but we believe it can be done. Reshaping the automobile city will entail restructuring the entire dominant civilization on the planet right now, one which follows a very strong materialistic pattern, with a tremendous amount of competition, machines and use of incredible amounts of energy. In contrast, an ecocity would have a physical form that responds to the same physical dictates that the human body does, or the body of any animal. If the city is scattered over vast distances, then it doesn't function effectively. The parts must be proportional and close enough together to work in harmony. "Access by proximity," a term used first by Register, refers to the necessity of having a system whose parts are in proper proportion to each other and its whole. It is often thought of in terms of transportation, but it can also be thought of as transportation of blood in the vascular system in the human being. In both cases, there is a complex interrelation of parts, like the organs in an organism and "land uses" in a city. In society, communication between people and exchange of goods work most easily and efficiently at short distances: access by proximity. If a city is designed so that it's spread over vast distances, access by proximity has been compromised. Instead access is achieved only at great expense of energy and technology. In other words, one must drive cars and ride streetcars, trains or buses for many miles to meet basic needs—instead of walking or biking a short distance.

Richard Register and Ecocity Builders has invented a number of ecocity reshaping tools that can assist us, as he says, to roll back sprawl and rebuild civilization. Then we can transform human settlements at all scales into ecologically healthy places for people and nature. In Register's upcoming book, *Ecocities*, he outlines four fundamental steps leading to the political and economic realization of an ecocity. He calls them the Four Steps to an Ecology of the Economy.

First, he says, we have to know what goes where. To determine this, we can design maps that illustrate a clear expression of the concept of ecocity anatomy. Register calls these "ecocity zoning maps." The maps indicate areas to be developed in more density and diversity—the future walkable centers based mostly on existing lively centers—and the areas in which to restore nature and agriculture—the zones farthest from those centers and most dependent upon private motorized transport. Such maps will provide general rebuilding guidance, defining the vision and broad parameters of what should be built and where. Register reminds us that we should undertake this mapping exercise knowing that it will require revision and refinement. However, he says we simply cannot wait until we have all the answers. Instead, we can start in on the task and expect to self-correct along the way.

When planning an ecocity zoning map, careful attention should be given to the local bioregion. Where are the existing creeks and waterways? Where could natural corridors make room for species to thrive and traverse their natural habitat freely? Where could parks and community gardens be expanded or buildings be removed to open up automobile dependent areas, then shifting the development rights to compact pedestrian centers?

The second step is to identify technologies, businesses and jobs that come together to provide a vital economy based on the ecocity-zoning map. Some such business would be those which construct mixed-use buildings and solar technologies, bicycles, streetcars and rail stations, greenhouses, rooftop and organic gardens. Obviously, planning for more parking structures, gas stations and single family subdivisions would not play into the economy of an ecologically healthy city. Register believes that "improving" fundamentally damaging technologies like the automobile is the main reason random improvements have done so little to stem the larger disasters that are overwhelming the planet today. He writes, "In fact in giving us false assurances and postponing important strategic decisions the "better" car may well be one of the major causes of the disasters reaching their present and projected scales. Making such random (usually lucrative) "improvements" has also taken the critical and rigorous edge off good science that could have really helped—and still can if we adopt a strategy that reorganizes human settlements as pedestrian/bicycle oriented centers served by transit to a modest degree."

The third step towards an ecologically healthy human habitat is to provide appropriate incentives. Our present automobile-based cities are heavily subsidized. It is estimated that for every dollar an automobile owner pays—about $8,000 per owner per year—taxpayers contribute another dollar in subsidies. This money goes to highway building and maintenance, pollution damage repair, the EPA's air and water clean up budget, government contributions to hospitalization of car accident victims, policing services, the cost of defense of "our" oil in the Middle East, and more. An ecocity system will need a new set of incentives in order to make it profitable to build a society in balance with nature. New laws and policies, regulations, taxes, fines, grants, contracts, loans and especially zoning ordinances and building codes will be needed to support the community defined by the ecocity maps.

In Berkeley, Ecocity Builders is currently advocating for the adoption of the Ecocity Amendment, a set of four sustainable land use policies we hope to have adopted into the updated Berkeley General Plan revision. The City of Berkeley's City Council is deliberating on our motion. If adopted, the Ecocity Amendment will open the door for future ecocity planning and rebuilding by encouraging ordinances that will boost the likelihood that the Heart of the City project will be built—and soon. True to the findings of the Bruntland report, if adopted, the Ecocity Amendment could do what Jane Holtz Kay calls for in her Spring 2001 editorial for *Orion Afield, Working for Nature and Community*: "It becomes more and more clear that only if they (or more proactively, we) can become advocates on the larger political and planning scale, activists outside our newly insulated, sustainable front doorways, can we consider ourselves builders of a true sustainability and not just hammer-wielders building little green islands in a sea of subdivided nature."

The Ecocity Amendment policies address environmental design, centers-oriented development, ecological demonstration projects like the Heart of the City Project and environmental restoration. It seeks to provide a structure that will develop an economic and social environment leading to improved environmental quality. At this time, over 100 mostly local groups and businesses have endorsed the policies, and real and lasting healthy change, we feel, is immanent as public acceptance grows. The adoption of the Ecocity Amendment will allow ecocity principles to be put to work. They will illustrate that higher density can have beautiful, ecologically informed design expression in buildings that work well with transit, sun angles, natural features like creek restorations and provide views to the local region in which natural areas would be expanding.

Step four in Register's Ecology of the Economy is simply the people. In Berkeley, there are hundreds of students and retired people who are desperate for the opportunity to live in reasonably priced housing in a downtown which is "ecologically" well located. They are ready and waiting to be part of a more effective city system, but until now, have been repeatedly shut out by neighborhood conservatives and anti-development environmentalists refusing to allow sufficient housing to be built. Getting past the illogical fears and old belief systems is not easy, but Ecocity Builders is counting on persistent education and positive outreach to make a change for the better.

One recent step in the right direction is a very successful newly constructed mixed-use seven-story building with eco-features designed by Ecocity Builders. The Gaia (Earth) building makes the case that well-designed development demonstrating mixed use, terracing, roof access, solar orientation and access to public transit complements the city and enhances its vitality and overall heath. We believe that the Gaia building, third tallest building in downtown, with its terrace and rooftop gardens, trellises and vines, trees and people elevated into the sky is historic upon completion: it's the first building to bring life up onto the top. It's sheer cheerfulness—despite (some would say)—its large scale makes it a very positive precedent for our Heart of the City ecological demonstration project, and other such projects everywhere.

Conclusion

Until we address the city from the foundation up, we can't build whole cultural/economic systems that work in balance with nature. The impact of maintaining a resource draining pattern of building without regard to living systems is wiping out species and degrading wild places that are necessary for all of our survival. It is our sincere hope that those who seek to preserve and protect wild places will look to the link between cities and nature and join with us in what we believe will be the most consequential ecological endeavor of the 21st century: the rebuilding of our cities and towns in balance with living systems.

Wilderness
and a Sense of Self

Ian McCallum

"Psyche" comes from the Latin word which means soul. Psychiatry then, as well as psychology, would therefore imply that they are therapies or disciplines of the soul and ultimately of the self. Psychotherapy is as old as the hills. Apollo, the Homeric god of the Sun and of Healing, the twin brother of Artemis, the goddess of the Wild, once spoke from his home at Delphi. He gave three simple admonitions with respect to personal healing:

> Know thy Self.
> Honor the gods.
> Do no thing in excess.

Psychologically, these admonitions are as true today as they were then. To do no thing in excess did not imply that we do everything in moderation, which is our usual understanding of the expression. How boring! We may have our excesses, he implied but do not have them all the time. To honor the gods was to recognize that they were in everything, the trees, the lands, the animals, the people. To know thy Self, implied a personal responsibility. In 1973, the biologist Theodosius Dobzhansky wrote: "Nothing in biology makes sense except in the light of evolution."

It is a statement that is both simple yet profound. One of those statements that you or I could have made, especially because it seems so obvious. After all, we all knew that, didn't we? Or did we? Perhaps we didn't want to know. I have a notion that our sense of self, our sense of who we are in the world, is intimately associated with a deep historical sense of landscape and of our links with the animals—some ancient memory of where we have come from and of the shared survival strategies of all living things. For some it is the desert and the wide open plains. Not just the sight of them, but the sound, the feel, the smell and the taste. For others it is the mountains and then there are those whose sense of self is intimately linked to ice and water. "This place is in my blood," they say. It is therefore a sense of home and to be without it is to suffer one of the most overlooked psychiatric conditions of our time—homesickness.

How many of us have not experienced that intermittent sense of demotivation, a loss of a sense of pleasure for things that normally please us, that sometimes disturbing sense of a lack of direction or meaning? And how many of us know the feeling "I need to get out of here"? Apollo would have advised thusly: "Go and visit my sister, Artemis, in the wild—get in touch with your soul … get in touch with the land and with your history." This implies both an outer and an inner journey. If there is anyone in the audience who vaguely understands the significance of the Aboriginal "walk-about," then you will know what I mean. For those who quietly celebrate the chilling night call of the spotted hyena or the shape and the shade of the *Acacia Tortillis*—the umbrella thorn— or Africa's night sky, then you will know where I am coming from or perhaps, more significantly, where I am headed.

It would seem to me that all living things are creatures of time and place and that at the level of human existence our sense of self and our sense of place are like the two intertwining threads of the DNA molecule. They are inextricably linked. They are the prerequisites to a notion that I would like to introduce during the course of this presentation—the notion of an ecological intelligence and with it, a language that can articulate our connection to all living things (including what we regard as inorganic and non-living matter—for this at another level is also alive). I believe this intelligence to be something not lost or forgotten, but a way of thinking that is emerging in response to the unprecedented environmental crises of our day. I see it as an intelligence that will contribute to a greater understanding of our significance and of our responsibilities as the peculiar species we are—the human animal.

I feel a great passion for this subject, although on so many levels I know so little about it. If permission to speak on this subject depended on the number of times I have been into the wild parts of Africa with its animals and peoples, I might have earned this privilege. And yet, whatever I say, I know will be inadequate. For a start, we struggle the find the right words, the right language to describe wilderness and to describe ourselves. We struggle with words like spirit, soul, gods and God—we think we know what they mean. But do we? There might be good reason for this struggle—perhaps we need to wrestle to find the right words to express a self that is authentically spiritual or filled with soul, a self that understands the concept and meaning of the word, God.

For a start, perhaps we need to remember that language, like the harnessing of fire, has been the evolutionary equivalent of the harnessing of the syllables of the wild, and that as we speak, we intrinsically speak for the wild. If this is the case, then let us wrestle like hell for the right words. Let us wrestle like hell to make our words more conscious and authentic. Jacob's long and wounding wrestle with the angel and his subsequent awakening to who and what his wild brother, Esau, was really about—that he was an ally and not an enemy, took a long time coming. So too, for me, has the subject of wilderness, landscape and a sense of self. It has been a great wrestle. As hostile, as indifferent and as dark as the wilderness has so often appeared to me, it refuses to let me go. I too, refuse to it let go. I simply cannot escape the sense that like the dark parts of the human psyche, wilderness is our ultimate ally, the ultimate mirror of who we are, of where we have come from and without which, we are nothing. It would seem to me that as we bless the wilderness, as we honor the gods, as we honor our evolution—so in turn, are we blessed, in that order.

What did Chief Seattle mean when he wrote to the U.S. President in his day that the land and the sky were not for sale, and that without the animals his people would die of a loneliness of spirit? What was Henry David Thoreau getting at when he wrote "in wilderness lies the preservation of mankind." And what about Carl Sandburg's poem, *Wilderness*?

Surely these are the voices of an ecological intelligence, an ecological Self. What did Laurens van der Post mean when he asked this question in 1982: "Why is it that whenever there is a call to assist in the preservation or conservation of an endangered species, men and women rally to this call?" This was his answer: "There is a subtle realization here, for the conservation of animals and plants are more important to human beings than to the former. These forms of life are vital for our survival," he said. "They are on show as a reflection and as a symbol of the qualities and the expression of man." We are the species that are both endangering and endangered. It was as if he had been speaking directly to me. I was deeply moved. Van der Post had reminded me that the conservation of the wilderness was at the same time the conservation of the body of mankind and of the whole earth. He was telling me that wilderness and my sense of self are inextricably linked. Bless you for that, Laurens, and damn you too.

Still, he would not let me go. Drawing me toward the image of a fire, to that great metaphor for consciousness, he silently reminded me of the significance of the night watch—keeping the fire alive. "Remember Ian, this is your last watch, make the most of it." Is this the voice of a fantasist and "no-good" as portrayed in a recent lopsided biography? Nobody before or since, has defined for me the essence of wilderness quite so succinctly, quite so poignantly, so personally, and this is the whole point—that wilderness be taken personally. It distresses me to hear that the Kruger National Park has not had to rely on a cent of taxpayer's money in the last few years. I think there is something wrong with that. It is our Park—our responsibility as well. We also need to learn how to pay for our own drinks!

And so, within a month of that meeting with van der Post, I found myself in the Umfolozi with Ian Player and his great friend, Maqubu Mtombela. It was there and then that I wrote the poem, *Echo*. For me the wrestle was truly under way. Here are a couple of verses:

> And the mountains and the streams and the sea....
> Am I the one who speaks for you
> Or is it you that speaks for me?
>
> And the eagles or the mantis and the trees ...
> Do you live your lives in the wild out there
> Or in the wild in the life of me?

"Ah, these are the lamentations of the romantic," some might say. And a part of me answers "Ja-nee—yes no." Yes, wilderness is indeed a metaphor for the unconscious, for the great mother, for the origins, and No, it is never just that. It is what it is. Yes, it can be a movable feast carried in our hearts and mind and No, it can never be moved, and neither should it. To have a memory of wilderness will never be enough—we have to go there also. And Yes, I am a romantic, but "let me reiterate" says the South African poet Stephen Watson, "romanticism was never about romanticism. It was and is rather, one expression of a perennial human tendency to protest against that which would confine and otherwise mutilate what used to be called the human soul."

May I remind you that the word "animal" comes from the Latin root "anima" which means breath or spirit or soul—that which animates. And let us remember also that poetry is and always has been, in its essence, a form of protest. Is it possible that ecological intelligence implies the art of knowing what it means to live poetically?

The animals are in our blood. The landscape is in our skin. But let us not forget that we are in their blood also—we too gnash and gnaw: we too have our alarm calls, our cries of territory, of sexual prowess and discovery. We too, experience fear, frustration and rage and we are not the only ones who die of a broken spirit. And we too are in the skin of the land—every element from silica and hydrogen to lithium, phosphorous and gold can be traced in the human body. We are the dust of the earth and of the stars. Say thank you quickly! Say thank you to every green leaf and plant for without them you and I would not exist.

Few people in this audience would argue our interdependence with the environment, with the living creatures of the World. But how many of us know just how closely and how delicately we are linked. For example, the difference in the chemical formula of the oxygen releasing chlorophyll molecules in plants and the oxygen binding hemoglobin molecules of mammalian blood is tantalizingly close, resting on the interchange of only two trace elements. Exchange the iron in hemoglobin for the magnesium in chlorophyll, then technically speaking we will become producers of oxygen. Do we know what it means to have a primate cousin, *Pan troglodytes*, and the chimpanzee, genetically defined as being 98% human?

We badly need an overall direction that can point us to a greater sense of Self, an ecological Self, an identity which can make sense of the debt and the reverence we owe to the animal kingdom, to wilderness and to humanity. Ours is a search for an identity that includes but is not limited by our usual understanding of who and what we are, namely our ego selves. Without the ego we cannot make sense of our world. We cannot stand outside of its boundaries, for to do so or to witness that in another, is to understand the meaning of psychosis. This can be extremely frightening. We cannot live effectively without the ego, for the world, as it is perceived by us, is ultimately defined by it. The ego, then, is an essential yet fragile personal complex of the psyche giving voice, orientation and reflection to that which is mostly conscious and personal to our individual lives. Within its boundaries, we are reminded of who and where we are, our names and addresses, where we are going and where we have been, etc. This is the ego self—a tiny island of dry land surrounded and supported by an evolutionary sea of life. It is a tenuous complex mostly afraid of the great depths of the psyche from which it has evolved and which ultimately supports it; often blind not only to the collective genetic memories of our species, but to our ancient interdependence with the very environment out of which it was born and which shaped it. This is not the Self that Apollo was referring to when he said, "Know thy Self." It was an Ecological Self that he was referring to and with it, an Ecological Mind, the mind that remembers how old and how young we actually are in the universe.

Barry Lopez refers to "La quarencia" as the Spanish word which describes the place on the ground where one feels secure—a place from which one's strength of character is drawn. It is not a passive place, he says. Instead, it is that immeasurable yet tangible "spot" in a bullring where a wounded bull goes to gather himself—the place he returns to after his painful encounters with the picadors and the banderilleros. To me, "la quarencia" is the wilderness—a place where I can lick my wounds and where I can reconnect to my ecological Self— to that self that grips the hand of Barry Lopez when he writes about the necessity of recognizing the spiritual and psychological dimensions of geography. His is a voice of ecological intelligence ... and there are others.

"All men are brothers," we like to say, half-wishing sometimes in secret it were not true. And is the evolutionary line from protozoan to Spinoza any less certain? That also may be true. We are obliged therefore to spread the news, painful and bitter though it may be for some to hear ... "that all living things are kindred," says Edward Abbey in his book, *Desert Solitaire*.

And so, as the genetic codes responsible for the variety of the earth's species are slowly unraveled and interpreted, the mist that has clung to our history, our sense of self and our responsibility as human beings, *homo sapiens sapiens*, appears to be lifting. Look, we are the human animal. We are not going anywhere—we've emerged. We are the younger brothers and sisters of Nature. This is our place. We are privileged. To recognize and to acknowledge the genetic similarities between us and our primate and other mammalian cousins, is at once sobering, exciting and essential. It is also something to celebrate.

However, if, as we have discovered, *Pan Troglodytes*, the chimpanzee, is 98% human, then we owe it to them and to ourselves to examine the 2% difference also. To ignore or to minimize it would be to overlook the significance of what it means to be a human animal. If, as it would seem, that human consciousness is defined in that tiny fraction then the difference between us and our nearest earthly relative, is at once close and colossal. Human consciousness, the capacity to deeply reflect, to abstract, to laugh and to live in the knowledge that we have to die, is, as far as we know, uniquely ours. It may well be a consciousness that is evolving yet, but it is nevertheless a quantum leap beyond the creativity and sociability of our primate friends and our other mammalian kin. If, to be humanly conscious, is indeed to function at another level, another orbit, then it carries with it a necessary responsibility.

Consciousness does not come without a price. I believe our responsibility is this—to be receptive to the emergence of an ecological intelligence, remembering where we have come from ... knowing at some deep level that we are dependent on the living forms that have emerged before us, and that without them we are nothing. We spin around the same core. If the image of the animal is that of the image of breath and spirit, is it not likely that that with our brothers and sisters of the wild, we too are an embodiment of that great spirit? Is there anything on earth that is not an expression of the pattern of God?

"And how shall we find the kingdom of heaven?" asked the disciples of the Master in one of the apocryphal gospels. "We are lost," they said. "Follow the birds and the beasts," came the reply. "They will lead you there."

Appendices

Major Accomplishments—
7th World Wilderness Congress

The 7th WWC was a roaring success ... from substantive international issues and accomplishments, to the cultural program, all the way through to the community outreach program to create revenue and exposure for local communities here in South Africa. We are pleased to give you a summary of the main accomplishments.

World Wilderness Summit Highlights

With 700 delegates from more than 44 nations the World Wilderness Summit was incredibly productive. Opened by the Minister of Environment of South Africa, our host country, here is a brief list of our accomplishments in the World Wilderness Summit after our first two days.

Global Environmental Facility Announces—
Two new grants to assist wilderness and wildlands conservation

- $1,000,000 to South Africa for the Baviaanskloof ("Baboon's Ridge") Wilderness Area—$1,000,000 to Angola to assist the Kissama Foundation work to rehabilitate Angola's Quiçama National Park.

Private Sector Wilderness

- The first wilderness area on private property in Africa—legally declared and with a wilderness management plan—was announced by Adrian Gardiner, owner of Shamwari Game Reserve in the Eastern Cape Province, near Port Elizabeth. Mr. Gardiner put 16% of his land, over 3,000 hectares (7,500 acres) under legal servitude to the Wilderness Foundation of South Africa, founded by Ian Player and headed by Andrew Muir.

New Wilderness Legislation and
Protected Areas—Namibia announces:

- New, national, wilderness legislation, and
- Proposed plans for a new Wilderness National Park in SW Namibia
- Proposed three nation, transfrontier, desert wilderness, stretching from Northern Cape Province of South Africa, all the way through Namibia, into Southern Angola.

Two New Fundraising Strategies for African Protected Areas

- My Acre of Africa—new strategy launched—Internet-based, public fundraising strategy for Southern African parks, Protected Areas and local communities (www.myacreofafrica.com).
- African Protected Areas Initiative—new strategy announced—to be developed and launched at 5th World Parks Congress in Durban in June 2003, this is an initiative of numerous international agencies, funders, and NGOs to address the need for more finance for all African Protected Areas.

Conservation Education, Private Sector Support

- Johnnic Holdings Ltd., South Africa's media giant and largest black-controlled company, announced that Conservation Education is now one of only two top priorities in its corporate social and community outreach program.

Professional Training

- 20 wildlands managers and wardens from 13 countries graduated from a special training course on wilderness management, associated with the 8th WWC.

Tropical Forests

U.S. Congressman E. Clay Shaw announced the imminent introduction into the U.S. Congress of a bill addressing the need to stem the tide of unsustainable logging of tropical forests, using a number of different financial mechanisms.

7th World Wilderness Congress Resolutions

8 November 2001

Resolution #1

Restoration of the Southern Cape Forests

WHEREAS

- Deforestation and the resultant extinction of species is a critical global problem, and is a major environmental issue in Africa, especially in the Congo Basin, Madagascar, and West Africa;

- In South Africa, the Southern Cape Forests, which represent a unique outlier of the Afro-montane forests, have been reduced to a small fraction of their original extent;

- The remaining isolated fragments are scattered throughout their former range and most are of insufficient size to ensure their biological and ecological integrity;

- These forest fragments are undergoing continuous degradation as a result of, for example, damage from recent fires in adjacent plantations on non-native pines and the planned widening of the Highway N2 through the Plaatbos Nature Reserve;

- No regeneration of these forests is taking place because of grazing pressure on cleared, formerly forested land and the planting of exotic tree species right up to the edge of the indigenous forest remnants;

- South Africa, because of its innovative conservation policies and long-standing statutory recognition of wilderness areas, is uniquely placed to pioneer the ecological restoration of indigenous forests in Africa as part of the vital task to achieve ecological and economic sustainability for Africa in the decades ahead; and

THEREFORE, the 7th World Wilderness Congress

- Congratulates the SA Government and agencies for replacing removing non-native plantations, and in some cases replacing them with indigenous forest species, from numerous important ecosystems such as the Eastern Shores of lake St Lucia;

- Recognizes the good work and excellent results of the Working for Water programme in involving local communities in such work; and

RESOLVES, that
The South African Government should further:
- Develop and implement a coordinated plan for the ecological restoration of the southern Cape Forests, to return the indigenous forest to suitable areas of its former extent (including some of the existing non-native pine plantations), and to link up the surviving forest fragments, thereby re-establishing a much larger contiguous and ecologically viable forest ecosystem;
- Involve the relevant agencies, such as SAN Parks and SAFCOL, non-governmental organizations and local communities in the drafting of the plan, to ensure that it meets both ecological targets and the economic needs of the people, through, for example, expanded ecotourism opportunities;
- Allocate adequate funding to employ disadvantaged people in the practical work of ecological restoration, such as planting native tree species and the removal of exotic ones, so that local communities become active partners in the return of their natural heritage;
- Make an initial announcement of its commitment to the restoration of the Southern Cape Forests at the major international conference, Restore the Earth, held at Findhorn, Scotland, 30th March—5th April 2002, launch a detailed plan at the World Summit on Sustainable Development in Johannesburg, September 2002, and present a progress report at the 8th World Wilderness Congress.

Resolution #2
Protection of Kakadu World Heritage Site
from the Jabiluka Uranium Mine
WHEREAS
- The Mirrar aboriginal traditional owners are opposed to the Jabiluka uranium Mine which is being constructed with an enclave of the Kakadu Heritage site, Australia;
- Many IUCN NGO members around the world are opposed to the Jabiluka uranium mine;
- The IUCN (World Conservation Union) has a policy of opposing mineral exploration and extraction within protected areas (IUCN Category 1–4) as adopted at the 2nd IUCN World Conservation Congress in Amman, Jordan October 2000;
- This policy was again reaffirmed by IUCN Council in October 2000;
- Despite this policy, the World Heritage Site Committee may be under the impression that IUCN (which is the advisory body to the World Heritage Committee on natural World Heritage values) does not oppose the construction and operation of the Jabiluka uranium mine within the enclave of the Kakadu World Heritage area;

THEREFORE, the 7th World Wilderness Congress
- Congratulates the Mirrar traditional owners for defending Kakadu from the threat posed by the Jabulika uranium mine to this outstanding World Heritage Site;
- Commends Rio Tinto for its decision not to proceed with Jabilika but urges immediate restoration of the mine site; and

RESOLVES, that
- NGOs around the world SHOULD continue in their efforts to ensure that the Jabilika uranium mine in never operated and the mine site is quickly rehabilitated for future incorporation back into the World Heritage site after agreement is reached with the traditional owners; and
- Further, calls on the IUCN to publicly and vigorously oppose the Jabiluka uranium mine and requests that IUCN make a statement to the World Heritage Committee at its meeting in Helsinki in December 2001 pointing out the serious threats posed by the Kakadu, calling for immediate rehabilitation of the mine site.

Resolution #3
Wilderness Values in East Europe and North Asia
WHEREAS
- Wilderness and wildland areas in eastern Europe and northern Asia have only sporadic protection and require more specific legislation for their protection and management;
- These areas provide many and valuable services to human communities; and
- Threats to and actual negative impacts upon these important areas are increasing;

THEREFORE the 7th World Wilderness Congress
- Congratulates The Kiev Ecological and Cultural Centre for their pioneering educational and other work in this region; and

RESOLVES, that
- The Kiev Ecological and Cultural Centre (Ukraine) further assume an active coordinating role for matters of wilderness and wildlands in the region, organize a regional conference on these issues in Eastern Europe, translate and publish the 7th World Wilderness Congress proceedings and other materials on wilderness; and report back on their activities in this regard at the 8th World Wilderness Congress.

Resolution #4
Providing Education, Research and Leadership to Ensure Sustainability of Wilderness Resources and Values in Alaska

WHEREAS
- In the circumpolar north, there remain today many local cultures that maintain relatively intact relationships with vast pristine ecosystems that are protected as wilderness or could be protected as wilderness;
- Protection of these areas is crucial to assure sustainability of these cultures and the wilderness resources on which they and their identities depend, and for their unique biodiversity and economic values;
- Alaskan wilderness areas were established by special legislation that ensures the rights of local people for continued access, but also assures the people of the U.S. that wilderness values will dominate in management decisions;
- These areas are also receiving increasing attention from, and may be threatened by, economic development interests such as rapidly increasing ecotourism and potential energy development;
- Over 50% of the U.S. National Wilderness Preservation System is located in Alaska, but there remain over 80 million acres of roadless public land in Alaska that are not protected as wilderness;
- Many protected areas have outdated plans which do not adequately address how biodiversity and economic values will be encouraged while supporting traditional means of livelihood and relationships with nature;

THEREFORE, the 7TH World Wilderness Congress
- Applauds the wilderness scientists, managers, educators, native representatives, non-governmental organizations and government officials from across the polar north countries (Norway, Finland, Canada, Denmark, Iceland, Russia and the U.S.) who came together in May of 2001 in Anchorage, Alaska, to determine the priorities for protecting wilderness places of the north.
- Supports the priorities they agreed upon, including the need for a center of excellence in Alaska to provide focus and leadership on northern wilderness issues;
- Agrees that such a center would provide continued coordination for identifying high priority research issues, provide guidance in accomplishing science needs, be a repository for research reports, management plans and data sets, be a source of the highest integrity for input to decisions about wilderness allocation and management, and a source of energy and coordinated resources in undertaking education and interpretation regarding the many values associated with northern wilderness; and hereby

RESOLVES to
- Encourage the People of Alaska, through their University System and in cooperation with the Aldo Leopold Wilderness Research Institute and the Arthur Carhart National Wilderness Training Center, to recognize the needs of ALL people of Alaska and ALL people of the rest of the U.S. by facilitating development of the University of Alaska Wildland Center. This Center should be

directed through cooperation among the native people of Alaska, academic and government scientists, nongovernmental organizations, energy and economic development interests, and public land managers and planners, striving toward meeting the needs for science and education in Alaska as an example and as a source of information and inspiration for the circumpolar north; and

- Further recommends that this important venture be a high priority of the University System of Alaska, state/national/international foundations and nongovernmental organizations with interest in wilderness, public land management agencies, energy development corporations, and the commercial recreation industry.

Resolution #5
Energy Development in Critical
Wilderness Ecosystems in the United States of America
WHEREAS
- The United States of America is the largest consumer of energy and the largest contributor to global warming pollution from the burning of fossil fuel;
- The USA could dramatically reduce its reliance on fossil fuels by adopting a national energy policy with a primary focus on conservation, energy efficiency and investment in clean renewable energy resources;
- The Bush Administration has refused to ratify the Kyoto Protocol on Global Climate change and is promoting an energy strategy that is primarily centred on relaxing environmental standards promoting nuclear power, and promoting new domestic oil development, including on public lands in or adjacent to critical wilderness ecosystems and other environmentally sensitive lands;

THEREFORE, the 7th World Wilderness
- Recognizes the importance of a sound energy policy for the United States and all nations, especially one which is based on principles of conservation and lowered dependence on imported fuels; and hereby

RESOLVES to
- Urge the United States of America to ratify and implement the Kyoto Protocol on global climate change and adopt a national energy policy that has primary reliance on conservation, energy efficiency and expanding clean renewable resources of energy, while reducing reliance on nuclear power and fossil fuels, while fully enforcing all existing environmental laws; and
- Call upon the government of the United States to specifically and fully protect the Artic National Wildlife Refuge (Alaska), the Greater Yellowstone Ecosystem (Idaho, Montana, Wyoming) and the Greater Glacier—Bob Marshall Ecosystem (Montana) from oil and gas development

by permanently withdrawing federal lands in these ecosystems from mineral development and designating all qualifying wildlands in these ecosystems as wilderness under the Wilderness Act.

Resoluion #6
Transkei, Eastern Cape SA — Education for Self Sustainability
WHEREAS

In Transkei, Eastern Cape, South Africa:
- Soil erosion has taken over the land resulting in deep gashes in the earth;
- People are poor and live in unfortunate conditions with little or no income;
- The land, cities and towns are practically ankle deep in litter and rubble;
- The residents have little knowledge and encouragement to establish better living conditions;

THEREFORE, the 7th World wilderness Congress
- Recognizes that lack of environmental self-sufficiency inevitably leads to degradation of wilderness and wildland areas;
- Supports the critical importance of poor rural and local peoples to be masters of their own beneficial environmental conditions; and hereby

RESOLVES that
- Local and regional government, with assistance from national agencies and international funders where possible, introduce to and educate the communities of the Transkei in, as many natural resource techniques as possible that restore ecological balance and self-sufficiency, including but not limited to permanent agriculture (perma-culture) systems.

Resolution #7
Provision of Wilderness Training
in Association with the World Wilderness Congress
WHEREAS
- The Wilderness Action Group of South Africa, in cooperation with the University of Natal and others, delivered a week-long pre 7th WWC training session for wilderness managers from ten African countries, India, Canada, Russia, and Brazil; and
- This training activity substantially enriched the WWC experience of the delegates and will contribute to improved wilderness management across a large region.

THEREFORE, the 7th World Wilderness Congress
- Congratulates The WILD Foundation, The Wilderness Foundation (SA), The Sierra Club and others for initiating and sponsoring this training;
- Thanks the trainers for donating their considerable time and expertise; and

RESOLVES, that
- In order to directly affect the management of wilderness areas worldwide, the organizers of the World Wilderness Congress should continue to organize a regional training programme in association with and in proximity to each World Wilderness Congress, and draw upon the professional strengths of the WWC delegation to provide training in a regional context appropriate to the location of the Congress.

Resolution #8
Successful Coexistence of People, Predators, Wildlife and Livestock
WHEREAS
- National parks and other protected areas are essential for conservation of biodiversity, but they are not sufficient on their own, and in particular are often too small to provide viable territories for large predators, so that non-protected area conservation is also essential for these species;
- This requires the active cooperation of local communities who recognize that parks have benefits beyond their immediate boundaries, and in particular that large predators and other wildlife are a key attraction for tourism;
- These communities are commonly dependent for their livelihood on livestock which they therefore need to protect from predation;
- For coexistence with predators this requires non-lethal methods for predator control, which can be achieved through restoring and maintaining healthy populations of prey wildlife species and by actively guarding livestock;

THEREFORE, the 7th World Wilderness Congress
- Recognizes that integrated systems for maintaining wildlife and livestock, which meet the needs of both humans and predators, are essential for the coexistence and conservation of communities and carnivores alike;
- Notes that successful models for such integrated human-livestock-wildlife-predator systems have been developed and applied by organisations such as those listed in Annexure A; and hereby

RESOLVES, that
- International agencies such as the Global Environment Facility of the World Bank, the United Nations Environment Program, and the World Conservation Union; and
- National, sub-national and local governments, assisted by non-government organisations, all of which currently fund projects to sustain critical biodiversity;
- Initiate and/or approve, and provide pilot funding for, a global program to establish integrated human-livestock-wildlife-predator systems throughout all relevant regions of the world, with a plan to be completed within 2 years and substantial implementation within 5 years.

Annexure A to 7th WWC Resolution #8
Models and examples for integrated human-livestock-wildlife-predator systems
- Cheetah Conservation Fund in Namibia
- International Snow Leopard Trust in Nepal and India
- WWF/USAID LIFE Project in Namibia
- Corbett Fund in India

Resolution #9
Development of Infrastructure of Higher Education Focused on Wilderness and Protected Area Management in Southern Africa
WHEREAS
- The University of Natal in cooperation with the University of Montana, have developed a protected area management degree and training programme within the province of KwaZulu-Natal;
- Wilderness legislation, wilderness areas and wilderness management plans currently exist in SA and are in the process of being expanded in that country and elsewhere in the region;

THEREFORE, the 7th World Wilderness Congress
- Congratulates the Universities involved for initiating this program;
- Recognizes that this level training and higher is necessary given the legal mandate of protected area managers in South Africa; and hereby

RESOLVES, that
South African universities and their international co-operators, develop and provide:
- A graduate degree program, aimed at the professional audience, with a focus on wilderness and protected area management in South Africa;
- An organized program of research to provide the reference material needed both for said degree and by a broader audience of protected area managers within Southern Africa;
- An information system to effectively organize, distribute and archive knowledge about the protected area system in Southern Africa, and
- Ongoing training to wilderness and protected area stewards responsible for development, administration and implementation of policy at all organizational levels.

Resolution #10
OCP Crude Oil Pipeline in Ecuador
WHEREAS
- The Amazon headwaters in Ecuador are an incomparable biological treasure house and home to unique indigenous communities;
- The biggest threat to this area is the ecological and social destruction accompanying the oil extraction industry;
- The proposed OCP crude oil pipeline would double the mount of oil

extracted from the area and destroy large tracts of wild nature including "protected areas" such as the Yasuni National Park, the Cuyabeno National Park, the Panacocha Reserve, and others' plus the traditional lands of Huaorani, Quichua, Cofan, Secoya and Siona peoples;

- As it traverses the Andes, the pipeline will of necessity pass through geologically unstable areas prone to earthquakes and landslides, following a route similar to the existing pipeline which has burst 48 times, spilled 75 million litres of oil, killed 30 people and polluted forests, rivers and farms;
- In late October 2001, local grassroots conservation groups blockaded the start of pipeline construction and appealed to the world conservation community for support;
- All attempts to influence the oil companies and the Ecuadorian government have failed;
- The main source of funding for the OCP project is WestLB, the largest publicly owned German bank;
- This project would never be allowed to proceed in Germany or anywhere else in the developed world;
- There is already considerable opposition to this project within WestLB itself;
- The German people have consistently shown a strong commitment to ecology in general and to rainforest conservation in particular;

THEREFORE, the 7th World Wilderness Congress
RESOLVES, that
- The Ecuadoran government withdraw its plan for this pipeline, and observe ecological and cultural needs in any new plan;
- No foreign donor agency or bank, including WestLB, provide financing for the OCP pipeline project; and
- German citizens actively and directly protest to WestLB, using a customer boycott if necessary.

Resolution #11
The Value of Experiences in Wilderness and Nature for Healing and Reconciliation of Human Differences
WHEREAS
- The wounds of anger and deprivation from social injustice and inequality are giving rise today, in part, to terrorism, war and seemingly irreconcilable conflicts over differences in beliefs, culture and religion;
- Escalating terrorism and war threaten the future of humanity and life as we know it, including visions and opportunities for conservation of nature;
- Scientific and social studies show us that human experience of wilderness and nature, alone and/or in groups, offer superb opportunities for healing the wounds of injustice and inequality, and for development of

human reconciliation and tolerance;
- This use of wilderness for healing and reconciliation of human differences is demonstrated in South African programmes in this regard during its transition to democracy, and in hundreds of wilderness therapy and personal growth programs worldwide;

THEREFORE, the 7th World Wilderness Congress hereby
RESOLVES, that
- The organizers of the World Wilderness Congress continue to highlight the values of wilderness and nature as places of healing anger and reconciliation of differences in the published proceedings of the 7th WWC and on the programme of future Congresses;
- Wilderness and Nature leaders worldwide be urged to feature these values in their meetings, conferences, symposia, other gatherings and media so as to increase awareness of their importance and to encourage new methods and applications for utilizing them;
- The United Nations (whose original formation dialogue utilized the inspiration of nature in the giant redwoods of the west coast on USA) take note of the values of wilderness and nature for healing and reconciliation, and that natural environments be used as a place for negotiation and dialogue to heal wounds and reconcile differences that threaten the world today;
- Relevant groups and organizations in South Africa – and the many hundreds of other groups worldwide—better promote their programmes which use wilderness for healing and reconciliation, so as to be recognized as pioneering examples and an inspiration to other nations and situations with similar challenges.

Resolution #12
Establishing a Global Network of Youth
Toward the 1st Youth World Wilderness Congress
WHEREAS
- Wilderness experiences are proven to be life-changing experiences for youth;
- There are many programmes internationally that bring youth into wilderness;
- Value would be added to these programmes if the students could learn/interact/dialogue with students in similar programmes from other countries and cultures;

THEREFORE, the 7th World Wilderness Congress hereby
RESOLVES
- Students from Imbewu Youth Wilderness Programme in South Africa (joint venture between South African National Parks and the Wilderness Leadership School) and the Wildlink Wilderness Education Project in

California, USA (joint venture between USDA Forest service, USDI National Park Service and Bureau of Land Management) and other interested programmes will begin to share their perspectives, experiences, and subsequent life decisions based on these experiences. At first this dialogue will take place via shared letters, photographs and video;

- Further, in one year a satellite internet discussion will take place between the students directed toward a Youth World Wilderness Congress to run concurrent with the next World Wilderness Congress. The group involved will seek funding from various sources to send youth delegates to the Congress.

Resolution #13
State of Indian Tiger
WHEREAS

- The Bengal Tiger continues to decline in numbers and viability;
- The Bengal Tiger is a flagship, wilderness-dependent species, and its decline signals an alarm for the well-being and future of its critically important wilderness habitat;
- Numerous international and Indian organizations are working on this, and international funding is available through existing organizations, corporations, NGO councils, and others;

THEREFORE, the 7th World Wilderness Congress

- Emphasizes that saving the Bengal Tiger may not be accomplished unless the national government of India makes it a priority now, as they did at one point in the past;
- Recognizes that coordination, cooperation and collaboration between the many agencies and institutions involved is also of paramount concern; and hereby

RESOLVES

- To convey these concerns directly to the Honourable Prime Minister of India, asking for his personal intervention at this critical stage for the future of the Bengal Tiger, to pull it back from the brink of extinction, and to assure a healthy tiger population and wilderness habitat for evermore as an icon of India and an irreplaceable gem of the world's biodiversity.

Resolution #14
Sunderbans Transfrontier Peace Park Shared by India and Bangladesh
WHEREAS

- The Sunderbans area is the delta of the Brahmaputra and Ganges Rivers, and is shared by India and Bangladesh;
- The Sunderbans supports an estimated population of 500 tigers, the most viable gene pool anywhere on the sub-continent;

THEREFORE, the 7th World Wilderness Congress hereby
RESOLVES that

- As a vital and important element in the plans to secure the long term survival of panthera tigris, the governments of India and Bangladesh work immediately with UNESCO and place the Sunderbans on the register as a World Heritage Site, and declare it the first transfrontier Peace Park in Asia.

Resolution #15
Himalayan Terai Arc
WHEREAS

- The Himalayan Terai Arc area forms an unbroken elephant and tiger corridor of more than 1000 kms along the foothills of the Himalayas, supporting over 1000 Asian elephants, more than 200 tigers, and numerous prey species.
- This area currently contains of five national parks—Rajaji, Corbett, Dudhwa in India and Shuklaphanta and Bardia in Nepal;
- The biological role and functioning of these parks, and their positive impact on conservation of biodiversity can be increased dramatically by creating corridors between them;

THEREFORE, the 7th World Wilderness Congress hereby
RESOLVES, that

- The Governments of India and Nepal prioritise, as an important part of the plan to save the tiger and elephant, the creation of corridors linking the national parks in the Himalayan Terai Arc, declare and manage these five parks as a transfrontier Peace Park between India and Nepal, while also working with UNESCO to declare this region a World Heritage Area.

Resolution #16
Management and Integrity of Wilderness Areas
WHEREAS

- The physical and conceptual integrity of wilderness is irrevocably linked to the efficiency and motivation of those responsible for its management and protection;
- Wilderness areas often require human input in terms of public involvement, education and management if they are to retain integrity as a specially protected area;
- These experts—"rangers," managers, etc.—need to be adequately trained, equipped, paid, motivated and led if they are to perform their duties properly;

THEREFORE, the 7th World Wilderness Congress hereby
RESOLVES, that

- Government agencies and other organizations—public or private—that propose or proclaim wilderness areas need to include in their planning the training and support of those people—i.e managers, rangers, and others—who will protect and manage the areas and help involve the local communities.

Resolution #17
Re-creation of Wilderness Areas in Great Britain
WHEREAS

- Changes in agriculture over the last few years are rendering this form of land use increasingly uneconomic in substantial areas of upland England, Wales and Scotland, resulting in progressive disintegration of local communities and heavy expense of taxpayer subsidy;
- Restoration of wildland areas and values is becoming increasingly important and will be a major focus of wilderness work in the 21st century;

THEREFORE, the 7th World Wilderness Congress

- Emphasizes that the restoration of Britain's wild heritage in general would catalyse wider support for re-creation of specific wilderness areas within industrialized countries, and reinforce the credibility of our assistance to developing countries in preserving their own wild lands and species; and hereby

RESOLVE, that

- United Kingdom governments, academic institutions and NGOs evaluate, demonstrate and promote:
- The establishment of wilderness zones in appropriate areas on a scale sufficient to sustain the reintroduction of major species lost to Great Britain, including boar, beaver, lynx and bear
- The development of related eco-tourism, outward bound and educational activities that have a minimal environmental impact yet offer long term economic opportunity to local communities.

Resolution #18
Landscape Approach as Wilderness Theme in Fragmented Ecosystems
WHEREAS

- Though a significant proportion of the world's terrestrial ecosystems have been highly fragmented, these fragmented systems contain significant proportion of the Earth's biodiversity;
- These fragmented ecosystems support the livelihoods of millions of people around the world;
- Strict protection efforts are increasingly hampered by conflict with development efforts;
- A broad, landscape–based approach involving wilderness concepts can enhance management effectiveness;

THEREFORE, the 7th World Wilderness Congress
- Endorses the landscape approach as a tool in advancing wilderness areas stewardship in fragmented landscapes to protect biodiversity; and hereby

RESOLVES, that
- Future Congresses will further emphasize the landscape approach, and create opportunities for effective dialogue and sharing experiences that promote and strengthen links between wilderness area management and protected area managers.

Resolution #19

Porto Dobela—Proposed Deep Water Port in Southern Mozambique
WHEREAS
- The Mozambican government has approved a proposal for a deep-water port to be constructed at Ponta Techobanine, immediately to the south of the 70,000 ha. Maputo Special (Elephant) Reserve (MSR) in southern Mozambique. (The concession requested is for an area of 25,000 ha., extending a considerable distance northwards as far as Ponta Milibangalala within the MSR, wherein besides the port a spectrum of light industrial, tourism and residential developments are planned.); and
- Through the proposed Lubombo TFCA (a component of the Lubombo Spatial Development Initiative's Lubombo Transfrontier Conservation and Resource Area protocols, signed by Mozambique, South Africa and Swaziland in June 2000), the MSR will be linked to the Tembe Elephant Park in South Africa through the protection of the pristine and largely unpopulated Futi Corridor;
- The MSR plus adjacent coastal areas from Portuguese Island southwards to Ponta do Ouro have been recommended as a proposed World Heritage Site (DNFFB/UNESCO 2000) that will link to the St Lucia Wetlands World Heritage Site;

THEREFORE, the 7th World Wilderness Congress
- Understands the need for sustainable economic planning and upliftment for local people in the area, but asserts that the jobs created by the scheme are not sustainable environmentally or economically;
- Recognizes that the area forms the core of the globally recognized Maputaland Centre of Plant Diversity, and is of enormous biological value, with substantial economic possibilities for local communities and the private sector in the field of ecotourism; but
- Concludes that the scheme, if it goes ahead, will indisputably attract very great numbers of job-seekers for whom there will be no planning in place (and who will perforce live off the land), and that the construction of the proposed port will seriously compromise the ecological integrity

of the area, as well as the objectives of the LSDI–TFCRA protocol, the TFCA Project, and any possible application for World Heritage status for the area; and hereby

RESOLVE
- The construction of the Porto Dobela deep water port is not planned on sound scientific and sustainable development principles, likely should not have been originally authorized, and must be the subject of a thorough international EIA conducted under the auspices of an independent organization such as the IUCN, and financed by the development consortium.

Resolution #20
Sao Sebastiao Penininsula, Mozambique

WHEREAS
- The government of Mozambique has approved for a South African businessman a nature tourism initiative in Mozambique's Sao Sebastiao Peninsula, which calls for the removal of over 2,000 people from the area, after which the area will be fenced and stocked with wildlife;
- The local people of the area, the Quewene have not been consulted properly and have registered a formal grievance with their District Administrator; and
- Clear indications exist of incompatibility of large wildlife ungulates with the typically acid grasslands of the east coast;

THEREFORE, the 7th World Wilderness Congress
- Understands that nature-based tourism, if done properly, is an important element of sustainable revenue for local rural communities;
- Commends the Mozambique government for trying to expand sustainable tourism; and hereby

RESOLVES, that
- The Government of Mozambique and private investors involved in the Sao Sebastiao Peninsula project should listen to and accommodate the expressed needs of the local inhabitants, follow internationally accepted standards for a comprehensive and independent EIA process, and adopt any and all recommendations of these two procedures including, if indicated, abandoning or relocating the project.

Resolution #21
The World Protected Areas Congress, Durban

WHEREAS
- Wilderness areas are or should be the nucleus of all protected areas;

- Wilderness will continue to grow in importance in this century due continued population growth, urbanization and technological advance
- WWC has worked with IUCN on definition of wilderness areas.

THEREFORE, the 7th World Wilderness Congress
- Fully Supports the Vth World Parks Congress in Durban; and

RESOLVES, that
- The World Commission on Protected Areas of the IUCN conduct a workshop at WPC devoted to wilderness in the 21st century.

Resolution #22
Wilderness as a Component of Environmental Education Curricula

WHEREAS
- Environmental education is being formalised to fit within the national qualification framework in South Africa; and
- Current wilderness education is not adequately represented within formal education programs;

THEREFORE, the 7th World Wilderness Congress
RESOLVES, that
- Relevant agencies and departments within South African national government incorporate wilderness education into the national educational framework.

Resolution #23
Legal Protection of Wilderness in South Africa

WHEREAS
- National wilderness legislation in South Africa is presently inadequate.
- There is an urgent need to provide secure legal protection for state, private and commercial land;

THEREFORE, the 7th World Wilderness Congress hereby
RESOLVES, that
- The Department of Environmental Affairs and Tourism implement national legislation to ensure that South African wilderness is protected adequately at national and provincial levels; including provision for wilderness on private and communal land.

Resolution #24
NGO Alliances for Wilderness Protection in South Africa and Other Countries

WHEREAS
- Efforts in wilderness protection are uncoordinated;
- With new wilderness NGO's being formed co-ordination and planning of wilderness protection actions is required;
- Co-operation is necessary to avoid conflict and to streamline actions;

THEREFORE, the 7th World Wilderness Congress hereby
RESOLVES, that
- Wilderness NGOs within South Africa and other countries should whenever possible collaborate, leverage their strengths through alliances, and form national and international coalitions to address important wilderness related issues.

Resolution #25
Protection of Wilderness Areas Under German Law
(Ref. Naturschutzgesetz Bdrucksache 14/6378) as of 14.09.2001
WHEREAS
- The German Nature Conservation Act is presently revised under Doc.-NR 14/6378 dated 14 September 2001-11-13;
- The draft revision does not include that wilderness should be preserved in its own right ("eigenwert der wildnis an sich");
- The draft does not address yet wilderness areas as defined by IUCN, such as Wilderness Area, Category 1b;

THEREFORE, the 7th World Wilderness Congress hereby
RESOLVES, that
- The protection of Wilderness "in its own right" (eisenwert der nature) not be deleted in the final document—NR 14/6378. The wording of the draft should stand without amendment. Further, the final wording should include reference to Wilderness Area Category (e.g. 1b) as defined by World Conservation Union (IUCN).

Resolution #26
World Heritage Society
WHEREAS
- According to a UNEP study some 50% of our presently "Living Languages" will be lost within the next 50 years;
- Those languages are those of indigenous people mainly living in close contact with wilderness areas;
- The loss of natural biospheres correlates with the loss of languages, i.e. cultures;

THEREFORE, the 7th World Wilderness Congress

RESOLVES, that

- The preservation cultural diversity in context with its natural environment is an issue of priority, is in need of greater public awareness and involvement, and may be well-served by formation of a World Heritage Society that recruits well-known and respected "ambassadors" from all walks of life to represent and promote this issue.

Resolution #27
Multiple Site Designations
of Wilderness Zones Within Protected Areas
WHEREAS

- In protected areas, wilderness zones are often isolated, single site designations rather than multiple zones or an extensive, continuous zone throughout the protected area;
- This type of wilderness zonation results in the erosion of a protected area's wild character through inappropriate developments/use adjacent to these areas;

THEREFORE, the 7th World Wilderness Congress

- Recognizes the importance of wilderness planning and management integrated with overall protected area management plans; and hereby

RESOLVES, that

- Land management agencies and NGO's adopt the principle of multiple site designation of wilderness zones, with corridors whenever possible, in protected areas.

Resolution #28
Recreational and Educational Developments and
the Leasing of Trading Rights and Concessions in and Adjacent to
Wilderness Zones Within SA National Parks
WHEREAS

- The National Parks Board of South Africa has the responsibility and mandate to conserve biological diversity and the natural heritage in the national parks for all South Africans and the world in perpetuity; and
- Accepted international park planning, development and wilderness criteria and standards are firmly established and accepted by members of the World Conservation Union (IUCN), of which SANP is a member; and
- SANP has entered into numerous recreational, educational, tourism and other concessions that involve developments within National Parks;

THEREFORE, the 7th World Wilderness Congress

- Congratulates the National Parks Board for seeking new and innovative ways to raise funds to strengthen, manage and expand SA National Parks; and hereby

RESOLVES, that
- The long term biological, social and financial interests of SA national parks is best served by SANP and other partners including My Acre of Africa to adhere to IUCN park planning guidelines and independent EIA procedures including processes of independent review and the submission of full financial disclosure prospectus; and, further;
- In respect of present and future leases, to implement a comprehensive strategic environmental assessment (SEA) with its peer review component, taking account of these present and future commercialisation plans and proposals in all SA National Parks.

Resolution #29
Wilderness Trails in German National Parks
WHEREAS
- German legislation does not permit any sort of camping within the boundaries of a National Park;
- The Bavarian National Park offers the potential for wilderness primitive (leave-no-trace) trails;

THEREFORE, the 7th World Wilderness Congress
- Congratulates the German Parks Authorities on their excellent commitment to managing their national parks; and hereby

RESOLVES, that
- German officials understand the value of the primitive wilderness trail experience, and allow such "leave-no-trace" trails within the Bavarian National Park, and further, to study and eventually re-introduce wilderness-dependent wildlife such as lynx, wolves and bear.

Resolution #30
Medicinal Plants and Traditional African Medicine
WHEREAS
- 80% African population uses medicinal plants;
- 80% African population has no access to validated "modern" medicine;
- Medicinal plants represent important economic and social development opportunities; and
- Medicinal plants fit into socio-economic, cultural, African mind and address some aspects of unmet public health needs (e.g., AIDS, cancer);

THERFORE, the 7th World Wilderness Congress hereby

RESOLVES, that

- All governments—national, regional and local—can assist the health, economic vitality, and social upliftment of their citizens by protecting and promoting the value of medicinal plants as a vital part of their natural biodiversity, creating sustainable means of medicinal plant production and processing, and assuring low-cost availability to especially the economically disadvantaged.

Resolution #31
Purchase of Land to Consolidate Groendal Wilderness Area
WHEREAS

- The existing Groendal Wilderness Area is not a "consolidated" area in terms of land continuity and, if not consolidated, faces the possibility of serious degradation such as water pollution, internal development, and visual and sound distress of future development;
- Consolidation would also lessen the threat of peripheral development, and would reduce management costs due to core:surface area ratio;
- A piece of private land in the middle of the wilderness area—purchase of which would effectively consolidate the southern and northern portions of Groendal—is for sale at approx R6000,000;

THEREFORE, the 7th World Wilderness Congress hereby
RESOLVES, that

- The Cape nature conservation authority responsible for the Groendal, and the (national) Department of Environmental Affairs and Tourism, and other relevant governmental agencies make the consolidation of Groendal a priority and, with the assistance of the private sector and NGOs allocate funds, launch an appeal, and persist until this is accomplished.

Resolution #32
Wilderness Areas Under Threat
by Multilateral and Bilateral Funding Agencies
WHEREAS

- Multilateral and bilateral funding agencies, principally the World Bank, continue financing governments and projects in biodiversity rich Third World Countries which often negatively impact wilderness areas through unsustainable exploitation and destructive social implications; such as:
- World Bank finance is being made available to commission more than 100 open pit coal mines in India, which affects the Hazaribagh-Palamau tiger and elephant corridors and adjoining forests.
- World Bank finance is also being made available to construct four lane highways through critical tiger forests in the Nallamalai hills, south of and contiguous to the Nagarjuna Sagar Tiger Reserve.

- Many other examples of equally destructive projects have been documented across the world that cause displacement of human populations, which in turn are forced to move into wildernesses and thus further increase the possibility of extinction for endangered wild species;

THEREFORE, the 7th World Wilderness Congresses hereby
RESOLVES, that
- The major international funding agencies, especially the World Bank, stop funding projects which negatively impact wildland areas, important wildlife and plant species, and the human communities dependent upon them; cancel or redirect loans where relevant.

Resolution #33
Wilderness and Jurisprudence
WHEREAS
- Recognizing the importance to the well-being of the wider community of life on earth which includes the human community, and the failure of existing regulatory systems to protect that wilderness adequately;
- Accepting that no wilderness will be safe in the long term unless we succeed in changing how society regulates human behavior;
- Acknowledging that such change will involve a fundamental reassessment of the legal philosophy (jurisprudence) of human cultures that currently dominate the world and requires the co-operation of all sections of human society;
- Believing that it is important to draw upon the wisdom of those indigenous peoples and local communities who have lived in harmonious and sustainable relationship with the natural world;

THEREFORE, the 7th World Wilderness Congress
- Emphasizes that it is not possible for humans to fulfil their role in the wider earth community unless we re-think the philosophical basis which underlies and informs the ways in which the dominant cultures in the world regulate themselves; and hereby

RESOLVES, that
- Delegates at this Congress, coordinated by the Gaia Foundation, will facilitate a process of re-evaluating the basis on which human societies regulate themselves, including calling upon the World Summit for Sustainable Development at its meeting in Johannesburg, South Africa in 2002; and further, will
- Initiate programs and provide resources to develop a jurisprudence that recognizes humans as inseparable from the planetary ecosystem and that for it to function properly, human societies must regulate their behavior

in a way that supports rather than undermines the integrity and health of the community of life on earth.

Resolution #34
Protection of Van Staden Nature Reserve
WHEREAS
- The Van Staden Nature Reserve (Port Elizabeth) is one of the oldest proclaimed nature reserves in South Africa;
- It harbours a valuable array of plant diversity and offers a unique experience to visitors;
- The Nelson Mandela Metropole Municipal Council has recently moved to deproclaim part of the reserve in order to make affordable, low-income housing for local residents;

THEREFORE, the 7th World Wilderness Congress
- Understands the need for affordable housing and for government action for the underpriviledged; yet
- Emphasizes that nature reserves are inviolate areas and de-proclamation is a non-acceptable action; and hereby

RESOLVES, that
- The Nelson Mandela Metropole Municipal Council should recognize the international environmental standard by maintaining the full and original boundaries and integrity of the Reserve, expand it when and where possible, and find alternate and more appropriate sites for the low-income, affordable housing required by local citizens.

Author Contact Information

Marcelin Agnagna
Nairobi
Kenya
marcelinagnagna@yahoo.fr

Jose Alves
P.O. Box 244
Kamieskroon 8241
South Africa
jalves@rarecenter.org

Gerard Bailly
24-26 Rue Louis Gaillet
Gentilly 94250
France
gbailly@afrique-initiatives.com

Mohamed Bakarr
World Agroforestry Center
United Nations Ave.
Gigini P.O. Box 30677-00100
Nairobi, Kenya
m.bakarr@cgiar.org

Mangasuthu Buthelezi
Minister of Home Affairs
P.O. Box 1
Mahlabathini 3865
South Africa

Trygve Cooper
Ministry of Environment & Tourism
P.O. Box 42
Luderitz
Namibia
trish@mweb.co.na

Richard Cowling
Professor
TERU
P.O. Box 1600
Port Elizabeth 6001
South Africa
rmc@kingsley.co.za

Dr. Iain Douglas-Hamilton
Save the Elephants
P.O. Box 54667
Nairobi
Kenya
save-eleph@aficaonline.co.ke

Dr. Mohamed El-Ashry
Global Environmental Facility
1818 H St. NW
Washington, D.C. 20433
USA
info@thegef.org

Elizabeth Estill
U.S. Forest Service
1720 Peachtree Rd. #760
Atlanta, Georgia 30367
USA
eestill@fs.fed.us

Dr. Michael Fay
Expeditions Council
1145–17th St. NW
Washington, D.C. 20036
USA
mfay@ngs.org

Alan Featherstone
Trees for Life
The Park
Forres, Moray
1V36 0T2
Scotland
trees@findhorn.org

Naxeem Goolam
P.O. Box 392
Pretoria 0003
South Africa
goolanmi@unisa.ac.za

Bruce Hamilton
Sierra Club
85 Second St., 2nd Floor
San Francisco, California 94105
USA
Bruce.Hamilton@sierraclub.org

Dr. Richard Jeo
Round River Conservation Studies
USA
rjeo@earthlink.net

David Johns
The Wildlands Project
P O Box 725
McMinnville, Oregon 97128-0725
USA
djohns@viclink.com

Johan Joubert
Shamwari Game Reserve
P.O. Box 91
Paterson 6130
South Africa
lynn@shamwari.com

Patience Koloko, Traditional Dr.
Traditional Healers Association
P.O. Box 82
Hammarsdale 3700
South Africa

Brenda Locke
Embocraft
P.O. Box 1363
Hillcrest 3650
South Africa
ngobet@mweb.co.za

Dr. Walter Lusigi
Global Environmental Facility
1818 H St. NW
Washington, D.C. 20433
USA
Wlusigi@worldbank.org

Maurice Mackenzie
Member of Parliament
3 Tanner Rd.
Pietermaritzburg 3201
South Africa
Maurice@iafrica.com

Philemon Malima
Minister of Environment & Tourism
Private Bag 13346
Windhoek
Namibia

Dr. Laurie Marker
Cheetah Conservation Fund
P.O. Box 247
Windhoek
Namibia
cheeta@iafrica.com.na

Alec Marr
The Wilderness Society
P.O. Box 188
Civic Square, ACT 3608
Australia
alec.marr@wilderness.org.au

Vance Martin
President
The WILD Foundation
P.O. Box 1380
Ojai, California 93024
USA
info@wild.org

Ian McCallum
Wilderness Leadership School
2 Capstone Close
Marina da Gama 7945
South Africa
soitgoes@iafrica.com

Malcolm McCulloch
moles@netactive.co.za

Dr. Simon Metcalfe
Four Corners Project
22 Woodholme Rd.
Emerald Hill,
EH 226 Zimbabwe
Metcalfe@mweb.co.zw

Kirstin Miller
Ecocities
1474 Seventh St.
UNICT
Berkeley, California 94710
USA
kleighmi@flash.net

Khulani Mkhize
CEO
Kwazulu Natal Wildlife
P.O. Box 13053
Cascades 3202
South Africa
kmkhize@kznncs.org.za

Valli Moosa
Minister of Environment
Pretoria, South Africa

Andrew Muir
Wilderness Foundation
P.O. Box 91
Paterson 6130
South Africa
andrew@sa.wild.org

Credo Mutwa
South Africa

Henry Mwima
Four Corners Project
P.O. Box 50844
Ridgeway
Lusaka
Zambia

Matti Nghikembua
Cheetah Conservation Fund
P.O. Box 247
Windhoek
Namibia
cheeta@iafrica.com.na

Dr. Ian Player
Wilderness Foundation
P.O. Box 53260
Yellowwood Park
4011 South Africa
icplayer@eastcoast.co.za

Gareth Pyne-James
My Acre of Africa
88 Napier Rd.
Parktown 2193
South Africa
gareth@myacreofafrica.org

Serge Rajaobelina
Fanamby
P.O. Box 88434
Antananarivo
Madagascar
s.rajaobelina@fanamby.org

Cyril Ramaphosa
My Acre of Africa
88 Napier Rd.
Parktown 2193
South Africa

Dr. David Rothenberg
New Jersey Institute of Technology
6 Fishkill Ave.
Cold Spring, New York 10516
USA
terranova@hudson.highlands.com

Bittu Sahgal
Sanctuary Magazine
602 Maker Chamber V, Nar.Pt.
Mumbai 40021
India
bittu@sanctuaryasia.com

Partha Sarathy
World Wilderness Trust
Hamsini 12 Cross
Rajmahal
Bangalore 560080 India
mpartha@vsnl.net

John Seed
Rainforest Information Center
P.O. Box 368
Lismore, NSW 2480
Australia
Johnseed1@ozemail.com.au

The Hon. E. Clay Shaw
Member of Congress
#2408 Rayburn HOB
Washington, D.C. 20515
USA

Dr. Vandana Shiva
Research Foundation for Science
A-60 Hauz Khas
New Delhi 110016
India
vshiva@vsnl.com

Dr. Michael Soulé
Wildlands Project
P O Box 2010
Hotchkiss, Colorado 81419
USA
soule@co.tds.net

Daudi Sumba
Four Corners
Box CT-570
Victoria Falls
Zimbabwe
daudi@telcovic.co.zw

Michael Sweatman
The WILD Foundation
P.O. Box 659
Stowe, Vermont 05672
USA
m@sweatman.com

Terry Tanner
Confederated Salish & Kootenai
P.O. Box 278
Pablo, Montana 59855
USA
terryt@cskt.org

Wouter Van Hoven
Professor
Center for Wildlife Management
University of Pretoria
Pretoria 0002
South Africa
vanhoven@ecolife.co.za

Dr. Willem Van Riet
Peace Parks Foundation
19 Frikkie de Beer Street
Aterbury Estates, Building #7
Pretoria 0181
South Africa
dfvriet@mweb.co.za

Ben-Erik Van Wyk
Professor
Dept of Botany
Rand Afrikaans University
P.O. Box 524, Auckland Park
Johannesburg 2006
South Africa
bevw@na.rau.ac.za

Dr. Martin Von Hildebrand
The Gaia Foundation
Carrera 4a No.26B-31 1
Santa Fe de Bogota
Santa Fe 001-10 Columbia
Gaia-amz@colnodo.apc.org

Executive Committee

7th World Wilderness Congress

Murphy Morobe (Chairperson), South African National Parks

Adrian Gardiner CEO, Shamwari Game Reserve (South Africa)

Maria Kapere Director of Resource Management, Ministry of Environment and Tourism, (Namibia)

Walter Lusigi Senior Advisor, Global Environmental Facility

Gwen Mahlangu MP, Chairperson of Environment and Tourism Portfolio Committee, National Assembly (Sourth Africa)

Khulani Mkhize CEO, KwaZulu-Natal Wildlife

Nomkhita Mona CEO, Eastern Cape Tourism Board (South Africa)

Partha Sarathy Chairman, World Wilderness Trust (India)

Fanyana Shiburi Daimler Chrysler (South Africa)

Andrew Muir (Director)

Vance G. Martin (Director, International)

Dr. Ian Player (Founder) *ex officio*

Staff: Jean Rigby, Rosanne Clark, Margaret Nichol, Lorraine Short, Mayra Collyer, Beverley Clarke, Margot Muir, Jacob Nduu, Molefe Motshwane, Bool Smuts, Michaela and Martin Peterson, and Carol Batrus